Italian Film in the Light of Neorealism

Italian Film in the Light of Neorealism

MILLICENT MARCUS

1986

PRINCETON UNIVERSITY PRESS

791.430945 MAR
9 6 441

Copyright © 1986 by Princeton University Press
Published by Princeton University Press, 41 William Street,
Princeton, New Jersey 08540
In the United Kingdom: Princeton University Press,
Chichester, West Sussex

LIBRARY OF CONGRESS CATALOGING-IN-PUBLICATION DATA

Marcus, Millicent Joy.
    Italian film in the light of neorealism.

    Bibliography: p.
    Includes index.
    1. Moving-pictures—Italy.   2. Realism in moving-
pictures.   I. Title.
PN1993.5.I88M28   1986   791.43'09'0912   86-91473
ISBN 0-691-05489-4 (alk. paper)
ISBN 0-691-10208-2 (pbk.)

Publication of this book has been aided by a grant from the
Paul Mellon Fund of Princeton University Press

This book has been composed in Linotron Sabon

Princeton University Press books are printed on acid-free
paper, and meet the guidelines for permanence and durability
of the Committee on Production Guidelines for Book
Longevity of the Council on Library Resources

Printed in the United States of America

9   8   7

To Jacob and Lucy

Contents

Illustrations

Acknowledgments

ALL FILMS, and neorealist films in particular, are collective ventures whose opening credits can only give the most abstract and schematic account of the collaborative efforts that went into their making. In a similar way, I offer my own "opening credits" with scant hope that they can ever express the full measure of my dependence on others to realize this project. First credits go to the funding agencies that supported me during a year of research and writing: the American Council of Learned Societies, whose award was made possible by the National Endowment for the Humanities; and the University of Texas University Research Institute.

One of the great difficulties in writing about film is procuring the "texts" which are often expensive to rent, and sometimes quite difficult to locate. In this regard, I have been extremely fortunate to have the help of Stephen Bearden, Texas Union Film Coordinator, who cheerfully brought to campus and projected so many of the movies needed for my research. I am also very grateful to William Weaver for his tireless efforts to trace obscure films, and to Vittorio Lorenzini, projectionist at the University of Siena, for helping me screen one of the movies that was not available in this country.

In preparing the manuscript, I have received a great deal of help, including a series of Special Research Grants from the University Research Institute. I am grateful to Mrs. Robert Stephenson for her expert typing, to Omega Clay for her design work, and to Mary Corliss, Film Stills Archivist at the Museum of Modern Art, for helping me procure the illustrations.

The staff of the Perry Castenada Library has been extremely supportive of my research. I would like to thank Jo

Anne Hawkins for giving me "a room of my own" and her Interlibrary Loan office for so heroically processing my many requests for esoterica.

Warmest thanks go to the staff of Princeton University Press, especially to Joanna Hitchcock for her sustained and sustaining interest in my project, and to my unerring copy editor, Marilyn Campbell. The two outside readers solicited by the Press offered comments and criticisms which were of great help to me in revising.

I would also like to express my appreciation to my departmental chairman, James Stephens, and to his assistant, Alice Hart, for their unstinting support of my project throughout its various phases; to Richard Grant for his research advice; and to Peter Bondanella, Ben Lawton, and Robert Sklar for their endorsements of my research plans from the very start. I am also grateful to Gian-Paolo Biasin who first encouraged me to plunge into film teaching and to embark on the road that would lead to this book. The many students who have taken my Italian cinema courses over the years have contributed to my thinking about film in ways too subtle and all-pervasive to acknowledge fully in my notes. To them, I offer special thanks for the sympathy and critical discernment with which they have received my ideas, and for sharing the wealth of their perceptions with me.

Final credit goes to my husband and colleague, Robert Hill, for doing 50 percent of the child-care, and 100 percent of the criticism and encouragement so necessary for the completion of this book.

Austin, Texas
September 1985

Preface

WHEN ROBERTO ROSSELLINI abandoned neorealism in the early 1950s for a cinema of greater subjectivity and depth, he was called a traitor to the movement he had been so instrumental in founding.[1] That such strong language should be used in matters of aesthetics may strike us as odd, until we realize that neorealism is far more than a mere episode in the history of style. Though every aesthetic embodies a cultural and philosophical outlook of its own ("une technique implique toujours une métaphysique," as Sartre put it) neorealism is a special case in which the relationship between style and implied world view is so deep and morally binding that the modification of one amounts to the virtual betrayal of the other. And since the world view of neorealism is very much linked to the events of the Resistance and the postwar reconstruction of Italy, it is no wonder that the term "traitor," with all its political and moral import, would be applied to one who would dare shift stylistic allegiances.

Vittorio De Sica's comments on *Shoeshine*, his first film of the postwar period, suggest the intensity of the social and ethical commitment that went into neorealist practice.

> The experience of the war was decisive for us all. Each felt the mad desire to throw away all the old stories of

[1] On Rossellini's presumed "tradimento" see Gianni Rondolino, *Rossellini* (Florence: La Nuova Italia, 1977), p. 39, and Lino Miccichè, "Per una verifica del neorealismo," in *Il neorealismo cinematografico italiano*, ed. L. Miccichè (Venice: Marsilio, 1975), p. 14. Lest this one term fail to convince us of the harsh moralizing tone of much criticism on neorealism, Gian Piero Brunetta remarks on the critical habit of conducting "summary trials against works and directors, considering entire groups accused of desertion as if worthy of the firing squad." See *Storia del cinema italiano dal 1945 agli anni ottanta* (Rome: Riuniti, 1982), p. 342.

the Italian cinema, to plant the camera in the midst of
real life, in the midst of all that struck our astonished
eyes. We sought to liberate ourselves from the weight
of our sins, we wanted to look ourselves in the face
and tell ourselves the truth, to discover what we really
were, and to seek salvation. . . . *Shoeshine* was a
small stone, a very small stone, contributed to the
moral reconstruction of our country.[2]

Though critics will later take issue with many of these points,
especially the claim to a radical break from prewar cinematic
modes and the pretense to documentary reportage, De Sica's
statement nonetheless stands as a cogent argument for the
inadequacy of a strictly stylistic approach to neorealism. As
the cinematic offspring of the Resistance (*Open City*, for example, was originally intended to commemorate the anti-
Fascist underground of Rome), neorealism became the repository of partisan hopes for social justice in the postwar Italian state.[3] Its means were at once epistemological, moral,
and political. The neorealist resolve "to plant the camera in
the midst of real life, in the midst of all that struck our astonished eyes" enabled the filmmakers and their audiences
to see an Italy that Mussolini had concealed for two full decades. "Twenty years of Fascism and therefore of absolute
closure vis-à-vis all types of representations of reality," claimed
Ettore Scola, "and then, starting from 1945, there appeared
all that could not be expressed in twenty years."[4] Neorealism became a way of knowing, an "instrument leading to
knowledge about reality," as Elio Petri called it.[5] Nor was

[2] *La table ronde* 149 (May 1960), 80.
[3] Though the Resistance was not an ideologically homogeneous movement, its supporters "held in common that a regression to the society out
of which Fascism in Italy first evolved was not what they were fighting for."
See David Overbey, ed., *Springtime in Italy: A Reader in Neo-Realism*
(Hamden, Conn.: Archon, 1979), p. 9.
[4] See the interview in Jean Gili, *Le cinéma italien* (Paris: Union Générale
d'Editions, 1978), p. 300.
[5] See Joan Mellen, "Cinema Is Not for an Elite but for the Masses: An
Interview with Elio Petri," *Cinéaste* 6 (1973), 10.

the neorealist revelation to remain a passive, intellectual one. "After the years of Fascist obscurantism and of provincial escapist films," Petri continued, "a cinema appeared which was looked on as a means toward liberation and to freedom."[6] Freedom from the sin of personal complicity with a corrupt moral order, freedom from the social injustices perpetrated by Fascism, but endemic to even the most seemingly benign uses of power—this is the ideal that De Sica invokes in his modest celebration of *Shoeshine*. Of utmost interest to us, however, is the metaphor with which De Sica concludes his observations. If the collective Italian conscience is figured as an edifice, devastated by years of Fascism and war, then the nature of De Sica's building materials must not escape our notice, for his "very small stone contributed to the moral reconstruction of our country" is, quite importantly, a film. The rebirth of the Italian national identity will thus owe as much to the cinema as it does to the various political and cultural movements we normally associate with the rise of a new social order. "Neorealism, as the artistic expression of a historical period represents an important revolutionary moment, not only of cinema, but of Italian thought," said Scola, who went on to extol film as the privileged medium for the conveyance of "that new way of thinking and of seeing reality, . . . that need to analyze ourselves, that necessity to follow man and his vital problems" which constitutes the moral and philosophical legacy of the Resistance.[7]

As a protagonist in the momentous upheavals of postwar Italian society, as the vehicle for a new national identity, and as the conscience of a country coming to terms with its recent historical past,[8] neorealism therefore demands an ap-

[6] Ibid.

[7] See the interview in Aldo Tassone, *Parla il cinema italiano, II* (Milan: Il Formichiere 1980), p. 314.

[8] On the relationship between neorealism and the collective conscience of the newly emergent postwar social order, see Pietro Germi and Giuseppe De Santis, "In Defense of Italian Cinema," in *Springtime*, ed. Overbey, pp. 215, 217, and 218; and Brunetta, *Storia del cinema italiano*, p. 319.

proach that goes far beyond mere considerations of style.[9] Its vast cultural and ideological reverberations are what make the movement so resistant to narrow definition and so opaque to critical methods, while continuing to attract scholars even thirty years after the official neorealist "demise" in the early 1950s. This also may explain the seemingly disproportionate impact of a movement that lasted only seven years, generated only twenty-one films,[10] failed at the box office, and fell short of its didactic and aesthetic aspirations.[11]

As one of those scholars who cannot resist the perpetual lure of neorealism, I, too, have made it my subject. But I have done so in a way that is perhaps best defined by explaining what it is not. This indeed is not a history, nor is it a systematic effort to trace the cultural, economic, or managerial influences on the film industry of the postwar years. It is an attempt, instead, to fathom the impact of neorealism on Italian cinema through selective analyses of exemplary works produced between 1945 and 1982. Nor does this study

[9] In this regard, see Luigi Chiarini, "A Discourse on Neo-Realism," in *Springtime*, ed. Overbey, pp. 139 and 140.

[10] According to Alfonso Canziani, between 1945 and 1950, 313 films were produced in Italy. Of these, 46 had "visione neorealista" and only 21 were of authentic "invenzione neorealista." See Alfonso Canziani and Cristina Bragaglia, *La stagione neorealista* (Bologna: Cooperative Libraria Universitaria, 1976), p. 9. For varying statistics, see Mira Liehm, *Passion and Defiance: Film in Italy from 1942 to the Present* (Berkeley and Los Angeles: University of California Press, 1984), p. 334 n. 5; and Peter Bondanella, *Italian Cinema from Neorealism to the Present* (New York: Ungar, 1983), p. 35.

[11] Lino Miccichè argues that the neorealists never succeeded in elevating the cinematic tastes of the Italian public. See "Per una verifica," in *Il neorealismo cinematografico italiano*, p. 22. As for its aesthetic aims, Cesare Zavattini wrote in 1952, when the movement had gone as far as it could go with *Umberto D*, that neorealism had not yet achieved its ideals. See "Alcune idee sul cinema," in *Umberto D* (Milan and Rome: Fratelli Bocca, 1954), pp. 10, 19. For a translation of this important essay, see "Some Ideas on the Cinema," in *Film: A Montage of Theories*, ed. Richard Dyer MacCann (New York: Dutton, 1966), pp. 216–28. Overbey edits together passages from "Alcune idee" along with those from two other Zavattini essays in "A Thesis on Neo-Realism," in *Springtime*, pp. 67–78. Subsequent references to "Alcune idee" will be to the English version in MacCann.

aspire to completeness—it just begins to sample the richness
and complexity of the neorealist imprint on subsequent cinematic expression in Italy. Should readers find that crucial
titles have been overlooked, or that a given director has been
ignored, I can only grant the validity of their objections and
regret that I had not the time nor space in these pages to
consider many more representative films of the period. But a
project of this kind, involving in-depth interpetation of selected works, cannot, by definition, be exhaustive unless it is
to abandon close reading for comprehensiveness and heter-
ogeneity of approach—goals that have already been quite ably,
and in some cases brilliantly, pursued by recent scholars in
the field.[12] Rather than dismiss such objections, then, let me
use them to argue the need for further study in the direction
I am proposing here, and to support the thesis of this book,
which is that neorealism constitutes *la via maestra* of Italian
film,[13] that it is the point of departure for all serious postwar
cinematic practice,[14] and that each director had to come to
terms with it in some way, whether in seeming imitation (the
early Olmi), in commercial exploitation (the middle Comencini), or in ostensible rejection (the recent Tavianis). The
sporadic outbursts of neo-neorealism *(The Organizer, Accattone,* and *Bandits at Orgosolo)* are only the most obvious
examples of a cinematic memory that will not disappear, and
that dictates, if not the outward form of the modern film
industry, at least its conscience.[15]

[12] See Bondanella, *Italian Cinema*; R. T. Witcombe, *The New Italian Cinema* (New York: Oxford, 1982); Brunetta, *Storia del cinema italiano*; and
Liehm, *Passion and Defiance.*

[13] See Giuseppe Ferrara, *Il nuovo cinema italiano* (Florence: Le Monnier,
1957), p. 278.

[14] See *Springtime*, ed. Overbey, p. 32. On the lasting impact of neorealism, both in Italy and abroad, see Liehm, *Passion and Defiance*, pp. 129–
31.

[15] Vittorio Taviani gave voice to this critical consensus when he referred
to "our best cinema . . . that which was born from the Resistance and from
neorealism." See Fulvio Accialini and Lucia Coluccelli, *I Taviani* (Florence:
La Nuova Italia, 1979), p. 9.

A historical/theoretical discussion of neorealism and its antecedents in earlier concepts of realism will be the subject of my introductory section. Part One includes the officially "terminal" films of neorealism (*Open City*, 1945, and *Umberto D*, 1952) as well as *Bicycle Thief*, which epitomizes the movement at its peak, and *Bitter Rice*, which adds a heterodox, melodramatic element to the standard neorealist aesthetic. In Part Two I consider films that exemplify the transition from neorealism proper to a broader, often highly personalized interpretation of cinematic realism. *Bread, Love, and Fantasy*, with its impoverished characters and squalid settings, is a good example of that Fifties phenomenon—*realismo rosa*—where neorealism degenerates into manner and poverty becomes the stuff of light comedy. Fellini extends the neorealist inquiry to include psychological and spiritual dimensions in *La strada*, while Antonioni in *Red Desert* elevates visual style to the level of a full-fledged thematic concern. In 1954, Visconti abandons present-day Italy (the neorealists' required setting) for the past in *Senso*, but justifies its contemporary relevance by a Gramscian argument for rewriting Risorgimento history. In Part Three, I treat films that return to the neorealist concern for contemporary social criticism. Olmi's *Il posto* quietly censures the myth of Italy's postwar economic "boom" by revealing the boredom and stagnation that await aspirants to white-collar security. Hypocrisy and sexual mores are the targets of *Seduced and Abandoned*, set in a Sicily which allows Germi to argue his case *in extremis*. Late Sixties' *contestazione* is the subject of Pasolini's *Teorema*, an oblique social commentary in allegorical guise, as it is the subject of Petri's *Investigation of a Citizen above Suspicion*, which takes antirevolutionary backlash to surrealistic lengths. In the Seventies and Eighties, I have been struck by an obsessive cinematic interest in the themes of Fascism and war, and these films will be the subject of my final section. From a distance of some thirty years, filmmakers have been able to return to this traumatic period with irony and critical detachment. Bertolucci's *The Conformist* is a study of the aberrant logic behind one man's complicity with Fascism, while eros and ideology battle for the soul of Everyman in Wertmuller's *Love and Anarchy*, set against the splendor and corruption of Mussolini's Rome. Rosi's *Christ Stopped at Eboli* takes us on a journey to another Italy—the peasant Italy of the southern interior—where Fascism is seen as yet one more episode in the long history of oppressive central governments seated in Rome. The Taviani brothers' *Night of the Shooting Stars* offers an ambivalent tribute to neorealism, embracing its privileged subject matter of war and resistance, while calling into question the neorealist pretension to documentary truth by invoking a style rich in cultural mythology and personal reminiscence. I conclude with Scola's *We All Loved Each Other So Much*, an affectionate, yet critical history of the mid-Forties to the mid-Seventies. Scola's retrospective provides the occasion for my own as I consider, along with him, in what ways the Italian cinema has fulfilled, and disappointed, the promise of neorealism.

Italian Film in the Light of Neorealism

Introduction

AN ITALIAN CRITIC once quipped that *neorealismo* was *realismo* with a *neo* (mole or blemish).[1] Though we may doubt the conclusions of this fanciful etymologizer, we would do well to follow his lead in breaking down the term into its constituent parts. If neorealism is a new or revised form of realism, it behooves us to consider the root concept in its complex, often contradictory aesthetic and philosophical manifestations. The difficulty of such a task becomes evident when we note that even a scholar of the stature of Erich Auerbach will have trouble pinning down the term, as René Wellek points out in his review of Auerbach's *Mimesis: The Representation of Reality in Western Literature*. Wellek argues that Auerbach uses realism in mutually exclusive ways, implying now those supremely agonizing moments of decision when a character most fatefully fulfills the meaning of his or her destiny, and now the character's immersion in the flux and change of everyday historical circumstance. But the first meaning of realism is an existential one, according to Wellek, derived from Kierkegaard, who was reacting against the historicism of Hegel, the progenitor of Auerbach's second interpretation of realism.[2] And Auerbach's confusion of terminology in no way exhausts the options, for realism can range from the heights of Platonic idealism in its application to the eternal world of Forms, to the depths of pragmatic self-interest, when we say "let's be realistic," meaning "let's set aside all norms of principled behavior in the pursuit of

---

[1] In Franco Venturini, "Origini del neorealismo," *Bianco e nero* 11 (February 1950), 51.

[2] See René Wellek, *Concepts of Criticism* (New Haven: Yale University Press, 1963), pp. 236–37. See also his article "Auerbach's Special Realism," *Kenyon Review* 16 (1954), 299–307.

amoral ends."[3] That a single term can embrace such antithetical meanings suggests that it requires a highly contextual approach, and that in isolation, as Harry Levin observes, realism is a contentless designation.[4]

In the history of style, therefore, realism is always defined
in opposition to something else, be it romanticism in nineteenth-century literature, modernism in twentieth-century art,
nominalism in medieval philosophy, or idealism in eigh-
teenth-century thought. In film, realism is set against expressionism, aestheticism, or more generally, against illusionism.[5] The oppositional relationship required by realism
throughout its history bears out André Bazin's claim that
"realism can only occupy in art a dialectical position—it is
more a reaction than a truth."[6] Realism, according to Levin,
is a recurrent response to the conventions and artifices of an
earlier style, checking the tendency of literature to turn in on
itself by forcing it into renewed contact with the world beyond the text.[7] Thus the history of literature is the record of
this continued oscillation between illusion and disillusion-

---

[3] For a paraphrase of this notion, see Harry Levin, "What Is Realism," in
Contexts of Criticism (Cambridge, Mass.: Harvard University Press, 1957),
p. 69.

[4] Ibid. On the slipperiness of the term "realism" and on the need for a
contextual approach, see *Springtime*, ed. Overbey, p. 20.

[5] Louis Giannetti sets realism against expressionism throughout his *Un-
derstanding Movies* (Englewood Cliffs, N.J.: Prentice-Hall, 1972). André
Bazin opposes realism to aestheticism in *What Is Cinema?*, Vol. 2 (Berkeley
and Los Angeles: University of California Press, 1972), p. 16. According to
Peter Bondanella, neorealism's primary preoccupation is the dialectic be-
tween reality and illusion. See his "Early Fellini: *Variety Lights, The White
Sheik, The Vitelloni*," in *Federico Fellini, Essays in Criticism* (New York:
Oxford, 1978), pp. 220–39 and "Neorealist Aesthetics and the Fantastic:
The Machine to Kill Bad People and *Miracle in Milan*," *Film Criticism* 3
(Winter 1979), 24–29.

[6] *What Is Cinema?*, 2:48.

[7] Harry Levin, *Gates of Horn: A Study of Five French Realists* (New York:
Oxford, 1963), p. 57. Alain Robbe-Grillet argues along similar lines in *For
a New Novel: Essays on Fiction*, trans. Richard Howard (New York: Grove
Press, 1965), p. 158.

ment, convention and parody, opacity and transparency of technique.[8] Levin hastens to add that realism is by no means innocent of the illusions and conventions it seeks to challenge in earlier styles, and that as soon as its disillusioning impulse is exhausted, it soon degenerates into manner, and yet another dialectic of illusion and disillusionment begins.[9]

It is important to note that in Bazin's and Levin's discussions, the primary consideration is the relationship of realism to other styles, rather than the relationship of the artistic representation to some extra-aesthetic "reality." Mimetic concerns are relevant to the extent that they define a style as more realistic than another one, in that the "what" of the representation takes precedence over the "how." But the mimetic accuracy of a work of art can never stand alone as the measure of realism, since no representation can give an unmediated rendering of objective reality. Even photography, which at its birth held the most representational promise of all the visual arts,[10] cannot help but distort reality in its transposition of three-dimensional space to a two-dimensional plane, in its isolation of objects from their larger physical context, and in its reduction of color to its chemical equivalents in a laboratory (or to black and white).[11] Documentary film, which improved on the already superior mimetic powers of photography by adding motion to the still visual record, was already contrived by the time of its early master, Robert Flaherty. Indeed, his celebrated *Nanook of the North* and *Man of Aran* were carefully staged to give a heightened sense of documentary truth, revealing the paradox that the reconstructed event often produces a "stronger

[8] Levin, *Gates*, p. 48.

[9] Ibid., p. 51.

[10] The photographic image is a "trace, something directly stenciled off the real . . . a material vestige of its subject." Susan Sontag, *On Photography* (New York: Dell, 1980), p. 154.

[11] See Siegfried Kracauer, *Theory of Film: The Redemption of Physical Reality* (New York: Oxford, 1979), p. 15.

illusion of reality" than the original.[12] André Bazin illustrates how the technology that substantially furthered the cause of realism in the cinema entailed a necessary loss in the authenticity of the filmmaking conditions themselves. Thus deep-focus photography, which enhanced the representational values of the medium by allowing all planes of the shot to appear in clear focus, required a studio setting and the concomitant forfeit of location shooting possibilities.[13] Similarly, the technology for postsynchronization gave the camera untrammeled freedom to explore the visual implications of a shot while necessitating an obvious loss in aural realism.[14]

Photography and film are limiting cases in the argument for realism through contrivance—if these, the media most potentially faithful to the real world, are inevitably distorting, what about those arts whose techniques require extensive transformations of their data at the very start? The inescapable conclusion is that all realism is predicated on illusions—illusions that, however, find their ultimate justification in their service to a higher truth: the revelation of the world order in a way that would otherwise escape our unaided notice. Even Zola will confess to manipulating his raw material in the very recording of it, but he does so in order better to reveal the workings of empirical reality. "Indeed we do start out from true facts, which are our indestructible basis, but, in order to demonstrate the mechanism of the facts, we have to produce and direct phenomena."[15]

Those who expect a one-to-one correspondence between

[12] Ibid., p. 35. Similarly, "to render the idea of reality it is often necessary to modify it," according to Vittorio Taviani. See Tassone, *Parla il cinema*, *II*, p. 368.

[13] Bazin, *What Is Cinema?* 2:28–29.

[14] Ibid., 2:29–30.

[15] "Nous partons bien des faits vrais, qui sont nôtre base indestructible; mais, pour montrer le mécanisme des faits, il faut que nous produisions et que nous dirigions les phénomènes." From the Preface to *Le roman expérimental* (1880), in *Anthology of Critical Prefaces to the Nineteenth-Century French Novel*, ed. Herbert S. Gershman and Kernan B. Whitworth, Jr. (Columbia, Mo.: University of Missouri Press, 1962), p. 168.

elements in the artwork and their referents in the material world, therefore, do a grave disservice to the realist aesthetic. What defines realism is a certain set of principles, such as Aristotle's laws of necessity and probability, which govern the internal relationships of the various parts of the representation and which are seen to have their source in the natural world. Thus when Aristotle upholds nature as the proper model for artistic imitation, he refers not to a series of objects in the physical universe, but to the movement from potentiality to actuality by which all things reach formal perfection. Since this ideal evolution, or *motus ad formam*, is hindered by the accidents and contingencies to which matter is subject, artists are able to improve upon their model by bringing to completion what nature necessarily leaves imperfect and flawed. In this way, Aristotelian mimesis is didactic and dynamic, unwilling to remain at the level of surface appearances. Aristotle argues that the ideal is indeed inherent in the real and artists should bear witness to this truth by purging nature of all obstacles to its perfect progress.

Classical realism, however, is a far cry from the theory that came to prevail in nineteenth-century France and provided the precedent against which the Italians would later react.[16] For the French realists in painting and literature, realism meant "impartiality, impassivity, scrupulous objectivity, rejection of *a priori* metaphysical or epistemological prejudice, the confining of the artist to the accurate observation and notation of empirical phenomena, and the description of how, and not why, things happen."[17] Naturalism, which was only distinguished from realism much later on,[18] took the scientific pretensions of the earlier movement to their extreme, using current theories of genetic and environmental

---

[16] It was during the eighteenth century that realism underwent the radical change which was to produce our modern understanding of the term. See Wellek, *Concepts*, p. 225.

[17] Linda Nochlin, *Realism* (New York: Penguin, 1978), p. 43.

[18] Wellek, *Concepts*, p. 233.

determinism as the basis for literary practice. "In a word," wrote Zola in his introduction to *Le roman expérimental*,

> . . . we must work on characters, passions, human and social facts as the chemist and the physicist work on raw substances, as the physiologist works on living bodies. Determinism dominates everything. It is scientific investigation, experimental reasoning, that combats one by one the hypotheses of the idealists and that replaces the novels of pure imagination by novels of observation and experimentation.[19]

The insistence on a strictly materialistic approach to the human condition and the concomitant denial of any principle of transcendence complete the rupture between nineteenth-century realism and its ancient and medieval counterparts. Yet these seemingly irreconcilable outlooks do have some points in common which would entitle us to group them together as theories of realism in opposition to medieval nominalism, or modern idealism, for example. All realisms share certain assumptions about the objective world: that it exists, that it can be known, and that its existence is entirely separable from the processes by which we come to know it.[20] Realist theory holds that the material universe is governed by a set of laws and principles accessible to human reason and that the highest priority attaches to our rational study of its workings. Practitioners of realism in literature, from Dante to Zola, have sought to render humanity in the context of the material world in such a way that its inner-

---

[19]"En un mot, nous devons opérer sur les caractères, sur les passions, sur les faits humains et sociaux, comme le chimiste et le physicien opèrent sur les corps bruts, comme le physiologiste opère sur les corps vivants. Le determinisme domine tout. C'est l'investigation scientifique, c'est le raisonnement expérimental qui combat une à une les hypothèses des idéalistes, et qui remplace les romans de pure imagination par les romans d'observation et d'expérimentation." *Anthology of Critical Prefaces*, p. 172.

[20]F. D. Wilhelmsen, "Realism," *New Catholic Encyclopedia*, 1967 ed., p. 110.

most workings are revealed. If writers are able to achieve the true "critical realist perspective," as Georg Lukács describes it, then a certain set of political implications will necessarily follow. For Lukács, the realist perspective means a grasp of the underlying dynamics of historical development, a corresponding vision of the future which will emerge from the movement of history so discerned, and a belief that the social order is modifiable and therefore perfectable.[21] As opposed to modernism, which holds a static view of the world order and hence despairs of our power to change it, critical realism (and later socialist realism) points out the dynamism of historical change so that we may more consciously and intelligently act to forge our own destiny. Though Lukács's theory of critical perspective obviously serves the ends of his Marxist ideology, it nonetheless bears the stamp of an Aristotelian faith in the ideal movement to a perfect end within the natural order. Indeed, I would argue that the survival of classical realism goes far to explain the inconsistencies and contradictions of modern realist theory, which demands that art be at once objective and politically *engagé*, that it be disinterested yet didactic, limited to the phenomena of empirical experience yet attuned to the underlying patterns that determine it, a styleless record of material reality yet formed and harmonized by human reason. These disparate claims on the artwork testify to the continual pull of classical realism on the one hand, and nineteenth-century scientism on the other. The quest for an ideal movement toward perfection in the world order and the role of the work of art to bear witness to, and convince us of, its presence would explain the didactic, politically interested, synthetic impulse of the tradition. Nineteenth-century realism, with its denial of preconceived systems of meaning and its insistence on a scientifically verifiable, objective approach to the material world, would ex-

[21] Georg Lukács, *Realism in Our Time: Literature and the Class Struggle,* trans. John and Necke Mander (New York and Evanston: Harper & Row, 1964), pp. 57ff.

plain the disinterested, styleless, superficial tendencies of the theory.

Where do the Italians stand in all this, and specifically in what form will future neorealists have access to the traditions of realist thought? A study of the work of Francesco De Sanctis, the great Risorgimento critic whose pronouncements became virtually normative for generations of his compatriots, suggests that the survival of classical realism in the nineteenth century explains the basis of the Italian reaction to contemporary French naturalism. Thus De Sanctis regrets "a certain pleasure today in cherishing more the animal than the human part, and by dint of wanting to prove that man was born from the monkey, we end up considering more the monkey than the man."[22] Darwinism and the general tendency to privilege the biological determinants of life above all others have reduced thought to its chemical constituents, morality to temperament, idea to instinct, fantasy to mechanics, and passions to appetites.[23] In *verismo*, the Italian version of naturalism, De Sanctis mourns the rejection of the Risorgimento ideals of patriotism, humanity, and liberty, calling the style depraved and even misnamed, since the emphasis on the ugly and the squalid is necessarily a distortion of truth.[24] But De Sanctis is too judicious and insightful entirely to dismiss the most important theoretical current of his time, so he makes an implicit distinction between good and bad realism whereby he can reject its extreme elements and preserve what conforms to his notions of human dignity and propriety. Good realism tells the story of man's conquest of his animal self through the cultivation of his rational and spiritual faculties, thus counterbalancing the tendencies of contemporary philosophy to overabstraction and the tenden-

[22] Francesco De Sanctis, "L'ideale," in *La poesia cavalleresca e scritti vari*, ed. Mario Petrini (Bari: Laterza, 1954), p. 311.

[23] Ibid., p. 312.

[24] De Sanctis, "Studio sopra Emilio Zola," in *Saggi critici*, ed. Luigi Russo (Bari: Laterza, 1952), p. 253.

cies of art to traditionalism and conventionality.[25] The movement, however, soon replaced these old excesses with some of its own, sanctioning corruption and depravity in those who would take its polemical stance seriously as a prescription for license in word and deed. "There is progress in science, and there is decadence in life."[26] Perhaps most suggestive of De Sanctis's ambivalence toward realism is his treatment of the foremost French naturalist in his "Studio sopra Emilio Zola" (1878). An ardent admirer of the novelist, De Sanctis has difficulty reconciling his enthusiasm for the *oeuvre* with his antipathy toward its theoretical underpinnings. In the throes of this critical dilemma, De Sanctis goes to great lengths to separate the man from his theory, arguing that Zola's novels succeed despite the naturalism they bespeak. "If we want to understand and to enjoy Zola, we must forget his idea."[27]

Luigi Capuana, the foremost theorist of realism in nineteenth-century Italy, performs a similar operation on Zola, claiming that the novelist never took his theory seriously, but that he simply needed a slogan to promote his work. Thus, Capuana rejects the theoretical implications of the novelist's scientism, while hailing the impersonality and objectivity of his method.[28] In this, he is very much like his friend and colleague Giovanni Verga, the most celebrated exponent of Italian *verismo*, who will serve as a very important model for the incipient neorealist movement some half-century later. What Verga objects to in the French realists is their exclusive attention to the material world and their sensory apprehension of it. "I confess to you," he wrote Capuana in 1874, "that I do not like *Madame Bovary*, not because the excessive realism irks me, but because in the realism there is only that

[25] Ibid., pp. 256–57.
[26] Ibid., p. 257.
[27] Ibid., p. 251.
[28] See Luigi Capuana, *Gli "ismi" contemporanei*, ed. Giorgio Luti (Milan: Fratelli Fabbri, 1973), p. 44.

of the senses, indeed, the worst is that the passions of those characters last the duration of a sensation."[29] Like Capuana, Verga enthusiastically accepts the methods of impersonal observation and artistic nonintervention implied in the French scientific approach. In the preface to his story "L'Amante di Gramigna," which amounts to a manifesto of *verismo*, Verga promises to put the reader "face to face with the naked fact," to execute the analysis "with scientific scruples" and to emerge with a "science of the heart." Dramatic impact will be sacrificed to scientific demonstration and the work will become a self-evident, autonomous whole "without maintaining any point of contact with its author, any stain of original sin."[30] The impress of scientism also marks the introduction to a projected five-volume cycle of novels about the human condition, to be entitled *I vinti*, of which only two, *I Malavoglia* and *Maestro Don-Gesualdo*, were ever completed. Verga explains that he will begin his study of humanity in its most primitive forms since "the mechanism of the passions that determine it [human activity] in those low spheres is less complicated and will therefore be observed with greater precision."[31] Verga's peasant Sicily offers the laboratory conditions most conducive to clinical observation of man's fate since the simplicity of its subjects enables the experimenter to keep his number of variables to a minimum.

All this sounds extremely inhuman and reductive, until we recognize that touch of classical realism in the final passage of Verga's introduction, which calls into question the unmi-

[29] Giovanni Verga, "Storia de *I Malavoglia*, carteggio con l'editore e con Luigi Capuana con una notizia di L. e V. Perroni," *Nuova antologia* 75 (March 1940), 110.

[30] "Faccia a faccia col fatto nudo," "con scrupolo scientifico," "scienza del cuore umano," "senza serbare alcun punto di contatto col suo autore, alcuna macchia del peccato d'origine." Giovanni Verga, *Tutte le novelle*, Vol. 1 (Verona: Mondadori, 1967), pp. 168–69.

[31] "Il meccanismo delle passioni che la determinano [l'attività umana] in quelle basse sfere è meno complicato e potrà quindi osservarsi con maggior precisione." Giovanni Verga, *I Malavoglia* (Verona: Mondadori, 1968), p. 51.

tigated naturalism of the immediately preceding argument. "Whoever observes this spectacle does not have the right to judge it, it is already a lot if he succeeds in withdrawing, for an instant, from the battlefield to study it without passion, and to render the scene neatly, with the appropriate colors, such as to give the representation of reality as it was, or *as it should have been* [emphasis mine]."[32] In this concluding verb, Verga gives his strategy away. Far from representing unmanipulated material phenomena, Verga's narrative world will reveal the inner laws and principles that human destiny obeys when allowed to follow its ideal course to completion. Here, Verga reveals a considerable debt to Aristotelian mimetic theory in which art presents a clarified image of nature by purging it of those accidents and contingencies that hinder the progress to formal perfection. Capuana makes this Aristotelian legacy even clearer when he argues that "the Novel . . . should not want to do anything other than to draw out living creatures from any material, put them in the world with the same variety, the same prodigality as Nature, but superior to those of Nature because not subject to the bondage of contingency and the fatality of death."[33]

Nineteenth-century Italian realism reveals an eclectic mixture of elements drawn from the various, sometimes contradictory manifestations of the theory as it underwent its long history of evolution and transformation from the ancient Greeks to the contemporary French. By assimilating the scientific methodology of the French naturalists, the Italians were able to keep abreast of the latest developments in realist theory. At the same time, by rejecting the strictly material, deterministic elements of naturalism, they were able to retain the Aristotelian belief in a permanent, ideal order inherent in

[32] "Chi osserva questo spettacolo non ha il diritto di giudicarlo, è già molto se riesce a trarsi un istante fuori del campo della lotta per studiarla senza passione, e rendere la scena nettamente, coi colori adatti, tale da dare la rappresentazione della realtà com'è stata, o come avrebbe dovuto essere." Ibid., p. 53.

[33] Capuana, *Gli "ismi" contemporanei*, p. 46.

the world of matter and men. This conservative, yet flexible approach to realism has continued in Italy up through the twentieth century. It lives in the simultaneous claims of absolute, scientific objectivity on the one hand, and a quest for underlying patterns of significance on the other. Thus Roberto Rossellini will argue that neorealist cinema must represent reality with statistical and scientific concern,[34] while at the same time it must grasp "the intelligence of things . . . because to give the true value to anything means to have apprehended its authentic and universal significance."[35] Similarly, neorealist literature is torn between the rival claims of the *is* and the *ought* of history—to describe objective reality a posteriori or to represent it in terms of an ideal movement to perfection.[36]

In 1941, on the eve of the first proto-neorealist film season (*Ossessione, I bambini ci guardano,* and *Quattro passi fra le nuvole* were to come out the next year), a quarrel took place in the pages of the periodical *Cinema* that renegotiated the terms of the debate within nineteenth-century Italian realist thought. In "Verità e poesia: Verga e il cinema italiano,"[37] Giuseppe De Santis and Mario Alicata issued a plea for the return to realist literary models as the source of cinematic inspiration. "Realism," wrote De Santis and Alicata, "not as

[34] According to Rossellini, neorealism expresses "a need that is proper to modern man, to tell things as they are, to understand reality, I would say, in a pitilessly concrete way, conforming to that typically contemporary interest, for statistical and scientific results." Quoted in Mario Verdone, "Colloquio sul neorealismo," *Bianco e nero,* No. 2 (1952), 8.

[35] Quoted in Verdone "Colloquio," p. 8. The recurrence of the term "truth" in writings on neorealism attests to this desire to penetrate surface appearances in quest of hidden, universal meanings. Thus, Mario Gromo says of neorealism, "what came to life was less a new realism and more a new truth." Quoted in Liehm, *Passion and Defiance,* p. 135. Similarly, Sergio Amidei claims that "ours has been not the cinema of neorealism, but the cinema of truth." Quoted in Mino Monicelli, *Cinema italiano: Ma cos'è questa crisi?* (Bari: Laterza, 1979), p. 23.

[36] See Alfonso Procaccini, "Neorealism: Description/Prescription," *Yale Italian Studies* 2 (Winter 1978), 55.

[37] Giuseppe De Santis and Mario Alicata, "Verità e poesia: Verga e il cinema italiano," *Cinema,* 10 October 1941, 216–17.

passive obeisance to a static, objective truth, but as a creative force, in fantasy, of a history of events and of persons, is the true and eternal measure of every narrative expression."[38] With this carefully qualified notion of realism, De Santis and Alicata do to the nineteenth-century tradition what Verga and Capuana did to the French naturalists—they purge the theory of its exclusively scientific perspective. Their rejection of a passive, literal-minded transcription of the phenomenal world in favor of a dynamic interpretation of its underlying forces suggests the critics' preference for a classical over a naturalistic approach to realism in art. But their view does not go uncontested, as Fausto Montesanti reveals in his polemic response to the Alicata–De Santis editorial. A cinematic purist who believes that film must free itself from contamination by the other arts, Montesanti's primary quarrel with the Alicata–De Santis position is its plea for literary mediations. But underlying Montesanti's argument against literary intrusions into film is a very different interpretation of realism from that entertained by his adversaries in the pages of *Cinema*. In his observation that cinema came into its own when its theatrical conventions were slowly substituted by "precise constructions and objects taken from reality" he is basing cinematic realism, as Kracauer will some two decades later, on the quality that distinguishes film from the sister arts—its power physically to replicate the objective world.[39] The very properties of the medium itself dictate a naturalistic approach, according to Montesanti, who insists that truth is a surface phenomenon, immediately accessible to the senses, and hence to the filmic medium, making literature an uninvited guest in the *camera oscura*. "Truth is not hidden," wrote Montesanti, "it is enough to read it on the face of a passerby, as if between the lines of a newspaper item."[40]

"We too . . . want to bring our movie camera into the

[38] In "Verità e poesia," p. 216.
[39] Fausto Montesanti, "Della ispirazione cinematografica," *Cinema*, 10 November 1941), 281.
[40] Ibid.

streets, fields, ports, factories of our country," answered De
Santis and Alicata in "Ancora di Verga e del cinema italiano." "We too are convinced that one day we will create
our most beautiful film following the slow and tired step of
the worker who returns home."[41] Though this passage seems
to concede Montesanti his point about unmediated naturalistic reportage, De Santis and Alicata have projected his goal
onto an indefinite future by positing a "one day" so vague
and remote that it seems more a wistful chimera than an
imminent possibility. The purpose of this delaying strategy is
obvious—what must take place between now and the fulfillment of Montesanti's objective is a serious and systematic
study of literary models. Cinema must learn the lessons of
nineteenth-century literary realism before it can find its own
unmediated realist vocation.

Those lessons are perhaps best expressed by Francesco De
Sanctis in his plea for the embrace of realism as a corrective
to the problems besieging the late nineteenth-century Italian
sensibility. I will quote his remarks at length, since they so
well summarize the contemporary Italian approach to realism and anticipate the neorealists' contribution to a long and
rich tradition.

> Its substance is this, that in art it is necessary to give a
> larger part to the natural and animal forces of man, to
> chase away the dream and substitute action, if we want
> to restore our youth, to form our will, to strengthen
> our fiber. Realism that resembles an orgy is poetry of
> impotent and depraved old men; it is not the restora-
> tion of youth. . . . And the form of realism is this,
> that it be robust, clear, concrete, but such that within
> it appear all the phenomena of consciousness. Man
> must do, not say, what he thinks. But his thought must
> appear through the action, as the instinct of the animal

[41] Giuseppe De Santis and Mario Alicata, "Ancora di Verga e del cinema
italiano," *Cinema*, 25 November 1941, 315.

appears in its movements. This is the objective form, the life of things. The artist is like the great actor who forgets himself and reproduces the character exactly as nature formed him. Galileo, precursor of realism even in art, called this naturalness and simplicity. . . . For a fantastic race, friend of phrases and pomp, educated in Arcady and in rhetoric, as ours generally is, realism is an excellent antidote.[42]

According to De Sanctis, realism is a kind of cultural fountain of youth which rejuvenates a collective temperament fallen into artistic senility and decay. But the critic is quick to temper his enthusiasm with some implicit warnings—it is not all realisms that afford such cultural reawakenings, for indeed the wrong realism can have the opposite effect, making us more decrepit and impotent than ever in orgies of unmitigated materialism. Here we recognize the old expedient of dividing realisms into the good and the bad in order to salvage what is acceptable in modern theory while rejecting that part of it which precludes adherence to classical norms. In the injunction to transparency—to representing material things as they reveal higher truths—we can see the traces of classical realism at work, and when De Sanctis invokes nature as the model of artistic imitation, it is not the deterministic, strictly phenomenal nature of the naturalists but the vehicle of supersensory truths of the ancients. Even when De Sanctis pays obeisance to the scientific pretensions of contemporary French realism, he revealingly invokes Galileo, who is neither French nor contemporary.

It is this Italianized form of nineteenth-century realism, with its cautious synthesis of ancient and modern theory, that the neorealists will adopt in framing their approach to literature and film. But in choosing realism, the generation of the 1940s was by no means looking strictly behind; now the style was to prove its affinity for new cultural awakenings. With the

[42]De Sanctis, "Zola e L'assommoir," in Saggi critici, pp. 298–99.

fall of the Mussolini regime a month away, and the longed-for new order fast approaching, Umberto Barbaro was to issue his famous challenge: "If we in Italy wish to abandon once and for all our trashy histories, our rehashes of the 19th century, and our trifling comedies, we must try the cinema of realism."[43]

THE TERM NEOREALISM began its career as a literary designation, coined by Arnaldo Bocelli in 1930 to describe the style that arose in reaction to the autobiographical lyricism and elegiac introversion of contemporary Italian letters. In contrast, neorealism offered a "strenuously analytic, crude, dramatic representation of a human condition tormented between will and inclination by the anguish of the senses, the conventions of bourgeois life, the emptiness and boredom of existence; and a language founded no longer on the *how* but on the *what*, sunk as deeply as possible into 'things,' adhering to the 'object.' "[44] Though far less conspicuous than its cinematic counterpart, the literary movement of neorealism boasted some of the most distinguished figures in twentieth-century Italian culture, including Alberto Moravia, Elio Vittorini, Cesare Pavese, and Vasco Pratolini, in its prewar and postwar ranks. Despite the scarcity of cross-influences between the literature and cinema of neorealism, the two media shared enough common source material to enable us to consider them parallel manifestations of the same aesthetic and ideological impulses.[45] Many of the following stylistic considerations are thus as pertinent to literary neorealism as they are to its more celebrated cinematic equivalent.

[43] Quoted in Pierre Leprohon, *The Italian Cinema*, trans. Roger Greaves and Oliver Stallybrass (New York: Praeger, 1972), p. 86.

[44] Arnaldo Bocelli, *Letteratura del '900* (Palermo: Salvatore Sciascia, 1975), pp. 366–67.

[45] On the paucity of interactions between the literature and cinema of neorealism, see Roy Armes, *Patterns of Realism* (South Brunswick and New York: A. S. Barnes, 1971), p. 27. According to Francesco Flora, "cinemat-

Already in 1933, Leo Longanesi anticipated Barbaro's call
for a cinema of realism when he endorsed a filmmaking approach free of artifice, unhampered by fixed screenplays, inspired by real-life subjects, and resolved to tell the unvar-
nished truth.[46] The cause of realism was taken up again by
a group of young contributors to the journal *Cinema*, who
favored screenplays about the conditions of the working
classes, set in the factories and in the fields, told with attention to the minutiae of their everyday lives.[47] Giovanni Verga
provided the narrative prototype for the *Cinema* writers who
sought an alternative to the clichés and falsehoods of the
Fascist film industry and who found in the Sicily of *verismo*
the authenticity so lacking in contemporary cultural models.[48]
Luchino Visconti, the standard-bearer of the *Cinema* group,
was to embody its ideals in his first film. Heeding the pre-
scriptions of Mario Alicata and Guiseppe De Santis, Visconti
chose a Verga story, "L'Amante di Gramigna," for his
screenplay, but the prestige of the Sicilian author was of little
avail in getting past the Fascist censors, who thought better
of approving a film about banditry and self-degradation.
Fortunately, the censors failed to see the equally subversive
threat in the screenplay for *Ossessione* (based on James Cain's
novel *The Postman Always Rings Twice*), allowing Visconti
to make a film whose revelations of passion and provincial
squalor diametrically opposed the regime's ideas of artistic
propriety. Along with Alessandro Blasetti's *Quattro passi fra
le nuvole* and Vittorio De Sica's *I bambini ci guardano*, *Ossessione* was considered the harbinger of that realist recur-

---

ographic and literary neorealism were born from the same research and
experience." In *Inchiesta sul neorealismo*, ed. Carlo Bo (Turin: Edizione
Radio Italiana, 1951), p. 76.

[46] See Leo Longanesi, "L'occhio di vetro," in *Dai telefoni bianchi al neorealismo*, ed. Massimo Mida and Lorenzo Quaglietti (Bari: Laterza, 1980),
p. 118.

[47] See François Debreczeni, "Origines et évolution du néo-réalisme," *Etudes
cinématographiques* 32–35 (Summer 1964), 29.

[48] Ibid.

rence which was to produce its first full-fledged postwar example three years later in Rossellini's *Open City*.

But this opening to realism did not arise *ex nihilo* in 1942 like Minerva from the head of Jupiter, nor was it a sudden reaction to the falsifications of the Fascist cinema, for the Italian film industry had always paid obeisance to the realist possibilities implicit in the medium. From the very dawn of the industry, Italian filmmakers had sought at least physical realism in their fidelity to detail in historical reconstructions, in their occasional use of existing antiquities as settings for their "costume films," and in a kind of philological passion for authenticity.[49] In some cases, the early cinema's commitment to realism went beyond such surface accuracy to the quest for underlying social truths that we have come to identify with the classical realist tradition. Thus, amidst the historical extravaganzas and bourgeois melodramas of the Italian silent era, there appeared a smattering of films of undoubtedly realist descent. These included *Sperduti nel buio* and *Teresa Raquin* by Nino Martoglio, *Assunta Spina* by Gustavo Serena, and *Cavalleria rusticana* by Ubaldo Maria Del Colle, all made between 1914 and 1916, and all indebted to the "naturalism of the southern tradition" as it was formulated in literature by Giovanni Verga, Luigi Capuana, and others.[50] In the late 1920s, the two filmmakers who dominated the industry for a decade, Alessandro Blasetti and Mario Camerini, produced several works of a decidedly realist bent. Blasetti's *Sole* (1928), about Mussolini's draining of the Pontine marshes, and Camerini's *Rotaie* (1929), about two men in search of employment, look ahead to neorealism in their technique—location shooting, nonprofes-

[49] See Gian Piero Brunetta, "La migrazione dei generi dalla biblioteca alla filmoteca dell'italiano," *Italian Quarterly* 21 (Summer 1980), 86; and Liehm, *Passion and Defiance*, p. 9.

[50] This is Umberto Barbaro's perception, as quoted by Mario Quaragnolo in *Dove va il cinema italiano?* (Milan: Pan Editrice, 1972), p. 8. For a more detailed discussion of the "Neapolitan school" of filmmaking in the silent era, see Liehm, *Passion and Defiance*, pp. 12–16.

sional cast—as well as in their subject matter—contemporary problems in a working-class milieu.[51] Blasetti's *1860* (made in 1934) anticipates historical neorealism,[52] while his *Quattro passi fra le nuvole* joins the triumvirate of 1942 films that directly prefigured neorealism.

It would be naive, however, to proceed with a study of neorealism as if its validity and meaning were beyond question. Instead, the term has become the subject of considerable controversy, ranging from those who dismiss it as a figment of the critical imagination[53] to those who extol it as the highest expression of the postwar Italian world view.[54] Even among the upholders of neorealism (and these are by far the majority) there is much debate about definitions, rules, and influences. In the interests of time and space, I will limit myself to those arguments that bear most directly on our present concerns.

Claiming that neorealism is indeed a school, Georges Sadoul compiles a list of five characteristics prerequisite to such a designation: clearly delineated geographic and temporal boundaries, a group of masters and disciples, and a set of rules.[55] Neorealism meets the first two qualifications in its almost exclusive confinement to Rome between the years 1945 and 1952. Among its masters are Vittorio De Sica, Cesare Zavattini, Luchino Visconti, and Roberto Rossellini, while

[51] See Brandon French, "The Continuity of the Italian Cinema," *Yale Italian Studies* 2 (Winter 1978), 61–62.

[52] See Leprohon, *The Italian Cinema*, p. 222.

[53] Such critics admit that four or five remarkable films did emerge out of the immediate postwar industry, but that they resulted from a serendipitous combination of forces, including the talent of Rossellini and De Sica, and the straitened circumstances that necessitated the technical expedients associated with neorealist style. See Nicola Chiaromonte, "Italian Movies," *Partisan Review* 16 (June 1949), 628; Enrico Emanuelli's remarks in *Inchiesta sul neorealismo*, ed. Bo, p. 71; and Brunetta, *Storia*, p. 21.

[54] As does, for example, Brunello Rondi throughout his *Il neorealismo italiano* (Parma: Guanda, 1956).

[55] Cited in Mario Verdone, *Il cinema neorealista da Rossellini a Pasolini* (Palermo: Celebes, 1977), p. 27.

Luigi Zampa, Pietro Germi, Renato Castellani, Giuseppe De
Santis, and Aldo Vergano form the ranks of its disciples. The
rules governing neorealist practice would include location
shooting, lengthy takes, unobtrusive editing, natural lighting,
a predominance of medium and long shots, respect for the
continuity of time and space, use of contemporary, true-to-
life subjects, an uncontrived, open-ended plot, working-class
protagonists, a nonprofessional cast, dialogue in the vernacular, active viewer involvement, and implied social criticism.[56] But this is where a definition of neorealism encounters its most formidable problems, for the stylistic differences
among its individual practitioners are often greater than their
conformity to a given set of rules. Furthermore, neorealist
filmmakers never constituted a formal group, such as the Fu-
turists or the French *nouvelle vague* filmmakers, who sub-
scribed to a commonly agreed-upon aesthetic code.[57] "It's
not that one day we sat down at a table on Via Veneto,"
explained De Sica, "Rossellini, Visconti, myself, and the others and said: 'now let's create neorealism.' "[58] Critical formulation of neorealist rules came only after the fact—it did
not furnish any a priori basis for cinematic practice. When
Zavattini defined neorealism in his famous essay "Some Ideas

[56] Apropos the cinema's dissident voice, Zavattini remarked "the most
renewing part of neorealism, even in a theoretical sense, was (too briefly)
the consciousness of its duty always to trace first of all the negative points
of our reality." In Monicelli *Cinema italiano: Ma cos'è questa crisi?*, p. 162.
For the requirements of realist cinema in general, see Giannetti, *Understanding Movies*, pp. 91–96. On the time–space continuum of realism, see
Bazin, *What Is Cinema?*, 2:28. See also François Debreczeni, "La technique
du néo-réalisme," *Etudes cinématographiques* 32–35 (Summer 1964), 121–
22.

[57] On Futurism and its cinematic products, see Liehm, *Passion and Defiance*, pp. 16–19. On the absence of an aesthetic program for neorealist
practice, see Bondanella, *Italian Cinema*, p. 34. Nor was there ideological
homogeneity among neorealists, according to Brunetta, *Storia*, p. 321. On
the divergent cultural backgrounds and preparations of the major neorealist
directors, see Brunetta, *Storia*, p. 323.

[58] Quoted in Brunetta, *Storia*, p. 367.

on the Cinema,"[59] his was not the analysis of a disinterested critic but of a scriptwriter seeking theoretical justification for the particular aesthetic of his own work in *Shoeshine, Bicycle Thief,* and *Umberto D.* Thus no filmmaker of the so-called neorealist tendency will consistently manifest all the hallmarks of the style as institutionalized by the critical literature, nor will the received definition necessarily distinguish neorealist performances from other examples of documentary or realist fiction filmmaking.

However, if we go beyond technical considerations to the ethical impetus behind neorealism, we are apt to discover far more of a consensus among artists of the period and to find ample reason for grouping them together as upholders of a certain school, tendency, or style, broadly construed. Indeed, for many critics, neorealism is first and foremost a moral statement,[60] "una nuova poesia morale" whose purpose was to promote a true objectivity—one that would force viewers to abandon the limitations of a strictly personal perspective and to embrace the reality of the "others," be they persons or things, with all the ethical responsibility that such a vision entails.[61] This shared moral commitment united filmmakers "from above," dissolving their petty stylistic differences into basic agreement on the larger issues of human concerns and general world view.[62] Such a moral consensus among stylistically separate practitioners of neorealism leads one critic to the conclusion that it was never an aesthetic code at all, but strictly an ethical one.[63]

[59] See "Some Ideas," pp. 216–28.

[60] François Debreczeni, "L'esthetique du néoréalisme," *Etudes cinématographiques* 32–35 (Summer 1964), 73; Liehm, *Passion and Defiance,* p. 73; Chiarini, "A Discourse on Neo-Realism," in *Springtime,* ed. Overbey, p. 159; and Bondanella, *Italian Cinema,* p. 74.

[61] Rondi, *Neorealismo,* p. 27.

[62] Ibid., p. 130.

[63] Miccichè, "Per una verifica," in *Il neorealismo cinematografico italiano,* p. 27. Numerous others speak to this dimension of neorealism. See, for

Neorealist morality is perhaps best understood in relation to its nineteenth-century literary inspiration in Verga. When the Sicilian writer promises to give "la rappresentazione della realtà com'è stata o come avrebbe dovuto essere" (the representation of reality as it has been or as it should have been)[64] his insistence on an ideal course of human history, which may or may not be expressed by the factual record, suggests the influence of classical realism on an artist not fully committed to the naturalists' creed. This conflict between the scientific objectivity of naturalism and the humanistic survivals of classical realism continues into the twentieth century, but it takes a different form in the neorealists. For them, the influence of classical realism does not stop at Verga's recognition of the discrepancy between the way things are and the way they should be, but goes on to demand an end to that discrepancy, or in Sandro Petraglia's words, "cambiare le cose da come sono a come dovrebbero e potrebbero essere" ("to change things from the way they are to the way they should and could be").[65] In the difference between Petraglia's locution and Verga's resides the entire distinction between nineteenth-century Italian *verismo* and its twentieth-century counterpart. Verga's use of past tense verbs gives the objects of his representation a fixity and closure that defies any possibility of modification, while Petraglia leaves that option open in his choice of present and conditional verbs. The temporal disparity between Verga's act of writing and the events he records suggests a distance which is not only historical but

example, Bo, ed., *Inchiesta sul neorealismo*, p. 5; and Sergio Pacifici, "Notes toward a Definition of Neorealism," *Yale French Studies* 17 (1956), 50.

[64] *I Malavoglia*, p. 53.

[65] Sandro Petraglia, "Cesare Zavattini teorico del neorealismo," in *Il neorealismo cinematografico italiano*, p. 217. On the neorealist aspiration to social change, see Chiarini, "A Discourse on Neo-Realism," pp. 139, 167; Giuseppe Ferrara, "Neo-Realism: Yesterday," pp. 201–202; and the editor's introduction, p. 10, all in *Springtime*, ed. Overbey.

performative—his writing takes place in a world that is separate from and helpless to change the world of his characters.[66] The neorealist, on the other hand, considers himself part of the world he records—he is in it and a determinant of it, intervening in the present so that the conditional verbs will one day merit the unqualified future tense, and eventually even the present tense itself. Most significant is Petraglia's addition of *potere* (to be able to) to the Verghian list of *essere* (to be), and *dovere* (to have to), suggesting that the conflict between the way things are and the way they ought to be is reconcilable by appropriate social action.

What transpired to convert Verga's passive resignation into neorealist activism was, of course, the Resistance.[67] This movement gave its generation the confidence to believe that the ideal could impinge upon the real and that man could forge his own destiny in accordance with his highest moral promptings. Art, which for Verga bore passive witness to the underlying dynamism of the historical process, becomes the instrument for motivating radical change in the hands of the neorealists. That vestige of classical realism which fused with nineteenth-century positivism to form Verga's aesthetic is thus taken one step further by the neorealists, who develop the cognitive program into an incentive for action. The scientific pretensions of nineteenth-century naturalism survive in the neorealist aspiration to an objective, disinterested analysis of the social order. But where Verga could maintain the pretense of scientific impartiality because of his resigned acceptance of the status quo, the neorealists could not uphold

[66] Verga indeed renounced any pretensions to correct the injustices that were his constant thematic preoccupation. See Romano Luperini, *Verga e le strutture narrative del realismo* (Padua: Liviana, 1976), p. 99, and Visconti's remarks quoted in Carlo Lizzani, *Storia del cinema italiano 1895–1961* (Florence: Parenti, 1961), p. 451.

[67] On neorealism's birth in the Resistance, see Zavattini, "A Thesis on Neo-Realism," p. 68; Ferrara, "Neo-Realism: Yesterday," p. 199; Luigi Chiarini, "Neo-Realism Betrayed," p. 208, all in *Springtime*, ed. Overbey.

this pretext against the weight of their urgent didacticism. Needless to say, the neorealists' commitment to social change did not endear them to the guardians of the postwar status quo.[68] Despite their reluctance, for the most part, to embrace a Marxist perspective,[69] the filmmakers maintained a resolutely antiestablishment stance and presented an image of Italy that was anything but comforting to Italian officialdom. "We are in rags?" wrote Alberto Lattuada in 1945. "Let's show everyone our rags. We are defeated? Let's look at our disasters. How much are we obligated to the Mafia? to hypocritical bigotry? to conformity, to irresponsibility, to bad breeding? Let's pay all our debts with a ferocious love of honesty and the world will participate, moved by this great contest with the truth."[70] Small wonder that the established authorities felt threatened by these revelations and labeled such films as *Paisan, Caccia tragica* and *La terra trema* antagonistic to the national interest.[71] Thus *Bicycle Thief* was attacked by the Vatican newspaper *L'osservatore romano* as being uncharitable to Catholic charities, while De Sica's exposé of the Roman prison system in *Shoeshine* guaranteed that no director would even gain entrance to an Italian jail for filmmaking purposes again.[72] *Umberto D* earned Giulio Andreotti's opprobrium as De Sica's "wretched service to his fatherland, which is also the fatherland of . . . progressive social legislation."[73]

[68] See Guido Aristarco, "Del senno di poi sono piene le fosse," in *Antologia di "Cinema nuovo" 1952–1958*, ed. G. Aristarco (Florence: Guaraldi, 1975), p. 7.

[69] For Marxist criticisms of neorealism, see Mario Cannella, "Ideology and Aesthetic Hypotheses in the Criticism of Neorealism," *Screen* 14 (Winter 1973–74), 5–60; and Liehm, *Passion and Defiance*, pp. 92–94.

[70] Quoted in Lizzani, *Storia del cinema italiano*, p. 392.

[71] See Carlo Lizzani, *Il cinema italiano 1895–1979*, 2 vols. (Rome: Riuniti, 1979), 1:141.

[72] See Chiaromonte, "Italian Movies," p. 626, and Pierre Leprohon, *Vittorio De Sica* (Paris: Seghers, 1966), pp. 45–46.

[73] For the full text of Andreotti's letter to De Sica, see Giuseppe Ferrara, *Il nuovo cinema italiano*, pp. 286–87.

Unfortunately, the success of neorealism's dissident stance was such that it provoked the state's most lethal retaliatory measures. Censors excised objectionable material[74] or denied export to films that presented Italy in an unflattering light, in compliance with the provisions of the Andreotti Law of 1949.[75] Since domestic consumption could never generate enough revenues to meet neorealist production costs, the refusal of access to foreign markets was a sure promise of financial failure.[76] Those who persevered in making neorealist films did so at great financial risk, as Vittorio De Sica was quick to point out.[77] Whether or not these establishment pressures against neorealism were causal in its eventual decline, they nonetheless bear witness to the potency of the movement's dissident voice and to its fatal effect on a medium so dependent upon broad-based public and institutional support.[78]

There are many explanations for the waning of neorealism, some of which have been mentioned in the preceding pages: its refusal to embrace a Marxist perspective; the state and commercial pressures to tame its ferocity; and the survival of prewar stylistic modes.[79] But I would argue that the responsibility lies elsewhere, in the very principles that gave the movement such strength and nobility of purpose—its as-

[74] This was the case, for example, with Antonioni's *I vinti*, one of whose episodes had to be completely altered because it contained material that was deemed politically unacceptable. See Lizzani, *Il cinema italiano*, p. 172.

[75] See Armes, *Patterns of Realism*, p. 28; Liehm, *Passion and Defiance*, pp. 90–91; and *Springtime*, ed. Overbey, p. 28.

[76] Armes, *Patterns of Realism*, p. 28. On the importance of foreign markets, see Rossellini's "Ten Years of Cinema," in *Springtime*, ed. Overbey, p. 94.

[77] See his interview in Charles Thomas Samuels, *Encountering Directors* (New York: G. P. Putnam's Sons, 1972), pp. 146, 147, 157, 162.

[78] See Chiarini, "A Discourse on Neo-Realism," in *Springtime*, ed. Overbey, p. 157.

[79] On the vestigial Fascist influences within the industry, see Miccichè, "Per una verifica," in *Il neorealismo cinematografico italiano*, p. 15. For a survey of the causes of neorealism's decline, see Liehm, *Passion and Defiance*, pp. 101–102; Brunetta, *Storia*, pp. 334–36. See also Chiarini, "A

piration to change the world. For the danger of an art directed toward extraaesthetic ends is that its career is contingent upon the whim of historical circumstance, which can snuff it out as quickly and as arbitrarily as it brought it to life. Neorealism's birth in the Resistance may have endowed the movement with its considerable dignity and power, but it also brought about its inevitable demise when the Christian Democratic victory over the Popular Front in 1948 revealed that the forces of reaction had defeated the forces for change. No longer a protagonist in the historical process of renewal, neorealism could not retrench or revert to a Verghian position of passive witness to social injustice. Instead, it went underground, allowing a pseudo-version of itself to take over in the form of "rosy realism," which mimicked the external trappings of the neorealist model without any of the attendant commitment to social analysis and consequent corrective action. When the "boom" of the 1950s began to wind down and to reveal the fragility of its economic base, the genius of neorealism reappeared in the early 1960s to provide cinematic examples of pointed social satire. The crisis of 1968 sustained this impetus with films that returned to the original subjects of neorealism—Fascism and war—seen now from a distance of several decades with all the ironies and occasions for self-scrutiny that such a perspective affords.

Italian cinema may have lost its immediate postwar optimism about the attempt to shape political reality according to a moral idea, but it never lost its deep and abiding commitment to the dignity of that attempt, nor has the movement ceased to examine the reasons for its failure. By way of proof, we have only to look at the entire postwar produc-

---

Discourse on Neorealism," pp. 139 and 161; Ferrara, "Neo-Realism: Yesterday," p. 205; De Santis, "In Defense of the Italian Cinema," p. 217; and Ferrara, "Neo-Realism: Today," p. 221, all in *Springtime*, ed. Overbey.

tion of the Italian film industry, which has continued to acknowledge, in whatever respectful or irreverent ways, its
lasting debt to neorealism.[80]

[80] On the impact of neorealism on subsequent Italian film production, see
French, "Continuity of Italian Cinema," p. 64; Canziani and Bragaglia, *La
stagione*, p. 15; Miccichè, "Per una verifica," in *Il neorealismo cinematografico italiano*, p. 10; Lizzani, *Il cinema italiano*, pp. 163–263, and Peter
Brunette, "Recent Italian Film," *Italian Quarterly* 25 (Spring 1984), 61–62.

PART I

Neorealism Proper

I Rossellini's *Open City*: The founding

WHEN MANFREDI, the partisan leader who has been captured by the Nazis at the end of *Open City*, refuses to divulge the secrets of the Committee of National Liberation, explaining that he wants to live up to the heroism of his comrades who died for their silence, the Gestapo leader, Bergmann, immediately stereotypes him as grandiloquent and insincere. "You Italians, whatever party you belong to, are all addicted to rhetoric. But I'm quite sure that you will see things my way before dawn."[1] Bergmann is proven twice wrong, both in his certainty that Manfredi will break under torture and in his characterization of all Italians as creatures of rhetoric whose deeds will never match their extravagant promises. The Nazi chief's accusation, however, is not limited to the bravado of political prisoners under Gestapo interrogation, for it extends to all of Fascist Italy, whose penchant for rhetoric was so well exploited by that archjournalist and manipulator of headlines, Benito Mussolini. Not only was rhetoric the most important subject in Italian high schools, but it was the very foundation of the national legal profession, whose members populated the ranks of the Fascist hierarchy.[2] Mussolini spoke directly to this Italian love of the grand gesture, of the *bella figura*, whose form became an end in itself, regardless of the speaker's ability to make good on his promises.

[1] Roberto Rossellini, *The War Trilogy*, trans. Judith Green (New York: Grossman, 1973), p. 126. All quotes from the screenplay will come from this edition and subsequent page references will appear in the text.

[2] See Edward Tannenbaum, *The Fascist Experience*, (New York: Basic Books, 1972), p. 216.

By linking Manfredi's imminent martyrdom to Bergmann's indictment of Italian rhetorical excesses, Rossellini
makes the partisan's death an expiation of that cultural
weakness, and a prophecy of a new national style free of
empty bombast.[3] In truth, Manfredi's deeds are entirely
commensurate with his words, for he acts in accordance with
his pledge to reveal no partisan confidences, and his behavior
under torture is the very antithesis of rhetorical in his commitment to absolute silence. Even when his supreme defiance
could give vent to words as Bergmann allows him one last
chance to speak and save his life, Manfredi does not deign
to utter his contempt but spits in the interrogator's face, and
thus condemns himself to the worst possible death.

In Manfredi's antirhetorical stance, Rossellini embodies his
own polemic response to a cinematic tradition of historical
extravaganzas, white telephone comedies, and propaganda
films. *Open City* was to be the repudiation of an industry as
wedded to rhetoric as the Mussolini regime under which it
flourished. The filmmaker's most obvious antirhetorical ploy
was to dispose of all the physical trappings of prewar cinema, making a virtue of the necessity imposed upon him by
the straitened circumstances of a wartorn industry. The lack
of studio space, the absence of sophisticated equipment, and
the scarcity of film stock forced Rossellini to adopt the simplicity of means that was responsible for the authentic and
uncontrived look of his finished product. His resort to location shooting and to understated lighting contributed to the
newsreel quality which has often been ascribed to *Open City*,
while the inconsistency of the film stock, bought in bits and
pieces from street vendors, and the unstable electric current,
which sometimes fell as much as 15 to 20 volts in mid-shoot-

---

[3] Much has been written about neorealism's antirhetorical stance. See, for
example, Chiarini, "A Discourse on Neo-Realism," in *Springtime*, ed. Overbey,
p. 151. Bruno Torri calls *Open City* a film "senza retorica" in *Cinema
italiano: Dalla realtà alle metafore* (Palermo: Palumbo, 1973), p. 13. Pio
Baldelli echoes this sentiment in *Cinema dell'ambiguità* (Rome: La Nuova
Sinistra, 1971), p. 59.

ing, gave the film a roughness and a spontaneity matching the very historical circumstances of its birth.[4] For Rossellini these technical difficulties did not present obstacles so much as challenges, propelling him on to ever more inventive solutions and establishing that talent for improvisation which would constitute one of the greatest strengths, and limitations of his career.[5]

Open City is not only antirhetorical in its technical simplicity, but in its subject matter as well. The term "chronicle" has been applied again and again to describe the experiences of a group of Resistance fighters, set in Rome between the onset of the Nazi occupation in September 1943 and the Allied liberation of the city in June 1944.[6] The film tells the story of Giorgio Manfredi, a Resistance leader; Francesco, a printer for an underground newspaper; Pina, his fiancée and organizer of the neighborhood women; Marcello, her activist son; and Don Pietro, priest and committed partisan. In their pursuit are the Gestapo forces of occupied Rome, led by Bergmann and his henchwoman, the evil and seductive Ingrid. The link between the two groups is Marina, Manfredi's ex-mistress, who is corrupted by Nazi drugs and Ingrid's caresses. The film opens with the arrival of a German search party at the apartment of Manfredi, who manages to escape over the rooftops and find refuge with Francesco on the eve of his wedding to Pina. When a group of child terrorists dynamites a gasoline truck, Nazi attention is called to the neighborhood and a roundup of partisans follows. Manfredi manages to elude capture again, but Francesco is caught and

[4] See Vernon Jarratt, *The Italian Cinema* (London: The Falcon Press, 1951), p. 58.

[5] For an example of producer objections to Rossellini's improvisational technique, and for the director's defense of his *modus operandi*, see Rossellini, "Ten Years of Cinema," in *Springtime*, ed. Overbey, p. 103.

[6] See, for example, Luigi Malerba and Carmine Siniscalo, eds., *Cinquanta anni di cinema italiano* (Rome: Bestetti, 1954), p. 54. The film's attempt to chronicle recent historical events is made explicit in its original title, *Storie d'ieri*. See Liehm, *Passion and Defiance*, p. 64.

Pina, in her desperate pursuit of the truck that carries her fiancé away, is killed by machine-gun fire. After the prisoners are freed by partisan ambush, Manfredi, who had led the assault, and Francesco seek refuge at the apartment of Marina. Rebuffed by a moralizing and unforgiving Manfredi, Marina betrays his escape plans to the SS. Now it is Francesco who eludes capture, while Manfredi, Don Pietro, and an Austrian deserter are carted off to Gestapo headquarters. In their refusal to divulge anti-Fascist secrets all three meet their deaths—the deserter by suicide, Manfredi by torture, and Don Pietro by execution.

Though the events of the narrative are certainly fictionalized, the term chronicle is not misapplied, for the story is a pastiche of actual occurrences fused into a coherent whole whose general fidelity to the historical record far outweighs its recourse to any formal or aestheticizing effects.[7] "We made *Open City*," wrote Sergio Amidei in 1947, "under the impression, the suggestion, and the influence of what we had just lived through. More than that, we all have been the instrument of the will of the underground army that was anxious to write its page for the book of history."[8] Indeed, the historical roots of the narrative are deep and pervasive, extending from the fact of the Nazi occupation itself to many

[7] Recent American criticism has converged on the antirealistic elements of *Open City*. According to Martin Walsh, "*Rome, Open City; The Rise to Power of Louis XIV:* Re-evaluating Rossellini," *Jump Cut*, 20 July 1977, 13–15; and Peter Brunette, "Just How Brechtian Is Rossellini?" *Film Criticism* 3 (Winter 1979), 37, Rossellini's failure to make explicit the terms of his cinematic discourse and his insistence on the transparency of his medium have earned him the label of "illusionist," who pawns off his fictions as if they were realities in the best tradition of Hollywood. It follows that the only filmmakers who could possibly escape such charges of illusionism would be those highly self-conscious ones who make the language of the medium a major thematic preoccupation, leading to the *reductio ad absurdum* that the only valid subject for realist cinema is the impossibility of realist cinema.

[8] Sergio Amidei, "*Open City* Revisited," *The New York Times*, 16 February 1947, sec. 10, 5.

of the particulars of the narrative action.[9] Manfredi's initial
flight from the Nazis was inspired by Amidei's own rooftop
escape, the execution of Don Pietro was drawn from that of
an actual partisan priest, the death of Pina was based on an
incident witnessed by the actor Aldo Fabrizi, and the bombing of the gasoline truck was modeled on an actual episode
of the Resistance youth.

The characters' authenticity is of two sorts, deriving either
from the concrete historical figures they impersonate or the
popular types they represent. Authentic in the former way is
Bergmann, a composite of Gestapo chief Herbert Kappler and
Nazi commander Eugen Dollmann; Don Pietro, a fictional
rendering of Don Morosini, the activist priest whose story
was to be the original subject of a short documentary film;
and Manfredi, a figure of Resistance leader Celeste Negar-
ville.[10] Lacking in concrete historical counterparts, the more
"popular" characters are authentic in another way—embodying various aspects of the city's reaction to the Nazi
occupation.[11] Francesco represents the underground press and
hence the city's commitment to keep information flowing in
order to counter the partial and highly doctored coverage of
the Fascist news, and to further the spread of Resistance ideals.
Pina, as one of the organizers of the neighborhood women,
represents the spirit of popular insurrection against the occupying forces, while Lauretta, Pina's sister, and Marina

[9] On the authenticity of the film's facts and historical figures, see Armes,
Patterns of Realism, p. 68, and Jarratt, *Italian Cinema*, p. 59. According to
Giuseppe Ferrara, even some of the dialogue is historically authentic. See *Il
nuovo cinema italiano*, p. 106. Such historicity is what leads Ferrara to call
Open City "the first authentic example . . . of historical film," p. 108.

[10] The idea for the film began as a short documentary on the activist priest,
and then came to include a second documentary on the child-resistance
movement in a fusion of the two subjects with other interpolated fictional
material. See Armes, *Patterns of Realism*, p. 68.

[11] According to Fernaldo Di Giammatteo, such characters "synthesize a
historic situation," thus creating the "choral" nature of *Open City*. Cited
in Ferrara, *Il nuovo cinema italiano*, p. 109.

dramatize the weakness and corruptibility of those who found collaboration the easier route. It is through these last two, both daughters of the working classes, that Rossellini avoids sentimentalizing the proletariat, showing that for every Pina there is a Lauretta or a Marina, ready to exploit the situation for selfish and mercenary ends. Indeed, he goes to some lengths to establish the working-class origins of the two women, making Lauretta the family member who is ashamed of her humble origins, and Marina a childhood crony who has made it in the show world through Fascist connections. Thus Rossellini does not allow us to ascribe Marina's complicity to any bourgeois decadence, nor to a lifelong dependence on luxury, but instead to a personality weakness that makes her succumb to the seductions of drugs, fur coats, and lush surroundings.

The fact that Pina and Marina both share the same humble origins cannot be overstressed, for it shows that Rossellini holds Marina fully responsible for her choices, making Pina the standard against which this traitress is constantly measured. The consequences of two sets of moral decisions are embodied in these two women who are compared to each other throughout the film in terms of physical appearance, amorous expectations, emotional style, and cinematic precedents. Marina is a throwback to the *femme fatale* or the diva tradition of prewar Italian cinema. We first see her in bed against a luxurious headboard with a cockleshell design, which leads our gaze to her as the center of a glamorous set. We learn later what this elegant image costs her to maintain in the midst of a wartime economy. Her showgirl salary suffices to pay for her silk stockings and cigarettes alone, and necessitates a more lucrative sideline to cover the cost of room and board. Plain, unpretentious Pina, on the other hand, is a reverse diva who dresses in bobby socks and allows herself the luxury of silk stockings only once, on her wedding day. Whereas Marina first appears to us alone in a private space, Pina is introduced to us as she emerges from a crowd, establishing her status as a *popolana* whose identity is very much bound up with the community of which she is both organizer and member. Her language, with its dialectal cadences and colloquialisms is another social indicator, which locates her squarely in the popular midst. Marina instead speaks a neutral, nonregional Italian in keeping with her pretensions to social mobility. As the quintessential *popolana*, Pina incarnates the strength and self-possession that we see evidenced throughout the neighborhood, especially in the scene of the Nazi raid where women stand up to the German soldiers with great anger and personal dignity. Paradoxically, Pina's very strength is what leads to her destruction, for it will not let her watch as the Nazis cart off Francesco, but compels her to run after him and face the ensuing barrage of machine-gun fire. While Pina dies in the name of strength and defiance, Marina survives because of her weakness, and when confronted by the spectacle of her dead lover Manfredi, she merely faints in a coward's version of Pina's heroic death.

Perhaps the most telling commentary on the differences between the two women emerges from parallel conversations with their respective partners in love. To get any privacy, Pina and Francesco must talk on the stairwell outside their apartments, and although Pina is exhausted and demoralized by her feud with Lauretta, Francesco is able to encourage her with his partisan prophecies of a better world. Theirs is a tender and idealistic exchange punctuated by humorous recollections and hopeful foreshadowings. The analogous conversation between Marina and Manfredi is diametrically opposed in staging, substance, and tone. Set in Marina's diva boudoir, the discussion quickly degenerates into accusations and counteraccusations of the bitterest and most vindictive sort, ending in a stalemate of rigid, mutually defensive positions that admit of no compromise or progress. Where the dialogue between Pina and Francesco is future-oriented and transcends the dilemmas of self, that of Marina and Man-

fredi is limited to egocentric concerns that confine them to
an immobile present. Underlying the interpersonal success of
the one woman and the emotional bankruptcy of the other
is their divergent approach to love itself, which Pina sees as
an internal drive set in motion by an act of free will, while
Marina sees it as an external force that tyrannizes those who
become its prey. For Pina, the woman in love is an active
determinant of her fate and is morally accountable for the
course of her passion, while Marina sees herself as the passive victim of an uncontrollable power to which she abdicates all personal responsibility. Pina reveals her activist stance
in responding to Manfredi's nostalgia for Marina's simple,
working-class roots. When he concludes "she's not the right
kind of woman for me. Maybe if I'd known her before, when
she lived in Via Tiburtina. . . ." Pina replies, "Well, a woman
can always change, especially when she's in love" (26–27).
While Pina sees the woman as the author of her own amorous transformation, Marina attributes love's alchemy to another source. "If you'd really loved me," she tells Manfredi,
"you'd have changed me" (110), thus externalizing the cause
of her moral decline, just as later she will project onto drugs
and the enticements of Ingrid all responsibility for her forthcoming betrayals. Marina's concept of love as a transcendent
and destructive passion is given words by the song overheard
in her dressing room while she ransacks her purse for nar-
cotics. "At Copacabana, at Copacabana, on moonlit nights,
the woman who loves you kisses you, takes you, holds you,
enfolds you, inflames you with love. At Copacabana they
steal your heart, at Copacabana is the life of love" (40–41).
The exotic setting, loss of self, the forfeit of control, all identify this as the predatory passion that subsumes the beloved
into another order of being where conscience and consciousness are left behind. Ironically, it is Ingrid, appearing at the
end of the scene with caresses and more drugs, who fulfills
this "Copacabana" sentiment, playing the *femme fatale* to

1. *Deeply moved, Pina (Anna Magnani) listens as Francesco (F. Grand-Jacquet)
expresses his hope for the good outcome of the partisan struggle.*

Marina, and revealing the exploitative and dehumanizing implications of such a passion.[12]

The transformations worked by love, be they the malignant, externally imposed ones of Marina, or the purifying, internally motivated ones of Pina, are not limited to the thematic level of the film, but also reveal important formal and symbolic applications. Indeed, the entire film may be said to be about transformations—of people, of genres, and of the systems of signification that typify a culture. Rossellini's interest in the second and third kinds of transformations is what makes him the founder of a new cinematic mode and of a new cultural vision—in short, it is what makes him the first neorealist.

The generic transformation is the most obvious and the easiest to identify, thanks to Rossellini's own celebration of the "spontaneous creations of the actors: of Anna Magnani and of Aldo Fabrizi in particular."[13] He goes on to cite their debt to the vaudeville stage, which offered such valuable training to the leads in his film, making the regional theater, both in its popular manifestations (the variety shows or *avanspettacoli*), and in its more formal, literary versions (the dialectal plays of Eduardo de Filippo, for example), one of the most important influences on *Open City*. Indeed, this source explains much in the tone and staging of the film, from the use of dialect itself to the slapstick humor, which is handled so brilliantly and appropriately to provide relief in moments of almost unbearable dramatic intensity. Thus, the anxiety generated by the Nazi roundup is lightened by Don Pietro's faked administration of the last rites to the old man who provides his and Marcello's excuse for entering the tenement under Nazi surveillance to confiscate the contents of the boy terrorists' arsenal. Rather than dissipate the dra-

---

[12] The primacy of the sentimental theme in the film is suggested by Armes, who argues "in one sense indeed it would be perfectly valid to view the film as a study of the success and failure of love." *Patterns of Realism*, p. 74.

[13] Quoted in Verdone, "Colloquio sul neorealismo," p. 8.

matic tension of the scene, this interlude both heightens and eventually resolves it by providing the unexpected comic ending to a seemingly impossible predicament. When the old man sees Don Pietro about to give extreme unction, he rebels with every ounce of the considerable life-energy remaining in him. With the soldiers about to enter any minute and the old man's panic rising, Don Pietro has no time to lose. Rossellini spares us the actual scene of the priest's knocking the man unconscious with a frying pan, since the violence of such a spectacle would diminish our delight and surprise at the good outcome of his expedient.

Another homage to the slapstick tradition of regional theater is the scene of the boys' homecoming after their successful demolition of the gasoline truck. Puffed up by their daring, they face the parental consequences of their postcurfew return with bravado, only to be spanked ignobly like the small children they really are. Rossellini uses the architecture of the tenement to great advantage as each landing provides a resounding punishment for the children who live on it. Again Rossellini spares us the gory details, focusing instead on the other children whose faces register the fact of the punishments suffered by their comrades within. As the group of survivors dwindles at each landing, the facial expressions deteriorate with the knowledge that "we're next." The sequence is brilliant not only in its mixture of comic and cinematic effects, but in the wonderful irony that condemns those who defied Nazi authority to the tyranny of parental authority, which not only afflicts, but (far worse) infantilizes, its victims.

The regional theater is also discernible in the many details of domestic life that appear independent of the plot, yet that greatly enhance the sense of the quotidian pervading the film. Thus the spectacle of two girls' carrying a demijohn of water down the stairs of the tenement as Manfredi waits for Pina to get the apartment key has no other purpose than to show us an aspect of life as lived. Similarly, Pina makes the bed as she talks to Manfredi, a streetcar passes while Marcello leads Don Pietro home, the soccer game goes on after Don Pietro entrusts its supervision to another boy, and numerous other details conspire to show that this world continues to exist even after Rossellini's camera crew has left the scene.[14]

The film promises, then, to be a domestic idyll in the tradition of Italian regional theater, replete with familiar detail, local color, love interest, slapstick humor, and a classical comic resolution in the marriage of Pina and Francesco.[15] Midway into the story, however, these generic expectations are violently reversed by the death of Pina, which shocks us out of our comic complacency and shifts the film into a tragic mode.[16] In this transformation of genres, Rossellini reveals that the potential domestic comedies of contemporary life were turned into tragedies by contact with the world beyond the hearth; indeed, that history would not leave the private space alone, or to put it another way, that given the times, Pina could never simply remain the comfortable Donna Rosa of Eduardo de Filippo's *Sabato, domenica e lunedi*. Neorealism may be said to begin with the death of Pina, which forces her story to open to history and forsake any easy withdrawal into literary formulas and predictable plots.[17]

As a measure of this generic transformation, we have only to look at the various uses to which humor is put throughout the film. In the first half of the story, where the modes of the regional theater prevail, we have popular banter of a fairly neutral, standard sort. Agostino, the sexton of Don Pietro's

[14] For further striking examples of this *quotidianità*, see Liehm, *Passion and Defiance*, p. 64.

[15] On the expectations for a comic happy outcome, see Baldelli, *Cinema dell'ambiguità*, pp. 52–53.

[16] On the critical tradition of dividing the film in half, see Ferrara, *Il nuovo cinema italiano*, pp. 113–14. I agree with Ferrara, who deplores the tendency to privilege the mode of the first half and condemn that of the second. On the other hand, Bondanella, *Italian Cinema*, p. 39, sees the entire film as a mixture of tragicomic elements.

[17] On Pina's death as the film's opening out to history, see Ferrara, "Neo-Realism: Yesterday," in *Springtime*, ed. Overbey, p. 202.

church, is the source, and the object, of much clerical humor, sparked initially by his enthusiastic, if unauthorized, participation in the raid on the neighborhood bakery. When Agostino snatches a roll from one woman's share of the spoils, she protests, "Hey Agostino, why don't you go get some yourself?" "I can't, I'm a sexton," he answers, "I'd end up in Hell," to which the woman replies as she retrieves her roll, "then you'll eat your cake in Paradise" (16). Later, the joke continues when Don Pietro and Marcello bump into an Agostino laden with bread, who explains that the bakers were celebrating that morning. "I don't know what holiday it was. Not even the baker knew. Excuse me, Don Pietro, I have to go" (30–31). The clerical humor takes a visual turn in the religious shop above the basement headquarters of the Resistance press. Don Pietro's sensibilities are offended by the juxtaposition of a statue of San Rocco and that of a voluptuous nude. At first he turns the nude away, giving San Rocco the benefit of an equally appetizing dorsal view, when he realizes that it is the saint who needs repositioning, not the nude.

This benign, almost childlike humor gives way to sarcasm and mockery in the second half of the film where it serves as a coping mechanism for a people in the throes of despair. During the raid on the tenement, the soldiers tell one woman not to worry about leaving her laundry behind. "Get outside. No one's going to touch your stuff. We're here!" "Of course, how stupid of me," she answers. I didn't think of that" (82), relishing the irony of a situation that ensures the safety of her dirty clothes, while threatening the lives of her husband, brothers, or sons. We find a similar handling of sarcasm in the restaurant scene when two German soldiers bring live sheep to provide the meat for their main course. Flavio, the proprietor, objects, "I'm a cook, not a butcher," and when the soldiers offer to slaughter the animals themselves, he comments, "Oh yes, you people are specialists" (98).

A minor character who appears once in each half of the film, well illustrates the change in humorous usage that accompanies the more general shift from domestic comedy to public tragedy. The paralyzed old man makes his first cameo appearance during the family quarrel on the eve of Pina's wedding. Oblivious to the emotional fireworks in the adjoining room, he voices his exclusive concern for the fate of the wedding cake and for the *mangiata* (gorging) which will constitute his part in the next day's festivities. This delightful hedonism becomes something much more poignant in the second half of the film, when the old man appears in another comic scene whose stakes are much higher and whose thematic implications much more serious. His refusal to "play dead" as Don Pietro and Marcello seek to hide Romoletto's weapons under his sheets signals the will to life and to resistance that characterized the people in their finest and most desperate hour. The fact that the old man is not named, and that he is paralyzed and sick, makes him an emblem of that Rome which was damaged and helpless, yet unwilling to surrender either to superior military force, or to its own will to die.

Thus the emblematic figure of the old man corroborates what the film's title suggested all along—that the protagonist of the story is Rome itself, as a place, as a people, and as a historical entity.[18] The several maps of the city that recur throughout the film serve to remind us of its thematic importance and of the plurality of meanings that attach to it. The first map we see is in Bergmann's office, providing the background for the conversation between the Gestapo chief and the Fascist police commissioner about the ensuing dragnet for partisan leaders. This map represents the Nazi–Fascist image of Rome—a city to be drawn and quartered for

---

[18] Gianni Rondolino points out how Rossellini combines individual story with recent Roman history "in such a way as to compose a sort of fresco in which the story of each one is confounded with that of the entire city." See *Rossellini*, p. 52.

its audacity in resisting the occupation sanctioned by international law. Significantly, the map is divided into many subsections in accordance with the Schröder plan to smoke out resisters, but also in accordance with the more general technique of separating the people from each other in the time-honored tradition of divide and conquer. The second map of Rome is located in Francesco's apartment and it labels centers of underground activism. In diametrical opposition to Bergmann's map, Francesco's aspires to unify and coordinate the various Resistance strongholds by sharing intelligence through the underground press as well as through personal contacts. It is perhaps no accident that Manfredi's tortured, blood-lined face, which we see again and again in closeup at the end of the film, recalls the contours of these two maps and the two "Romes" they represent, lacerated by years of war and the most recent struggles for military dominance.

In working with the image of the city, however, Rossellini must perform an important act of recuperation, for he cannot forget that Mussolini had made of Rome a symbol and a justification for all his imperialist exploits. The title *duce*, the ancient Roman salute, the classicizing architecture, the claim to the Mediterranean as *mare nostro*, and the *fasce* themselves show how Mussolini used the trappings of antiquity to adorn his campaign for power. "Rome must appear marvelous to all the peoples of the world," he said in 1926,

> vast, ordered, potent, as it was at the time of the early empire of Augustus. You will continue to free the trunk of the great oak of all that still encumbers it. You will make passages around the Theater of Marcellus, the Campidoglio, the Pantheon: all that grew around them in the centuries of decadence must disappear. You will also liberate the temples of Christian Rome from profane and parasitic constructions. The ancient monuments of our history must loom in the

necessary solitude. Hence, the third Rome will spread over other hills, along the banks of the sacred river as far as the beaches of the Tyrrhenian Sea.[19]

The Fascist state thus constitutes *la terza Roma*, typologically fulfilling the figures of Augustan Rome and Christian Rome that Mussolini sees as his historical models. All that intervenes between these climactic moments of political and spiritual supremacy is seen as decadent, parasitic growth, although elsewhere, Mussolini is quick to invoke other historic precedents, such as the Risorgimento or the heroics of World War I as prefigurations of his Fascist state.[20] The city, referred to significantly, if pretentiously, as *L'Urbe* and *caput mundi* represents, above all, the notion of empire, and when Il Duce alludes to Christian Rome, it is to the Renaissance popes whose archaeological passion for antiquities matched Mussolini's own.[21]

Rossellini must somehow undo this damage to the dignity and integrity of Rome as a historical idea before he can use it to further his anti-Fascist intent. The filmmaker's strategy of revoking Mussolini's title to the symbols of antiquity and then appropriating them for his own purposes explains the symmetry of the triumphal marches that introduce and conclude the film. *Open City* begins with the procession of German soldiers into a square of the occupied city and ends with the return of the young boys into Rome on the Via Trionfale

---

[19] Quoted in Francesco Sapori, *L'arte e il duce* (Milan: Mondadori, 1932), p. 1.

[20] Garibaldi is thus called "dittatore" (p. 119) and is lionized in the official Fascist celebration of the fiftieth anniversary of his death, while Mazzini is seen as one of the prophets of the perfect Italian state as embodied in Fascism (p. 187). A monument to the soldiers fallen in World War I culminates in a triumphal image of Mussolini (p. 115). All in Sapori, *L'arte e il duce.*

[21] Ibid., p. 10. For further analysis of the function of the figure of Rome in Fascist rhetoric, see Arthur R. Evans, Jr., "La croce e il coltello: Malaparte and the March on Rome, A Note on the Rhetoric of Fascism," *Italian Quarterly* 23 (Winter 1982), 50.

(Triumphal Way). Theirs is the corrective to the initial march of the occupying troops as the boys reclaim their city for the future of justice and hope that their political activism bespeaks. Another clue to Rossellini's interpretive strategy is the identity of the boys' leader—he is Romoletto, whose symbolic significance is twofold, both in its allusion to the myth of Rome's founding, and in its revelation of the Fascist taste for naming children after classical heroes.[22] The filmmaker is thus able to challenge Mussolini's mythomania by revising the myth according to anti-Fascist ideals.[23] Like Mussolini, Rossellini's Romoletto will look to the past for his model and his justification in refounding the city, but he will select republican Rome, rather than imperial Rome, as his historical exemplar. The boy's physical mutilation serves as a reminder that post-Fascist Rome operates under the literal and figurative handicaps incurred by the events of its immediate past. Like Romulus' aboriginal city, Romoletto's will also be founded on fratricidal blood in the bitter civil war between Nazi–Fascist collaborators and the finally triumphant soldiers of the partisan cause.

However, we would be seriously remiss if we were to advance a strictly secular interpretation of the image of the city. Indeed, to do so, we would have to relegate Don Pietro to a merely ornamental role in the narration, and to ignore the considerable external evidence of Rossellini's Christian humanism.[24] But Don Pietro's central position in the film, the shy and indirect protestations of faith made by other characters, and the constant allusions to the relationship between

[22] See Ben Lawton, "Italian Neorealism: A Mirror Construction of Reality," *Film Criticism* 3 (Winter 1979), 14.

[23] This side of Mussolini's antiquarianism is evidenced by the celebration of Hellenic myths in Agrigento under the direction of Ettore Romagnoli (p. 41) and the Duce's interest in those archaeological findings that were most suggestive of Rome's mythic past (p. 26). Both in Sapori, *L'arte e il duce.*

[24] According to Bondanella, *Italian Cinema,* p. 38, it is the Christian humanist message which prevails in *Open City,* taking precedence over any realist social analysis.

Church and political activism all argue for the inclusion of the religious theme in any serious reading of *Open City*. We should begin, however, by positing the distinction that Rossellini himself upholds between the Church as institution and the Christian faith not always perfectly embodied by its worldly agents.[25] Indeed, the Church as political entity comes under repeated attack by Rossellini for its neutrality, a stance necessitated by the signing of the Lateran Treaty between Mussolini and the Vatican in 1929. Marcello's truancy from catechism class is thus ascribed to the Church's aloofness from the anti-Fascist struggle. "How come you never come to the oratory anymore?" asks Don Pietro. "How can a guy go waste time at the oratory, the way things are" (29) is Marcello's partisan rejoinder. Later, when Don Pietro tells the printer Gino that he had offered Manfredi asylum in the monastery of San Giovanni e Paolo, the response is a tacit criticism of the Church's political nonalignment. "I know, Father, but there are only a few of us, and if everybody goes into the monasteries . . ." (38).

Despite this contempt for certain aspects of the institutionalized faith, Rossellini nonetheless evidences a deep respect for the power and the dignity of the Christian message. Pina herself is a believer who finds the idea of a religious wedding far more congenial than a civil ceremony under the auspices of Fascist authority. Her informal confession to Don Pietro, as she accompanies him to the rendezvous with Manfredi's partisan contact, shows how unnecessary the formal trappings of Church worship are to the sincere expression of religious sentiment. And despite her "fallen" condition as an unwed mother who dies without those sacraments which would entitle her to some portion of sanctifying grace, Rossellini accords her the dignity of a saint. Her death is fol-

---

[25] James Agee's failure to honor this distinction is what leads him to question the validity of Rossellini's Marxist–Christian synthesis at the end of *Open City*. For his doubts about Rossellini's ideological optimism, see *The Nation*, 13 April 1946, 443.

lowed soon after by a scene in church where the desperate prayer to the Madonna seems addressed to Pina herself: "Mater Purissima . . . Mater Castissima . . . Mater Inviolata . . . Mater Intemerata . . . Mater Amabilis . . . Mater Admirabilis . . . ora pro nobis . . . ora pro nobis" (102–103). Pina's presence, even in death, is felt throughout the second part of the film, not only as the standard against which the other female characters are measured, but as a figure who watches over the action, indeed, who even intercedes in answer to the congregational plea "ora pro nobis." It is she, in a sense, who saves Francesco's life when Marcello delays his would-be stepfather's final departure for the monastery to give him Pina's scarf. This momentary hesitation spares Francesco the fate that Don Pietro, Manfredi, and the Austrian have to suffer, giving Pina's scarf a kind of talismanic effect on the lives of the man and boy she loved, and conferring upon her a quasi-mystical power to intervene in their behalf.

Even Manfredi, a communist and hence "an atheist and an enemy" (130) of the faith (at least as Bergmann would have it), tries to make confession to Don Pietro after their capture by the SS. "I have to tell you the truth. I'm not the man you think I am. I'm . . ." (124), he begins, only to be interrupted by the Austrian deserter who announces the approach of the Nazi guards. Manfredi's and Pina's impulse to confess to Don Pietro derives less from the fact that he is a Church official than that he is the best possible embodiment of the Christian imperative to social justice. As such, he redeems the Church by showing that its political neutrality constitutes by no means the sole interpretation of the Christian mandate.[26] Far from condemning the film to a narrow pietism, Don Pietro opens it up to a plurality of moral perspectives by vindicating not only the heterodoxy of Church

[26] Indeed, the historical counterpart to Don Pietro, Don Morosini, was not alone in his dissent. See the comments of Fausto Amodei as reported in Ferrara, *Il nuovo cinema italiano*, p. 115.

doctrine but also the multiple bases of political action in the secular domain. Whether the participants in the struggle are Marxists, humanists, monarchists, or Christian soldiers does not matter as long as the fight is directed toward the divinely sanctioned end of social justice. When Bergmann questions the propriety of Don Pietro's collaboration with a communist, he explains "I am a Catholic priest and I believe that a man who fights for justice and liberty walks in the pathways of the Lord—and the pathways of the Lord are infinite" (130). Don Pietro invokes divine authority not to privilege his own ideological position, but to show that petty sectarian differences are of no account when viewed *sub specie aeternitatis*. Don Pietro's Rome will thus be an open city in the truest sense of the word, accommodating a multiplicity of perspectives in a society that refuses all absolutes except those of freedom and social justice.[27]

Don Pietro's role in the story and his final martyrdom to the partisan cause make Romoletto's refounding of the city a rebirth as well. When the boys march back to Rome after witnessing the priest's execution, they do so against the backdrop of St. Peter's in the closing shot of the film.[28] This monument ("San Pietro" in Italian) is a visual allusion, of course, to Don Pietro and it suggests that the ideals for which he died—secular activism under the aegis of Christian spirituality—will govern the liberated city, just as Rome herself spreads out under the dome of St. Peter's in Rossellini's final *mise-en-scène*. Rome thus becomes the symbol of regeneration in its threefold typology—as capital of the pagan past,

---

[27] On the film's presentation of a plurality of perspectives and on its refusal to privilege any one, univocal truth, see Brunetta, *Storia*, pp. 321 and 373. Indeed, this interpretation of the film's title as a plea for ideological openness is corroborated by the group of Marxist dissidents who, in the wake of the Hungarian revolution of 1956, began a journal called *Città aperta* in which disaffected members of the PCI could voice views which differed from the straight party line.

[28] On the spiritual implications of this shot, see Bondanella, *Italian Cinema*, pp. 41–42.

as headquarters of the Christian present, and as a figure of the Kingdom of God to be founded on earth at the end of time. This apocalyptic element is introduced at the moment of Don Pietro's execution when the young priest in attendance recites from the Lord's Prayer "adveniat regnum tuum: ("may thy kingdom come" [155]) in a promise of that future when the secular ideals of the classical past will fuse with the spiritual ideals of the Christian present to form that Rome "onde Cristo è romano" ("where Christ is a Roman" [*Purg.* XXXII, 102]).

Though Rossellini's film spoke with an optimism and a faith appropriate to the events of 1945, subsequent developments have proved him more a dreamer than a prophet. No leader emerged to carry out this synthesis of Marxism and Catholic humanism, and no social order arose to fulfill his political imaginings.[29] Yet *Open City* had enough power and momentum to sustain its vision and to inspire an entire cinematic movement dedicated to its realization. Later filmmakers would modify the particulars of the vision, but none would question its essential rightness nor its urgent claim to repeated artistic expression. Rossellini and his colleagues may not have founded the social order of their political dreams, but they did found a cinematic movement whose adherents constituted a citizenry of its own, as loyal and as committed, in many instances, as the Romolettos and the Marcellos of the neorealists' visionary city.

[29] Not surprisingly, Rossellini came under attack by Marxists for propagating this "fairy tale of national agreement on the part of opposed forces and hierarchies." Baldelli, *Cinema dell'ambiguità*, p. 84. For Rossellini's ideological waffling in *Open City*, see the same volume, pp. 76–88.

2 De Sica's *Bicycle Thief*: Casting shadows on the visionary city

SOON AFTER ANTONIO RICCI reports the theft of his bicycle to the authorities, a journalist, looking for a story, asks
an officer at police headquarters if there is any news. When
the officer answers, "No, nothing, just a bicycle,"[1] the audience is suddenly confronted with a violent clash of perspectives. From the point of view of the police and the press, the
bicycle theft lacks any of the sensationalism, squalor, or violence that recommends crime to the public notice. For Antonio, and for the viewers, who have come to see the crucial
importance of the bicycle to one family's well-being, the police officer's dismissal is the cruelest of understatements. But
the clash of perspectives implies far more than the mere disparity between the public and private claims of events—it
reveals the historical distance that separates *Bicycle Thief* from
Open City, and suggests the challenges faced by De Sica and
Zavattini in updating the neorealist aesthetic.[2] Though both
Open City and *Bicycle Thief* may be considered chronicles
in that they document contemporary social circumstances,
Rossellini's film was endowed with drama and urgency by

---

[1] *The Bicycle Thief: A Film by Vittorio De Sica*, trans. Simon Hartog
(New York: Simon and Schuster, 1968), p. 35. All quotes from the screenplay will be from this edition. Subsequent page references will appear in the
text.

[2] Though Zavattini was the official scriptwriter and De Sica the official
director of *Bicycle Thief*, so neat a division of labor belies the truly collaborative nature of their partnership. When I refer to De Sica alone in these
pages, I do so out of convenience, and not out of a desire to slight Zavattini's contribution to this and the other films on which the two men collaborated.

the very nature of the history it recorded, while De Sica's story reflected, instead, the banality of the stabilized postwar condition. Where Nazi occupation, torture, underground resistance, and guerrilla warfare gave *Open City* its natural dynamic power, hunger, unemployment, and despair provided De Sica and Zavattini with subject matter of far less obvious dramatic potential.[3] But Zavattini made a virtue of necessity, arguing that the dramatically poor subject matter was by definition the richer in truth, devoid of the distractions and fabrications of conventional narrative structure.[4] In De Sica's words, "my purpose, I was saying, is to find the element of drama in daily situations, the marvelous in the news, indeed, in the local news, considered by most people as worn-out materials."[5]

Such statements may be helpful in telling us why *Bicycle Thief* is not *Open City*, but they do nothing to locate the source of the film's poetic power, nor to explain why it is that we recoil in horror at the police officer's belittling of Antonio's loss. Although the comment "no, nothing, just a bicycle" is on one level a valid assessment of the incident, its unfairness, on other levels, is an insult to our very notions of human justice. What the police officer's reductiveness does is to underscore, by contrast, the filmmaker's strategy of semantic layering, whereby the storyline becomes the vehicle for multiple levels of meaning. Unlike this-for-that allegory, however, the literal level is not swallowed up by its figurative significance, but maintains its autonomy as a document of a concrete historical condition. Yet the simultaneous and parallel meanings it generates on psychological, sociopolitical, and philosophical levels serve to give every cinematic event

---

[3] Leprohon comments on how the filmmakers succeeded in shifting the neorealist themes from those of Resistance and liberation to the banality of postwar restoration. See *Vittorio De Sica*, p. 37.

[4] See Zavattini's "Some Ideas on the Cinema," p. 217.

[5] Cited in "De Sica su De Sica," *Bianco e nero* 36 (September–December 1975), 259.

such interpretive complexity that what appears at first glance
to be a simple narrative construction upon close critical scrutiny reveals the highest degree of literariness.[6] Such deceptive
simplicity, or self-concealing art, makes the film, like Antonio's bicycle, the bearer of far heavier and more sophisticated cargo than its fragile exterior would immediately suggest. But before we examine this literary strategy, we would
do well to consider the concrete cinematic vehicle whose
technical form reveals the same self-concealing art that typifies De Sica's approach to meaning.

Here, again, comparisons with *Open City* are in order.
Just as historical circumstances gave the events of *Open City*
its natural drama, so too did they dictate its technical style.
The primitive equipment that Rossellini had at his disposal,
the absence of studio facilities, and the improvised mode of
production were all direct correlates of the very historical
events that the film records. But by 1948, filmmaking was
no longer the obstacle-ridden process that it was in the immediate aftermath of the Allied liberation. On the contrary,
technical possibilities were wide open to De Sica and Zavattini, who made of *Bicycle Thief* a neorealist superspectacle,
complete with a big budget, a cast of hundreds, and a metic-
ulously worked out shooting style. The film cost 100 million
lire—a sizable sum by contemporary Italian production standards, owing in large part to the vast number of extras who
had to be kept on retainer until perfect filming conditions
were met.[7] De Sica and Zavattini took six months to prepare
the script, discussing every image and carefully selecting the
best possible locations for the action to unfold. Shooting was
done with painstaking care to maximize visual complexity,

[6] On the interpretive richness of every image in the film, see André Bazin,
Vittorio De Sica (Parma: Guanda, 1953), p. 19.
[7] On the opulence and meticulousness of the film's production, see Armes,
Patterns of Realism, pp. 152–55, and Bondanella, *Italian Cinema*, p. 57.
On the multiplicity of camera angles and the plurality of the filmmaker's
perspectives, see Baldelli, *Cinema dell'ambiguità*, p. 235.

while concealing the art that went into its making. Rossellini's expedients in *Open City* had come to be stylistic norms for neorealism, generating such a taste for simplicity, location shooting, and authorial nonintervention that subsequent filmmakers were forced into creating, through elaborate technical means, an illusion of technical poverty. *Bicycle Thief* is a prime example of the self-concealing art that neorealists were required to practice in the pursuit of Rossellinian austerity, where the impression of effortlessness and stylistic transparency were not achieved without calculated effort.[8] This is not to say that De Sica's careful aesthetic is in bad faith. On the contrary, it reflects a conscious ideological *prise de position* against the spectacular conventions of the commercial cinema—a rejection that is made explicit in two episodes in *Bicycle Thief*. When a co-worker curses the Sunday rain and complains that there is nothing to do but go to the movies—a singularly boring prospect for him—he is arguing for the irrelevance of commercial cinema to the common plight.[9] It is significant, too, that Antonio's troubles begin as he is putting up a publicity poster for Rita Hayworth's new film, suggesting the marked contrast between commercial cinematic fantasies and the real survival problems besetting the Italian public.[10] In fact, in the very process of putting up the poster, Antonio suffers the crisis that prevents *Bicycle Thief* from ever becoming a consumable family idyll. Antonio will not be able to rescue himself and his dependents

[8] As Jean Cocteau observed, "the miracle is in having effaced the work." Cited in Henri Agel, *Vittorio de Sica* (Paris: Editions Universitaires, 1955), pp. 99–100.

[9] Ben Lawton cites this remark and the Rita Hayworth poster as examples of De Sica's self-reflexive commentary on the nature of his medium. See "Italian Neorealism: A Mirror Construction of Reality," p. 18; and Bondanella, *Italian Cinema*, p. 57.

[10] In an interview with Charles Thomas Samuels, De Sica makes explicit the disparity between this Hollywood image and Antonio's world. See *Encountering Directors*, p. 153.

from their desperate poverty by dint of perseverence, hard work, and good luck, as the hypothetical Hollywood equivalent, produced by David O. Selznick and starring Cary Grant, would require.[11] The literal level of the film could be summarized in two lines on the local page of a Roman newspaper. "Man's bike stolen on first day back to work after two years' unemployment. Bike prerequisite to job."[12] The film tells of an odyssey through Rome by Antonio Ricci, soon joined by his son Bruno, in search of the lost vehicle. Their itinerary includes the police station, trade union headquarters, the open markets of Piazza Vittorio and Porta Portese, a mendicants' church where one of the thief's contacts goes for a free lunch, the apartment of the soothsayer Santona, a brothel, and, finally, Via Panico where the thief is found but not apprehended. In the final episode, Antonio attempts to steal a bike himself, is caught, but soon released while his astonished and ultimately forgiving son looks on.

Like the deceptively simple visual style of *Bicycle Thief*, which conceals a wealth of technical artistry, its banal narrative hides a plentitude of meanings. Most affecting is the psychological relationship that evolves between Antonio and his son Bruno as the search for the bicycle unfolds.[13] It is this level that engages the sympathies of the viewers, for Bruno's witness provides a constant reminder of what is at stake should Antonio fail in his quest. Bruno serves as an internal chorus, mutely commenting on the action from an innocent

[11]David O. Selznick offered to finance *Bicycle Thief* provided that Cary Grant play the lead. See Bondanella, *Italian Cinema*, p. 57, and Leprohon, *De Sica*, p. 35.

[12]"The whole story would not deserve two lines in a stray dog column," remarks Bazin in *What Is Cinema?*, 2:50. In this regard see Jean Cocteau's comments, cited in Agel, *De Sica*, p. 71.

[13]That the father–son relationship is the most emotionally gripping part of the film, there is considerable critical agreement. See, for example, Luigi Comencini's observations in "Li capiva," *Bianco e nero* 36 (September–December 1975), 123, and Bazin's very moving pages in *What Is Cinema?*, 2:53–54.

child's perspective on some occasions, and from a surprisingly adult one on others.[14] His presence in the film is an inspired addition to the literary source, the novel *Ladri di biciclette* by Luigi Bartolini, whose protagonist is a childless loner. Bruno's companionship adds immense richness to the story by providing another surface against which the narrative action rebounds, so that each event is given triple impact as it affects the man's consciousness, the child's, and the interaction between the two.

Psychologically, *Bicycle Thief* traces the evolution of the father–son relationship from disparity and dependence on external mediations to full self-definition and equality. The bicycle is the emblem of all those cultural and material forces that determine the relationship from without. When the vehicle is retrieved from hock at the beginning of the film, it enables Antonio to be a conventional patriarch, requiring obedience and respect now that he is once more the chief provider for his dependents' material well-being. And if the direct relationship between the bike and Antonio's power to support the family were not obvious enough, De Sica literalizes it in two scenes where the newly reinstated paterfamilias carries first his wife Maria, and then Bruno, on its handlebars. The political significance of the bike in the family context, and the way it structures the relationship between father and son, is rendered visually in the scene that introduces Bruno to us in the film. He is first shown behind the spokes of the wheel as he polishes the bike in a point-of-view shot taken from Antonio's perspective. The boy's effort to restore the bike's original luster is an obvious projection of his desire to rehabilitate his father's parental authority, as his adoring mimicry of Antonio throughout this scene suggests. Bruno imitates his father's toilet in a way so exaggerated as to suggest parody if it were not for his utter sincerity

[14] On Bruno's role as internal chorus, as witness and conscience, see Leprohon, *De Sica*, p. 40, and Bazin, *What Is Cinema?*, 2:53.

and delight in seeing his father repossess his former exemplary status within the family. What makes Bruno's filial subordination especially striking is the fact that it involves a forfeit of his own precocious adulthood—during Antonio's extended unemployment, Bruno had been the only family breadwinner in his job as gas station attendant. Throughout the film, vestiges of his precocity remain as Bruno intermittently plays the adult to Antonio's child—when he does the higher mathematics of his father's stipend calculations in the restaurant scene, when he has the prudence to get a policeman to defuse a hostile crowd in Via Panico, and when he solicitously closes the window shutters to protect his baby sibling from the morning sun. It is perhaps with some relief, and certainly without rancor, that Bruno relinquishes his premature adulthood when the bike is retrieved at the film's start and the traditional family hierarchy is reconstituted once more.

There is a further detail in Bruno's introductory scene that merits careful critical attention if we are to establish the terms of the father–son relationship. "Papa, did you see what they did?" Bruno asks in dismay. "No, what?" "A dent!" "Perhaps it was there before." "No, it wasn't . . . I'd have complained to them" (28). Referring most obviously to Antonio's paternal dominion predicated on the bike and the earning power it betokens, the dent suggests the permanent, if minor damage, done to his authority by two years on the dole. Were this a conventional commercial film, however, where concrete details are all governed by considerations of plot, we would expect the dent to reappear later on in the story and to play a part in the narrative resolution. We could envision a happy ending, for example, in which Bruno identifies the otherwise disguised frame by this characteristic disfiguration. But the dent looks ahead to no such optimistic turn of events. If anything, it foreshadows the greater damage that Antonio allows his bike to suffer in the theft itself. Bruno's activist rejoinder ("I'd have complained to them") in which he registers an implicit criticism of his father's passivity, anticipates the later scene outside the mendicants' church when the child reprimands his father for letting the thief's contact get away. What the dent reveals, then, is the vast difference between a film aesthetic which privileges considerations of plot and one in which metaphoric meanings are given equal dignity and weight. In developing the psychological dimension of the story, De Sica and Zavattini must solve two problems built into their very material: 1) how to reveal the shifts and subtleties of interpersonal relationships in working-class characters little given to verbalizing their sentiments; and 2) how to do so in a way that is appropriate to the medium of film. The film-makers' solutions offer perhaps the greatest evidence of that cinematic poetry for which *Bicycle Thief* has been so rightly acclaimed. Accordingly, De Sica and Zavattini choose two physical analogues to the relational changes going on between father and son. The first is visual cuing, by which Bruno will literally look up to Antonio to observe the paternal reactions on which he should model his own. This visual cuing, as a sign of Bruno's uncritical acceptance of his father's authority, is significantly disrupted at several points in the film. When Antonio takes out his frustrations on his son and slaps him with little apparent cause, Bruno refuses all visual contact with Antonio for some time. This averting of the eyes, as Bruno's retaliation for Antonio's blow, reveals how important the earlier visual cuing had been in defining the father–son hierarchy, and thus reaffirms the hierarchy itself. Only at the end of the film, when Antonio's decision to steal a bike robs him of his paternal authority, does Bruno's gaze at him reveal the radically changed terms of their relationship. His eyes first stare in horror at the spectacle of his father turned thief. But when he emerges at his father's side as the crowd harasses Antonio, Bruno looks up in concern and fear for the well-being of his fellow traveler. His upward glance, so reminiscent of the earlier ones throughout the film, is vastly different in the kind of information that Bruno seeks from it. Previously the conduit for behavioral directives, the glance now reveals the fallibility and contingency of the disgraced parental model. With this knowledge, Bruno is deprived of all conventional ways of thinking about Antonio. He cannot condemn him as a common criminal since the man is, after all, his father. Yet Antonio has abdicated any claim to patriarchal respect by violating the legal sanctions on which all authority rests. Thus when Bruno slips his hand into Antonio's at the end of the film, he is offering his father an entirely new relationship—one that no longer needs the mediation of the bicycle, whose physical absence throughout the film has heralded its real emotional irrelevance to this final shared understanding. The financial and political power that the bicycle represented within the family in reestablishing the old hierarchy is no longer the basis of the relationship between Antonio and Bruno. And the quest for the missing bike need no longer be the pretext for the day of important searching and mutual self-discovery that Antonio and Bruno spend together.

In addition to visual cuing, De Sica and Zavattini have also used gait to figure the shifts in Antonio's relationship with his son. "Before choosing this particular child," Bazin said of Enzo Staiola who played Bruno in the film, "De Sica did not ask him to perform, just to walk. He wanted to play off the striding gait of the man against the short, trotting steps of the child. . . . It would be no exaggeration to say that *Ladri di biciclette* is the story of a walk through Rome by a father and his son."[15] Where the visual cuing reveals Bruno's side of the relationship, the striding emphasizes Antonio's. He often walks well ahead of Bruno in a revelation of the self-absorption that at times endangers his son's very well-being. Thus Antonio fails to notice that Bruno has fallen in the rain, and as the soaked child brushes himself off, his

[15] See Bazin, *What Is Cinema?*, 2:54–55.

2. *Bruno (Enzo Staiola) refuses to make eye contact with his father (Lamberto Maggiorani) after Antonio takes out his frustration by unfairly striking his son.*

father distractedly asks why all this flailing of arms. "I fell down" (51), shouts Bruno, distressed as much by his accident as by his father's-apparent obliviousness to it. Toward the film's end, Bruno is twice nearly run over in the traffic of Rome as Antonio heedlessly forges ahead to fulfill his new criminal resolve. Bruno's constant efforts to keep pace with his father are interrupted by the same incident that interfered with his visual cuing. After Antonio reprimands Bruno, the boy walks as far from his father as possible, interposing a row of trees himself and the source of his undeserved reproof. At the end of the film, as Bruno and Antonio establish their new relationship of equality, their gait reflects this psychological change. They now walk abreast, holding hands; their disparate strides have accommodated themselves to the differing needs of the man and the boy.

Bazin's apt description of *Bicycle Thief* as "a walk through Rome by a father and his son" is not limited to topography, however. The film is also a walk through Rome's social institutions, whose indifference to Antonio's plight forms the basis of De Sica's sociopolitical critique.[16] The law, the Church, and the trade union all fail to alleviate the very problems they were established to correct, forcing Antonio to resort to unconventional, and, finally, self-defeating modes of redress. His trip to the police station proves that the law is less interested in protecting the property rights of the citizens than in suppressing their civil liberties, as the officers rush out to quell a demonstration while giving no help to Antonio in retrieving his stolen goods. The law becomes an impersonal, *pro forma* means for registering injustice without doing anything about it, while the attendant human suffering is entirely dismissed as the officers minimize the significance of Antonio's loss.

The trade union proves to be just as indifferent to the in-

---

[16]On the failure of social service organizations to address the common plight, see Leprohon, *De Sica*, p. 39. On institutional and popular indifference to Antonio's predicament, see Agel, *De Sica*, p. 83.

dividual suffering of its constituents as the legal system is.
When Antonio rushes into headquarters in search of his colleague Baiocco, he interrupts a speaker who voices the usual
pieties about worker welfare. The utterly abstract and impersonal nature of this commitment is dramatized by the
speaker's snarling retort to Antonio. "Hey . . . quiet please.
. . . If you don't want to listen to this, go somewhere else"
(41). Though Baiocco does all that he can to help his friend,
he acts not as an ambassador of the union's will to help its
members, but as a single individual, empowered by compassion alone, lacking the kind of institutional support that could
give his aid the weight to succeed.[17]

Just as the union failed to address Antonio's material plight,
the Church offers no spiritual sustenance in his despair. The
Quaker do-gooders, as Bazin calls them,[18] not only enable
the old man who is the thief's contact to get away, but they
degrade Antonio along with the other mendicants whom they
process through their church in an assembly-line operation
of shaving, soul-saving, and lunch. Despite Antonio's attempts to distinguish himself from the beggars who must be
shorn and shriven before they can be fed, he is constantly
mistaken for one of them, responding with an emphatic "no"
when asked if he wants to be shaved before being herded
with the others into Mass. The Church's charitable efforts
are portrayed as not only inadequate to the task of rehabili-
tating a war-ravaged population, but downright dehumanizing in its wholesale approach to processing bodies and souls.[19]

In order for the film's social criticism to work, however,
Antonio's plight must not be seen as unique. Accordingly,
De Sica and Zavattini offer a series of visual essays on the

[17] Baldelli sees in this disparity between Baiocco's individual sympathy for
Antonio's plight and the union's collective indifference an example of the
failure of worker solidarity and the absence of a class consciousness in the
Italian populace. See *Cinema dell'ambiguità*, p. 216.

[18] Bazin, *What Is Cinema?*, 2:52.

[19] The Vatican was quick to take umbrage at De Sica's critical assault. See
Leprohon, *De Sica*, p. 45.

commonality of Ricci's condition.[20] Any tendency to see the protagonists as exceptions to the impoverished masses is discouraged early in the film when Antonio and Maria pawn their wedding sheets in order to redeem their bicycle from hock. If we think that this difficult sacrifice will be enough to set them apart from the crowd and to rescue them from destitution, we are wrong, as a dizzying tilt-shot reveals when it follows the pawnshop attendant up to the top of a mountain of shelves filled with similarly pawned trousseau linens. In a later visual essay, Antonio's story is universalized by the multitudes of used bicycles shown at the open markets on the day after the theft. The evidence that these bicycles are being dismantled, painted, reassembled, and generally disguised suggests that most of them arrived at Piazza Vittorio and Porta Portese by dishonest means. One vendor's sneering comment, "well, we all know that in Piazza Vittorio there's nothing but honest people" (48), suggests a strong presumption to the contrary. A further visual essay on the plurality of Antonio's plight occurs in the police station as the constable stands before a background of cubbyholes in which scores of similar theft reports are filed. The fact that none of the characters in the film acts surprised when Antonio tells of the crime further testifies to the frequency of such mishaps.

There is, however, another Rome, set against the masses of Antonio's fellow sufferers. This is the middle-class city of churchgoers, restaurant patrons, and soccer fans who are engaged in the leisure activities of a typical Roman Sunday. What this suggests is that recent history has afflicted only the lower classes and that the bourgeoisie enjoys a kind of ahistorical status, that their lives are exempt from the devastations of war and its aftermath and are obedient only to the regular rhythms of the work week, with its ritual Sabbath rewards. The exclusivity of this caste is, of course, the

---

[20] On the universality of Antonio's predicament, see Bondanella, *Italian Cinema*, p. 60; and Ferrara, *Il nuovo cinema italiano*, pp. 228–29.

theme of the entire film, which argues, in Catch 22 fashion, that one must be rich enough to own a bike in order to get the job that will provide the means to buy the very vehicle on which the job is predicated. Put more simply, one must already have a foot in the door of capitalism in order to enter that privileged domain. It is as if an invisible barrier separated the Riccis from the middle-class exemplars in the film, and indeed that barrier becomes almost palpable in the restaurant scene where Antonio and Bruno are seated next to an affluent family of conspicuous consumers. While Antonio mentally compares his earning power to that of the paterfamilias at the next table, the smug son makes his judgment of Bruno explicit in contemptuous glances and table manners exaggerated to the point of buffoonery.[21] It is the waiter, however, who makes the definitive class distinction between the Riccis and their neighbors, denying Antonio and Bruno a tablecloth and failing to lay out the silverware, in marked contrast to the amenities heaped on the more prosperous customers. Visually, De Sica need say no more about the impenetrability of the middle class to Antonio's aspirations.

The foregoing considerations have by no means exhausted the interpretive richness of De Sica's film, which abounds in metaphysical as well as psychological and sociopolitical truths. Now that social institutions have failed Antonio, he must seek alternative ways to understand and control his fate.[22] Once the law is discredited by the impotence of its enforcers, Antonio avails himself of the occult, which he had once viewed with such contempt when Maria had paid off her debt to the soothsayer, La Santona. "As if these witches had any control

---

[21] Baldelli offers a subtle reading of this scene whose humor tempers the harsh polemics inherent in juxtaposing rich and poor. See *Cinema dell'ambiguità*, p. 220.

[22] On the film's metaphysical inquiry, see Bondanella, *Italian Cinema*, p. 61. Agel characterizes the film's philosophical message as one of "fatalisme" in which Antonio is powerless to affect his negative destiny. See his *De Sica*, p. 82.

over people's lives. It's just idiotic," sneered Antonio "and who found this job then? Her or me?" (27). In a rather artful transition, Antonio reverts to the soothsayer later in the film when events have so humbled him that he can admit "we won't find it, even with the aid of the saints" (73). A cut to the scene in the soothsayer's apartment makes explicit Antonio's implied association of La Santona with *santi* (saints) in an anticlerical maneuver by De Sica and Zavattini to show how easily belief in one kind of supernatural power can be transferred to less orthodox objects of faith. This time, Antonio finds himself a suppliant among the other desperate followers of La Santona, rather than a cynical observer convinced of his own unaided power to succeed.[23] Though the fortuneteller must interpret her oracular utterances to her other clients, informing the ugly man with the unresponsive fiancée, for example, that he must sow his seeds in another field and then applying the metaphor to the problem of unrequited love, she speaks unambiguously to Antonio, telling him "either you will find it immediately or you will never find it" (76). This reply, like that of the officers at the police station, throws Antonio back on his own resources, and fails to offer either the specific practical advice or the morale-building support that he requires in this moment of crisis. Broadly interpreted, both parts of La Santona's prophecy come true, since Antonio immediately finds the thief, and at the same time, loses forever the possibility of recuperating the bike. Indeed, no sooner do father and son leave La Santona's than they spot their prey and chase him to his neighborhood in Via Panico, where the hostility of the community and Antonio's inability to marshal allies makes it impossible for him to pursue his course of justice.

---

[23] Baldelli finds in this return to La Santona one of the few weaknesses of the film. He faults it as precious, overly literary, and out of character for Antonio who had earlier scorned Maria's womanly superstition. See *Cinema dell'ambiguità*, pp. 239–40. For a cogent refutation of Baldelli's criticism, see Ferrara, *Il nuovo cinema italiano*, pp. 224–25.

Although De Sica and Zavattini borrow the name of the neighborhood directly from Bartolini's novel, they take full advantage of its poetic implications. Via Panico is indeed the place where Antonio is thrown into the emotional turmoil which the god Pan inspired in unwary travelers of antiquity. But Antonio's turmoil is more than psychological—it affects his moral and cognitive faculties as well. The events in Via Panico destroy all the principles on which Antonio predicates his quest, making the distinctions between victim and victimizer, prey and predator, right and wrong, meaningless in a world undone by confusion and doubt. The occurrence most subversive to Antonio's moral order is the confrontation with the thief in a context that gives the criminal an identity and a background as tragic as the protagonist's own. Up to this point, the thief has been a nameless, faceless villain, devoid of any humanity and target of our unmitigated hate. In Via Panico, we learn the thief's name from the lips of his mother, whose poverty and despair cannot help but soften our judgment of her son's misdeeds. De Sica does not sentimentalize the thief and his family, however, for this is no fantasy world where victim and victimizer embrace in ultimate recognition of universal brotherhood, nor does he prettify the picture with quaint poverty and cherubic urchins to elicit our sympathies and make us ashamed of our oversimplified impulses to love or to hate. The thief remains unattractive, as do the snarling mother and the contemptuous sister in the squalid apartment whose dank atmosphere we can almost feel and whose pitiful story we probably already know. De Sica evokes less sympathy for the thief's plight than understanding—this is a cold, hard fact which the film presents to us as a material part of the equation that will determine Antonio's next move. Our awareness that the thief has himself been long unemployed and is responsible for supporting a destitute family further diminishes the distance between Alfredo and Antonio, between criminal and victim of crime.

The second, and more decisive blow to Antonio's moral order is what he discovers about the nature of justice in Via Panico. When the police officer asks Antonio, "Do you have a witness?" and Antonio replies, "I am a witness" (89), the officer says "look down there. . . . All those people are witnesses for him" (90). Antonio learns that justice is by no means an absolute, but that it is a function of the crowd—an entirely relative, situational concept that favors those already blessed with power, wealth, friends, or good luck. This devastating lesson enables Antonio to shed the morality which had previously distinguished him from the criminal object of his manhunt, making the Italian plural title of the film, *Bicycle Thieves* (as opposed to the misleading singular in English) a commentary on the sociopathic effects of life in the postwar era. Though Bartolini's novel has the same title, its plural is a far less momentous one, reflecting the narrator's condescending opinion of the Roman rabble, rather than a disturbing indictment of a society whose most fundamental principles are called into question.

Having abandoned any naive belief in social justice, and having exhausted the possibilities of the occult, Antonio casts about for other ways to take charge of his faltering destiny. If the universe is as arbitrary and as random as the events in Via Panico suggest, then Antonio could try to comply with the forces of chance and anticipate the next throw of the dice, according to the game of hazard which he had refereed at the entrance to La Santona's in the first part of the film. The game of chance merges with another kind of game—that of agility and speed—to form the final, catastrophic course of action which will end Antonio's quest. A sports subplot has developed in the second half of the film around the soccer match between Modena and Rome to be played that Sunday afternoon.[24] Heralded by the truckload of Modena

[24]Franco La Polla notes that the entire second half of the film is characterized by the tension between Ricci's desperate quest and the festivities of the Sunday soccer game. See "La città e lo spazio," *Bianco e nero* 36 (September–December 1975), 69.

supporters who pass them by on a bridge, the game provides
Antonio with a pretext for humoring Bruno after their recent
quarrel by deferring to the boy's superior knowledge of sports.
"Is Modena a good team?" (69) Antonio asks his son, to
which Bruno shakes his head in the negative, only mildly
appeased. Later, the subject recurs when a radio broadcast
announcing the day's soccer scores is overheard on the way
to La Santona's. And indeed, it is no accident that the final
act of Antonio's drama is played out against the backdrop
of the soccer game, for this provides the analogue to the protagonist's choice of tactics.[25] The setting offers multiple in-
centives to action in the rows of bicycles parked outside the
stadium, the mounting volume of audience excitement within,
and, finally, the spectacle of bicycle racers whizzing past the
desperate man and boy on the curb. In a universe where human justice and the supernatural are of no avail, Antonio
decides to align himself with the forces of luck and brute
strength that govern the world of games. But like the Modena team, whose hopeful fans we saw on the way to the
stadium and whose dejected followers we see leaving it, Antonio is not favored by Lady Fortune when he attempts to
steal a bicycle himself, nor is his physical prowess any match
for the many runners who converge on him in answer to the
owner's cries for aid. Unlike the incident of his own bike's
theft, this time help for the victim is forthcoming, and witnesses to the crime are numerous, including, most tragically,
the new thief's own son.

Though the events of Via Panico and the collapse of Antonio's hierarchy of values give his fall a tragic necessity, we
still view it through the horrified and disbelieving eyes of
Bruno. The crisis is doubly shocking, both in its violation of
our own ethical standards and in its subversion of our need
to identify with the protagonist and to see his actions in

[25] Armes observes that the soccer game provides a counterpoint to Antonio's moral struggle (*Patterns of Realism*, p. 153) whereas I would argue
that it offers a model for his final choice of a "survival-of-the-fittest" philosophy.

morally absolute terms. When Simon Hartog compares Antonio to "the lone Western hero, or the tough detective . . .
searching for justice,"[26] he forgets that the Hollywood genre
heroes not only require audience identification, but take great
pains to justify its vote of confidence through happy, or at
least cathartic and consoling, plot resolutions. By violently
shocking us out of our unexamined identification with the
protagonist, De Sica is challenging not only our naive assumptions about poetic justice, but our most intimate film-
viewing needs. Our sympathies were similarly violated by
Rossellini when he removed Pina from the stage midway into
Open City and disappointed our expectations for a conventional comic outcome. But Rossellini's generic revolution left
the audience's moral sensibilities intact, whereas De Sica
challenges even these, leaving us a vision whose only certainty is a son's miraculous love of a father stripped of all
mystifications and cant.

The three years that intervened between *Open City* and
Bicycle Thief took its toll on the optimism which typified the
inaugural film of the neorealist season. By 1948, it was clear
that Rossellini's visionary city would never be founded and
that his hopeful synthesis of Marxist and Catholic ideals was
a fantast's dream. De Sica's and Zavattini's pessimism is as
much a reflection of this historic disappointment as of their
more somber poetic temperaments, and in their image of the
city of Rome, they make explicit the vast distance separating
Rossellini's vision from their own.[27] As a physical setting,
Rossellini's city is a familiar one, consisting of well-known
monuments—St. Peter's, the Spanish Steps—and areas that
we visit time and again in the film—the Prenestino neighborhood of the Resistance fighters, and the rooms of the Gestapo in Via Tasso. Rossellini's city is a centered, coherent

[26] See the introduction to *The Bicycle Thief*, p. 8.

[27] "An undeniable protagonist . . . of De Sica's cinema in this period is the
city," observes La Polla. See his discussion of the role of the city in *Bicycle
Thief* on pp. 69–70 of "La città e lo spazio." Of special interest is his
identification of the city as a moral space, p. 82.

space whose overview we get in the two maps which show Nazi and partisan Rome. We always have a sense of where we are and how this location relates to the city as a whole and to its historical progression from past, to present, to future. De Sica's Rome, instead, is a fragmented, decentered space with few familiar landmarks and no sense of cohesion. With the exception of La Santona's apartment and Antonio's tenement, we never return to the same place twice, nor does De Sica ever give us any establishing shots to tell us where we are. Rome is presented as a maze, full of endlessly twisting and turning streets that dead-end or lead into yet more labyrinthine byways, and Antonio's movements are as aimless and as random as the streets themselves.[28] In the scene following the downpour at Porta Portese, Rome becomes a setting worthy of Ariosto, where hidden secrets and dangers seem to lurk around every corner and shadowy presences materialize in the raincleansed air. This is also a Rome of thick walls with few windows which either shut in Antonio's face, or open onto yet other windows and walls, suggesting the impenetrability of the city to his quest. De Sica's camera takes great advantage of Rome's predominant architectural motif, its arches, to convey the heaviness and inevitability of Antonio's fate. The union headquarters, the poster office, the restaurant, the tunnel through which Antonio chases the thief's decoy, and the bridge under which he runs to see the boy dragged from the Tiber, are built on the principle of the Roman arch with all its implications of solidity and stasis.[29] The inhabitants of this city are the logical extensions of so oppressive and fragmented a space. They are uniformly irritable, from the priest who knocks Bruno over the head in the confessional of the mendicants' church, to the performers

[28] On the labyrinthine nature of the narrative and the urban space of *Bicycle Thief*, see Brunetta, *Storia*, p. 387.

[29] For other observations on the symbolic use of the physical topology of Rome, see Liehm, *Passion and Defiance*, p. 76.

who cannot seem to hit the right note in the vaudeville rehearsal. It is no accident that the word on which they constantly stumble is *gente* (people) and that Baiocco must continually remind them to end the lyric on a downbeat. Two
tobacco salesmen in Piazza Vittorio, who have nothing to do
with the plot, argue for unknown reasons while Bruno's em-
ployer at the gasoline pump refuses to acknowledge the boy's
cheerful "good morning." The film is full of irascible crowds,
from the throng of unemployed who resent Antonio's sole
acquisition of a job at the opening of the film, to the mobs
of people boarding the bus, or waiting in line to get water
from the tenement well. Antonio is never part of these crowds,
for they are conglomerates of isolated selves whose predicament divides rather than unites them in mutual competition
for the scant resources of the unreconstructed city.[30]

Nothing could be more distant from Rossellini's popular
Rome whose solidarity and fellow feeling culminated in the
heroics of the partisan struggle. The demise of postwar
idealism and the egocentricity of a population beset with
shortages have changed Rossellini's collectivity into an angry, unwelcoming mob. But perhaps the most striking measure of the distance separating *Open City* and *Bicycle Thief*
is De Sica's rejection of Rossellini's synthesizing conclusion.
Where narrative events pointed ahead to the political and
spiritual fulfillments of Rossellini's Christian–Marxist typology, De Sica's various semantic levels sharply diverge at his
film's termination. The narrative remains inconclusive while
the sociopolitical and philosophical levels reach the dead end
to which the film's pessimism invariably leads. The filmmaker's modicum of hope is reserved for one level alone, as the
personal relationship between father and son reaches its sub-

[30] On the film's depiction of a hostile citizenry and its pessimistic approach to class solidarity, see Bondanella, *Italian Cinema*, pp. 59–60, and
Leprohon, *De Sica*, p. 39. Lizzani sees in *Bicycle Thief* "a tired, threadbare
society, and precisely because of this, more cruel and desperate, strained by
the quest for new forms of solidarity and civil cooperation." See *Il cinema
italiano*, p. 129.

lime conclusion. But the very isolation of this happy ending amid the profusion of negative ones on other levels serves to polarize De Sica's final view.[31] Bruno's ultimate acceptance of his fallen father, despite the social and even cosmic conspiracy against him, makes the boy's generosity remarkable to the point of heroism. Conversely, the world's utter imperviousness to Bruno's humanizing example shows how unbridgeable is the gap between personal ideals and the larger world order. In the closing shot of the film, as Bruno and Antonio merge with the crowd, the ignorance and indifference of the masses to the crisis just experienced by father and son constitute De Sica's final denunciation. As Bruno walks back into the city, he can entertain none of the hope for social justice and spiritual rebirth that characterized the young activists' triumphal march home in *Open City*. All that remains for Bruno is his own miraculous capacity for love—a gift that will have no impact beyond the immediate private domain.

[31] On the rift between the film's psychological conclusion and its political and philosophical ones, see Bondanella, *Italian Cinema*, p. 62, and Leprohon, *De Sica*, p. 40. The distinction between De Sica "social pessimist" and "human optimist" which emerges at the film's end is not unique to *Bicycle Thief*, but typifies his entire cinematic career according to Philip V. Cannistraro in "Ideological Continuity and Cultural Coherence," *Bianco e nero* 36 (September–December 1975), 19. On the variant political readings of this ending, from optimistic to nihilistic, see Agel, *De Sica*, pp. 85–86.

3 De Santis's *Bitter Rice*: A neorealist hybrid

THOUGH IDEOLOGICALLY the most doctrinaire of the neo-realists in his militant commitment to the PCI, De Santis was the first major director to introduce heterodox elements into the new postwar film idiom. In defying the aesthetic strictures of neorealism, De Santis sought to decentralize a style that was moving ever inward toward purity and refinement (according to Henri Focillon's paradigm for the life cycle of forms in art).[1] The vehement antiformalism that pervades his critical writings reveals the filmmaker's adherence to what he terms neorealist "content" and his simultaneous refusal to honor the rigid set of rules that had become the standard of virtue for neorealist practice. In the *crisaioli* (crisis-mongers), who are always gleefully forecasting the death of neorealism, De Santis pillories the advocates of this limiting formalism who condemn any film that does not conform to their highly codified notion of style. "They are the ones who dissect a film into infinitesimal particles, and talk of 'framing imbalances,' of 'internal rhythm,' of 'external dynamics' and then they forget, for all that, to inquire into the most urgent meaning of a film, that which constitutes its human and poetic value, comprises its substance, and from which its own figurative values take root."[2] In his play on the word *valore* (value), De Santis exposes the flaw in the formalists' approach and proclaims his own divergent hierarchy of interpretive importance. It is the content of the film that reveals its "human and poetic value" and only once this basis

[1] See Henri Focillon, *Life of Forms in Art* (New York: Wittenborn, 1948), pp. 10–12.
[2] See Giuseppe De Santis, "È in crisi il neorealismo," in Lizzani, *Storia del cinema italiano*, p. 345.

of meaning has been established do the work's formal aspects, its "figurative values" make sense. Though the first use of the term has moral force while the second does not, the formalists err by mistaking the one for the other, so that the figurative values become the measure of ethical, as well as aesthetic, worth. Thus the morally charged notions of impurity, contamination, deviance, and so forth are applied to films that fail to comply with the formalists' canon of stylistic acceptability. De Santis, instead, is arguing for the interpretive priority of content which, once its neorealist legitimacy is established, will then justify any departures from received notions of form.

To qualify as neorealist content, a film must not only portray "the world of the humbled and the injured"[3] but it must do so by adopting a certain perspective on it. "The lens of the movie camera—like that of history—recorded the displacement of the driving forces of Italian life: the lens was displaced from a unilateral vision of the middle-class world . . . in order to focus on another, vaster world."[4] De Santis's neorealism will not be any static record of injustice, but will show the dynamism of historical forces as one order struggles to replace its predecessor in a vision of social process reminiscent of Lukács's own. Nor can neorealism itself remain in stasis, for it too must grow and evolve in accordance with the social order it seeks to record. This progressive approach to neorealism is what leads De Santis to call for a "supercession" of De Sica's achievements in *Bicycle Thief* or Germi's in *The Path of Hope*, where the authors remained at the level of denunciation without proposing any alternatives to the social ills they diagnosed.[5] But the formalist critics of neorealism would hold back the ideological progress of the movement by limiting the practitioners to the aesthetic codes appropriate to a previous phase of its development.

[3] Ibid., p. 347.
[4] Ibid.
[5] See ibid., p. 350.

Only through technical experimentation and the incorpora-
tion of variant tendencies will the style be able to go beyond
its earlier achievements to document, and exemplify, the new
social forces at work in a changing world. De Santis's neorealism will thus be an inclusive style which does not fear
heterodoxy, opposing the exclusivist tendencies of the formalists, whose purism leads ineluctably from *Bicycle Thief*
to *Umberto D*, from classical balance to terminal simplicity
and refinement.

Thus when the train pulls out of the station of Turin for
the countryside of Vercelli in *Bitter Rice*, De Santis is vindicating the freedom of his neorealist venture, not only from
the urban-centered themes of many of his predecessors, but
from the formal constraints that the neorealist past imposed
on its subsequent practitioners. De Santis's journey away from
the city is also a journey into his own, very personal brand
of neorealism, with its blend of melodrama and social analysis, of epic effects and documentary reportage, of mythic permanence and popular culture.[6] His is a grand design whose
disparate parts often coexist in uneasy communion, prompting the considerable critical discomfort to which his defensive posture testifies. It is not my intention here to join the
chorus of critical doubt, or to pass judgment on the success
of his experiment in *Bitter Rice* and elsewhere, but rather to
discuss De Santis's ambitious strategy as it bears on the history of neorealism.

Bitter Rice is the story of two young couples, set during
the season of the rice harvest in northern Italy. Francesca,
mistress of petty thief Walter, finds herself on one of the
trains carrying the *mondine*, or female rice harvesters, to the
fields of Vercelli. Silvana, a seasoned *mondina*, yet innocent
in the ways of the world, takes Francesa under her wing and
gets her employment as a *clandestina*—one who is hired
without a proper contract for work. At the rice fields, Fran-

---

[6] There is much critical commentary on De Santis's heterodox approach.
See, for example, Alberto Farassino, *Giuseppe De Santis* (Milan: Moizzi,
1978), p. 26; and Brunetta, *Storia*, p. 328.

cesca is soon joined by her lover Walter who eventually jilts her for Silvana, while planning to steal all the fruits of the impending harvest. In the meantime, Francesca takes up with Silvana's ex-fiancé Marco, a career army sergeant once billeted in the dormitory where the *mondine* now lodge. On the final day of the harvest, as Walter prepares the theft of the rice, he convinces Silvana to flood the fields and divert attention from his criminal maneuvers. The two couples confront each other in the slaughterhouse of the farm where Walter is killed by Silvana when she learns that he has deceived her with a gift of false jewels. Overwhelmed by guilt and remorse, Silvana jumps to her death and earns the belated pardon of the co-workers she had betrayed.

As this plot summary amply suggests, melodrama is the most obvious intrusion into the purity of the received neorealist aesthetic in *Bitter Rice*. Critics have also pointed out the influences of other cinematic genres on De Santis, including the gangster film, the western, and even the musical.[7] But perhaps the most striking intrusion is that of the overt eroticism which Silvana, played by the visually opulent Silvana Mangano, introduces into the otherwise chaste neorealist canon. Though neorealism acknowledged the sexuality of its characters in the premarital pregnancies of Pina in *Open City*, and of Maria in *Umberto D*, for example, it never made eroticism one of the driving forces of the narrative action, nor did it parade the physical attributes of its protagonists, the way De Santis does in *Bitter Rice*.[8]

If this were all there were to the film, however, reviewers would be justified in panning it as pulpy melodrama and cheap sensationalism,[9] but two considerations work against such a

---

[7] See Bondanella, *Italian Cinema*, p. 82; and Farassino, *De Santis*, pp. 70, 72, and 73.

[8] On the puritanical response of the Italian Left of the film's overt eroticism, see Farassino, *De Santis*, p. 24; and Stefano Masi, *De Santis* (Florence: La Nuova Italia, 1981), pp. 3 and 4.

[9] Thus Leprohon faults De Santis for his "novelettish plots" and for pandering to the lowest common denominator of public tastes (*Italian Cinema*, p. 106), and Torri argues that the filmmaker never transcends the limits of

blanket critical dismissal. The setting alone is enough to justify De Santis's project, for it acquaints the viewer with an
Italy little known, and of the rarest beauty, while salvaging
the film's dignity by constantly reminding us of the indis-
soluble bond between the characters and their natural environment. In many ways, *Bitter Rice* may be considered De
Santis's answer to his own plea "For an Italian Landscape"
issued in 1941, where he celebrates

> that atmosphere, impossible to create artificially, in
> which our most intimate being participates precisely by
> virtue of the extraordinary and marvelous nature that,
> together with the characters' actions, takes place under
> our eyes. But otherwise how could it be possible to un-
> derstand and interpret man, if we isolate him from the
> elements in which he lives every day, with which he
> communicates every day.[10]

The primacy of the setting is evident in De Santis's very
opening scene, which moves from the detail of water gushing
over the dikes to a high-angle shot of the rice fields, laced
with human figures holding hands, moving now to the left
to show a second field similarly adorned with figures, now
to the right, and down to the water level where the shot
began.[11] This grand panorama gives the film not only its epic
dimension, but a moral one as well, conferring upon the

---

melodrama (*Cinema italiano*, p. 38). Many reviewers feel that De Santis
compromises his noble didactic intentions in his use of melodrama and eroticism. See Canziani and Bragaglia, *La stagione*, pp. 142–43; Armes, *Patterns of Realism*, p. 129; and in the American press: *New Yorker*, 30 September 1950, 61; *New Republic*, 9 October 1950, 30; *Commonweal*, 6
October 1950, 632; *Rotarian* 78 (March 1951), 36; and *Newsweek*, 18
September 1950, 92.

[10] See "Per un paesaggio italiano," in Lizzani, *Storia del cinema italiano*,
p. 335.

[11] De Santis's aggressive and flamboyant camerawork reveals another way
in which he departs from the neorealists' canon. See Brunetta, *Storia*, p.
329; and Bondanella, *Italian Cinema*, p. 83.

women who slave in the paddies a dignity and righteousness grievously lacking in the men, who are usually associated with the indoors, or uncultivated outdoor spaces. Even Silvana, the tarnished heroine who separates herself from her colleagues through recalcitrance or downright perversity, is constantly ennobled by her mere presence in the spectacular natural setting, be she standing alone as the others go off to confront the "bosses," or running away in shame and hysteria after submitting to the sexual onslaughts of Walter.

Another way in which *Bitter Rice* transcends its own melodramatic premises is by making melodrama one of the thematic concerns of the film and then bringing it into balance with a competing tendency, that of documentary realism. The juxtaposition of these rival impulses is evident from the very opening titles, which pretentiously announce that

> . . . man sought two things since the dawn of time—food and love. Rice, man's oldest grain, must still be pulled from watery fields and each stalk replaced by a shoot for the next year's harvest. Hard work requiring delicate hands—the same hands that can thread a needle and rock a cradle. Such a harvest requiring human labor may reap lives as well as rice. This film tells two stories: one of hard work and the other of the flow of emotions created by thousands of women who pick and plant, pick and plant for forty days. And it tells, too, of their long, long nights.

The two stories that the film proposes to tell, that of food and that of love, reveal the division of De Santis's loyalties between the claims of documentary reportage, on the one hand, and those of melodrama on the other.[12] In the very opening scenes, the dual nature of his venture emerges as he juxtaposes the two narrative modes that will define the generic tensions of the entire film. An announcer from Radio

[12] On the expository promise of a mixed documentary/melodramatic mode, see Bondanella, *Italian Cinema*, p. 83.

Turin introduces the scene in the train station as he describes to his listening audience the departure of multitudes of women of all ages and subclasses of proletarian Italy for the *mondariso*, or rice harvest season. To authenticate his report, the announcer proceeds to interview a randomly selected woman, named Severina da Cervi, about the impressions, needs, and ideals of the *mondine* while the camera explores the general commotion and excitement of the departure scene. With this introduction, De Santis offers one alternative for what his film could be: a documentary about the world of the rice harvest, seen from the detached perspective of the media commentator who makes general observations and chooses representatives at random to serve as vehicles for his impressionistic report.[13] No sooner does De Santis establish this model for his film, however, than he subverts it by a sudden shift into a very different narrative mode. The soundtrack abandons the radio announcer's interview to give us the dialogue of the two figures who are now on camera—men whom we would be far more apt to find in a gangster film than in the frames of a documentary. Though both are sinister figures—one wears dark glasses, the other a dark suit—they turn out to be plainclothesmen giving chase to their gangster prey, Walter. Their presence transforms the railroad station from the starting point of a documentary investigation into the *locus communis* of romance, adventure, and escape that it is in contemporary popular culture.

We may ask at this point why De Santis chooses to tell two stories rather than one? Why the story of food and love, rather than food alone? Why the story of Silvana Meliga rather than that of Severina da Cervi? The answer lies partially in the limits of the documentary approach as De Santis por-

---

[13] On the identification of De Santis's perspective with that of the radio announcer, see Farassino, *De Santis*, p. 56. In this radio commentary, Masi finds not a pure model for the documentary aspect of De Santis's aesthetic, but rather a model for the filmmaker's own mixed generic aspirations. "What is this exceptional transmission of which the radio announcer speaks? It is, simply, reality; a reality around which the radio medium seeks spectacle." See Masi, *De Santis*, p. 48.

trays it in his opening scene. For one thing, the radio news reporter remains in Turin—he does not board the train and leave the city behind for a forty-day sojourn in the country-side. He can never penetrate the surface level of the experi-ence—the departure, the return, the statistics of time, money, and yield—those elements which have the most bearing on the life of the city and which are most easily translated into documentary terms. Secondly, and more insidiously, the eye-witness news report necessarily distorts and falsifies the event it is covering by presenting the part for the whole (the leave-taking, the interview with one *mondina*), implying that those aspects which are inaccessible to its recording facilities are either trivial or nonexistent. Judging from the media cover-age of the departure scene, with its truckloads of waving girls, its Fiat workers coming for the send-off with candy and cheers, the *mondariso* is nothing more than a forty-day girl scout excursion or a summer camp for the needy, offering Italian women a chance to get away for awhile, make new friends, and commune with nature. The truth is grievously, if unin-tentionally, lost in this type of media coverage whose super-ficiality and bondage to the terms of urban life cannot allow it to penetrate further than the train station in Turin. Why not replace the arbitrarily chosen, and only apparently rep-resentative Severina da Cervi with Silvana Meliga, whose links with melodrama might even better qualify her, as De Santis would argue, to be our guide to the *mondariso?*[14]

A further explanation for De Santis's resort to melodrama may be found in his critical writings, where he invokes Gramsci's notion of "national-popular literature" as a model for his own filmmaking venture.[15] Literature must root itself

[14] "Art is not the reproduction of simple documents. By contenting our-selves with planting the movie camera in the streets or in the houses we can only attain a completely exterior realism. In my opinion, realism does not at all exclude a fiction, nor all the classically cinematographic means." Cited in Brunetta, *Storia*, p. 328.

[15] See Giuseppe De Santis, "De Santis scrive," in Lizzani, *Storia del cin-ema italiano*, p. 360. It is to be noted, however, that De Santis was not aware of Gramsci's writings at the time of *Bitter Rice*, but had arrived at

in popular culture, wrote Gramsci, so that a film aspiring to the Gramscian ideal will speak to the working classes as well as to members of the intellectual elite. By appropriating the modes of melodrama, De Santis is thus appealing to a popular audience whose curiosity would hardly be piqued by an invitation to documentary realism.[16] Nor is this a simple example of sugarcoated didacticism, for De Santis's teaching calls into question its sugarcoating by associating melodrama with its most debased form in pulp fiction. Silvana is an avid reader of photo-romances and her attraction to Francesca derives from her belief that this dark lady with "a past" is obviously a character out of *Grand Hotel*. Silvana "reads" the adventures of Francesca and Walter just as she reads the pages of her magazine, whose title, not insignificantly, echoes the name of the locale where the couple stole a valuable necklace, according to the headlines of the tabloid press. Later, when Walter lures Silvana into criminal complicity with the gift of the stolen necklace, he also promises her a vacation in a grand hotel, playing openly on her photo-romance notions of adventure and chic. Her casting of Walter as a character in *Grand Hotel* is confirmed when she asks him, "Do you wear a mask?" anticipating in its naiveté Wanda's fantasies in *The White Sheik*, though Fellini's heroine has the good luck to succumb to a less sinister lothario.

The source of Silvana's attraction to the glamorous couple is best illustrated in the scene of her first encounter with Francesca. De Santis's sequence could have been lifted directly from photo-romance: a closeup of the stolen jewels followed by the image of a shifty-eyed beauty who hides them in a handkerchief when she hears a knock at the door. Outside the train compartment stands Silvana, her face buried in

---

similiar conclusions by his own, empirical means. See Masi, *De Santis*, pp. 10 and 47.

[16] In fact, the film had considerable box office appeal in Italy (as opposed to most neorealist works), and was also a great international success. See Farassino, *De Santis*, p. 26, for statistics.

a copy of *Grand Hotel.* Were the scene shot from Silvana's point of view, we would see a page of photo-romance give way to the image of Francesca, reinforcing Silvana's belief that she is witnessing the real-life counterpart of her beloved stories. "They don't invent anything," she tells Francesca. "It's all true stuff." When Silvana speculates out loud about the couple's antics earlier in the station, Francesca retorts, "Did you learn that from your little newspaper?"

If the interview with Severina da Cervi offers one alternative for De Santis's film, the photo-romance represents the other. Not only is this media format technically similar to film, since both tell stories through a succession of juxtaposed stills, it also shares a similar hold on the popular imagination.[17] In another model for the melodramatic aspect of his film, De Santis recalls the folk ancestor of photo-romance—the professional composer of love letters, who offers to write one for Silvana, "without misspellings," full of "originality, sentiment, and passion." By modeling his film on these examples of popular romance, De Santis is appealing to the Silvanas of his viewing public, but he does so in the hope of ultimately discrediting the very source of this attraction.[18] Silvana becomes an object lesson in the dangers of reading life like the pages of *Grand Hotel*: the handsome masked man does not always carry off the beautiful girl into lands of plenty where everything is electric and the sounds of boogie-woogie fill the air. Silvana's romanticizing vision is contradicted throughout the film, as much by juxtaposed

---

[17] Ben Lawton calls photo-romance "that printed medium which is both mendacious and yet most closely resembles film." See "Neorealism: A Mirror Construction of Reality," p. 19.

[18] Lawton points out how De Santis has it both ways, insuring the commercial success of his film "by the faithful adherence to the code of Grand Hotel" (ibid.) while attacking it as false and manipulative. On De Santis's use of popular genres to maximize his contact with the viewing public, see Farassino, *De Santis*, p. 69. For the filmmaker's comments on his desire to communicate with the simplest as well as the most educated filmgoers, see Masi, *De Santis*, p. 42.

imagery as by events themselves. When Walter says to Francesca, "all trains are traps," in a line truly worthy of photoromance, the camera tells us otherwise, panning from the glamorous portrait of the criminal couple framed in the doorway of the train, to glimpsed scenes of ordinary travelers doing very ordinary things—shaving, brushing their teeth, or getting dressed. For them, trains are not places of adventure and love, they are modes of conveyance which simply facilitate the business of living—a business that goes on as usual not only at either end of the journey, but during its uneventful course. Similarly, the romance of Silvana's first encounter with Walter, on the makeshift dance floor of the railroad station as he joins her spontaneously in the boogie-woogie, is undercut by the primitivism and documentary realism of another "dance" going on behind them—the procession of women along a ridge carrying their suitcases on their heads on their way to work the *mondariso*.[19]

The two opposed narrative modes collide again on the train when Silvana gets Francesca hired as a *clandestina* and the melodrama of their relationship begins. De Santis does not dwell exclusively on their storybook interaction in this scene, but forces us instead to survey the other less glamorous passengers of the freight car, including a woman gulping down some wine, another voraciously eating a sandwich, and a third powdering her nose while complaining of the stench of nearby horse manure. This collision of modes is perhaps best dramatized in the dormitory episode where Francesca explains to Silvana the sordid details of her past. The photo-romance story that emerges—service in a wealthy household, dismissal due to pregnancy, a stillborn baby, seduction into a life of crime—is constantly interrupted by the events in the dormitory itself, events whose compelling realism throws into violent relief the melodramatic conventions of Francesca's story. Her confession is first interrupted by the shouts of a

---

[19]This is an example of the "background–foreground composition" that Liehm attributes to much of *Bitter Rice*. See *Passion and Defiance*, p. 80.

delegation going to negotiate with the bosses about the status of the *clandestine*; it is interrupted a second time by a co-worker who complains of having to use a horse syringe for her own medicinal injections; and a third time by Gabriela's vomiting—symptom of a problem beyond mere indigestion—and finally by Andreina's announcement that the bosses have capitulated to the collective demands of the *mondine*. We realize, by the end of the episode, that a far more important drama has reached its climax behind the scenes than the one Francesca has narrated to us on camera, and that Silvana's voyeuristic interest in the tainted woman blinds her, and us, to its superior claim on our attentions.[20]

The demands of these two different narratives are mutually exclusive, and when Silvana opts for the melodramatic one, she not only forfeits any positive role in the second story, but becomes a traitor to it. Silvana's absorption in her solipsistic fantasies disqualifies her from participating in the other story, whose end is solidarity and the communal ideal. She stands apart and alone every time that the *mondine* make common cause: when they reconcile the infighting between *clandestine* and regulars by deciding to confront the bosses as a united front, when they leave the rain-drenched fields in solidarity with the ailing Gabriela, and when they abandon the harvest festivities together to save the new rice plantings from the flooding that Silvana, of course, has unloosed. In fact, we never see Silvana toiling alongside her co-workers at all. In the scene that best "documents" the ordeal of the *mondine*, Silvana leaves her comrades to ride the horse-drawn cart with Nanni, the mute, and distribute the new rice shoots to the others, or again, when they all opt to work in the rain at Andreina's behest, Silvana is off being seduced by Walter. Alone, too, she has been the constant object of collective admiration in the two dance scenes where her chewing gum and her boogie-woogie express an entire generation's infat-

---

[20] Farassino, *De Santis*, p. 55, sees in the constant interruptions of Francesca's story an allusion to the discontinuity of serialized photo-romances.

uation with America.[21] In both scenes, it is Walter who turns
her solo performance into a pas de deux, revealing that he is
the fitting partner for her melodramatic fantasies, the perfect
accessory to her romantic image of self. Popular enthusiasm
for Silvana's charms culminates in the ferocious ironies of
the Miss Mondina contest, a pathetic attempt to bring peasant culture in touch with the latest trends from overseas.
Without the fiction of a beauty contest, and without the title
of "Miss," this rite could pass for any pagan harvest festival,
with Silvana impersonating the presiding female deity of the
land. Had Walter not come along to wrench Silvana from
her roots, the Miss Mondina crown might have fulfilled her
longings for recognition and pseudo-American glamor while
keeping her in the domestic cultural context which could
sustain and nourish her best.[22] Without the intrusion of Walter, the Miss Mondina celebration would have provided the
comic resolution to Silvana's cultural dilemma, synthesizing
peasant tradition with modern fads, local customs with the
new trends from abroad.

Another possible comic resolution for Silvana is offered by
the wedding of one of the *mondine* to her fiancé at the opening of the harvest festivities. The ceremony does not come as
a complete surprise, for De Santis has made us privy to a
premarital discussion of theirs in the scene of the midnight
assignations at the walls of the farm. When presented with
the choice of a cow or its cash equivalent for the dowry, this
man had unhesitatingly preferred the animal, exposing, in

[21] This is one of the most critically noted aspects of *Bitter Rice*. On the
"American way of life" as protagonist of the film, see Farassino, *De Santis*,
p. 84. On De Santis's ambivalence toward America as the source of both
morally corrupting influences and of the Hollywood genres which he lovingly assimilates into his film idiom, see Bondanella, *Italian Cinema*, pp.
82–83. For De Santis's own views on American cinema, see Masi, *De Santis*, pp. 8–9.

[22] Silvana's incarnation of two opposing cultural codes—that of the peasant work ethic and that of the Hollywood *femme fatale*, is discussed by
Andrea Martini and Marco Melani, "De Santis," in *Il neorealismo cinema-
tographico italiano*, ed Miccichè, p. 308.

his levelheadedness, the vanity and frivolity of the rhinestone necklace or the honeymoon at a grand hotel as the basis for a new life in love.

Silvana's would-be apotheosis as Miss Mondina becomes a double mockery, both of the provincials' pretensions to chic, and of Silvana herself, who has subverted her own coronation by betraying the community's vote of confidence in her. It is appropriate that the scene of her crowning end with the image of her alone on the platform, bereft of the admiring crowd which has run off to save the rice, doomed to walk along the pier into the imaginary audience in a crude parody of Miss America's triumphant march. Unlike the tears of the American contest winner, however, Silvana's represent true pain in the knowledge of what she has just done. Her apparent ascent to the throne of Miss Mondina is an ironic inversion of the moral descent into betrayal and criminal complicity that preceded it—a descent whose physical counterpart is Silvana's plunge to death from the festival tower. Only through a self-inflicted death can she expiate her sin of betrayal and reintegrate herself into the community whose solidarity she had refused all along and whose pardon she comes to ask too late.

Does De Santis hold Silvana morally accountable for her fall, or does he see her as the helpless victim of uncontrollable circumstance? When one of her co-workers says of her, "she's crazy, but she's not bad," are we supposed to exonerate Silvana of all blame for her tragic end or are we supposed to expect of her, as Marco does, a conscious decision to seize control of her fate? When he tells Silvana, "there's still time," during the slaughterhouse scene, "they're out there saving the rice," it is as if he were the good angel of medieval allegory, fighting for her soul against the blandishments of the devil in Walter's guise. Marco himself has come around to a very different way of thinking about human destiny and the moral responsibility for it. A fatalist at first, he spoke of "marked roads" and faces that revealed the prognosis of a life. "It's all a question of faces. I've seen thousands of them. Each has its destiny. No one can do anything about it." Francesca's road is marked, he insists, while Silvana's leads to a future of matrimonial bliss with himself across the seas in Latin America—interestingly, not the "all-electric" America of Silvana's dreams. As superficial and as opinionated a reader of human experience in his way as Silvana is in hers, Marco eventually abandons his determinism and allows for the radical changes that both women will undergo during their forty-day stint in the rice fields. Indeed, Silvana and Francesca will literally change places during the course of the film, not only in terms of their relationships with men, but in their moral positions as well. Silvana begins as the innocent, untried maiden of the provinces whose deterioration is balanced by Francesca's equal and opposite progress toward redemption.[23] Silvana's itinerary and Francesca's intersect midway into the film when the two women seem to switch identities in the scene of Francesca's confession. As she recounts her sordid past, Francesca seems to be divesting herself of it, ending on a note of praise for Marco, Walter's foil and the antithesis of all she has ever previously desired. Silvana, oblivious to the self-critical tone of Francesca's confession, reacts only to its mystique. "At least you've been around. I'm stuck here," she responds. Throughout this interview, De Santis has shot the two women in closeup, positioning their heads together in a rather striking composition, so that when they switch places throughout the scene (three times, to be exact) he offers a visual commentary on their interchange of roles. To enhance the chiastic relationship between the two women's experiences, De Santis makes the end of Silvana's story the beginning of Francesca's. She knows at the outset what Silvana finds out only at the conclusion, and this knowledge leads the tainted woman to rebuild a life with system and purpose. The discovery, which is so devastating

---

[23] Canziani analyzes the relationship of these two destinies that intersect and then achieve diametrically opposed results. See his *La stagione*, p. 142.

3. *As Francesca (Doris Dowling, right) confesses her scarlet past to Silvana (Silvana Mangano), the two women virtually exchange destinies.*

to Silvana (that the necklace is false), occasions relief in Francesca early in the film, for she has already given up the delusions that the other woman so stubbornly maintains. Francesca makes explicit her quest for purification and salvation through work when she tells Walter, "this is the only clean place I've ever been," in a pun on the Italian term *mondariso* meaning literally "to clean the rice," making the term *mondina* mean, significantly, "little cleaner."[24] When Marco muses during a lull in the slaughterhouse showdown, "I guess I wasn't destined to have the Madonna," the implication is that he got instead the Magdalene, a fallen woman redeemed by the influence of a good man. In shedding the sins of her "previous life" Francesca also makes an important literary transition, leaving behind her status as a protagonist in melodrama to welcome her newly acquired realist credentials. Thus she features prominently in all the scenes of drudgery in the rice fields, working cheerfully with her colleagues under the worst possible conditions. Though she has occasional melodramatic lapses—her confrontation with Walter over his new liaison in crime, and the shootout in the slaughterhouse—these strengthen, rather than subvert, her new generic affiliations.

Melodrama has functioned not only as the antagonist in this battle of genres, it has also provided analogies to the larger social forces that De Santis's film seeks to document. The exploitation of the peasants by the managerial classes is echoed on the melodramatic level by Walter's parasitic relationships with his various female associates. "Women are useful to him," Francesca tells Silvana on the train, and indeed this truth has already been thrice borne out in the station where Walter embraced his mistress to head off his pursuers in search of a lone escapee, used her as a screen against their possible gunfire, and danced the boogie-woogie with Silvana to further confound the chase. Walter's constant need

---

[24] On the redemptive power of work for Francesca, see ibid., p. 141.

to be shielded is taken to grotesque extremes in the slaughterhouse where he hides behind a huge side of beef, suggesting its equivalence, in his own mind, to the various women he had used as similar protective devices. When Walter tracks Francesca down at the rice fields, it is obviously neither for love nor for the necklace, which he knows by now is false, but to continue to live off of her in the absence of the requisite pride or competence to sustain himself in the world. Even in his travels with the other nameless vagabond on the way to Vercelli, Walter is parasitic, providing only the knife for their shared meal while his companion, of course, provides the bread. Francesca gives him her own rations once he settles into his rent-free quarters in the granary, where he presides over his court of five—the two women and his three henchmen, Nanni, Beppe, and Aristide.

Though by far the most flamboyant and malevolent, Walter is not the only male parasite in the film. His partners in crime, who are ready to feed on the harvest fruits of the *mondine*, have really been exploiting the women all along. Beppe and Aristide are the agents who promote the *clandestine* in exchange for 10 percent of their take, despite the fact that their sponsorship does nothing to convince the bosses to hire noncontracted labor. Other parasitic beneficiaries of the women's work are the *caporali* or the taskmasters who whip the *mondine* into action, prohibit their talking on the job, and do everything possible to maximize the rice yield, regardless of the human cost. Though we never see the actual bosses, they constitute the end term of this parasitic progression. Their invisibility in the film is a measure of the vast distance between workers and management, between the producers of capital and those who can dispose of it.

Through all this, the rice field has served as far more than a merely decorative backdrop. It has offered the pretext for the documentary dimension of the film, with its vivid images of the women holding hands in geometric patterns throughout the landscape, the opening of the dikes to flood the fields, the distribution of the straw hats which fly through the air like so many frisbees, the filling of the mattresses with straw, the lunches eaten standing up as a relief from the bent-over posture of work, and the game of three stones played in the dormitory on a rainy day. De Santis also takes full advantage of the symbolic possibilities of the *mondariso* with its simultaneous requirements of planting and harvest, of renewals and ends. "Rice, man's oldest grain," the titles tell us, "must still be pulled from watery fields and each stalk replaced by a shoot for next year's harvest." As if to reinforce the symbolism of the process, the *caporali* shout: "Youngsters will transplant and old hands will husk," making explicit the metaphoric link between the organic cycle and the ages of man. It is from this abstract, universalizing perspective that De Santis is able to organize and reconcile the various tensions of the film so that melodrama and realism cease to be binary oppositions and organize themselves instead in so many concentric circles reflecting their exemplar in the natural world.[25]

On the most concrete level, that of individual story, Silvana's death makes way for the new life of Francesca who by the film's end has gained her predecessor's original claim to personal honor and to Marco's affections. On the political level, Silvana's suicide serves to redeem and revive the collectivity whose ideals she has dared to defy. Her co-workers signal their acceptance of her sacrifice by sharing their rice with her, just as they had shared the ordeal of its harvest. In this final gesture of pardon, her apostasy is all but cancelled out and what is remembered about Silvana are the generous impulses—those which led her to sponsor Francesca, to hand over her portion of rice to Gabriela, and to give up her life when only her death could further the collective cause. With this fusion of personal and political themes at the film's end, De Santis resolves the generic tensions as well, leaving be-

---

[25] On the abstract, universalizing tendencies of De Santis's aesthetic, see Martini and Melani, "De Santis," in *Il neorealismo cinematografico italiano*, ed. Miccichè, p. 310.

hind the terms of melodrama and documentary realism to adopt a social realist perspective. The final two-shot of Francesca and Marco, with their satchels over their shoulders as they prepare to face a hopeful future, empties them of their individuality and makes them icons of the new genre into which the film has passed. The low camera angle, Francesca's white shirt, the resolute facial expressions, and their posing against the horizon all conspire to make them heroic types representing the popular will to defeat exploitation and injustice.[26] If the reigning virtue in this new genre is to be solidarity, it must be achieved at the sacrifice of the individuality and self-absorption so celebrated by the melodramatic mode. With Silvana's death, this ethos is extinguished along with its generic champion in melodrama, resolving the tension between the rival genres that has characterized the entire film, in favor of social realism. But De Santis's ending refuses the brash revolutionary promise of doctrinaire social realism just as it refuses the resignation and despair of those neorealist films, like *Bicycle Thief*, which merely describe the problem. Silvana's self-sacrifice and Francesca's new life bring no radical change in the system, which will continue to exploit workers for the benefit of those who control the means of production. Nor will the cycle of annual return to the *mondariso* under backbreaking and less than lucrative conditions stop because Silvana has died and Francesca has gone off with Marco. What De Santis does offer is the guarded hope that the *mondine* will return to the rice fields next year in full possession of the truths learned this season, so that the cyclical repetition of past injustice can be gradually transformed into linear progress toward reform. The rice which her co-workers strew over Silvana's dead body will bear its fruit in future harvests, when the rewards of this painfully forged solidarity will finally be reaped in social justice and economic fair play.

[26] On the adherence of this final image to the iconography of social realism, see Brunetta, *Storia*, p. 425.

4 De Sica's *Umberto D*: Dark victory for neorealism

JUST AS *Open City* reveals an explicit awareness, on Rossellini's part, of the new cinematic movement that his film so dramatically inaugurates, *Umberto D* is very much about the movement as it is now drawing to an end. The film is at once a celebration of neorealism and a lament for its death, a pure embodiment of its ideals and the terminus beyond which the movement could not go without lapsing into repetition or mere self-embroidery.[1] What some critics have called lyricism and others crepuscularism may be attributed to this elegiac mood, which characterizes De Sica's and Zavattini's attitude toward the cinematic era they are so consciously bringing to a close.[2] Indeed, the bells which chime at the opening of *Umberto D* sound a funereal note when linked with the subsequent image of a cortege moving slowly down a city street flanked by a single line of cars proceeding with miraculous solemnity and order for the traffic of Rome. The itinerary begun by *Open City*, with its climactic shot of the young boys marching back into the city to forge a better world, has come to its bitter fulfillment in this parade of old men protesting the inadequacy of their pensions in a society that has disappointed the neorealists' reformatory hopes. "We have worked all our lives," reads one of the protest signs, announcing the dual themes of social injustice and old age

---

[1] According to Torri, *Umberto D* and *Two Pennyworth of Hope* form "terminal points in a road closed by now, beyond which it is not possible to proceed." See *Cinema italiano*, p. 47.

[2] Thus Torri calls the film "an occasion for poetry in addition to civic commitment." See *Cinema italiano*, p. 48. Mario Gromo considers the minimal storyline on which De Sica and Zavattini have courageously built an entire film a "pathetic, crepuscular sketch." See *Cinquanta anni di cinema italiano*, ed. Malerba and Siniscalco, p. 61.

that locate *Umberto D* on the losing end of the neorealists' inaugural promise.

Far from the future of solidarity and progressivism anticipated by Marcello's and Romoletto's activist stance, Umberto's present bears witness to the failure of social change and popular attempts at corrective action.[3] The protest is pitifully ineffective, beset with obstacles from without and misunderstandings from within, as visually expressed by the bus that turns into the midst of the marchers and easily destroys the unity of their advancing front.[4] The demonstrators never even reach the goal of city hall, but are intercepted by police who scold them for daring to march without a permit. When the old men let loose with a barrage of angry shouts, De Sica's camera is harsh and leering, showing not only the policemen's unflattering views of the crowd, but the filmmaker's own judgment on the futility and impotence of their efforts at redress. The cacophonous soundtrack, which lets us distinguish no single utterance of their grievances, shows that the men speak without a unified voice, and the closeups of toothless mouths make them caricatures of complaining old age. A similar scene in *Bicycle Thief* showed an angry group of unemployed men shouting their frustration when Antonio Ricci alone got a job, but De Sica's camera was more sympathetic than it is toward these raging old men. No less unattractive, however, are the police, who engage in a disproportionate show of force and whose mock military maneuvers suggest that this is a society at war with itself. In fact, the old men must hide in a doorway until the guards disperse and only then can they venture back onto the streets, alien to their own social order. But this defeat will not motivate

[3] The general comparison between Rossellini's political optimism in *Open City* and De Sica's disappointment in *Umberto D* is made by Nick Barbaro in his review of *Umberto D*, *Cinema Texas Program Notes* 12 (Spring 1977), 18.

[4] On these visualizations of the demonstrator's ineffectuality, see Armes, *Patterns of Realism*, p. 157.

them to regroup their forces and engage in further cam-
paigns for justice, since the very premise of collective action
has been lost in the scuffle. "Scoundrels," inveighs one of the
old men. "Who, the police?" asks Umberto. "No, the organizers of the protest—they should have had a permit," he
replies, granting the establishment the power to make all the
rules, even those that prohibit its citizens from breaking the
rules according to the imperatives of civil disobedience.

Though Umberto himself seems to champion the need for
solidarity in defending the protest organizers against these
misplaced charges, his own subsequent actions reveal a
grievous inability to set aside the claims of the self and to
act in concert with others. The very next scene shows how
Umberto aborts a burgeoning friendship by trying to sell his
watch to a fellow demonstrator, Orazio Valenti, without
reading the obvious signs of the other man's financially straitened circumstances. When Orazio answers defensively, "I have
one," Umberto is impervious to the sudden change in the
other man's tone and presses insensitively on. "What kind?"
Orazio's evasive, "it's good, it has a gold case," only occasions an equally proud falsehood from Umberto, who explains, "I have two, that's why I'm selling one." Orazio takes
unceremonious leave of Umberto at this point, bringing to
an end what could have been a mutually supportive relationship for two men who share not only the same plight, but
the same style of coping with it. In the next scene, Umberto's
insensitivity makes him a nuisance to the other customers of
the soup kitchen when he inconveniences everyone around
him in a conspiracy to feed his dog Flick, unbeknownst to
the waitress. He uses his table partners not only as co-con-
spirators, but as possible buyers for the ever-marketable watch,
forgetting, of course, that the other men are eating at the
soup kitchen only because they are as destitute as he.

In his campaign to avoid eviction by raising the 15,000
lire that he owes the landlady in back rent, Umberto is oblivious to the common plight that unites all the participants

in the demonstration and all the patrons of the soup kitchen, seeing in them, instead, potential contributors to his own empty coffer. The only character in the story who is not instrumentalized by Umberto is Maria, the servant, who is also a victim in the landlady's dictatorial household. Umberto takes a paternal, or grandpaternal interest in this illiterate girl from the provinces, offering her lessons in grammar and showing concern for her predicament as an unwed mother-to-be. Maria fully reciprocates, showing him many small attentions, from her visit to him in the hospital with a gift of a banana, to the slice of cake she brings him from the landlady's engagement party, to her insistence on getting up to bid him farewell on several early morning occasions. In their subjugation to the landlady's tyranny, Umberto and Maria have a great deal in common, especially their deadlines for expulsion from the premises: Umberto will be evicted by the end of the month, and Maria as soon as her pregnancy becomes obvious. If the landlady represents the interests of the new middle class of postwar Italy, as De Sica has made explicit in his own comments on the film,[5] then Umberto and Maria represent two disenfranchised social categories, the old and the "subproletariat" who suffer at the hands of the rising bourgeoisie. Indeed, it is the landlady's middle-class aspirations that dictate her intolerance for the old man and the maid—her parvenu notions of propriety would never allow her to harbor an unwed mother in her midst, just as her burgeoning prosperity requires that she remodel her apartment and convert Umberto's bedroom into an elegant receiving room commensurate with her newly achieved social status. This new status will be inestimably enhanced by her marriage to the owner of the cinema next door. "She'll get into the movies free," Maria tells Umberto in a remark which suggests that the landlady's empire is expanding considerably in this marriage to a neighboring "lord."

[5] See Vittorio De Sica, "Analyzing *Umberto D*," *The New York Times*, 30 October 1955, Sec. 10, p. 5.

Despite their many shared experiences and feelings, or perhaps because of them, the relationship between Umberto and
Maria is the most flagrant example of the failure of solidarity in the entire film. When Umberto takes his leave and Maria
asks if she can visit him some time, the hint of a happy ending is there, but when Umberto says, "You change places
too," the logical follow-up—"You come with me"—is never
made.[6] De Sica himself suggests the possibility of such a comic
resolution to Umberto's problems.

> When everything is at a dead end, when there is no
> more hope of getting help from anybody, it is just then
> that Umberto could have found a way out. By taking
> the girl out of this house, being a father to her. Two,
> or three, together might solve their problems. Nothing
> of this sort happened. Human beings have this primi-
> tive, perennial, ancient fault of not understanding one
> another, of not communicating with each other.[7]

De Sica's surrender to the isolation of the human condition
and the impossibility of true solidarity marks the distance
between *Open City* and *Umberto D*, between the harbinger
of a new social order committed to the populist ideals of the
Resistance and the elegiac look back at the hope which history had failed to fulfill.[8] *Open City* and the first neorealists
argued that Italy had been irrevocably changed by the Nazi–
Fascist occupation and the campaign for liberation and that
Italians would never forget the unifying lessons it taught. But
the landlady, De Sica's paragon of the new middle class, has
conveniently forgotten the truths of the war years, when she
used to call Umberto "grandpa" and he would give her his
rations of food. "After the war," Umberto tells the man in

---

[6] As Giuseppe Ferrara argues, "the two solitudes are so much more desperate because the girl could find salvation with the old man, and he could
find in her affection a reason for living." *Il nuovo cinema italiano*, p. 281.

[7] "Analyzing *Umberto D*," sec. 10, p. 5.

[8] See the remarks by B. Singerman in *Etudes cinématographiques* 32–35
(Summer 1964), 165–66.

the hospital bed to the left of his, "she went crazy," merci-
lessly rebuilding her depleted empire at the expense of her
former companion in the privations of war. For the landlady, and her counterparts throughout reconstructed Italy,
the war was something to put behind them or to dismiss
from memory in a denial of the solidarity and fellow feeling
of that exceptional time.[9]

Implicit in De Sica's attack on the new Italy is a recognition that neorealism, in its strict 1940s form, has no place in
it. Just as Umberto has no more right to his room in Via
Martini Della Battaglia No. 14, so too his film will have no
run in the movie theater next door, the Cinema Iride, whose
proprietor the landlady will marry. This built-in projection
of public failure became a self-fulfilling prophecy, for *Umberto D* was indeed a commercial loss, discouraging future
production of films in the strict neorealist vein. We would
be wrong, however, to ascribe the film's public reception to
external changes in Italian society alone, for *Umberto D's*
aesthetic severity is also responsible.[10] De Sica's and Zavattini's neorealist cinema has constituted an ever purer and more
refined application of the theory that Zavattini was to for-
mulate the very year of *Umberto D's* release.[11] His ideal of
a film that is utterly devoid of a dramatic superstructure and
that dignifies the ordinary and the unexceptional by taking
"any moment of human life" and showing "how 'striking'
that moment is"[12] finds its closest possible realization in

[9] Tino Ranieri sees in this the very basis of De Sica's neorealist pessimism.
"But his voice should be heeded also because De Sica, among the directors
of postwar Italy, is the first to feel and to communicate that many things
have not changed, that the difference resides only in the freedom to say that
they have not changed." See "De Sica neorealista," in *Il neorealismo cinematografico italiano*, ed. Miccichè, p. 303.

[10] On the public's rejection of *Umberto D* for its exploration of "the zero
degree of reality," see Brunetta, *Storia*, p. 390. Also see Bondanella, *Italian
Cinema*, p. 62.

[11] The famous essay, "Alcune idee sul cinema," first appeared in *La rivista
del cinema italiano*, December 1952.

[12] See Zavattini, "Some Ideas on the Cinema," p. 221.

Umberto D.[13] De Sica has used the term *uncompromising* to describe his film, which makes no concessions to commercial demands for spectacle, drama, and emotional catharsis.[14] In a sense, the filmmaker defied the public to identify, or even to empathize with Umberto in any way, choosing a subject that has little audience appeal, and a protagonist who is "at the limit of the unpleasant; . . . he is not the 'poor old man' whom we see begging on street corners and who whimpers to make us feel sorry for him. He is closed and hostile; it seems that he has lost contact with the world from which he comes."[15] Indeed, it is De Sica's and Zavattini's supreme achievement that they succeed, almost despite Umberto, in bringing us around to his cause and that they do so through no recourse to conventional melodramatic means. That this man, whose self-involvement and senile quirks so alienated us at first, can make us care so deeply about his solitary fate, is a tribute to his compassionate and accepting treatment at the hands of De Sica, whose dedication of the film to his father, Umberto De Sica, reveals a personal interest successfully sublimated to the requirements of a realist approach.[16]

Zavattini himself admits, however, that *Umberto D* is no perfect application of his theoretical precepts. Though purer than *Paisan, Open City, Shoeshine, Bicycle Thief,* and *La Terra Trema,* which still depend on an "invented story," *Umberto D* presents "reality as an analyzed fact . . . but the presentation is still traditional."[17] Critics have been quick to point out that there is, indeed, a plot "marked by a feeble

[13] This is what led Bazin to apply his metaphor of the asymptote to the relationship between neorealist practice and theory, or between neorealist practice and reality itself. See *What Is Cinema?*, 2:82.

[14] See "Analyzing *Umberto D*," sec. 10, p. 5.

[15] Quoted in Lizzani, *Il cinema italiano*, p. 132. On this refusal to appeal to our sympathies, see Baldelli, *Cinema dell'ambiguità*, p. 246; and Bondanella, *Italian Cinema*, p. 63.

[16] On De Sica's dedication of *Umberto D* to his father, see Armes, *Patterns of Realism*, p. 157.

[17] Zavattini, "Some Ideas on the Cinema," p. 221.

dramatic progression and this progression of events leads to an interior tension, if not to a tension of facts."[18] "Holding *Umberto D* together is the kind of emotional crisis which one can imagine a conventional film treating (if with other stylistic methods) namely a few days during which a man is driven to the verge of suicide."[19] Obviously, this is not a film about ninety minutes in the life of a man in which nothing happens, according to Zavattini's ideal for realist cinema, nor is it an accumulation of uneventful moments linked together to give the sense of quotidian reality.[20] *Umberto D* is a series of life-shaping occurrences: an old man, reduced to penury, is threatened with eviction for failure to pay back rent, takes ill and is hospitalized, returns to his lodgings to find his room semi-demolished and his dog missing, rescues the dog from extermination at the pound, contemplates suicide but reneges at the last minute out of concern for the welfare of his pet. Furthermore, the film chronicles critical events in the lives of the two most important secondary characters: pregnancy for Maria and imminent marriage for the landlady. It is not so much the absence of the extraordinary, then, that accounts for *Umberto D*'s impression of authenticity, but the "dedramatization"[21] of inherently dramatic moments which De Sica refuses to order in any hierarchy of importance.[22] Maria is the spokesperson for this strategy of "dedramatization" when she tells Umberto she is pregnant in the same matter-of-fact tone that she uses to complain of the ants in her kitchen. Umberto's middle-class ideas of propriety and

[18] Karel Reisz in *Etudes cinématographiques* 32–35 (Summer 1964), 162.

[19] Armes, *Patterns of Realism*, p. 160. Bazin writes similarly, "if we take just the theme of the film we can reduce it to a seemingly 'populist' melodrama with social pretensions, an appeal on behalf of the middle class." *What Is Cinema?*, 2:80.

[20] See Zavattini, "Intervento al convegno di Perugia," in Lizzani, *Storia del cinema italiano*, p. 465.

[21] This is Pierre Leprohon's term. See *The Italian Cinema*, p. 131. For an elaboration of this notion, see Leprohon's *Vittorio De Sica*, p. 57.

[22] On this "ontological equality," which destroys the possibility of dramatic structuring, see Bazin, *What Is Cinema?*, 2:81.

perhaps his innate sense that such a confession requires a heightened rhetorical mode lead him to exclaim: "Pregnant, and you say it like that?" "How should I say it?" answers Maria, making explicit De Sica's policy of emotional leveling by refusing to give undue dramatic weight to her revelation. The film actually includes three love stories, including Maria's, but its restraint with respect to the dramatic opportunities they offer, and its use of the other two erotic "subplots" as foils for Maria's and Umberto's adventures, only serve to make clearer the filmmaker's own divergent narrative strategy. The other two love stories, if they can be called that, involve the middle-class characters who appropriate all the melodramatic possibilities of the culture at hand. There is the adulterous couple who use Umberto's room by the hour with the landlady's blessing, and there is the landlady herself and her new fiancé. Both couples posture and pose in very studied ways: while Olga, the landlady, is singing her arias, Paolo, her betrothed, is perched affectedly on the arm of her sitting-room chair, and as they take their leave after the engagement party, she pouts prettily when he fails to kiss her goodnight. The ploy works—"Dear," he intones as he grants her a perfunctory peck on the cheek in a scene which Olga and Paolo probably think worthy of the Cinema Iride, but which De Sica exposes for all its insincerity and absence of passion.

The adulterers are equally theatrical as they take their conventional roles to stylized extremes. The dark, handsome woman slinks down the hall in cloak and feathered hat, followed a few paces behind by her lover, as if such separate exiting could allay any suspicions that their behavior might arouse. Maria, who refuses to dramatize her own situation, is the amused public for their posturings as she looks through the keyhole of Umberto's room into the adjoining parlor where the adulterous couple have withdrawn. The camera makes us privy to what Maria herself sees—a glamorous cameo of a man standing in swirls of cigarette smoke looking unresponsively off while the woman sits beside him, pressing his hand in her own. "Answer, answer!" are the only lines we hear, but we can well reconstruct the melodramatic scenario that this glimpse into the parlor suggests. It is as if a scene from another film found its way by mistake into *Umberto D*, serving, in its incongruity, as a foil for De Sica's resolutely undramatic storytelling mode. In a parallel episode later on, when Maria tells the soldier from Naples that she is pregnant and he walks away in mute rejection of any responsibility for her predicament, all the melodramatic trappings of the earlier scene are stripped away and only the harsh realities remain. The secrecy of the adulterers' setting is contrasted to the open market scene of Maria's encounter—the stylized pose, the cigarette smoke, and the keyhole framing of the earlier scene are opposed to the unglamorous, straightforward *mise-en-scène* of the later one, just as the uninformative, minimal dialogue of the adulterers is contrasted to Maria's blunt statement of fact.

Umberto finds himself inadvertently in the midst of these three love stories and his intervention in any one of them would radically change not only the plot of the film, but its genre. Were he to intercede on behalf of Maria, as he promises he will in the hospital, he would indeed be establishing a paternal authority over her which would tie their destinies together and guarantee the film if not a comic ending, at least an exemplary status as a lesson in the virtues of solidarity. Were Umberto to intervene in the landlady's engagement, denouncing her as an ingrate and a bawd, or were he to expose the adulteress whom he sees several times after her assignation, the film would degenerate into a silly melodrama, worthy indeed of a run at the Cinema Iride. But instead, the three erotic subplots remain tangential to Umberto's story, offering temptations into other genres that the film valiantly resists in defense of its stylistic virginity.

And yet, in its near-perfect embodiment of the precepts of neorealism, *Umberto D* also signals its breakdown. Not only have De Sica and Zavattini abandoned the cause of solidarity and the working-class themes of the postwar school, but they have also violated the pretense to objective reportage, which bore witness to the documentary aspirations of the neorealist founding fathers. The predominance of medium shots, the unobtrusive camera movements, and the minimal editing bespoke the fixed, external, neutral point of view typical of neorealist cinema. It is this absolute authority that begins to break down in *Umberto D* as perspectives shift and reality begins to take on a multiplicity of faces, according to its variant contexts and the particular biases of the observer. Critical attention has been called to the zoom shot from Umberto's window to the cobblestones below as the most obvious violation of neorealist technique in its obtrusive camerawork and its subjectivity—this is Umberto's consideration of a plunge to death as the resolution of his dilemma.[23] Another non-neorealist shot is that of the snarling bulldog in the kennel, presenting Umberto's (or Flick's?) subjective point of view on the inhospitality of this rest home for dogs. A third blatantly subjective set of images is the panorama from the trolley car which takes Umberto from the apartment on Via San Martini della Battaglia to Flick's presumed destination on Via Leccosa. The views of the city are seen through the eyes of a man who is regarding them for the last time, whose resolve to end his life cannot prevent this surge of last-minute nostalgia. But these shots are not the only violations of neorealist objectivity, for they point to a whole pattern, both psychological and cinematic, of ambivalent optics and shifting points of view.[24]

Umberto's condition itself is shown through a plurality of perspectives. When we first see him alone after the fiasco of the watch-vending episode, he is depicted simply as a dignified old man, dressed in middle-class finery, taking his dog

[23] On this zoom shot, and other technical violations of neorealist decorum, see Barbaro, "*Umberto D*," pp. 17–18.

[24] On the complexity of De Sica's cinematography in *Umberto D*, see Bondanella, *Italian Cinema*, p. 63.

for a Sunday walk. The music itself is festive, reinforcing this
sense of a Sabbath outing devoid of the financial worries intimated in the previous scenes and fulfilled in the subsequent
ones. The film is punctuated with such idyllic moments, whose
musical commentaries accord with the gay *mise-en-scène*:
Umberto's lighthearted tripping up the steps of a garden after
his hospital release, and his cavorting with Flick in the love-
liness of the children's park at the film's end. If we were
seeing Umberto out of context, in these carefree moments
alone, we would consider him a jolly pensioner enjoying his
leisure, as the Commendatore assumes when he asks after
Umberto's well-being. "I'm retired, I survive, I don't do anything." "Lucky you, who does nothing," remarks the Commendatore in a judgment as partial and as misrepresentative
as our own would be were we to see Umberto only during
these select moments. In a complex shot that reveals the
Commendatore's flawed point of view, Umberto's image is
reflected on the window of the bus which the other man has
already boarded. Embarrassed because he has nothing to say,
the Commendatore stands at the window looking down,
creating the optical illusion that he is contemplating Umberto's reflected image which, of course, we see but he cannot.
The illusion is, however, an accurate indication of the Commendatore's attitude toward Umberto—both condescending
and distorted—for he sees not the man, but his own version
of this idle pensioner trying to make a claim on his reluctant
attentions.

   Indeed, the play of perspectives is constant throughout the
film, making Umberto the object of humorous, pathetic, or
critical treatment according to the shifting point of view. Initially, De Sica posits an alienating distance between protagonist and public, presenting Umberto as the eccentric, self-
involved old man of the first three scenes. But a radical shift
of perspective occurs during the famous episode of Umberto's preparation for bed, an example of the *temps morts*[25]

---

[25] This is Armes's term, *Patterns of Realism*, p. 160.

that constitute so important a part of the film's dedramatiz-
ing technique. During this long sequence, which is interrupted by Maria's comings and goings, and a trip to the
bookstall, nothing really happens to advance the storyline,
yet its very dramatic insignificance concentrates our attention on the protagonist himself as the author of the small
gesture and the organizer of this quotidian space. Without
resorting to the more overt manipulative techniques of conventional cinema, De Sica and Zavattini succeed in drawing
us into Umberto's interior world by making us cohabitants
of his room—the room that has become an external expression of his innermost self, literalizing the old metaphor of
the chambers of the mind.[26] This *topos*, which underwrites
the entire scene of Umberto's preparations for bed (as well
as Maria's famous scene in the kitchen the next morning) is
introduced by the protagonist's entrance into the room after
the adulterers adjourn to the parlor. Umberto's fastidious actions—removing the handkerchief from the light, airing the
room, turning the pillow, smoothing the bed—reveal as much
his moral revulsion at what has just gone on there as his
desire to reappropriate this space for himself, making it once
more the ideal image of an inner psychic order. By letting us
observe this ritual of reclamation, we watch the metaphor
unfold, witnesses to the figurative link between Umberto's
interior life and its exterior manifestation in the "cameretta"
doomed to extinction by the landlady's empire-building
schemes. The famous scene later in the film, where the zoom
shot to the cobblestones reveals Umberto's death wish, concludes with a shot of Umberto through the hole in the wall
of the semi-demolished room, taken by a camera in the ad-

[26] The *topos* is an example of the "house of the body" tradition which,
according to Robert Durling in his lecture entitled "Boccaccio and the House
of the Body," delivered at the meeting of the American Association of University Professors of Italian, University of Illinois, Champaign, 21 November 1980, goes back to Plato's *Timaeus* and is used extensively in Ovid. The
chambers-of-the-mind metaphor finds specific application in Petrarch's son-
net 234, "O cameretta che già fosti un porto."

joining parlor.[27] The two shots are causally linked—the former is a logical result of the latter—as Umberto's suicide pact follows from the destruction of the psychic order figured in the room. This portrait of Umberto framed by the hole in the wall reverses the shooting direction, and the generic implications, of the earlier portrait of the adulterous couple framed by the keyhole. Though as artful as the glamorous couple's shot, Umberto's reveals all the vast distance separating his film from the one that would tell their story. For them, the elegant keyhole frame and the parlor setting are environmental props whose conventionality simply primes us for the predictable plotting of melodrama. For Umberto, the hole-in-the-wall framing and the dreary bachelor room are themselves the story[28]—they not only locate Umberto physically, but contain and determine him in his rush toward material and emotional ruin. Though Umberto's portrait is shot from the same distance as the couple's portrait (each from a room away), our sudden remoteness from his reveals, by contrast, how close we have come to this character and how well De Sica's interiorizing technique has worked, while we remain utterly detached from the adulterers.

The morning scene of Maria in the kitchen serves a similar interiorizing function. Like the bedroom for Umberto, this is Maria's personal space which she claims as her own through a series of small, ritualized gestures, from her fiery and watery campaign against the ants, to her lighting the stove and grinding the morning coffee. The movement into her mind is done with delicacy and tact through a subjective camera shot which, when it returns to an "objective" view of Maria, does so with new compassion and understanding. We merge with Maria's point of view early in the scene as she looks out the

[27] On the violation of neorealist technique implicit in this shot, see Barbaro "*Umberto D*," p. 18.

[28] It is unclear whether Umberto is a bachelor or a widower but, as De Sica remarks, the specifics of his past are immaterial since all that should concern us is his present solitude. See "Analyzing *Umberto D*," sec. 10, p. 5.

kitchen window onto the adjoining rooftops where she sees a stray cat—her momentary counterpart in its solitude and homelessness. When Maria returns to the stove and touches her breast to test for palpable signs of her pregnancy, we share with her the burgeoning realization of her desperate plight. These two scenes, which have been so justly celebrated for their naturalism, do much more than simply introduce us to the ordinary and uneventful quality of Umberto's and Maria's daily routines, for they reveal the characters to us in almost embarrassing intimacy—an intimacy far more revealing than confessional dialogue or intense dramatic encounters could afford.[29] Umberto's bedroom and Maria's kitchen serve as stages for the private enactments of their innermost selves, freed from the pretenses and defenses of public life. Despite the intimacy of these vignettes, De Sica and Zavattini never cast us in the role of voyeurs, peeping through keyholes into secret rooms, nor are we made to feel like unauthorized intruders into an alien land, but instead are eased into the characters' own perspectives, becoming "roommates" in the metaphoric chambers of their minds. Once this merging of perspectives is achieved, we begin to see much of Umberto's surroundings through his particular optic. The central hallway of the apartment is always shot frontally, from a low angle so that we feel at once dwarfed and oppressed by the heavy-ceilinged space in accordance with Umberto's own subjugation to physical circumstance. The positioning of the central hallway also suggests infinite, hidden depths in the landlady's portion of the apartment, which lies at the vanishing point of the *mise-en-scène*, while Umberto's bedroom and Maria's kitchen flank the front of the hallway that gives onto the photographic plane. We realize too that all the events we witness in the apartment that include Umberto are filtered

---

[29] Bazin considers these two scenes perfect examples of the "cinema of duration" that is Zavattini's neorealist ideal. See Bazin, *Vittorio De Sica*, p. 16 n.

4. *Umberto's bedroom, once the outward image of his psychic order and material security, is now about to be remodeled according to a plan that will have no place for him.*

through his perspective, so that sights and sounds are exaggerated as if they were assaults on his fevered senses. In his illness and insomnia, he is like Proust's Aunt Eulalie for whom the sickroom details and the comings and goings of the servant Françoise take on macrocosmic significance. For Umberto, no sooner does the landlady's pretentious singing stop than the fanfare of the Cinema Iride starts up, and the soundtrack magnifies these sounds to accord with the heightened perception of his overwrought state. Two of the love stories which unfold around Umberto have musical motifs that seem to converge on his room. The landlady's singing amounts to a kind of mating call as she vocally preens and postures for her fiancé, while Maria constantly comes running to the sound of the bugle that summons the soldiers into formation outside Umberto's window.

Once this merging of perspectives is established, there are moments of backing off in which we achieve enough distance on Umberto to laugh at him or to censure his conduct. Thus, even the interiorizing strategy of the bedroom scene is arrested by a momentary step back from Umberto as we laugh at his slapstick antics with the thermometer that has disappeared down the legs of his pants. Another source of humor is Umberto's face-offs with Olga, which include a dialogue of defiant "ha-ha's" between the two in a spoof of the landlady's own operatic exertions. A second episode of silly sparring occurs when Umberto returns home with the recently retrieved Flick and jumps out in front of Olga, berating her before an unsympathetic audience of onlookers. Later, our laughter is tinged with pathos when Umberto tries to beg and then is compelled by pride to deny his eleemosynary appeals. In a scene reminiscent of Chaplin, Umberto turns his outstretched hand palms down, pretending to a passer-by about to make him a donation that he was merely testing for rain.[30] When he delegates the job of begging to Flick, who

---

[30] On the Chaplinesque affinities of the film, see Armes, *Patterns of Realism*, p. 160.

sits on his hind legs and holds his master's hat in his teeth, Umberto withdraws to the porch of the Pantheon and pretends to be reading a letter. It is then that the Commendatore walks by and questions Flick's acrobatics, but Umberto only dismisses the dog's trick as a game, unwilling to admit his disgrace to his former supervisor in the Ministry of Public Works. The amusement occasioned by this Chaplinesque interlude is different from that of the thermometer or the soup kitchen, where his antics were motivated by senile self-absorption or physical awkwardness, for here, they reflect an admirable pride that the other beggars, in their aggressiveness, have easily discarded. The mendicant who harangues passers-by ("I have seven dependents, seven") and the one who buys Umberto's gold watch with all his morning's earnings are foils, in their shamelessness, for Umberto's sense of lost dignity.

This humorous distance from Umberto, be it tempered with pathos, or hardened with critical detachment, gives way to direct censure of him in his moments of supreme insensitivity to others. Though we sympathize with his frenzy over Flick's absence from home, we cannot countenance Umberto's brutal interrogation of Maria in the immediate aftermath of her abandonment by the soldier from Naples, nor can we condone his obliviousness to the next man in line at the pound who is unable to pay the retrieval fee for his dog.[31] Though Umberto is obviously unaware that Maria has just been jilted, or that the man will lose his dog to the gas chambers, De Sica's decision to give us this information which he withholds from the protagonist nonetheless serves to dramatize this character's self-absorption and to make us judge him accordingly. Yet, at the moment of Umberto's reunion with Flick in the pound, we are drawn into full sympathy with the character once more and forgive him his human failings.

If it were not for the filmmaker's complex and shifting

---

[31] Nick Barbaro cites this, among other examples of Umberto's failure of solidarity. See his "*Umberto D*," p. 20.

attitude toward the protagonist, *Umberto D* could easily rigidify into a thesis film about the plight of the socially disenfranchised, both the elderly and the so-called "subproletariat." There are the makings of a thesis film in Umberto's admonition to Maria about her failure to do her homework. "Some things happen because we don't know grammar. All exploit the ignorant." But not even grammar will help those for whom society has no more use, as the public official suggests when he shouts to the protesters, "You don't have a permit," as if they had no permission to exist in the eyes of a production-oriented establishment. Indeed, the film is full of withering social commentary in its attacks on the mercenary and hypocritical bourgeoisie embodied in the landlady who is so proper with her fiancé yet has no compunctions about leasing out Umberto's room for 1,000 lire per hour. The hospital patient in the bed to Umberto's right is visited by two sons who show the expected concern over their father's condition when the nun is there, but lapse into cheerful chatter about money the minute she is gone. The Church gets a broadside in the nun who can be talked into keeping Umberto in the hospital for an extra week provided he make the proper show of Christian reverence. When the nun holds out the rosary to him as if it were a trinket for a child, her carrot-and-stick approach to religious piety is only too obvious.[32] Like the pauper's Mass in *Bicycle Thief* where beggars are enticed into prayer with the promise of Sunday dinner, De Sica's Church makes unabashed use of the claims of the body to win the loyalty of the soul. Perhaps the most lethal social commentary is implicit in the scene at the dog pound, whose murderous efficiency, huge staff, and sophisticated physical plant are a terrible indictment of a society which lavishes such care and expense on the disposal of animals but cannot manage to fund increased pensions for its elderly.

[32] On the religious hypocrisy exposed in this scene, see Canziani and Bragaglia, *La stagione*, p. 101.

As in *Bicycle Thief*, no programmatic solution is offered to the social ills diagnosed by the film, but *Umberto D* does not even hold out the shred of hope in solidarity that we discerned in Bruno's forgiveness of Antonio at the conclusion of the earlier film.[33] Though both stories end with betrayals followed by reconciliations (in Umberto's case, he violates Flick's trust in attempting to commit a "double suicide" but wins him back in the end), it is significant that Bruno's human witness to Antonio's tragedy is replaced by a dog in *Umberto D*. The substitution is devastating, and gives the lie to the critical consensus that considers this final scene an upbeat ending to Umberto's story.[34] On the contrary, the protagonist's mood at the conclusion of the film suggests the gaiety that lies beyond tragedy, like Yeat's actors who

> If worthy their prominent part in the play,
> Do not break up their lines to weep.
> They know that Hamlet and Lear are gay;
> Gaiety transfiguring all that dread.[35]

And like Yeats's gay Chinamen carved in lapis lazuli at the end of his poem, it is the permanence of the artwork itself that consoles the tragic vision. Such an ending to De Sica's film constitutes at once the ultimate affirmation and the demise of neorealism, for it takes us out of the realm of history and into the realm of art in a total reversal of realist priorities, while positing the power of that art to help us change the world in accordance with the neorealists' injunction to social action. This double and seemingly contradictory conclusion is the result of a shift in emphasis from thematic to formal solutions to Umberto's plight. Indeed, within the terms of fiction, we can envision no answer for his predicament,

[33] See Singerman, "*Umberto D*," pp. 165–66.

[34] See for example, Canziani and Bragaglia, *La stagione*, p. 102; and Leprohon, *Vittorio De Sica*, p. 62.

[35] From William Butler Yeats, "Lapis Lazuli," in *Selected Poems and Two Plays of William Butler Yeats*, ed. W. L. Rosenthal (New York: Macmillan, 1964), p. 159.

either in self-inflicted death, or life in a flophouse, or a return to Via San Martini della Battaglia to retrieve Maria. This inability to project a future for the protagonist beyond the final frames of *Umberto D* throws our attention back on the film as aesthetic object in a violation of the neorealist insistence on artistic transparency. However, the isolation and incomprehension that Umberto suffers can be overcome by the approach to experience manifested on the film's formal level. In hypothesizing the perfect realist film of ninety uneventful minutes in the life of a man, Zavattini writes:

. . . each of these frames will be equally intense and revealing, it will no longer be just a bridge to the next frame, but will vibrate within itself like a microcosm. Then our attention will become continuous, and I would say perpetual, as one man's must be toward another man.[36]

Thus it is the style of the film, rather than the personal or political implications of its story, which offers a corrective to the atomization and solitude of the social order it depicts. The Zavattinian attentiveness to the conditions of others is exemplified by the formal attributes of *Umberto D*, especially in its *temps morts* sequences and in its general strategy of dedramatization, which assign as much importance to the minutae of our daily routines as to the life-shaping events of which plots are made.

With *Umberto D*, De Sica and Zavattini have not abandoned the revolutionary promise of the first neorealists, they have simply shifted the burden from the level of narrative content to that of cinematic form. While it is enough to read the screenplay of *Open City* to appreciate Rossellini's didactic intent, *Umberto D* must be screened before it can teach

[36]See "Intervento al convegno di Perugia," in Lizzani, *Storia del cinema italiano*, p. 465.

us how to regard mankind with Zavattinian attentiveness.[37]
This withdrawal into form as the agent of social change is
not so much a rejection of the neorealists' venture as a modernization of it. Rossellini's visionary city was further from
realization in 1952 than it had been in the immediate aftermath of war when anything seemed possible and the memory of the liberation was still fresh. The working-class emphasis and the allusions to Resistance ideals no longer spoke
to an Italy eager to put the "bad old days" behind it, like
Umberto's landlady, and enjoy the fruits of reconstruction.
By making the form the new repository of neorealist meaning, De Sica and Zavattini put an end to the classical neorealism of content, and rendered possible instead Fellini's,
Antonioni's, and Visconti's application of its stylistic precepts to subjects hitherto excluded from serious postwar cinematic treatment.

Significantly, there is no child at the end of *Umberto D* to
embody the hopes for a better future, there is only an old
man whose refusal either to die or to prolong an unviable
existence reflects the dilemma of neorealism itself toward the
end of its first decade of life.

[37]Kracauer cites *Umberto D* as an example of a truly cinematic narration,
as opposed to Renato Castellani's *Romeo and Juliet* (1954) whose story is
detachable from its medium. See his *Theory of Film*, p. 221.

PART II

Transitions

5 Comencini's *Bread, Love, and Fantasy*: Consumable realism

"BOMBARDMENT?" ASKS Marshal Carotenuto as he surveys the wreckage of a building in the village of Saliena to which he has just been assigned as chief *carabiniere*. "No, earthquake," answers one of his guides in this introductory tour of the town. When yet a second ruin appears before Carotenuto's astonished eyes, he is wary of repeating his earlier mistake. "Earthquake?" he now asks. "No, bombardment," he is told, in confirmation of his original guess.

This exchange is rich in promise for a thematic and generic approach to *Bread, Love, and Fantasy*. The comic device of repetition and reversal suggests that Comencini intends to amuse and divert us, to give us "a pleasing spectacle—not a vulgar one—based on an amusing and good-natured caricature,"[1] according to Luigi Chiarini's formulation. On the other hand, the content of the joke is not without critical sting in its allusion to the man-made and natural devastations of southern Italian life. Comencini thereby locates the film in a precise historical and economic context—one that hints strongly at the failure of postwar reconstruction to clear up the rubble, let alone to remake the social structure in a way which would buttress the population against its besetting disasters.

Comencini was certainly not the first to introduce comedy into the realist aesthetic. Indeed, as Carlo Lizzani points out, it had already appeared in isolated instances within the context of many classic neorealist works.[2] Slapstick moments

---

[1] Cited in Jean Gili, *Luigi Comencini* (Paris: Edilig, 1981), p. 24.

[2] See *Il cinema italiano*, p. 153. Here, Lizzani proposes the very suggestive thesis that the sketchy, light comic, popularizing elements of the prewar cinema, which persisted in neorealism, but constituted a minor part of a far

abounded in *Open City*, and though fewer in number, humorous touches did lighten the pathos of *Bicycle Thief* and *Umberto D*. De Sica and Zavattini sought to vary the neorealist formula with surrealist fantasy elements in *Miracle in Milan*.[3] Sentimental comedy became the prevailing mode in *Two Pennyworth of Hope* (1952) whose very title gave away the new optimistic emphasis that Renato Castellani was to impart to Italian realism.[4] Though Castellani held to the letter of neorealist practice, using nonprofessional actors, an authentic popular setting, regional dialect, unobtrusive cinematography, and an uncontrived storyline, his insistence upon a happy ending suggested arbitrary, facile solutions for the very intransigent social problems his story promised to explore. With the success of *Two Pennyworth*, Castellani launched the new vogue for "rosy realism," which Luigi Comencini perfected in *Bread, Love, and Fantasy* in 1953 and its sequel *Bread, Love, and Jealousy* in 1954. Nor were Castellani and Comencini the only directors interested in rosy realism, for Dino Risi was to consolidate his directorial fame in this genre with *Bread, Love, and . . .* (1955) and *Poor, but Beautiful* (1956). Such was the success of the bread-and-love formula that a Spanish director, Xavier Seto, was to try his hand in the genre with *Bread, Love, and Andalusia* set in Spain in 1959. But perhaps the most illustrious offshoot of rosy realism is the *commedia all'italiana*,[5] a genre that was to dominate Italian commercial production of the late 1950s and 1960s, launching the acting careers of such stars as Sophia Loren, Marcello Mastroianni, Nino Manfredi, Ugo Tog-

---

more serious and comprehensive aesthetic, emerged once more in the 1950s, after the fall of neorealism, to dominate cinematic style.

[3] For a discussion of this generic hybrid, see Bondanella, "Neorealist Aesthetics and The Fantastic: *The Machine to Kill Bad People* and *Miracle in Milan*."

[4] On the beginnings of rosy realism, see Liehm, *Passion and Defiance*, p. 89. On the relationship between *Two Pennyworth* and *Bread, Love, and Fantasy*, see Guido Aristarco, "I cascami," in *Antologia di "Cinema nuovo*," ed Aristarco, pp. 742ff.

[5] See Bondanella, *Italian Cinema*, p. 89.

nazzi, while establishing the directorial skills of Lina Wertmuller and Ettore Scola, among others. Franco Brusati was
to recall rosy realism in his ingeniously titled *Bread and
Chocolate* (1973), about the plight of the Italian guest workers in Switzerland. What is significant is Brusati's omission
of *amore* from the rosy realists' conventional tripartite titles.
Though love is by no means absent from his plot, the title's
failure to include it may be Brusati's attempt to distance
himself from his rosy predecessors' bias toward the overly
sentimental.

In its combination of comic and realist strategies, Comencini's aesthetic raises some serious critical questions. Does
the humor work to deepen and sharpen his social inquiry, or
does it serve instead to lighten and trivialize the problems it
is supposed to probe? Does the comic approach help to ex-
tend the realist teaching to a broader audience or does it
permit that audience to ignore its didactic justification?[6]

The considerable debate surrounding Comencini's film has
centered on the various answers to these questions given by
neorealist critics, on the one hand, and the defenders of the
genres populaires, as Jean Gili calls them, on the other.[7] For
those who hold up straightforward documentarist neorealism as the standard against which any deviation amounts to
heresy, *Bread, Love, and Fantasy* is indeed a betrayal, a bastard child, a pandering to the public's desire for cinematic
escape.[8] For those who instead see in the *genres populaires*
a dialogue between filmmaker and public, which can ultimately work toward the making of social consciousness,
Bread, Love, and Fantasy is defensible indeed.[9] Somewhere

[6] On Comencini's aspiration to a cinema of vast audience appeal, see the
interview in Monicelli, *Cinema italiano: Ma cos'è questa crisi?*, p. 54.

[7] See Gili, *Luigi Comencini*, p. 26.

[8] See, for example, Aldo Tassone, *Parla il cinema italiano, I* (Milan: Il
Formichiere, 1979), pp. 87–88; Aristarco, "I cascami," pp. 741ff.; Lino
Miccichè, "Dal neorealismo al cinema del centrismo," in *Materiali sul cin-
ema italiano degli anni '50* (Pesaro: Melchiorri, 1978), p. 9.

[9] See Gili, *Luigi Comencini*, p. 26. Brunetta, for different reasons, is also
somewhat "softer" on Comencini than the neorealist critics, seeing in *Bread,*

between these two extreme views lies a fair assessment of
Comencini's achievement—one that will require a careful examination of his realist–comic strategy and a close reading
of the resulting film before a balanced judgment can be
reached.

Bread, Love, and Fantasy tells the story of two courtships
whose intertwinings and parallelisms conclude in a dual happy
ending. In the first love plot, the middle-aged Marshal Carotenuto seeks the favors of Annarella, the municipal midwife
whose monthly trips to Rome, plus her absence of family
attachments, make her the object of intense curiosity on the
part of the town gossips. Carotenuto is neither immune to
her charms nor indifferent to her mystery, and he manages
to woo Annarella by offering her transportation on her
professional rounds. But when the courtship becomes too serious, Annarella backs off for reasons that ultimately explain
her monthly excursions to the capital and her spinster status.
She is an unwed mother who supports her son in Rome
through midwifery in the provinces. Such is Carotenuto's love
(and his honesty about his own amorous wanderings) that
he proposes marriage despite her tainted past.

In the second love plot, Carabiniere Giuseppe Stelluti, young
draftee from the Veneto serving his military duty under Carotenuto, seeks the hand of Maria de Ritis, called La Bersagliera, the poorest and most beautiful maiden in Saliena. In
love with La Bersagliera for eight months, he has been unable to press his suit for fear of violating the carabinieri's
prohibition against romancing the women of the town. Once
such a passion is made public, the guilty officer is subject to
immediate transferral. When Carotenuto assigns Stelluti to
rendezvous with La Bersagliera, the young man finally over-
comes his scruples and declares his love. Though he feels

Love, and Fantasy a work that is at once realist in its insistence on the
theme of poverty, and very literary in its recall of Goldonian theater. See
his Storia, pp. 467–68.

that he must now report his new status to Carotenuto, the marshal refuses to listen to him until after the festival of Sant'Antonio when the engagement will be made public in the presence of Stelluti's mother, newly arrived from the Veneto, and the entire chorus of rejoicing villagers. "The film was born from a casual encounter of mine with Margadonna [the co-scriptwriter]," Comencini said of *Bread, Love and Fantasy,*

> and from the reading of his book of sketches . . . of life in the Abruzzi, and from the desire of both of us to use them for a well-made play according to the rules of classical comedy. I remember that we reread Beaumarchais. Yet, like Beaumarchais . . . we also wanted to create a comedy that exposed to the public the conflicts and the contradictions of Italian society.[10]

This important account of the inspiration for *Bread, Love, and Fantasy* reveals the dual realist–comic impulse that will typify Comencini's aesthetic. His aspiration to reveal the inner dynamics of the historical process, full of discordant and colliding material forces, is reminiscent of the critical realism of Lukács, which was heartily embraced by the Italian Left of the 1950s.[11] In Beaumarchais, whose plays indicted the privileged elite of his day, Comencini chose as a model one who achieved the synthesis of classical comedy and social criticism, which is the filmmaker's own stated objective.

Later in the same interview, Comencini reveals two of the four reasons that undermined the success of the realist part of his strategy. First, and most deeply disturbing, was the debilitating effect of censorship on the initial inspiration of the film. Producers wanted to have nothing to do with a work that might cast doubt on the nation's armed forces. As one

[10] See *Materiali sul cinema italiano degli anni '50*, p. 249.
[11] On the Left's exclusive interest in the aesthetic theory of Lukács to the exclusion of Brecht, for example, see Micciché, "Dal neorealismo al cinema del centrismo," in *Materiali*, pp. 6–7.

producer explained: "I cannot make a film denigrating the military that defends my property."[12] It is this kind of objection that must have been in Comencini's mind when he introduced his film with the following titles:

> The occurrence that we are about to recount is imaginary. But nonetheless it is a human occurrence. The characters live it in the uniforms of the *carabinieri*, but not for this do they cease to be men and as such, they feel, love, and suffer the same as all of you.

With these lines, Comencini seeks to reassure his public and his backers that his film is anything but a criticism of the *carabinieri*—indeed, that it is not *about* them at all, but about universal human passions. The fact that his characters wear military garb is a matter of indifference to the storyline and to its interpretation. "When, however, their humanity transcends the limits of the immutable disciplinary norms," the titles continue, "they know how to come to their senses, according to their tradition, which is the luminous patrimony of the Army." Here, Comencini qualifies his original denial of the military's relevance to the plot. The *carabinieri* uniforms are more than gratuitous costumes, he admits, but where the military has thematic application, all will redound to the glory of that institution.

These titles are unfortunate in several ways. Their pompous rhetoric, so typical of the retrograde, Restoration mentality of the 1950s,[13] puts the film in league with the very forces of censorship that Comencini is seeking to appease. Even if this apology has nothing to do with the film it is trying to protect from the censor's scrutiny, it nonetheless creates certain viewer expectations which cannot help but

[12] Quoted by Comencini in *Materiali sul cinema italiano degli anni '50*, p. 250.

[13] "Restoration" is the term used to express the disappointment of the Left in the cultural backlash of the Fifties, which repudiated the values of the Resistance and made postwar reconstruction into a return to the pre-Fascist social order.

condition the aesthetic experience. We are primed to expect an epopee of the Italian police whose prowess will be tested in physical and moral combat of heroic proportions. Instead, the only law enforcement that takes place in *Bread, Love, and Fantasy* is the suppression of domestic skirmishes: La Bersagliera and her rival Paoletta come to blows in a flea market, and Annarella must be protected from anxious fathers who want to hold her hostage during their wives' long labors. Otherwise, the *carabinieri* are shown lounging about, whiling the time away in love-longing and sloth. Thus, because of the grandiose opening titles, the film turns into a joke on itself, continually mocking and trivializing its initial heroic stance at the expense of the *carabinieri* tradition it is supposed to be glorifying. Were it not for the opening titles, the status of the *carabinieri* would not be our explicit concern. We are only aware of its degeneration from a heroic ideal because our attention has been called to it by the initial rhetorical premise.

Pro-*carabinieri* censorship is responsible for the compromise of Comencini's realist intent in a still more important way. The original story idea called for "the encounter of a marshal of the *carabinieri* from the North with the reality of a poor town of the South, developed, on the whole, with a slightly black sense of humor and even with dramatic moments."[14] The film was thus to be about the education of an outsider into the economic and historic truths of postreconstruction Italy, and it was to bring into play all the virulent tensions of the North–South dichotomy, which lends itself so well to Lukácsian analysis.

Such a scenario, however, was unacceptable to Comencini's producers, whose objection to slander against the military really hides a deeper objection to the proposed revelation of social injustice in the disparities between North and South. The producer who finally agreed to back Comencini

---

[14] Quoted in *Materiali*, p. 249.

did so on one condition: that he cast Vittorio De Sica in the role of chief *carabiniere.* "The executive producer, in order to feel more reassured, had the script read, without my knowing it, by the commanding general of the *carabinieri*, who gave his assent only because 'De Sica would have made that marshal a sympathetic character.' "[15] Comencini's original choice for the role had been Gino Cervi, an actor whose seriousness would have given considerable weight to the educational theme of the film.[16] Cervi might have succeeded in taking us on an interior journey into the mind of a man who, by dint of exposure to an alien world, grows in knowledge and in moral responsibility. De Sica's suaveness and charm keeps us on the outside, and throws the emphasis on the sentimental, affective elements of the plot, obscuring its considerable intellectual, moral possibilities.[17] Indeed, in the story as we have it, no dramatic action arises out of the knowledge of poverty and suffering which is supposed to be the realist baggage of the film, unless it is Carotenuto's decision to renounce his predatory appetite for La Bersagliera and settle into legal domesticity with Annarella. Since La Bersagliera is a kind of personification of the town in her extreme poverty, Carotenuto's decision not to exploit her plight, but to sponsor instead her marriage to Stelluti, could signify a new, higher awareness of his moral responsibilities to the less privileged members of his society. With a different kind of actor, the socio-moral dimension of his decision to forfeit his lecherous pursuit might be brought into sharper relief. Instead, De Sica gives his choice a purely sentimental motivation. He is moved by pity for La Bersagliera's plight, and by a higher love for Annarella, and not by any new-found social conscience.

[15] Quoted in ibid., p. 250.

[16] On Comencini's preference for Cervi, see Gili, *Le cinèma italien*, p. 120.

[17] Comencini himself admits that this casting choice, which was forced upon him, makes the film "vaudeville, the story of a scoundrel from the South who doesn't discover a damned thing." In Tassone, *Parla il cinema*, I, p. 100.

Furthermore, De Sica's presence in the film works to undermine Comencini's realist aspirations in yet another way. When Zavattini articulated the neorealists' prohibition against the casting of professionals in his "Some Ideas on the Cinema,"[18] he did so not only because amateurs turn in a less contrived, more credible performance, but also because professional recitations are necessarily contaminated in the public mind by the memory of characters played by the same actors in the past. This is surely the case with Vittorio De Sica's Carotenuto who is, in many ways, a middle-aged version of the young ladies' man who graced so many of Mario Camerini's 1930s sentimental comedies. The memory of De Sica's prewar career as a matinee idol and the assurance that in twenty years his appeal for the ladies has not diminished is not only part of the joke of his name (he is still *carotenuto*—held dear) but is also made explicit early in *Bread, Love, and Fantasy* when the wife of his predecessor in Saliena encourages the marshal to marry. "At my age?" Carotenuto asks. "You must have great success with women," she affirms. "You are the classic type of the heartbreaker." And with this allusion to the romantic stereotype that De Sica the matinee idol was instrumental in creating, the passage establishes the generic antecedents of *Bread, Love, and Fantasy* in the prewar sentimental comedies of the actor's own past.[19]

The final obstacles to the achievement of Comencini's realist intent are implicit in the filmmaker's own original statement of purpose. In explaining that the subject was inspired by a book of *bozzetti* or sketches of life in the Abruzzi, Comencini uses the very term of opprobrium so often applied by neorealist critics to condemn the frivolity of Fifties film production. When they object to *bozzettismo*, these critics are referring not only to the degeneration of story into so many charming, folkloristic vignettes, but they are also regretting

[18] Zavattini, "Some Ideas on the Cinema," p. 227.
[19] On the throwback to Thirties cinema, see Aristarco, "I cascami," in *Antologia*, ed. Aristarco, pp. 744 and 746.

the diminution of the overarching neorealist design, with its comprehensive and cohesive historical vision, into fragments that aspire to nothing more than their own preciosity. Comencini's admission that his textual source was indeed a book of sketches suggests the aptness of this charge on the part of his neorealist critics.

Of course, the other literary model for *Bread, Love, and Fantasy* is the tradition of classical comedy in general, and of Beaumarchais in particular, which explains the artful, highly contrived nature of its storyline. Both courtships conform to the structural formula for the classical comic plot which has remained remarkably faithful to its prototype in Greek New Comedy.[20] "What normally happens," according to Northrop Frye, "is that a young man wants a young woman, that his desire is resisted by some opposition, usually paternal, and that near the end of the play some twist in plot enables the hero to have his will."[21] In the love story of Stelluti and La Bersagliera, this structure is easily discerned. The blocking force is Carotenuto who assumes a parental role in his association with established authority and who must therefore enforce the military prohibition against romancing the women of the town. In the case of Carotenuto's own sentimental quest, the blocking force is the social stigma attached to unwed mothers—a prejudice that convinced Annarella of her unworthiness to receive the marshal's attentions. In either case, it is Carotenuto's will that prevails, overriding the military ruling on the one hand, transcending the social bias on the other.

Divine intervention in the dramatic action, another property of classic comic structure, is also much in evidence in *Bread, Love, and Fantasy*. Comencini's use of Sant'Antonio to figure the operations of divine providence in human affairs is an ingenious choice, since this saint's holy jurisdiction

---

[20] See Northrop Frye, *Anatomy of Criticism* (Princeton, N.J.: Princeton University Press, 1973), p. 163.
[21] Ibid.

extends over most of the action of the film. As Apostle of Charity, patron saint of lovers, of marriage, of women in confinement, and of animals, Sant'Antonio combines so many of the interests of this plot that his benevolent power becomes analogous with the very principle of comic resolution.

In all his good deeds Carotenuto seems to be acting as Sant'Antonio's agent within the world of the film, seeing to the health of La Bersagliera's donkey the night that she spends in jail, helping Annarella tend her women in childbirth, and leaving La Bersagliera 5,000 lire during her family's pilgrimage to the saint's shrine. Furthermore, Carotenuto's role as the saint's earthly agent is twice made explicit in dialogue. "Marshal, you have been the hand of Sant'Antonio," cries La Bersagliera's mother, thanking him for detaining her daughter overnight in jail while the rest of the family was away on pilgrimage so that Sant'Antonio could visit their home undetected and leave them the 5,000 lire. Later, when the mother sends her children to arrange a tryst between La Bersagliera and Carotenuto the children exclaim, "You are as good as Sant'Antonio," equating the patron saint of lovers and charity with the potential amorous alleviator of their sister's poverty. Soon thereafter, when the village priest Don Emedio exhorts Carotenuto to suppress his appetite for La Bersagliera and to help sponsor her engagement to Stelluti, the conversation takes place before the image of Sant'Antonio, whose presence seems to have a sobering influence on the once disordered passions of the marshal. Don Emedio is in fact adorning the statue for the festival of Sant'Antonio which is soon to occur. Thanks to the timing of the festival, Stelluti is able to enjoy La Bersagliera's company for an extra few days before being transferred out of town to complete his tour of duty. It is also thanks to the festival that Annarella, who had hidden herself away for several days, finally appears on her balcony and emboldens Carotenuto to make his declaration of love. La Bersagliera's mother had once told Carotenuto, "Kiss Sant'Antonio and he will perform a miracle for you"—a prophecy that finds its fulfillment in the film's comic ending. When Carotenuto ignores Sant'Antonio for the spectacle of Annarella at the balcony, his maid reprimands him, "if you prayed to Sant'Antonio, it would be better." Little does she realize that by seconding La Bersagliera's nuptial hopes, and by pursuing his own marital ambitions with Annarella, Carotenuto is indeed doing the saint's divine will.

Bread, Love, and Fantasy, like the classical comedy of Frye's formulation, ends festively, with one celebration in progress—that of Sant'Antonio—and two on the way—the twin nuptials. But festivals are events which occur outside the linear flow of human history; they are exempt from the flux and change of chronological events. When festive moments give closure to plots, as they usually do in comedy, they call attention to the artifice and contrivance of the foregoing narration. "Happy endings do not impress us as true, but as desirable, and they are brought about by manipulation,"[22] observes Frye in an argument which suggests why the formal requirements of classical comedy are incompatible with those of realism. The realist mode depends upon the fiction of open-endedness—its text must appear to be coextensive with the world "out there" in order to support its plea for social responsibility and corrective action. For an *engagé* aesthetic to work, it must promote the illusion of free movement across textual borders. Comedy, with its unabashed artifice, its arbitrary manipulation of plot, and its celebration of formal boundaries, is by its very nature antagonistic to the realists' representational needs.

A stubborn resistance to structural change, and a love of form for its own sake, make classical comedy an essentially conservative mode in its image of society as well as in its own aesthetic principles. The marriage ceremony that concludes most comedies offers the promise of a new commu-

22 Ibid., p. 170.

nity *in nucleo* which will reaffirm the ideal of a social order based on the most rudimentary legal and blood ties between its constituent members. Though comedies often identify problems in the contemporary status quo, their resolutions never include reformatory action, nor a plea for a redress of grievances, since this would detract from the stability and the universality of the happy ending. Beaumarchais's *Marriage of Figaro*, which must have served as one of Comencini's inspiring texts, is vehement in its attack on the onerous *droit de seigneur*, which entitled the lord of the manor to be the first to possess his vassals' brides. It is this feudal privilege that acts as the blocking force to the marriage of Figaro and Suzanne, and only when Count Almaviva forfeits his right does the plot reach its happy nuptial conclusion. But the comic ending does nothing to change the principle of *droit de seigneur*, nor is there any evidence that Almaviva will forgo his privilege on future occasions, let alone legislate to deny his aristocratic peers their seignorial rights. Beaumarchais's resolution is a very partial one which does not really begin to redress the social injustice it so rightly condemns.

If comedy indeed seeks to establish a new society to replace a corrupt, older order as Frye suggests, it does so not by instituting progressive social change, but by returning to an earlier phase of social evolution—that of the legendary Golden Age.[23] Thus Carotenuto abandons the degenerate, predatory, cosmopolitan values of the modern world for the simpler, more authentic domestic ideals of rural life in Saliena, making the town a timeless, Utopian dream with no need for progress or remedial social action. What *Bread, Love, and Fantasy* turns out to be, then, is an ahistorical classic comedy with a patina of realism that has no actual bearing on its conservative comic ideology.

Now we are prepared to consider Comencini's various attempts at realist inquiry and the reasons for their failure within

[23] Ibid., p. 171

the context of his generic experiment. The film opens with a series of shots that could come right out of the neorealist lexicon of images from popular life: an old bus driving along a country road; the revelation of the harshness and austerity of the surrounding landscape; the arrival in an impoverished hilltop town. Carotenuto emerges from the bus with no visual fanfare, preceded by a line of undistinguished, unglamorous figures of neorealist descent. Gina Lollobrigida, as La Bersagliera, also makes an understated first appearance on the screen, riding her donkey behind the group of *carabinieri* who occupy the foreground of the *mise-en-scène*. But the film does not live up to the realist promise of its opening moments, as the treatment of La Bersagliera makes abundantly clear. Though Comencini scrupulously avoids glamorizing her poverty—dressing her literally in rags, refusing her shoes, tying her hair in pigtails, and placing her on the rump of a donkey—her florid face and voluptuous figure suggest that she is neither the victim of overwork nor of a substandard diet. Her threadbare image, astride the donkey, far from dramatizing her poverty, becomes so stylized through repetition that it constitutes a visual icon, devoid of all socioeconomic referents. Unlike Pina, whose dreary clothes and ankle socks were the index of a concrete historic condition in *Open City*, La Bersagliera's poor trappings are reduced to so much window-dressing—ornaments to her person that can be changed with the changing storyline. When we enter her house, along with Carotenuto, Comencini indeed does not shrink from showing us its true squalor, but the emotional musical commentary, and the chief *carabiniere*'s reassuring presence suggest that this poverty is not permanent—that it will be remedied by dramatic means.

It is La Bersagliera, then, who incarnates the poverty theme of the film and, as such, she becomes the key to Comencini's generic experiment in realist comedy. Not only is she the visual personification of indigence, but its temperamental victim as well in her frequent angry outbursts, which are at-

5. *Gina Lollobrigida plays La Bersagliera, whose rags, pigtails, and donkey become so stylized that they cease to denote poverty and suggest instead the charming rusticity that will make Marshal Carotenuto (Vittorio De Sica) one of her many admirers.*

tributed to "too much poverty" by the sympathetic, often fellow-suffering, people of the town. La Bersagliera is herself quite aware of the source of her rage and she spells it out as often as possible. When Carotenuto asks her if she is over her anger at Paoletta, La Bersagliera answers that poor people are always angry, and when the parish priest Don Emedio promises infernal rewards for the landlord Don Concezio, La Beragliera answers "for poor people, Don Eme', Hell is right here." With her political consciousness raised and with her anger as a motivating force, we expect La Bersagliera to channel those impulses into some form of social action. Indeed rebellion, or at least civil disobedience, seems to be fermenting in her mind during her unfair incarceration in the wake of a brawl with Paoletta. But this incipient outrage gives way to amorousness, and the initial image of La Bersagliera as a furious, caged animal is replaced by the sultry and seductive one of the beautiful wench lying on the prison floor, singing her heart out for love. Of course, it is romance that domesticates La Bersagliera, just as it will eventually remedy her desperate poverty through marriage. Nor is this solution limited to La Bersagliera's isolated example, for she has, throughout the story, embodied the economic straits of the entire village. "La Bersagliera has the problem of being the most beautiful and the poorest of the town," Don Emedio tells Carotenuto in a formulation which links the sentimental impulse of the plot to the film's historic and economic inquiry. The suggestion is not only that La Bersagliera's plight is amenable to a sentimental–comic cure, but that as the personification of the town's hardships, her rescue from indigence will somehow magically alleviate the sufferings of all Saliena.

In characterizing the wealthy landowner Don Concezio, Comencini further reveals the suppression of realist generic requirements in the overriding interests of comedy. Obese, strident, and hypochondriacal, Don Concezio is the incarnation of all that is wrong with the class system of the South.

Twice he erupts into the action of the film, bullying and intimidating his dependents, but in each instance Comencini refuses to confront this agent of social injustice, choosing instead to exploit Don Concezio for his comic potential by reducing him to the stock villain of slapstick. Accordingly, when Don Concezio accuses La Bersagliera of stealing his plums, she answers with a barrage of verbal abuse, in what could be the beginning of long overdue popular insurrection against the tyrannical overlord. The villagers, however, fail to take their cue from her, choosing instead to chant under their breath "Possa crepar, possa crepar" ("May he die, may he die") in a revelation of their impotence and passivity. Later on, the townspeople beg Sant'Antonio to "fallo crepar" ("make him die") in a comic variant of the earlier plea. The effect of the anti-Don Concezio humor, however, is to dull the impact of the landlord's iniquities and to show how well the people cope with their anger through communal wish fulfillment fantasy.

Saliena, as a collective protagonist and as a physical setting, becomes an important measure of Comencini's generic intentions. In its passivity, its nonrebellion, and its acceptance of an unjust status quo, the town reveals the futility of the neorealist attempt to elicit an activist response in the Italian public. From the very start of the film, we are told that Saliena is quiet, as opposed to other areas of Italy where peasant uprisings are the norm. Carotenuto has just finished an arduous tour of duty in Emilia-Romagna before taking up service in the South. Here, he is immediately reassured, he will have nothing to do but make love. Later, in an interview with Don Emedio whose thematic importance warrants lengthy citation, Carotenuto learns the "why" of this political calm.

DON EMEDIO:: This is a town that does not offer
distractions. A quiet town. No one strikes, no one
rebels.

CAROTENUTO:: Why, you'd like them to rebel?
DON EMEDIO:: No, what good would it do? They say
   in your newspapers that in Puglia, in Sicily, the peasants are rebelling, striking, to get land, and it almost
   makes me want to cry because at least they have
   hope. But here, for over fifty years the land has
   belonged to the peasants, therefore nothing can
   happen.
CAROTENUTO:: Progressive town?
DON EMEDIO:: Yes, progressive in poverty. Marshal, I
   have been parish priest in Saliena for forty years and
   I swear to you that to shatter this populace it takes a
   force. . . . We survive by deluding ourselves that we
   survive. Perhaps Providence has established that this
   town must disappear and we are dying little by little,
   day by day, without knowing it.

In another kind of film, this anguished commentary by a
concerned observer would constitute a call to arms, a plea
to raise the collective political consciousness to action, to bring
a halt to the gradual slippage and decline which is leading
the town to extinction.[24] But in Comencini's film, this passage remains itself a dead end, a realist addendum to an incompatible comic text.

If the previous passage suggests one possible direction in
which the film could move (but does not), the concluding
interchange suggests yet another potentially realist plotline.

CAROTENUTO:: By the way, Father, do earthquakes
   occur here often? I saw some ruins.
DON EMEDIO:: Every year a little quake, but without
   grave consequences. And every ten or fifteen years, a
   truly big quake.

[24] Adriano Aprà sees the physical instability of Saliena as "symbol of an
impossible Italy, of an Italy, anyhow, destined to disappear." As such Saliena points to the purely cinematographic, artificial status of the film's resolution. See "Comencini e Risi: Elogio del mestiere," in *Il cinema italiano
degli anni '50*, ed. Giorgio Tinazzi (Venice: Marsilio, 1979), p. 206.

CAROTENUTO:: How long has it been since the last big quake?

DON EMEDIO:: A long time. It appears that we're ready. This year or the next, we'll dance.

This ominous forecast, after the opening spectacle of a shattered townscape, puts the possibility of recurrent earthquakes in the forefront of the viewers' awareness. We expect the film to document the anxieties of life on the "brink" and the devastations of life in the aftermath. But the only tremors this film ever records are the metaphoric ones of the heart. The seismographic observations, however, are not completely without purpose. They do serve to focus attention on the physical landscape itself which Comencini photographs to marvelous advantage in what constitutes his greatest debt to neorealism.[25] No matter how ornamental and superficial his thematic use of the setting is, his cinematographic appropriation of it is masterful. The action and characters are firmly ensconced in the streets, the piazzas, and the stone buildings of Saliena and Comencini exploits the various vertical levels of the town to give maximal visual and dramatic interest to his *mise-en-scène*.[26] During the sequence of the sham miracle, for example, when La Bersagliera's mother gathers her cronies to worship at a makeshift shrine of Sant'Antonio, representatives of both civil and ecclesiastic authorities stand above the throng on a steep embankment to condemn this usurpation of divine prerogatives by the laity. First Carotenuto appears on the embankment to reprimand the crowd, and then Don Emedio, who delivers a tedious little sermon on theological protocol, is visually buttressed by the hillside behind him as he looks down on the erring flock. When the

[25] On the role of landscape in rosy realism, see Ernesto Laura, *Comedy Italian Style* (Rome: A.N.I.C.A., n.d.), p. 28.

[26] Though Saliena is supposed to be a town in the Abruzzi, *Bread, Love, and Fantasy* was actually shot in Castel San Pietro, a hill town in Lazio above Palestrina. See Aristarco, "I cascami," in *Antologia*, ed. Aristarco, p. 742.

devout finally disband, they file slowly up the same hillside in penitential silence.

The many vertical levels provided by the topography of the hilltop town offer just as many vantage points from which the action can be observed. Saliena teems with voyeurs who gather spontaneously in piazzas, balconies, and hillsides to observe the action (often through binoculars) and to gossip about the protagonists' amorous exploits—both real and imaginary. When Carotenuto is given his introductory tour of the town, he jokes about the ubiquitous crowd of observers whose alertness to their neighbors' lives will "facilitate the investigation." Just as he makes this remark, a crowd gathers on a terrace above him with such perfect timing and choreography that, were this a musical comedy, the obligatory production number would follow.

What all this suggests is that the town has ceased to be the on-site location for a neorealist inquiry and has become instead a theater for the performance of an ahistorical classical comedy. Perhaps nowhere in the film is this generic identity more evident than in the final scene of the nocturnal festival of Sant'Antonio in which both couples unite against the background of the town, whose buildings are outlined by strings of lights and whose sky is illuminated by fireworks. The final image of the town could be a studio set in Cinecittà, a miniature diorama, or a postcard—it has lost any semblance of a three-dimensional space capable of accommodating authentic, moving, historically rooted human lives. In contrast to the opening image of the rickety old bus, fit for the conveyance of real human beings into believable worlds, this final *mise-en-scène* shows the vast distance that Comencini has traveled from neorealism toward a theater of comic sentimentality.

Now we are prepared to reconsider the significance of the title, whose third element, *fantasia*, offers the interpretive key to Comencini's filmmaking strategy. A glance at any comprehensive Italian dictionary will reveal the richness and moral ambiguity of this term, whose most neutral sense—"faculty, virtue, creative power of the spirit that produces dreams illusions, abstractions etc."[27]—can give rise to the morally positive notion of artistic creation, or the morally suspect one of deviation from objective truth. Comencini uses all these shades of meaning as he takes us on a semantic itinerary which ultimately explains his own sentimental–comic aesthetic.

In a conversational exchange between Carotenuto and a nameless pauper, *fantasia* reveals its first, though by no means its exclusive, significance for the film.

PAUPER:: Happy Sunday, Marshal.
CAROTENUTO:: Happy Sunday. What are you eating?
PAUPER:: Bread.
CAROTENUTO:: And what are you putting on it?
PAUPER:: Fantasy, Marshal.
CAROTENUTO:: Happy eating.
PAUPER:: Thanks.

It is important to note that this dialogue takes place immediately after the rather serious one between Carotenuto and Don Emedio in which the town's problems of poverty, natural devastation, and the slow slide to extinction are all brought to the forefront of our attention. In this context, the marshal's interest in the pauper and the latter's response dramatize the very truths articulated by Don Emedio just moments before. That the pauper must season his bread with *fantasia* suggests the absence of the material additions which would constitute a decent diet. *Fantasia* must take the place of meat, cheese, or other nutritious supplements, suggesting that this man, whose facelessness and namelessness qualify him for emblematic status in the film, lives on the very brink of subsistence, like Saliena itself, according to the priest's dire prognostications.

[27] See Salvatore Battaglia, *Grande dizionario della lingua italiana*, vol. 5 (Turin: Unione Tipografica Editrice Torinese, 1968), p. 643.

Since this dialogue occurs early on, it implies several, mutually exclusive possibilities that Comencini could choose to explore. He could examine the tragic-realistic implications of this man's struggle for something to put on his bread, or he could continue the cheerful, breeziness of tone which allows Carotenuto to dismiss the man's plight with a good-natured *buon appetito*. After all, poverty is always with us and the Italians have the guilt-alleviating virtue of being able to sing, dance, and joke on an empty stomach.

The next two occurrences of *fantasia* both set the film firmly in the direction of sentimental comedy, though they do so in rather ambiguous ways. When La Bersagliera informs Carotenuto that the whole town knows of his infatuation for Annarella, he answers, "Your town operates too much on fantasy," suggesting the pejorative association of the term with factual distortion, rumor, and untruth. In a similar vein, when Carotenuto asks Annarella if her heart is committed to another, she answers, "You have too much fantasy," implying that he is harboring false suspicions about her love life. What is significant is that in each instance, *fantasia* is used to refer not just to any kind of misconception, but to ones based on romantic expectations for the protagonists' behavior. In the eyes of the villagers who function as dramatic chorus and public, Carotenuto and Annarella are protagonists in the town's own sentimental comedy, and at the end, Carotenuto expresses his awareness that he conforms to his audience's expectations. "What will people say?" asks Annarella, for whom public censure is something to be feared. "They'll say that the marshal is crazy about the midwife," answers Carotenuto, for whom public expectations are more prescriptive than condemnatory. And indeed, the chief witness of the goings-on, the one who has watched it all, from closeup, or from afar through binoculars, announces, "The marshal is crazy about the midwife," in a repetition which reveals the exact matching of performers' and public's desires.

Now we can return to the first *fantasia* dialogue with a

new understanding of its significance. When Carotenuto asks the pauper what he puts on his bread and the response is *fantasia*, we realize from the perspective of the ending that this is no neorealist exposé of the failure of postwar reconstruction, but rather that it is a metacinematic statement about how Comencini is going beyond his neorealist predecessors. His film will not be about bread, it will be about love, though the story just happens to take place in a society where bread is in short supply. *Fantasia* explains how stories about bread become stories about love, or in other words, how neorealism is transformed into rosy realism. *Fantasia* is the public desire for sentimental comedy, as expressed by the townspeople themselves who wanted Carotenuto and Annarella to act out a certain scenario for romance. It was Comencini's correct intuition that the prewar genre had come of age once again, that the Italian public of 1953, feeling the stirrings of the economic miracle and tired of rehashes of the postwar past, was ready for something new (or very old) and was happy to withdraw from harsh neorealist truth into sentimental comic reassurances.[28]

---

[28] In fact, the film was Italy's best box office draw for the 1953–54 season.

6 Fellini's *La strada*: Transcending neorealism

THROUGHOUT THE 1950s, the term crisis appears with some frequency in writings on neorealism. Whether it is De Santis denying the dire prophecies of the *crisaioli*, or Aristarco attributing the crisis of the cinema to the crisis of Italian society at large, the consensus seems to be that neorealism is undergoing radical changes whose effects will drastically alter its chances for survival.[1] The use of the term is significant, not only for what it tells us about the heightened emotionalism of the debate on neorealism, but also for the dramatic analogy itself, which suggests that the course of neorealism will be like the plot of a conventional play with its own rising action, turning point, and denouement. Those who proclaim the crisis of neorealism base their reading on the first half of the "play" and probably have some guesses as to how the drama will be resolved. It is ironic that a movement hostile to the conventions of dramatic plotting should become a character in its own theater of comic redemption or tragic demise, as if to compensate for the absence of drama in neorealist narrative structure.

Aristarco actually has two scenarios for the fate of postwar Italian cinema—one whose crisis yields happy results and one whose fortunes suffer a tragic downfall. The hero of the first scenario is Visconti, whose *Senso* (1954) signals the maturation of neorealism into realism, of chronicle into his-

---

[1] De Santis contradicts the *crisaioli* in "È in crisi il neorealismo," in Lizzani, *Storia*, pp. 345ff. Aristarco's crisis diagnosis appears in "Guido Aristarco Answers Fellini" in *Federico Fellini: Essays in Criticism*, ed. Bondanella, p. 65. Carlo Lizzani speaks of "crisis of language" and attributes its causes to the "crisis of story" and to the "crisis of character." See *Il cinema italiano*, p. 199.

tory, of *naturalismo zoliano* into *realismo balzachiano*, while
the villain of the second is Fellini, whose *La strada* reverts
to prewar attitudes of individualism, mysticism, and the quest
for pure style.[2] For Aristarco, realism must provide a politi-
cal-economic analysis of contemporary social structures so
that man can use his reason to "dominate and modify his
world, to solve problems within himself and outside himself."[3] Fellini's refusal to consider the historical forces that
shape the social order and his mystical abdication of control
over human destiny makes him a traitor to the neorealist
cause and an agent of its possible demise.

The formidable opponents of this theoretical position are
André Bazin and, of course, Fellini himself. Both argue against
the crisis approach to neorealism in the 1950s, seeing not a
turning point in its fortunes, but an essential continuity between the neorealist classics of the 1940s and the aesthetic
of Fellini's early films.[4] What both Fellini and Bazin object
to is the Marxist critics' appropriation of neorealism for their
own ideological purposes, making of it a "neo–socialist–realism" obedient to their highly partisan needs.[5] "Certain
people still think neorealism is fit to show only certain kinds
of reality," Fellini remarks, "and they insist that this is social
reality. It is a program, to show only certain aspects of life."[6]
The "certain people" are Aristarco, Chiarini, and the other
contributors to *Cinema nuovo*, a Marxist film journal of the

[2]For his celebration of realism in Visconti, see Guido Aristarco, "Esperienza culturale ed esperienza originale in Luchino Visconti," introduction to
the screenplay of *Rocco e i suoi fratelli*, ed. G. Aristarco and G. Carancini
(Bologna: Cappelli, 1960), esp. pp. 20–21. For his denunciation of *La strada*,
see his essay "Aristarco Answers Fellini," pp. 60–66. Lizzani has a similar
overview of the two directions taken by Italian cinema of the Fifties. See *Il
cinema italiano*, p. 197.

[3]See "Aristarco Answers Fellini," p. 64.

[4]One need not be an anticommunist to posit a continuity between Fellini's Fifties films and neorealism. See the comments of French Marxist critic
Georges Sadoul cited in Lizzani, *Il cinema italiano*, p. 201.

[5]See André Bazin, "*La strada*" in *Federico Fellini*, ed. Bondanella, p. 57.

[6]See "The Road Beyond Neorealism," p. 380.

Fifties, which had set itself up as the sole trustee of the neo-realists' truth. Both Fellini and Bazin trace this critical bias to the historical onset of neorealism when an exclusive concern for social problems was indeed appropriate to Italy's postwar condition. "Italy has had the luck, like Russia around 1925," writes Bazin, "to find herself in a situation in which a certain cinematographic genius began to spring forth and this genius was moving in the direction of social progress and the liberation of men."[7] It is natural, he continues, that the guardians of this trend would want to preserve its political progressivism by doctrinaire means, even after the initial impetus for the movement had died away. Fellini is less generous. "Later, the leftist press capitalized on this inadvertent one-sidedness by saying that the only valid thing to do in films is to show what happens around you."[8] He then issues a twofold attack on the Marxist interpretation: first in its exclusive privileging of social reality and second in its misplaced emphasis on subject matter as the sole standard of neorealist truth. Instead, neorealism should embrace "not just social reality, but spiritual reality, metaphysical reality, all that there is within man. . . . In a certain sense, everything is realistic. I see no dividing line between imagination and reality."[9] Bazin gives the apt label of "neorealism of the person" to this holistic approach, which considers the problematics of human existence apart from its sociopolitical determinants and unbound to the particulars of historical context.[10]

In fact, one of the many meanings of the road image in *La strada* might well be Fellini's journey from the classical neorealism of the 1940s to a new version of it, whether we call it "neorealism of the person" as Bazin does, or "phenomenological realism" after Amédée Ayfre.[11] Fellini's point of

[7] See Bazin in *Federico Fellini*, ed Bondanella, p. 56.
[8] See "The Road Beyond Neorealism," p. 380.
[9] In *Fellini on Fellini*, trans. Isabel Quigley (New York: Dell, 1976), p. 152.
[10] See *Federico Fellini*, ed. Bondanella, p. 57.
[11] Ayfre's proposed analogy between phenomenology and neorealism holds considerable promise for Fellini criticism. On his theory of phenomenolog-

departure for this journey is indeed the strictly construed neorealism of the Marxists—that form which "was mistaken for social realism. When people saw a badly made shack, they mistook it for neorealism. When they saw two tramps, they said 'neorealism.'!"[12] Indeed, the shack and the tramps are there in *La strada*—not only is Zampanò's moto-trailer a moving hovel, but Gelsomina's numerous family lives in a dilapidated hut whose roof repairs will be funded by the 10,000 lire earned from her sale to Zampanò. Her mother and younger sisters are in rags and Gelsomina herself is barefoot as Zampanò later gloats when he tells the circus manager, "I taught her everything; I gave her shoes." Poverty is the very impetus for the action—it is what forces Gelsomina's mother to sell her into virtual slavery as she had her older daughter Rosa, who died in Zampanò's service. "Remember Zampanò who took Rosa?" the mother asks Gelsomina. "We don't know where she's buried." The fatal consequences of employment with Zampanò show how drastic the mother's decision is and how desperate her situation must be to release another daughter to the same possible death. With such a beginning, the film could become an essay on the devastations of poverty which condemns its victims to cycles of bondage and death and prevents their ever escaping the margins of society. "The road" of Gelsomina never takes her to a better condition of material independence or social integration and she remains bereft of any of those things that would enable her to survive in the physical world. *La strada* indeed meets the conditions for a thesis film on poverty and social injustice, but it never remains that, leaving behind the conventional neorealist point of departure on its road to a far different poetic.

On the literal level, the road signifies the life of itinerant

---

ical realism, see "Néo-réalisme et phénoménologie," *Cahiers du cinéma* 3 (November 1952), 6–18 and "Du premier au second néo-réalisme," *Etudes cinématographiques* 32–35 (Summer 1964), 55–72.

[12] See the interview with Fellini in Samuels, *Encountering Directors*, p. 126.

entertainers that Zampanò and Gelsomina lead in their journey through the country. During the course of their travels they meet another wandering performer, Il Matto, who has several scuffles with Zampanò and is finally bludgeoned to death by the strongman in a roadside brawl. Gelsomina's frail psyche breaks under the burden of this experience and Zampanò abandons her along the way, only to learn years later that she was taken ill in a coastal town where she died an anonymous death.

That this is not a standard neorealist journey, such as the one in *Paisan*, or *The Path of Hope*, is proved by the total absence of concrete spatial and temporal markers to root the story in history. Only once are we given a geographic referent, and that is to Rome, though we remain in the anonymous suburbs of the city and never see any of its landmarks. Mention is made of one monument, San Paolo Fuori Le Mura (St. Paul Outside the Walls), whose very name makes it peripheral to the city, in keeping with the marginal status of the narrative action and its characters. With regard to time, the ESSO sign in the background of the first campsite suggests that this is a postwar setting, as does the redheaded prostitute's admiring question, "Is it American?" when presented with the spectacle of Zampanò's moto-trailer and scene of their imminent lovemaking. These minimal spatiotemporal allusions are hardly essential to the plot and their removal would occasion absolutely no modifications of the story, which is as deracinated as its very characters. Edouard de Laurot points out that Zampanò's refusal to specify his origins—he answers Gelsomina's question, "Where do you come from?" with the noncommital, "From my part of the country" and "Where were you born?" with "In my father's house"—reveals as much his rootlessness as his conversational perversity.[13] Unbound in time and space, Fellini's story thus announces its departure from neorealist historicity and its

[13] See Edouard de Laurot, "*La strada*: A Poem on Saintly Folly," *Film Culture* 2 (1956), 12.

preference for an ahistorical rendering of the human condition.

Nor do Gelsomina and Zampanò trace the kind of journey through society that Antonio and Bruno do in *Bicycle Thief* where Italy's major institutions—her law enforcement agencies, Church, and trade unions—are all systematically examined and found wanting.

Wary of arguments for the social determinants of humanity's plight, Fellini deliberately precludes any such misinterpretations of his inquiry by avoiding the city altogether and routing his journey through small towns, suburbs, and the countryside.[14] A social institution that does come under his scrutiny, however, is the Church, but he chooses one of the least institutionalized aspects of it, that of the nuns who change convents every two years in a renunciation of the very propertied interests which typify the secular world. Fellini's glimpse of the monastic vocation serves less as a social commentary on the Church than as an analogue to the totality of Gelsomina's own selfless commitment—an analogy that the nun makes explicit when she observes, "You follow your bridegroom, I follow mine." If Fellini criticizes the institutionalized Church at all, it is in the scene of the religious procession where he scrupulously shows us the cardboard back as well as the front of the holy images, suggesting that the ecclesiastical world is as guilty of showmanship and illusionism as is Il Matto who, in the very next scene, has his own apotheosis on the high wire connecting the church façade to the tavern across the street.

Another social institution that receives passing attention is the family unit in the wedding scene, though this, like the convent, serves less as an object of social criticism than as a comment on Gelsomina's marginality. The sacrament of marriage, the opportunities for childbearing, the consolations of the extended family and community life are all denied Gelsomina as she remains literally on the periphery of

---

[14] On the marginal settings of *La strada*, see ibid., p. 13.

this festive space, dancing alone to the beat of Zampanò's drum. Later that evening, when Zampanò performs his own postnuptial exertions, Gelsomina will not even be his consort, for he has found a partner and benefactress in the weddingfeast cook who has survived two husbands and has their wardrobes to bestow on willing surrogates.

But beside these passing and somewhat oblique commentaries on the Church and the family, *La strada* remains a film indifferent to the social and historical concerns of orthodox neorealism. On the other hand, a characteristic that *La strada* shares with its neorealist ancestors is a mistrust for conventional dramatic form. Like *Bicycle Thief*, the film has an episodic structure in which each event constitutes a self-sufficient unit, joining others in sequence to create a cumulative, rather than a linear, sense of meaning.[15] There is no cause-and-effect linkage of events, and actions are governed neither by the laws of psychological verisimilitude nor by those of poetic justice. For example, the logic of the emotions would dictate that Gelsomina leave Zampanò for a life in the circus or a partnership with Il Matto. Surely these represent far more attractive alternatives than the precarious independence she chooses when she actually does run away from Zampanò earlier in the film. The fact that she would escape once, under such poor conditions, and would refuse to later on when the alternatives would be so much more appealing, runs counter to our sense of plausibility. Nor does any concept of poetic justice rule the action, for such a principle would dictate that events punish Zampanò in accordance with the hints furnished by the narration. Legal apprehension for murder is indeed a possibility, since Zampanò's earlier scuffle with Il Matto and his consequent night in jail had put him on record as an enemy of the victim and one who would not stop at violence to express his antipathies. When Zampanò reassures Gelsomina "no one's looking for us," he gives

[15] See ibid., p. 12.

voice to his own fears of police detection and raises our audience expectations accordingly. During the final staging of
his chain-breaking act, we expect the tired, aging, and broken Zampanò to burst an artery or lose his sight as he had
so fatefully warned in his opening performance. "If a vein
bursts, I'll spit blood. A man in Milan went blind during this
act. When one loses his sight, it's finished." In a figurative
sense, of course, Zampanò never had any sight to begin with,
blind as he was to anything beyond his immediate sensory
experience of the world. It is during the fifth and final repetition of his act, as he is learning the true meaning of his loss
of Gelsomina, that he gains a vision he never possessed, in
an ironic reversal of his preperformance prophecies. Thus
Fellini's rejection of conventional poetic justice is in the service of Zampanò's climatic self-illumination. Should external
events impose their justice on him, he would never arrive at
the state of awareness and remorse that the final scene on
the beach affords. Bazin is right when he observes that "events
do not 'happen' in Fellini's world; they 'befall' its inhabitants, that is to say, they occur as an effect of 'vertical' gravity, not in conformity to the laws of 'horizontal' causality.
Thus the Fellinian character does not evolve; he ripens."[16]

Though the distrust of conventional dramatic structure
aligns Fellini with his neorealist ancestors, what he chooses
as an alternative only redistances him from this heritage. Unlike Rossellini, who takes the historical record as his point
of departure in *Open City* and *Paisan*, or De Sica who uses
the *piccola cronaca* or one-line newspaper item as his impetus in *Bicycle Thief*, Fellini turns to the modes of folk drama
and mime to provide the model for his film. The most obvious borrowing is from the commedia dell'arte tradition as
the costumes and stylized role-playing immediately reveal. Il
Matto belongs to the Arlecchino family with his motley costume, his wit, refinement, and acrobatic skill. Zampanò, in-

[16] See Bazin, *What Is Cinema?*, 2:84–85.

stead, is a descendant of Pulcinella in his churlishness and his utter lack of grace. Whenever they come in contact with one another, these two cannot help but perform their commedia dell'arte routines, enacting in their offstage lives the very roles they play in the circus tent or the makeshift arena of the roadside show. "I have nothing against him," Il Matto tells Gelsomina, "but when I see him, I can't resist teasing him," and Zampanò cannot resist retaliating with all the considerable brute force at his disposal. A degraded form of the commedia dell'arte is the clown act that follows Zampanò's chain-breaking exercise in the road show. "She's afraid of my *ciufile*," gloats Zampanò. "You say *fucile* [rifle], not *ciufile*, ignoramus," answers Gelsomina to the delighted applause of the audience. "Where are the ducks?" asks Zampanò, undaunted. When Gelsomina quacks, and Zampanò pretends to shoot at her, the rifle backfires in a prophecy of how his violence and insensitivity will some day redound to himself, just as the earlier skit showed how Gelsomina would emerge with the greater understanding and insight of the two, despite her seemingly limited mental capacities. Thus the commedia dell'arte acts serve as *in nuce* versions of the film at large, not in its material unfolding, but in the figurative significance of its action.

That the commedia dell'arte description is relevant not only to the roadshow skits and to the circus acts, but to the film as a whole, is suggested by the fidelity of all three characters to their theatrical personas, for Zampanò is always the heavy-handed brute, Gelsomina is always the educable naif, and Il Matto is always the mocking Ariel, offstage as well as on. Not only do all three remain "in character," they practically remain in costume, wearing toned-down versions of their theatrical garb throughout the film, as if their stage personas were simply heightened expressions of their unmasked selves.

Another folk analogue for the poetics of *La strada* is the medieval morality play, which explains the emblematic nature of the three main characters. The two male leads represent the polar extremes of the human condition, with Zampanò enacting the claims of the flesh and Il Matto impersonating his disembodied, ethereal opposite. When the other characters chide Zampanò, be it in anger or in jest ("The circus needs more animals," Il Matto tells him, or "You're a beast, you don't think," says Gelsomina), they make explicit his subhuman leanings. Indeed, Zampanò lives on an exclusively physical level, satisfying the primary appetites of food, sex, and sleep with little regard for the niceties of civilized society. Gelsomina's attempts to engage him in conversation are met either by grunts, monosyllables, or imperatives to silence, while the natural delicacy of her expressions of affection occasion Zampanò's mockery or indifference. The frequency with which Fellini shows the strongman either drunk or asleep reinforces our sense of this character's mental torpor, while his chain-breaking act constitutes the perfect expression of his bondage to the flesh and to the material limits of his condition. Though he succeeds in breaking out of the chains each time, the act provides no sense of release, for we know that Zampanò will have to don them again, that he will never escape the imprisonment of the flesh to which they metaphorically point.

As if his tightrope act were not enough to qualify Il Matto as a man of airy lightness in contrast to Zampanò's earthbound bulk, he also wears wings in an ambiguous costume whose stripes make him appear half angel, half bee. While Zampanò's sluggish intellect leaves him humorless and dull, Il Matto's mind is agile, able to make the connections prerequisite to wit. Musically, the two men are also opposed, as Il Matto plays the tiniest of violins and Zampanò blasts away on the trombone or beats on the drums. Il Matto's lightness finds its most poignant expression in his very fragility—a fragility that is expressed in his twice uttered prophecy of an early death.

It is within the polarities embodied by Zampanò and Il Matto that Gelsomina makes her journey from ignorance to full understanding and love.[17] At the start of the journey, Gelsomina's understanding is little better than Zampanò's. She is an unawakened, unthinking creature who operates on an instinctual level and is relegated, as Zampanò will be later on, to the animal realm. When Gelsomina's mother apologizes to Zampanò that her daughter "is a bit strange" the strongman answers reassuringly, "Don't worry, I can even teach dogs." As if to prove his mastery of animal subjects, he literally whips Gelsomina into obedience when she falters on her opening lines, "Zampanò has arrived."

But Gelsomina soon leaves Zampanò behind as she grows in understanding and love while he remains unchanged by the experiences of the road. If the film were to document her education alone, then it would indeed be a linear road directed toward a transcendent goal, but since it also tells the story of Zampanò's stasis, its trajectory is hindered by repetitions and returns. To account for the different dynamics of Gelsomina's and Zampanò's journeys, we may view their itinerary as a spiral in which they constantly cover the same ground, in accordance with Zampanò's repetition compulsion, but do so on a higher level of understanding, in accordance with Gelsomina's burgeoning awareness. Thus Zampanò's serial seductions teach him nothing about the transience of such physical consolations, nor the hurt they bring Gelsomina, who is only one in the list of his five bed partners throughout the story. She, on the other hand, progresses from the naive incomprehension of Zampanò's infidelity with La Rossa, the redheaded prostitute, to jealous hurt at his fling with the wedding-feast cook, to a mature acceptance of him, promiscuity notwithstanding, by the midpoint of the film.

The most obvious measure of Zampanò's stasis and Gelsomina's change is the chain-breaking act which is performed five times in symmetrical positions throughout the

---

[17] As a variant of this reading, Suzanne Budgen sees Gelsomina's journey as a coming of age. See her *Fellini* (London: British Film Institute, 1966), p. 11.

6. *Somewhat awed and bewildered, Gelsomina (Giulietta Masina) watches as Zampanò (Anthony Quinn) demonstrates his pectoral prowess.*

film. Twice near the beginning, twice toward the end, once at the midpoint of *La strada*, the act makes explicit Gelsomina's shifting relationship to the strongman, who remains himself unchanged, except for some grey hair at the temples and a certain vocal apathy in the last performance. Gelsomina, instead, has a radically different role to play during each act. Starting out as a star-struck spectator of the show, she becomes the leading lady by the second performance. Il Matto's intrusion into the world of Gelsomina and Zampanò is marked by his heckling of the third chain-breaking act when he interrupts with, "Zampanò, you're wanted on the phone." Though we do not see Gelsomina's part in this performance, we do see her in the very next scene rehearsing with Il Matto in an assertion of her new role as an independent artiste. Incapable of performing at all after the murder, Gelsomina's participation in the fourth act is limited to whimpering and repeating, "Il Matto is sick." Of course, the fifth act shows Zampanò alone, bereft of the partner whose loss he has just now begun to mourn. There will be no more chain-breakings and no more stasis now that Zampanò has finally grasped what Gelsomina had so painfully acquired on her long road to knowledge and love.

Zampanò's and Gelsomina's are not the only journeys in the film. Though we see very little of him, since he serves primarily as a foil for Zampanò and a catalyst for Gelsomina, Il Matto travels his own, tragically brief itinerary to self-knowledge and then to extinction. The purveyor of the gospel of usefulness, Il Matto suggests that he too would like to be of use, though he disguises that plea in denials which constantly defeat his purpose. "Do they want me?" he asks Gelsomina as the circus prepares to leave Rome. "Who needs them, anyway," he shrugs with a protective pride that would preclude his going to Colombaioni, the proprietor, to ask for reinstatement. When Il Matto offers Gelsomina the option of going off with him, her tacit refusal prompts him to add, "I don't need anyone," with a bravado that rings as false as

Zampanò's own drunken declaration of independence in the penultimate scene of the film. We sense, however, that Il Matto is fully aware of the hollowness of his claims to self-sufficiency and that Gelsomina's generosity and warmth have only fanned the flame of his own interpersonal need. The illumination he brings to Gelsomina must be self-illumination of the most painful kind, for Il Matto is powerless to end the terrible isolation of his own gypsy lot.

It is his interview with Gelsomina that marks both the turning point in her itinerary and the thematic center of the film. Il Matto's lesson to Gelsomina provides a kind of Archimedean point outside the narration which tells us retroactively how to construe the first half of the story and prepares us for an accurate interpretation of its ending. His teaching is, among other things, a lesson in reading, not only the literal language of Gelsomina's story, but the language of Fellini's journey beyond neorealism.

IL MATTO:: Everything in the world is good for something. Take . . . this stone, for example.
GELSOMINA:: Which one?
IL MATTO:: Uh, this one—it doesn't matter which. Even this little stone has a purpose.
GELSOMINA:: What's it good for?
IL MATTO:: I don't know what it's good for, this pebble, but it certainly has its use! If it were useless, then everything else would be useless—even the stars.

This teaching has the force of revelation for Gelsomina who learns through it that the human mind has infinite range, that it can move from the tiniest pebble to contemplate the vastness of the heavens, and that thought need not be earthbound or imprisoned by immediate material things. Until now, she has been like a prerational child, limited to the concrete data of the senses, unable to perform any mental operation that would exceed the specifics of her experience. When Il

Matto says, "Take this stone, for example," she must know exactly "which one?" and when he says it has a purpose, she must ask exactly, "What's it good for?" Il Matto frees Gelsomina's mind in the only way possible, for she is incapable of theorizing, but given a concrete example of a truth, can infer its abstract meaning. To be sure, she cannot remain on the level of theory for long, needing always to anchor herself in empirical experience, clutching hold of the pebble as a palpable reminder of the cosmic truth she has just learned. When Zampanò asks her why she came to fetch him from jail rather than leave with the circus, it is enough for Gelsomina to squeeze the pebble in mute affirmation of its meaning. Il Matto is the very embodiment of the mental agility he accords Gelsomina, for his figurative language bears constant witness to his own associational powers. "You look like an artichoke," "Zampanò barks like a dog," "he beats you like a donkey"—all these similes punctuate the very speech in which Il Matto teaches Gelsomina to think abstractly, to transcend the limits of the material world.

Zampanò, however, is unreceptive to the revelation that Gelsomina tries to share with him at the seaside pause in their journey. "Once I dreamt of going home; now, my house is with you," she confides. "Good discovery," Zampanò answers, "considering the hunger you suffered." "You're a beast," she replies, "You don't think." Gelsomina's disappointment could almost be a vernacular paraphrase of St. Augustine's attack on the bestiality of literal-mindedness.[18] For Zampanò has interpreted her metaphor in the most literal possible way, reducing her spiritual meaning to its material constituents of walls, roof, and hearth. He is incapable of rising above his carnal understanding to entertain any higher possible meanings—for Zampanò, a pebble is simply a pebble with no transcendent referent and no cosmic connections. It is his literal-mindedness and his materialism, as much

[18] See St. Augustine, "De doctrina christiana," in *Corpus christianorum*, 32 ed. Joseph Martin (Tournai: Brepols, 1962), 3.5.9, p. 83.

as his physical bulk, which reduces Zampanò to bestiality, denying him access to those higher mental faculties that are proper to man and raise him above his brute inferiors. In another instance of his reductivism, Zampanò misinterprets the true cause of Gelsomina's mental collapse. "What's wrong, no one's looking for us," he reassures her after Il Matto's murder, ascribing her imbalance to the most practical of causes—fear of legal retribution. Not even guilt, let alone any higher human response to untimely and violent death, seem to occur to Zampanò as possible causes of Gelsomina's malaise.

It takes a five-year separation, Gelsomina's own death, and eventually her return to him by song to convert Zampanò to the truth of her teachings. In the final scene on the beach, Zampanò finally looks up at the stars to complete his own itinerary from pure physicality to spiritual understanding, and perhaps even to grace. He has definitively burst the chains of his fleshly confinement in a belated sharing of Gelsomina's illumination. The sea, site of this conversion, has been Gelsomina's element throughout the film and here Zampanò indeed comes home, in accordance with her own metaphor for spiritual in-dwelling.[19]

At first glance, this ending might well support the critical charges of cheap mysticism that have been leveled at Fellini's work, but careful study of *La strada* reveals the wrongheadedness of such accusations.[20] Doubtless, the film argues that this is neither the only world nor necessarily the best world for human occupancy, but it never lapses into the *contemptus mundi* of the ascetic nor the retreat from human involvements of the emotionally vanquished. The film pursues a quest for transcendent meaning which then redounds to the concrete thing itself in a vindication of the dignity of this life.

[19] See Budgen, *Fellini*, p. 10.
[20] On the pejorative uses to which critics have subjected the term "mysticism" with regard to Fellini's work, see Aristarco, "Aristarco Answers Fellini," p. 65; and Lizzani, *Il cinema italiano*, pp. 192, 203.

Gelsomina's delight in the natural world is normative—her tomato garden or her examination of the roadside bugs all serve to dramatize the overlooked beauties of creation. Though the film lacks historical rootedness, it is nonetheless very physically rooted in the landscapes and roadscapes of its path through the country. The pebble of the parable becomes the stone which gives weight and mass to so many of the buildings in the film, from the barn where Gelsomina and Zampanò sleep after the wedding, to the convent, to the roadside ruins where Zampanò abandons Gelsomina in the glare of the winter sun. Even the most ethereal of characters, Il Matto, asserts his corporality in his tightrope act when he eats a plate of spaghetti in midair.

With the parable of the pebble, Fellini charts his road beyond neorealism. His filmmaking will not confine itself to the material conditions of life in a given time or place, according to the orthodox neorealist canon, but will transcend such limits to embrace "metaphysical reality, spiritual reality—all that there is in man." In a tribute to his wife Giulietta Masina that is reminiscent of Dante's promise to Beatrice at the end of *La vita nuova*, Fellini makes the actress his guide to the new territory not yet explored in postwar Italian cinema. "She has taken me over a certain threshold, through a certain gate, and made me penetrate into a landscape, into a territory that I have not yet described thoroughly and completely, but that I hope very much, if fancy leads me to it again, to be able to translate into images.[21] In *La strada*, Gelsomina performs precisely this function, leading us into another order of being beyond the normal range of human perception—an order that may be labeled the supernatural, the transcendent, the occult, or simply the unknown. Fellini offers no prior interpretation of this other dimension, he simply posits its existence and its importance for our experience of the sensible world. Thus the film is full of

[21] Quoted in Budgen, *Fellini*, p. 95.

"breakthrough" moments which offer intimations of a realm beyond: Gelsomina's wondrous encounter with Osvaldo, her witch's incantation over the campfire, the strange pantomime during Zampanò's drunken stupor when she imitates a tree or listens to a post. But Fellini keeps us balancing on the threshold while only Gelsomina is able to cross over, so that the mystery is affirmed but never "intruded upon."[22] Had Gelsomina gone off with Il Matto, we would have learned too much about that enchanted landscape to maintain a sense of its privacy and magic, but instead we remain, like Zampanò, on this side of the mystery. When he learns of Gelsomina's last years from the young girl who has been singing her song, the *mise-en-scène* situates Zampanò behind a fence, separated from the source of this sad revelation as he had been separated all along from the connectedness and synthetic force of Gelsomina's life.[23]

This passage from the empirical world into an implied beyond occasions a corresponding narrative transformation of considerable critical interest. The film bears witness to the making of a legend as Gelsomina's story passes into the realm of folklore for the villagers of the town where she died. Though unable to tell them her story when they found her ill on the beach, Gelsomina did play her song and this took the place of name and biography in identifying her for the town. The survival of the song after her death makes Gelsomina a kind of *spiritus loci*, exerting a tutelary power over her adoptive landscape. For Zampanò, and for us, who know the part of the story that the villagers do not, her passage into the realm of legend is the proper fulfillment of a life replete with "breakthrough" moments and preternatural gifts.

It is here that the constant allusions to Rosa reveal their logic, for they are not only indications of Gelsomina's jeal-

[22] Budgen says this of Fellini's treatment of Gelsomina, but it extends to the entire mystery of which she is a part. See ibid., p. 9.
[23] See Edward Murray, "*La strada*," in *Federico Fellini*, ed. Bondanella, p. 52.

ousy about Zampanò's prior attachments, but also a measure of the difference between a story which remains story (or implied story) and one which achieves the status of legend. Gelsomina asks Zampanò repeatedly about her older sister—did Rosa work like her, did Zampanò make love with Rosa, did Rosa know Il Matto—suggesting both Gelsomina's desire to surpass her sister in Zampanò's affections and perhaps, too, her fear of replicating her predecessor's fate. Indeed, their careers are sadly alike—both are sold into bondage to the same man as work partners and mistresses, both die a mysterious death, and both are buried in unknown graves. Both share the symbolism of their flower names with the implicit confinement to the natural cycles of flourishing and withering into a traceless death. Rosa's name is most suggestive of this natural transience with its metaphoric link to the philosophy of *carpe diem* and its affirmation of the finality of physical demise. Like her sister, Gelsomina withers and dies, but unlike Rosa, she passes into a realm of permanence in keeping with their surname, Costanzo (the masculine of constancy).

Though song is the means by which Gelsomina transcends her mortality, the film does not degenerate into a glorification of Art as the key to immortal life. Such a message would be not only self-congratulatory on Fellini's part, but would limit the mystery and allure of that other order to which his film so insistently points. Instead, this mystery must remain inviolate and unspoiled by any explanatory recourse to Franciscan pietism, pagan animism, or pantheism.[24] That Fellini's universe of meaning could be truly "open from above," that his itinerary from the pebble to the stars might continue indefinitely, occasions great critical discomfort and quests for theoretical closure. Of all the proposed "isms," the most appropriate, because the least binding, is Amédée Ayfre's phe-

[24]See Laurot, "*La strada*," p. 14.

nomenological realism, which keeps the mystery intact without reducing it to cheap mysticism.

In its declaration of freedom from neorealist constraints of subject matter and ideology, *La strada* cleared the way for other forays into areas previously considered "taboo" for serious cinematic treatment. Fellini's leap from the pebble to the stars allowed other directors to overstep neorealist boundaries in less risky ways, so that Visconti could venture into the historical past in *Senso* and Antonioni could venture into the literary province of middle-class psychology in *Le amiche*. As far as Fellini's own itinerary is concerned, *La strada* might be seen as the distant prelude to *8½* with its abolition of any "hierarchy of realms" through a paratactic ordering of dream, fantasy, memory, and actuality.[25] Neorealism, for Fellini, has not been so much abandoned as subsumed in a vision that takes in the stars but does not forget the pebbles that line the way in this world.[26]

[25] See J. P. Telotte, "*8½* and the Evolution of a Neorealist Narrative," *Film Criticism* 3 (Winter 1979), 75.

[26] Georges Sadoul concurs. "Far from betraying neorealism, Fellini enriched it by guiding it along a new path." *Dictionary of Films*, trans. Peter Morris (Berkeley and Los Angeles, University of California Press, 1972), p. 358.

7 Visconti's *Senso*: The Risorgimento according to Gramsci

ALTHOUGH ITS TRADITIONAL visual language and its conventional narrative mode promise to make *Senso* a universally accessible film, it is one of those works so bound to its own culture and to its time in history that a full appreciation of it by non-Italian audiences requires more preparation than any of the films considered thus far. Without such preparation, it is virtually impossible to understand the enormous enthusiasm this film inspired in some camps, the distress it caused in others, and the climactic place it occupied in the history of postwar Italian cinema.

Based on the nineteenth-century novella of the same title by Camillo Boito, *Senso* tells the story of Countess Livia Serpieri, whose allegiance to the cause of Italian nationalism gives way to a guilty passion for Lt. Franz Mahler, stationed in Venice during its Austrian occupation. An idler and a coward, Franz flees the battle front to seek refuge in Livia's country villa where he persuades his lady to help him obtain a medical discharge from the service. In order to bribe an army doctor into compliance, Livia gives Franz a sum of money originally destined for the Italian rebel forces. Released from military duty, Franz sets up housekeeping in Verona where he amuses himself with women and drink. When Livia pays her lover a surprise visit and finds him in the company of a beautiful young harlot, she reports him to the Austrian authorities who preside over his immediate execution.

Despite this straightforward storyline, *Senso* presents considerable difficulties for an American audience. Not the least of these problems is the casting of Farley Granger in the role

7. *Countess Livia Serpieri (Alida Valli) grants Lt. Franz Mahler (Farley Granger) refuge in her villa at Aldeno.*

of the Austrian lieutenant who seduces the Countess Livia
into betraying not only her husband but her country on the
eve of the Italian unification.[1] Because he is an American and
because he has a screen image alien to the one required for
the dashing Lieutenant Mahler, Granger is utterly unconvincing as the inspirer of a passion great enough to destroy
the virtuous Livia. Perhaps for Visconti and for Italian audiences his Americanness posed no hindrance to his credible
portrayal of the Austrian *homme fatal* and perhaps his for-
eignness lent exoticism, and hence credibility, to that performance.

Another drawback for American audiences, and non-Italian audiences in general, is ignorance of the nineteenth-century history on which this film so heavily relies. *Senso* pre-
supposes not only an acquaintance with the events of the
Risorgimento, which culminated in the expulsion of all foreign occupiers from the country and the unification of the
Italian state in 1870, but also with the official interpretations
of the historical episode from which Visconti's film radically
departs. What made *Senso* a cinematographic and political
event in 1954 was Visconti's audacity in challenging the received wisdom on the Risorgimento and in offering his own,
variant reading of this seminal chapter in modern Italian history. The film is a bold example of the kind of historiogra-
phy proposed by Gramsci in his essay on the Risorgimento
where he challenged the "sentimental and political interfer-
ences" and the "prejudices of every kind"[2] which turn Ri-

---

[1] Granger, however, was not Visconti's first choice for the part. He would
have preferred (understandably) Marlon Brando, but neither Brando nor
Ingrid Bergman (Visconti's choice for Livia) was available. See Bondanella,
Italian Cinema, p. 100, and Liehm, *Passion and Defiance*, p. 148 n.

[2] In Antonio Gramsci, *Il Risorgimento* (Turin: Einaudi, 1952), p. 44. Not
only was Visconti conversant with Gramsci, he considered the historian a
kind of mentor whose example provided the filmmaker with the historical–
political analyses that would typify his cinematic approach. See Visconti's
remarks in "Da Verga a Gramsci," in Lizzani, *Storia del cinema italiano*, p.
449. On *Senso* as a Gramscian interpretation of the Risorgimento, see Brunetta, *Storia*, p. 400.

sorgimento history into hagiography and myth. Admitting that all history is really "current politics *in nuce*"[3] which uses the past to legitimize the policies of the contemporary possessors of power and wealth, Gramsci calls for a reinterpretation of the Risorgimento as the basis for the intellectual and moral reform of the modern Italian state.[4] Such a reinterpretation must avoid the hero worship of standard histories and must expose the Risorgimento as "conquista regia e non movimento popolare" (royal conquest and not a popular movement) as the elementary school textbooks would have it.[5] "The famous Italian minority, by definition 'heroic' . . . that led the unitarian movement, in reality was concerned more with economic interests than with ideal formulas, and it fought more to prevent the people from intervening in the struggle and making it a social one . . . than against the enemies of unification."[6] Gramsci's refusal to honor the romanticized version of Italian unification held dear by the heirs of the Risorgimento moderates is equivalent, in its iconoclasm, to the Beardsian interpretation of our own Founding Fathers, which portrays them as more economically than idealistically motivated, more concerned with consolidating their own interests than with championing the rights and freedoms of all citizens.[7] Though there was no movie dramatizing Beard's revisionist insights into American history, the movie that dramatized Gramsci's was met with some distaste by Italian officials who hastened to censor the most damning passages and succeeded in removing the film's true revolutionary sting.[8] The offending scene occurs toward the

[3] *Il Risorgimento*, p. 114.

[4] See the preface to *Il Risorgimento*, p. xiii.

[5] See Lizzani, *Il cinema italiano*, p. 168.

[6] *Il Risorgimento*, p. 65.

[7] This theory of Charles Austin Beard is to be found in *An Economic Interpretation of the Constitution* (1913).

[8] On the extensive censorship of *Senso*, see Lizzani, *Il cinema italiano*, pp. 219–20; Bondanella, *Italian Cinema*, p. 99; and Liehm, *Passion and Defiance*, p. 150.

end of the film as Ussoni, a leader of the volunteer forces for the liberation of Italy, is turned down by the authorities of the royal army who want to preserve the Risorgimento as "conquista regia" and counter any efforts to make it "movimento popolare." When Meucci, the spokesman for the royal army, rejects Ussoni's volunteer corps, he claims to do so for strictly technical military reasons. "Wars are fought with a faithful, resolute, compact army. . . . Experience has always shown that volunteers enlisted in the regular army are of scant help, if armed and dispersed in skirmishes."[9] Ussoni's answer unmasks the political implications of this supposedly strategic decision. "Let's speak frankly, Captain. The order that you have transmitted to me reflects the repugnance of the entire army, beginning with General Lamarmora, for the revolutionary forces. It's clear that they want to exclude these forces from the war."[10]

Without this scene, Visconti's criticism of the Risorgimento is considerably weakened, though elements of it survive in the opportunism of Count Serpieri, Livia's husband, as he endorses first the Austrian imperial rulers' claims to power in Venice, and then the Italians', when it becomes clear that his compatriots will ultimately win out.[11] The count makes a conciliatory offer to the patriots, explaining, "I'm a Venetian born and bred, and you know perfectly well that all my interests and affections lie in this city. Now it's obvious that whichever way the war ends, Venice will certainly go to the Italian government . . . As you see, this is a very practical proposal and has nothing to do with passions or ideals or dreams that I do not share."[12] Visconti levels his most lethal attack on the "official" reading of the Risorgi-

[9] For the text of the censored scene, see Umberto Lisi, "Non dissero solo obbedisco," in *Antologia di "Cinema nuovo,"* ed. Aristarco, pp. 863–65.

[10] Ibid., pp. 863–64.

[11] On Serpieri's opportunism, see Bondanella, *Italian Cinema,* p. 99.

[12] *Visconti, Two Screenplays,* trans. Judith Green (New York: Orion, 1970), p. 139. All quotes from the screenplay come from this edition. Subsequent page references will appear in the text.

mento by making the Serpieris of Italy, with their *Realpolitik* approach to conserving power and wealth, prevail over the Ussonis with their selfless devotion to a nationalistic ideal.[13] Ussoni's impassioned sermon to Livia—"We haven't any rights any more, Livia, only duties. We must forget ourselves, Livia. I'm not afraid of sounding rhetorical. Italy's at war. It's our war . . . our revolution" (140)—is betrayed not only by her own guilty love for an Austrian soldier, which puts the self and its desires before all else, but also by Serpieri who will salute any flag and mouth any slogan in the interests of maintaining his class superiority. In Serpieri's triumph, Visconti exemplifies Gramsci's thesis that the Risorgimento was indeed a "passive revolution" wherein the power redounded to an already formed state, that of Piedmont, rather than to a new social group, as a pure revolution would require.[14] The leaders of the old order simply became the leaders of the new, assimilating, through the process of "transformism," the radical Partito D'Azione led by Garibaldi into the fabric of a constitutional monarchy, shaped by Cavour and governed by the Savoy dynasty.[15] Visconti's findings in *Senso* well accord with Gramsci's own condemnation of the Risorgimento leaders who "said that they would propose the creation of the modern State in Italy and they produced something bastard, they proposed to give rise to a diffuse and energetic ruling class and they did not succeed, [they proposed] to insert the people in the governmental picture and they did not succeed."[16]

But this by no means exhausts Visconti's Gramscian polemic against established interpretations of the Risorgimento. By making heroes out of the leaders of the Partito D'Azione, the standard histories divert popular attention from the col-

[13] See Geoffrey Nowell-Smith, *Luchino Visconti* (New York: Viking, 1973), p. 90.
[14] See *Il Risorgimento*, p.106.
[15] On "trasformismo," see ibid., p. 100.
[16] Ibid., p. 94.

lective actions and the subversive threat of this radical party, attributing its success to single, larger-than-life figures rather than to its ideological stance. Visconti, instead, resists any temptation to indulge in such Risorgimento hagiography by banishing Garibaldi and La Marmora to the edges of the story and concentrating on what Lukács calls "maintaining" rather than "world-historical" individuals.[17] Visconti's indirect reporting of Garibaldi's whereabouts and his various military successes through messengers allows him to subordinate epic action to personal reaction in a strategy which Lukács considers to be the very essence of the historical novel. What interests Visconti in *Senso* is not the Italian victories at Gaeta or Calatafimi, for example, but the irony of Livia's indifference to her country's military fate or her resentment of any combat that might endanger her beloved Franz. Perhaps most indicative of Visconti's revisionist strategy is his decision to make the Italian defeat at Custoza the military centerpiece of his film, rather than her victories at Gaeta or Calatafimi. It is as if a Hollywood filmmaker were to make a movie about the American Revolution, dwelling on the British victory at Brandywine as a way of challenging the standard histories of our own national birth. Visconti makes explicit his polemical reading of history in explaining the importance of Custoza to the original design of the film.

> It is towards the historical aspect that it was oriented
> first of all. I even wanted to call it *Custoza* after the
> name of a great Italian defeat. . . . The battle there-
> fore had originally a much greater importance. My
> idea was to draw a comprehensive portrait of Italian
> history against which the personal adventures of
> Countess Serpieri would stand out, though she was,
> basically, no more than the representative of a certain
> class. What interested me was to tell the story of a

---

[17] See Georg Lukács, *The Historical Novel*, trans. Hannah and Stanley Mitchell (London: Merlin Press, 1962), p. 43.

badly waged war fought by a single class and leading to disaster.[18]

Oddly enough, this passage seems to defy the actual facts of Risorgimento history by implying that Italy lost not only the battle of Custoza, but the entire war of independence. Indeed, for Visconti the Risorgimento may have been a military victory, but it was a political defeat—the "conquista regia" that precluded the "movimento popolare" of the radicals' dreams. In *Senso*, Custoza bears a synecdochal relationship to the entire unification campaign, revealing in miniature the failures that Gramsci ascribed to the Risorgimento as a whole and to the newly emergent nation-state.

For Italian audiences, whose knowledge of Risorgimento history would insure a full appreciation of Visconti's revisionist approach, *Senso* was not received without controversy. There were detractors not only in official circles, where the threat to the myth of Italian national identity called forth drastic defensive measures, but among the Marxists themselves whose reverence for Gramsci did not always override their monomaniacal devotion to neorealism. What incited the controversy was not Visconti's historical reading, but the fact that the film was a reading at all—that it stood several removes from its subject matter in a violation of neorealist imperatives to contemporary themes and unobtrusive style. Though *Senso* is obviously aesthetic worlds away from *Open City*, *Bicycle Thief*, and even Visconti's *La terra trema*, such was the power of the neorealist precedent that critics felt compelled to relate every artistically serious film to it. Thus, neorealism constitutes the absolute standard against which *Senso* is measured, and found wanting, by Chiarini and Zavattini who fault Visconti for abandoning the modern subject matter and stylistic transparency of the postwar school.[19]

---

[18] See Armes, *Patterns of Realism*, p. 109.

[19] See Chiarini, "Tradisce il neorealismo," pp. 882–88; and Zavattini, "Una grossa botta in testa al neorealismo," pp. 888–92, both in *Antologia*, ed. Aristarco.

When Aristarco defends the film against such charges, he does not deny the relevance of the neorealist standard, as we might expect, but broadens and alters that standard to fit the aesthetic requirements of *Senso*. Hence he argues that Visconti's film represents an evolution of neorealism, not its negation, as Chiarini claimed, marking the passage to a full-fledged realism in the nineteenth-century literary sense of the term.[20] Aristarco's argument implies a criticism of neorealism as necessarily superficial, purely descriptive, and limited to documenting a static present, whereas realism involves a deeper analysis of the dynamic forces that shape the historical process. In opposing Zavattinian neorealism to Viscontian realism, Aristaraco is simply renegotiating the tenuous truce reached by Italian thinkers of the nineteenth century between French naturalism, with its purely materialistic, scientific approach to phenomena, on the one hand, and the vestiges of classical realism, with its quest for underlying truths, on the other.[21]

The very things that most distance Visconti's film from unmediated neorealist reportage—his withdrawal into history and his use of extracinematic conventions—are not only justified by Aristarco's broadened definition of realism, they are celebrated by it. An analytic mode which is to *narrate* rather than *describe*, probing beneath the surface rather than limiting itself to purely material phenomena, must have the depth, breadth, fullness of characterization, and polemic stance that is best exemplified in literature by the novel.[22] For

[20] This oft-repeated argument of Aristarco can be found in "Esperienza culturale ed esperienza originale di Luchino Visconti," in *Rocco e i suoi fratelli*, pp. 32ff.; in "Dal neorealismo al realismo," p. 861; and "È realismo," pp. 895ff., both in *Antologia*, ed. Aristarco.

[21] For a more complete treatment of nineteenth-century Italian realist thought, see my Introduction.

[22] Hence Aristarco calls *Senso* a "romanzo cinematografico" in "Del senno di poi sono piene le fosse," in *Antologia*, ed. Aristarco, p. 91. On Visconti's preference for a novelistic filmmaking mode, see Tommaso Chiaretti, "La maniera di Visconti," in *Il neorealismo cinematografico italiano*, ed. Mic-

Chiarini and Zavattini, however, the immediacy of neorealism becomes a moral imperative, so that any abandonment of contemporary subject matter or direct cinematic reportage amounts to an abdication of the neorealists' ethical responsibility to raise the level of public consciousness and to motivate corrective social action. Chiarini deplores Visconti's intrusive style because it detracts from the film's moral impact, while Zavattini argues that only contemporary themes have the power to educate and politicize the filmgoing public. "The most substantial merit of neorealism was precisely this," wrote Zavattini, "to propose only subjects which were near in time and space, and in order to develop these, it was indispensable to insert oneself even physically into the fabric of the country, increasing, in geometric progression, the exchange of reports of knowledge among Italians."[23]

It is, of course, Gramsci who offers the best counterargument to Zavattini's criticism of Visconti's retreat into the archives. If the moral and intellectual reform of modern Italy must be predicated on a reinterpretation of the Risorgimento as "conquista regia e non movimento popolare" according to Gramsci, then the neorealists' reformatory mission can be inestimably advanced by such historical inquiries as Visconti's.[24] Lukács's studies of the historical novel further suggest how neorealist didacticism can be reconciled with forays into the past, when informed by what he calls the "necessary anachronism"—that is, the characters' expression of "feelings and thoughts about real historical relationships in a much

---

cichè, p. 285; Armes, *Patterns of Realism*, p. 120. On the appropriateness of the novel for the filmmaking needs of post-neorealist Italy, see Fabio Carpi, "Finita l'inchiesta si trova il romanzo," in *Antologia*, ed. Aristarco, pp. 902–903.

[23] Zavattini, "Una grossa botta in testa," p. 890.

[24] Accordingly, Vittorio Taviani writes, "it was inevitable, after having turned his gaze to the present, that he try to arrive at the roots of the political and social phenomenon . . . that is, he met with the Risorgimento as the historic moment that marks the birth of Italy as a modern nation." See "Tre guidizi su *Senso*," in *Antologia*, ed. Aristarco, pp. 881–82.

clearer way than the actual men and women of the time could have done."[25] In Serpieri's affiliation with the leaders of the occupying forces, and in Livia's passion for one of its officers, Visconti offers proof of Gramsci's favorite historiographic insight. All Risorgimento history, Gramsci argues, indeed all Italian history, is predicated on the myth that Italy has forever been a unified nation, and that foreign forces have simply suppressed the political manifestations of that unity.[26] What Visconti's film suggests is that indigenous class influences have divided Italy all along, inviting foreign occupation and resisting, for economic reasons, reunification. Indeed, the Serpieris have far more in common with the Austrian aristocrats than with inferior classes of Italians. Livia's initial loyalties to the movement for Italian independence stem more from her attraction to her aristocratic cousin Ussoni than from any innate devotion to nationalistic ideals. When her patriotism succumbs to the superior force of romantic passion for Franz, she is merely reverting to type, enacting the imperatives to courtly love which are the natural prerogatives of her class. Indeed, the scenes of her courtship and seduction by Franz, which could be criticized for their preciosity and their indulgence in literary clichés, constitute an important index of the tastes that define the European social elite. The couple's odyssey through the nocturnal city is a virtual repository of courtly love motifs, which create the illusion of a self-sufficient poetic cosmos, obedient to its own laws and exempt from the forces of historical change.

Livia has just bid farewell to her cousin Ussoni who has been consigned to a year's exile when she tells us in a voice-over, "I had a strange foreboding . . . of what his departure might mean . . . for me" (120) as if his presence were necessary not only to sustain her patriotism, but also to keep her in touch with her best self. The terminal qualifier "for

[25] Lukács, *The Historical Novel*, p. 63.
[26] See Gramsci, *Il Risorgimento*, p. 44.

me" suggests that the story is now leaving the objective, public realm of history and moving into the private world of sentiment and sensuality. Livia's nocturnal odyssey through the streets of Venice in the company of Franz becomes a metaphor for her moral errancy as under his aegis she abandons the virtuous path of chaste love and political commitment and becomes prey to her worst inclinations. Franz's strategy in seducing Livia away from Ussoni's cause is to transform all political issues into erotic ones and to empty his own military presence in Venice of its partisan implications. "Don't you think it would have been much better if you'd told me the other evening at the opera that Ussoni was your lover?" (121) Franz asks, attributing her anxiety for her cousin's safety to sexual motives alone. Though Livia resolves to maintain her honor and pride in the face of Franz's vulgarity, she capitulates by answering, "There's one thing I'd like you to know. Roberto Ussoni is not my lover," thus accepting the ground rules of his seductive game by deigning to refute him on his own terms. When they stumble upon the body of a murdered Austrian soldier, this too is emptied of its political significance when Franz offers a strictly erotic interpretation of the problems of the occupying forces. Though the dead man is a victim of the Italian resistance, Franz makes this politically charged murder an excuse for more sexual self-advertising. "You can see that . . . it's not very pleasant to be part of an army of occupation. One has to live among people who hate one. And as for us younger men, far from home, all alone, we end up courting their wives and their daughters" (124). The corpse ceases to function as a historical sign and becomes instead a poetic one: a *memento mori* which bids the lovers to seize the occasion in the face of an uncertain tomorrow. When Franz quotes Heine's verses, "'Tis the Judgment Day / the dead rise to eternal joy, or to eternal pain. / We still embrace, heedless of all, both Paradise and Hell" (126), he is revealing the generic conflict between the courtly love story of Livia and Franz and the historical novel that provides the larger literary context of *Senso*. The Heine passage suggests the ahistoricism of the courtly love code, which removes the couple from the realm of the ordinary and places it in a transcendent sphere of permanent, metaphysical desire. Yet the apocalyptic allusion in the Heine verses is not without historical force, for it reflects Franz's awareness that his class is doomed to extinction, that the Risorgimento will be an Armageddon for his kind.[27] "In a few years Austria will be finished," he tells Livia when she finds him drunk and debauched in Verona, "and a whole world will disappear. The one you and I belong to" (179).

The mediating position of Livia's maid Laura, who helps hide Franz, protects the secrecy of the couple's affair, and facilitates their meeting, is another index of the literary and class origins of this love. Laura descends from a long line of officious but efficient ladies' maids, from the Duenna in *The Romance of the Rose* to Juliet Capulet's Nurse, and she seems to have assimilated all the practical wisdom of her literary predecessors. Indeed, Laura is always several steps ahead of Livia, anticipating her mistress's needs and acting on her own initiatives to further the adulterous plot. When Livia finally realizes that Laura has discovered the affair, she naively fears for her own reputation. "So what," Franz reassures her. "That's what ladies' maids are for" (157), thus confirming the literary stereotype to which Laura so well conforms.

Another literary indicator is the allusion to Narcissus, which culminates the couple's nocturnal wanderings through the streets of Venice. When Franz perches on the edge of a well and admires his image in a mirror, this way of saying that he is vain and self-loving may strike us as overly artful until we realize that Visconti is forging yet more elaborate links between his characters and the courtly love tradition which

---

[27] On Franz's class consciousness, which makes him far more self-aware than Remigio (his counterpart in Boito's novella), see Aristarco, "È realismo," p. 897, and Italo Calvino, "Boito, un punto di partenza," in *Antologia*, ed. Aristarco, p. 880.

is their class inheritance. Narcissus has provided the informing myth for much courtly love literature, be it the celebra-
tory kind that finds in the lady's eye an idealizing mirror for
the lover or the condemnatory kind that sees in such worldly
desire man's love of himself in preference to his divine crea-
tor. It is significant that in adapting Boito's novella, Visconti
has transferred the mirror fetish from Livia to Franz, thus
giving it to the character who has the clearer consciousness
of class destiny. Just as Narcissus came to self-knowledge by
contemplating his image in the well, so the aristocracy came
to know itself through this special kind of loving—secret,
passionate, adulterous, accountable to no higher authority
and to no other law—which became a kind of caste trademark, distinguishing it from inferior classes whose loving was
ruled by religious, legal, and practical restraints. Thus when
Livia becomes an initiate of the cult of courtly love, she is
merely claiming her literary birthright as a lady of the titled
nobility.

Yet in the very enactment of the code that defines their
class ideal, Livia and Franz fall short of it. The courtly lover
must be a warrior as well as a suitor, spurred on to deeds of
military prowess by the desire to please his lady. Since Franz,
instead, uses Livia's love as a way of exempting himself from
battle, and she complies, they are both guilty of violating
their courtly imperatives: he to military proofs of his manhood, and she to inspiring them. Franz's desertion is not only
emasculating, but socially degrading, banishing him from that
class to which the practice of courtly love and his former
military position had entitled him. "Look, I'm not an officer
any more. And not even an gentleman," he rails at Livia.
"I'm a drunken deserter. What a stink" (175).

Courtly love is not the only ideal which is subject to deterioration and inner collapse during the course of *Senso*.
Indeed, the entire film may be seen as a study in the process
of decline, as Visconti's strategy in adapting the Boito novella suggests. Most of the filmmaker's changes are made in

the direction of "mobilizing" a static portrait of a certain social class by linking its fortunes to the historical forces at work in mid–nineteenth-century Veneto and analyzing the reciprocal effects of historical, cultural, and personal degeneration on this once splendid elite. "What is important," Calvino says of *Senso*, "is the drama of decadence in times of revolution, the 'cupio dissolvi' of a society, seen with the participation, together with the hatred, of one who knows it too well."[28] Boito's novella is an ahistorical love story that simply happens to take place on the eve of the Venetian independence from Austrian rule and could have just as easily been set during any other era of foreign occupation (and there are many to choose from). The vexed political situation has no bearing on the affair and serves merely as a technical device for resolving the plot—Livia can denounce her lover as a deserter to Austrian authorities and thereby exact revenge for his infidelity. Visconti's story, on the other hand, lives up to Lukács's definition of the historical novel wherein the "personal destinies of a number of human beings coincide and interweave within the determining context of an historical crisis."[29] A comparison of Boito's Livia with Visconti's reveals how the filmmaker has transformed a static, ahistorical character into a typical one, in Lukács's sense of the word, embodying the salient conflicts of her era and exemplifying the process by which the old order passes into the new.

The Livia of Boito's novella is a vain and frivolous woman who remains unchanged by the historical storms breaking around her as well as by the death-dealing emotions of her own private life. History is more a source of annoyance to her than of partisan concern. "Garibaldi, with his hordes of

---

[28] Calvino, "Boito, un punto di partenza," p. 879. Visconti's own aristocratic background is what generates his fascination (and identification) with the historical spectacle of upper-class decline—a phenomenon that he explores again in *The Leopard* and in a more debased way in *The Damned*.

[29] Lukács, *The Historical Novel*, p. 41.

red demons, wanted to slaughter all those who fell into his hands," she writes in a text that is otherwise indifferent to the burning historical issues of the times.[30] The story is told in the first person as Livia commits to her memoirs the account of her sordid affair with an Austrian soldier named Remigio Ruiz. This narrative is framed by her diary entries about a current flirtation with "the little lawyer Gino" who is first rejected by Livia, then becomes engaged to a respectable woman of his own social class, before returning to the countess's embraces. The framing situation reveals two things about Boito's Livia: that her treacherous affair with Remigio has not changed her at all; and that she merely uses it as a standard against which all subsequent suitors must be measured. When she looks back on her grand passion with nostalgia, it is Remigio's violence and vulgarity she misses most of all. "He squeezed my waist so as to crush me, and he bit my shoulders, making them bleed."[31] Such reminiscence leads to inevitable comparisons between Remigio's virile seductions and Gino's pale, anemic ones.

By having her speak in the first person, Boito allows Livia to damn herself. Not only is the brazen tone of her confession a judgment on her moral deficiencies, but so too are the misunderstood allusions and inappropriate responses with which the journal abounds. When Livia compares herself to the Roman matrons of Parini's "Ode on Dressing for the Guillotine," she mistakes the poet's critical stance for an admiring one, inadvertently revealing what kind of a target she herself is for authorial satire. In another witty misunderstanding, Livia obeys the Socratic injunction to "know thyself" by assiduously studying her image in the mirror—an activity that qualifies her for the title of "filosofessa perfetta"

---

[30] Garibaldi, con le sue orde di demonii rossi, voleva scannare tutti quelli che gli sarebbero capitati in mano." Camillo Boito, "Senso," in *Storielle vane* (Rome: Silva, 1971), p. 397.

[31] "Mi stringeva alla vita in modo da stritolarmi e mi mordeva le spalle facendomele sanguinare." Ibid,. p. 390.

("perfect philosopher-lady"). Perhaps the most damning entry in her journal is the final one in its juxtaposition of inappropriate commentary and misunderstood event. A witness to the execution of Remigio, she is momentarily dazzled by his naked torso stripped for the sharpshooters' fire. But when Remigio's whore throws herself on his corpse, Livia regains her composure, remembering the wound to her vanity that prompted this quest for revenge. "I was aware of my rights . . . calm in the pride of a difficult duty accomplished."[32] In this utterly improper use of moral language, Boito conceals his own judgment of Livia's character. Perhaps this vocabulary of duty and conscience was suggested to her by the military honor code to which Livia had appealed in her vindictiveness, or perhaps it bespeaks the "all's fair in love and war" philosophy to which she obviously subscribes. Nonetheless, Boito makes Livia her own worst judge by putting moral language to the service of a woman who prides herself on defying standard morality. The Bohemian soldier who spits in her face as Livia leaves the execution site constitutes a further authorial judgment on this murderess whose journal leaps to the present to report, with characteristic levity and detachment, that the new suitor Gino embraces her "almost with the vigor of the Lieutenant Remigio."[33]

Though Visconti borrows Boito's first-person narrative technique, he does so to entirely different effect. Where the novella's narrative mode serves as a distancing device and as an internal judgment on its protagonist, Visconti uses Livia's voice-overs as a way of establishing our shifting relationship to a character who undergoes a precipitous negative change. At first, the voice-overs command our sympathies and draw us into an identification with Livia, but gradually, as she descends into self-degradation and treason, they function as a

---

[32] "Avevo la coscienza del mio diretto . . . tranquilla nell'orgoglio di un difficile dovere compiuto." Ibid., p. 422.

[33] "Quasi con la vigoria del tenente Remigio." Ibid., p. 422.

measure of how involved we once were with this character who is now so morally repellent. Unlike Boito's Livia, who is never admirable, and therefore cannot fall in our estimation, Visconti's begins on a moral pedestal so lofty that her decline occasions surprise as well as distaste. To maximize the dimensions of her fall, Visconti adds a political element to it, making Livia a traitor to the patriotic cause from which she embezzles funds to finance Franz's desertion, whereas Boito's Livia has no public trust to betray and no audience expectations to disappoint.

In establishing the heights from which Livia will eventually fall, the film begins with the suggestion of a far different love story than the one she ultimately enacts with Franz. From her box at La Fenice theater, Livia looks down into the orchestra and catches the eye of a handsome civilian who rewards her attentions by tossing up a bunch of tricolored flowers. When Livia lifts the bouquet to her lips, she gives the stamp of a possible love interest to this token of patriotic fervor from her cousin Roberto Ussoni. At the same time, another man exemplifies a radically different approach to the floral demonstration of patriotism which takes place between the acts of *Il Trovatore*. "How entertaining!" remarks Franz Mahler. "This is the kind of war that suits the Italians: showers of confetti to the sound of mandolins" (109). It is their differential response to the patriotic gesture that sets the plot in motion, precipitating Ussoni's challenge to Franz, Franz's consequent denunciation of Ussoni, and Livia's attempt to intercede on behalf of her cousin. The proposal of a duel (which Ussoni would fight but Franz would not) represents, in germinal form, the military future of the entire story: Franz will flee combat later on while Ussoni will seek out battle against all military-bureaucratic odds. Indeed, Ussoni's long and circuitous journey to the battle front parallels and reverses Franz's odyssey through the nocturnal city which wins him the very love that will save him from combat.

Were the film to develop the love interest of Livia and

Ussoni, it would resemble the high melodrama of the Verdi opera that constitutes the background of the opening scene. Like his operatic exemplar Manrico, Ussoni promises to excel in battle and to pursue a selfless ideal. "He seems to be the type who's born to sacrifice for some noble cause!" (121) Franz says of Ussoni in acknowledging his rival's qualifications for Verdian heroic stature. Manrico's performance of "Di quella pira" as Visconti's expository titles fade suggests the fixed hierarchy of values that governs the world of *Il Trovatore* and that would presumably apply to the love story of Livia and Ussoni as well. Manrico's aria subordinates the claims of love (even those of a "casto amore" or chaste love) to a higher ideal—that of filial piety—when he delays his marriage to Leonora so that he can defend his mother's life, or die with her, just as Ussoni tells Livia "we must forget ourselves . . . Italy's at war. It's our war . . . our Revolution." If we add the standard metaphor of maternal Italy with her citizenry of "figli buoni" ("good children") into the equation, then the analogies between Manrico's and Ussoni's hierarchies of value become more obvious still.[34] For the Italian audience of *Il Trovatore* in *Senso*, this metaphor was alive enough to arouse patriotic choruses of "all'armi" ("to arms"), in response to Manrico's own battle cry on stage.

Visconti sets up this operatic paradigm of high melodrama only to show how far short of this ideal his own story will fall. *Senso* may be considered a degraded melodrama in its violation of the moral laws that govern the Verdian world.[35] The heroics of the sort which typify *Il Trovatore* are explicitly renounced by Franz who confesses, "we like elegant uniforms because they make us look good . . . we're all eager as long as it's only a matter of toasting our future victories,

[34] See Gramsci, *Il Risorgimento*, p. 68.

[35] Hence Nowell-Smith calls *Senso* an "impure" melodrama in its absence of clear-cut moral categories. See his *Visconti*, p. 83. Similarly, Guido Fink sees the film as a mediocre compromise of the melodramatic ethos. See "Conosca il sacrifizio: Visconti fra cinema e melodramma," in *Visconti: Il cinema*, ed. Adelio Ferrero (Modena: Comune di Modena, 1977), p. 91.

but we don't feel up to paying the price for what those victories cost" (151). Franz is like the "little boy playing soldier with a wooden sword" (149) of the dream he recounts to Livia when she gives him sanctuary at the Serpieri villa in Aldeno. Like a child, he enjoys the fancy trappings of military service but dreads its bloody realities. "I'm not your romantic hero" (179), he finally tells Livia, echoing their first interview in the Serpieri box of La Fenice. "I like it [opera] very much," Livia had told him. "I don't care for it offstage, though, or for people who act like melodramatic heroes" (116). What Franz insists in his final orgy of drunken lucidity in Verona is that Livia *does* care for opera off-stage and that she wants to be a Leonora to Franz's Manrico. During the episode in Aldeno when she resolves to give Franz the money destined for Ussoni's volunteer army, she enacts a twisted version of the melodramatic heroine's self-sacrifice. The heightened emotionalism of the lovers' encounter, and the lady's anguished choice between two opposing claims on her loyalties, give this scene a superficial likeness to melodrama while reversing the hierarchy of values implicit in the true melodramatic mode.

By introducing *Senso* with a spectacle within a spectacle, Visconti announces his interest in the relationship between staged melodrama and its offstage counterparts. "I love melodrama because it is situated right on the border between life and the theater. I have tried to render this predilection of mine in the first sequences of the film *Senso*."[36]

Not only in the opening scene, but throughout the film, *Senso* inhabits that boundary line between life and theater,[37] which explains Visconti's preoccupation with uniforms and veils, and the questions of personal identity underlying the costumes and political labels that the protagonists wear.

---

[36] Quoted in ibid., p. 88.

[37] Leprohon reveals how the high-angle camerawork of the opening theater scene, which makes us share the spectators' point of view, is continued throughout *Senso*. "The screen becomes a stage and is treated as such visually." See *The Italian Cinema*, p. 148.

Is Livia the Leonora of her melodramatic fantasy, or is she simply the older woman clinging to the self-delusions that Franz exposes when he tears off the veil during their encounter in Verona?[38] Is Franz truly a soldier who degenerates into a drunken nonentity when deprived of his epaulettes, or is he a coward who never merited the prestige of his uniform in the first place?

Indeed, the Risorgimento itself becomes a melodramatic performance with heroes, villains, and high-minded principles requiring a theatrical scenario of its own. It is no coincidence that the patriotic demonstration staged by Ussoni and his fellow activists takes place in La Fenice theater and is precipitated by Manrico's on-stage call to arms. Not only did Verdi's operas constitute the cultural vehicle for the country's burgeoning nationalistic sentiments, but its power to stir the democratic masses was analogous to the Risorgimento leaders' own propaganda campaign to capture the popular imagination. Thus La Fenice serves as the arena not only for a cultural performance, but also for a political one whose success is registered both by Ussoni who gloats, "they're waking up, they're waking up!" (112) and by Serpieri who fumes, "we cannot allow the Venice Theater to become a stage for revolutionary demonstrations" (114).

But just as *Il Trovatore* creates expectations and illusions about romantic love that the offstage affair of Livia and Franz cannot equal, so the Risorgimento myth propagated by the opera house demonstration falsifies the realities of the campaign for unification. The messenger Luca's political fantasies are analogous to Livia's melodramatic ones, when he insists, "we'll free our land ourselves without anybody's help"

[38] The importance of this "unmasking" cannot be overestimated. Visconti explains how his films are born from single obsessive images which then give rise to full-fledged narrations, and this is the one that inspired *Senso*. "I had constantly before my eyes, a woman dressed in black, presenting a face streaked with tears to the insults of her lover. That was to provide the determining scene of the denouement of the action: the encounter in Verona of Livia and Franz." See *La table ronde*, p. 84.

(156) in a naive belief that the Risorgimento will indeed be "movimento popolare" and not "conquista regia." Livia's degraded melodrama is thus the erotic counterpart of the degradation of the Risorgimento ideal as Gramsci exposed it. For this reason, Visconti chose to make a movie about Livia and Franz rather than one about Livia and Ussoni. What Visconti argues is that Verdian melodrama is not possible in a fallen, post-Risorgimento world where myths of absolute good, absolute evil, self-sacrifice, and heroism have given way to a reality of moral compromise and disillusionment. Franz's attraction for Livia proved the superior pull of class identity over the claims of nationalism—Livia would rather consort with another of her class and enjoy her literary–erotic birthright than burn with a chaste love for a man who would put her second to his political–moral vocation. It is the very survival of these class interests, as Livia embodies them, which subverted the Risorgimento ideal of "movimento popolare" and assured its preservation as "conquista regia," free from the true revolutionary threat that participatory democracy would entail. Thus the primacy of the Livia–Franz plot over the Livia–Ussoni one constitutes a Gramscian criticism of the Risorgimento in melodramatic terms.

Visconti had originally envisioned a very different opening for his film. The first scene was to take place in a Veronese hospital where a madwoman would spill out her story of a "sad and guilty love" (147).[39] Such a beginning would solve the problem of the narrative present from which Livia's voice-over derives—a problem that leaves the story as we have it disturbingly incomplete.[40] What happened between the final episode in Verona and the present, which motivates Livia to

[39] For this alternative beginning, see Jacques Doniol-Valcroze and Jean Domarchi, "Entretien avec Luchino Visconti par Jacques Doniol-Valcroze et Jean Domarchi," *Cahiers du cinéma* 16 (March 1959), 2.

[40] As Nowell-Smith observes, "the story is left in suspense and never reconnected with the hypothetical present tense of the voice off." See his *Visconti*, p. 87.

tell her desperate story? Has she resumed her former privileged status, like Boito's Livia, or has she undergone some
irreversible change in identity and quality of life? The confessional genre to which Livia's first-person narrative belongs
demands that we know the narrative present that determines
and explains the speaker's perspective on the past. Without
such information, Livia's voice seems to be suspended in some
postnarrative limbo which tells us nothing about the personal and political consequences of her "sad and guilty love,"
nor how we are to judge her narrative perspective on it. To
be sure, open-endedness is a legitimate structural ploy, as the
neorealists argue, but it is to be regretted in a story whose
generic affiliations with the confession require that the narrative point of departure be rigorously established.

Though Visconti's original opening would solve this interpretive problem, I would prefer it on no other grounds to
the present beginning with its virtuoso staging and its intri-
cate positioning of the story on the "border between life and
the theater." In the confluence of Verdian melodrama, Risorgimento idealism, and romantic love which animate the first
scene, Visconti has created a Golden Age moment of perfect
reciprocity and balance between the public and the private,
between culture and history. But to continue his story in this
high register would be to write Verdian melodrama in an age
when it was no longer appropriate, when to do so would be
to falsify the real historical forces that shape post-Risorgimento Italy. Verdi must be corrected by Gramsci, Leonora
must become Livia, before the Risorgimento can yield a politically useful subject for twentieth-century Italian art.

The Gramscian argument is perhaps the most successful in
reconciling *Senso* with the neorealist precedent which still, in
1954, held theoretical sovereignty over the Italian cinema.
By invoking Gramsci, Visconti is exonerated from charges of
an irresponsible retreat into the archives and is vindicated as
a historical novelist—in Lukács's sense of the term—who puts
history at the service of a modern political consciousness.
But the Gramscian argument fails to address the most trou-

blesome objection to *Senso*—that of its spectacular elements, which ally it with the more retrograde examples of prewar production: the costume films of the silent era, and later the calligraphers' exercises in pure style. This criticism of *Senso* is especially hard to refute because it rests on the assumption that aesthetic form determines thematic content and that a luxurious, self-congratulatory style full of extracinematic conventions will necessarily compromise any aspirations the artist may have to revolutionary meaning. Aristarco comes to Visconti's defense with several artful dodges, including the argument that such a vision is a realistic extension of the lovers' own world view,[41] and that the director's appropriation of pictorial, literary, and operatic conventions provides a formal analogy to the film's thematic conflict between the old order and the new.[42] Such defenses of the film's spectacular elements presuppose that Visconti uses them strategically, that he self-consciously manipulates his own spectacle from a critical distance that enables him to see it as a function of the very sensibility that he condemns in Livia and Franz. But Visconti has no such ironic detachment from his own creative process, nor does he judge in any way the dazzling, sensual surface of his film, which seems more an object of unqualified aesthetic delight than of ideological disdain.

Despite its troubled marriage of spectacular form and revolutionary content, *Senso* nonetheless served to broaden critical tolerance for film styles that did not exhibit the usual neorealist austerity. The use of color, calligraphic effects, and extracinematic conventions would no longer be grounds for immediately dismissing a film as regressive and ideologically suspect. Though Visconti will remain an anomaly for several decades, his aesthetic will find its admirers in the next cinematic "generation"—that of Bertolucci, Wertmuller, and Cavani—whose combination of neorealist commitment and stylistic virtuosity finds its bold and uneasy precedent in *Senso*.

[41] See Aristarco, "*Senso*," in *Antologia*, ed. Aristarco, p. 874.
[42] See Aristarco, "È realismo," p. 898.

8 Antonioni's *Red Desert*: Abstraction as the guiding idea

IF THE 1950S WAS the decade of the crisis of neorealism, it was also the decade of the proliferation of neorealisms, each with its own determining adjective and each with its justification for a style whose resemblance to the postwar films was not always immediately obvious. Thus we get "phenomenological neorealism" for Fellini's work, "lyrical" or "romantic neorealism" for Visconti's, and "interior neorealism" for Antonioni's.[1] Like the psychotherapist who can retrospectively find ample cause for his patient's nervous breakdown in the stresses that led up to it, yet was unable to predict the illness in advance, critics can look back on neorealism from the vantage point of Fellini's, Visconti's, or Antonioni's work and see in it the source for all three divergent aesthetics. Neorealism is somehow "reinvented" in retrospect each time it is called upon to justify a new stylistic departure, making it the absence of hierarchical significance, the openness to transcendent meaning that looks ahead to Fellini's approach, or the attention to the dynamics of the historical process that looks ahead to Visconti's, or the new way of putting oneself in relation to the world by means of

---

[1] On Fellini's phenomenological neorealism, see Ayfre, "Néo-réalisme et phénoménologie," pp. 6–18. On Visconti's lyrical or romantic neorealism, see Giuseppe Ferrara, *Luchino Visconti* (Paris: Seghers, 1963), pp. 46–47. On Antonioni's interior neorealism, see Lorenzo Cuccu, *La visione come problema: Forme e svolgimento del cinema di Antonioni* (Roma: Bulzoni, 1973), p. 160; Giorgio Tinazzi, *Antonioni* (Florence: La Nuova Italia, 1976), p. 34; and Michelangelo Antonioni, "La malattia dei sentimenti," in Lizzani, *Storia del cinema italiano*, p. 297.

a movie camera that anticipates Antonioni's.[2] The return to various aspects of neorealism to legitimize all important subsequent cinematic developments in Italy, even when those developments seem to contradict each other or to negate the neorealist example, is a testimony to the power of this precedent and to its elasticity.

Nor are critics the only ones to insist on the primacy of neorealist influence, for the filmmakers themselves follow suit, arguing that their styles are not radical breaks from neorealism, but gentle stretchings of its confines. "I began as one of the first exponents of neorealism," wrote Antonioni, "and now by concentrating on the internals of character and psychology I do not think I have deserted the movement, but rather have pointed a path towards extending its boundaries. Unlike early neorealist filmmakers, I am not trying to show reality, I am attempting to recreate realism."[3] Such a distinction between the neorealists' intent "to show reality" and his own ambition "to recreate realism" might sound like pure semantic quibbling, until we realize that this is Antonioni's way of performing for his own work what Aristarco did for Visconti's.

For both filmmakers, neorealism is condemned as "restrictive sociologism,"[4] unable to consider the deeper and broader issues that shape the historical process in Visconti's case, or the individual psyche in Antonioni's. When Antonioni says that he is extending neorealism by "attempting to recreate realism" he is really offering to go forward by going backward, that is, by returning to the cultural antecedents of the postwar movement and by taking them along a different evolutionary course. Aristarco, with his penchant for finding nineteenth-century literary analogues to the Italian cinema, invokes Flaubert, particularly the Flaubert of *L'éduca-*

[2] See Cuccu, *La visione*, p. 169.
[3] See Hollis Alpert, "A Talk with Antonioni," *Saturday Review*, 27 October 1962, 65.
[4] Tinazzi, *Antonioni*, p. 31.

tion sentimentale, as the model for Antonioni's representation of middle-class malaise.[5] The writer's portrayal of a life which suffers no major catastrophes, but which undergoes continual erosion from within, is the dynamic not only of *L'education sentimentale*, but of the modern novel in general, according to Aristarco, and it is in this tradition that Antonioni's filmmaking finds its proper place. But perhaps a more fruitful explanation for Antonioni's aesthetic would be the "transvaluation" of the realist concepts of truth and honesty that Nochlin sees occurring at the end of the nineteenth century in the plastic arts.[6] Whereas "truth and honesty" first described the realists' attempts to represent the external world as a natural or social entity, it later came to mean fidelity to the nature of the medium or to the artist's subjectivity itself, as the notion of an objective external order began to fall into disrepute.[7] Antonioni's emphasis on technique may be seen as just such a transvaluation of the realists' premium on truth and honesty of representation. Rejecting Zavattini's plea to conceal the hand of the artist and to make the medium transparent, Antonioni insists that his style be not only opaque and self-referential, but the primary vehicle of meaning, taking over the signifying function that drama or dialogue serve in the conventional cinema. Thus, as Cuccu argues, Antonioni's films are far from mere visual translations of a priori conceptual themes; they are representations of a twofold visual act which registers first a candid impression of an image and then seeks out its hidden meaning.[8] For Antonioni, cinema is vision in process, or as Cuccu calls it, "vision in development or *in fieri*,"[9] and such a process is always an interrogative one that denies prefabricated significance and opens

[5] See Guido Aristarco, "Cronaca di una crisi e forme strutturali dell'anima," in *Michelangelo Antonioni*, ed. Carlo Di Carlo (Rome: Edizioni di Bianco e nero, 1964), p. 222.
[6] See Nochlin, *Realism*, p. 230.
[7] Ibid., p. 236.
[8] See Cuccu, *La visione*, p. 155.
[9] Ibid., p. 147.

itself up to continual inquiry by cinematic means.[10] Putting it another way, Cameron and Wood admire Antonioni's "ability to think in film, as opposed to translating ideas into images,"[11] thus corroborating what Cuccu calls the preeminence of the visual moment over the "figurale-discorsivo-diegetico" ("figural-discursive-diegetic") one.[12]

In a passage that reads like a gloss for *Blow-Up ante litteram*, Antonioni describes reality as a palimpsest whose various layers must be visually unpeeled by the movie camera in the quest for ultimate truths. "We know that under the image revealed there is another which is truer to reality and under this image still another and yet again still another under this last one, right down to the true image of that reality, absolute, mysterious, which no one will ever see or perhaps right down to the decomposition of any image, of any reality."[13] Vision, for Antonioni, becomes a kind of meditational act capable of penetrating to the very core of reality, if there is a core, or revealing the final absence of any meaning to which the images ultimately point. This, of course, is Thomas's dilemma in *Blow-Up*: does the photograph within the photograph within the photograph—that of the corpse in the park—correspond to an external reality or is it a non-referential sign unable to be verified or to generate the chain of crime-detecting events that murder necessarily entails?

But more important for our study of *Red Desert* is the very nature of the visual act described in this passage, for it is one of abstraction, of probing so deeply into the nature of images that they decompose, becoming instead agglomerations of pure color, line, and shape.[14] This explains Anto-

---

[10] Ibid., p. 171.

[11] Ian Cameron and Robin Wood, *Antonioni* (New York: Praeger, 1971), p. 112.

[12] See Cuccu, *La visione*, pp. 147 and 149.

[13] In Samuels, *Encountering Directors*, p. 23.

[14] In speaking of *Red Desert*, Antonioni explains the appropriateness of an abstract style. "The story demanded shots of a reality that had become abstract, of a subject that had become color." Pierre Billard, "An Interview

nioni's fondness for shooting angles or lens distortions which transform the ordinary and the banal into objects of surpassing aesthetic interest, so that the factories of Ravenna become striking abstract compositions of color and design, "more beautiful than a row of trees which every eye has already seen to the point of monotony."[15] A taste for abstraction also explains why Antonioni tends to break up his shots into small visual cells, as he does in the factory, looking down at his two male protagonists through a grating, or using split compositions to divide the *mise-en-scène*. It is through abstraction that Antonioni is able to suggest connections among otherwise disparate settings—settings that would conjure up antithetical expectations in the conventional cinema. Thus, Antonioni makes a norm of the factory, whose brightly colored pipes give the composition a fragmented and painterly quality, just as do the balusters in Giuliana's house, the bed frame in Corrado's hotel room, and the pipes on the freighter he is preparing to load for Patagonia.[16]

When Antonioni has Giuliana ask her friends, "What should I do with my eyes, what should I look at?"[17] he is raising his visual style to the level of a full-fledged thematic concern, and is making Giuliana its embodiment within the film.[18]

---

with Michelangelo Antonioni," in *L'avventura: A Film by Michelangelo Antonioni*, ed. George Amberg (New York: Grove Press, 1969), p. 240.

[15] Andrew Sarris, *Interviews with Film Directors* (New York: Avon, 1970), p. 23.

[16] Thus Stanley Kauffmann sees in the film "a buried history of modern painting . . . from the Impressionists through Mondrian to Hopper and Wyeth." See *The New Republic*, 20 February 1965, 30–31. Liehm notes the special influences of the Italian abstract painter Alberto Burri on Antonioni's visual style. See her *Passion and Defiance*, pp. 228–29.

[17] Michelangelo Antonioni, *Il deserto rosso*, ed. Carlo Di Carlo (Bologna: Cappelli, 1978), p. 79. All quotations will be from this edition, and subsequent page references will appear in the text. The translations are mine.

[18] For an excellent account of Antonioni's visual and narrative strategies in *Red Desert*, see Giannetti, *Understanding Movies*, the pictorial insert between pp. 112–13. On Antonioni's abstract shooting techniques, see Bondanella, *Italian Cinema*, p. 220.

That we are seeing the world through her abstracting vision there can be no doubt, as Tinazzi says when he calls *Red Desert* a film "in subjective camera"[19] and as Cameron and Wood suggest when they explain how a composition which includes Giuliana in sharp focus looking at a background in soft focus is a compressed version of a conventional pair of shots: the closeup of a character, followed by an image of what that character is seeing through his or her own eyes.[20] By using Giuliana as his visual receptor within the film, Antonioni is exemplifying Pasolini's notion of "free indirect subjective" which is the cinematic equivalent of the free indirect discourse in literature.[21] It is by means of this technique that cinema realizes its highest poetic possibilities, according to Pasolini, freeing itself from the restrictions of conventional narrative form and allowing itself to return to its expressive source in preconscious thought.[22] Unlike Cameron and Wood, who fault Antonioni's placement of a neurotic woman at the center of his statement about the contemporary world,[23] Pasolini applauds this choice, for the neurotic's vision gives Antonioni an excuse to indulge his extravagant aestheticism and thereby to achieve "the greatest poetic liberty—a liberty which precisely borders (and this is why it is intoxicating) upon the arbitrary."[24]

If Giuliana's abstracting vision is equivalent to Antonioni's, then her story is an explanation, though in no literal-minded way, of how his own visual style came to be. By grounding his vision in a character who has a tendency to look with wonder and fear at the things around her, Antonioni suggests a prior phase of his own perceptual develop-

---

[19] Tinazzi, *Antonioni*, p. 100.

[20] Cameron and Wood, *Antonioni*, p. 120.

[21] Pier Paolo Pasolini, "The Cinema of Poetry," in *Movies and Methods*, ed. Bill Nichols (Berkeley and Los Angeles: University of California Press, 1976), p. 549.

[22] Ibid., p. 552.

[23] Cameron and Wood, *Antonioni*, p. 124.

[24] Pasolini, "Cinema of Poetry," p. 553.

ment. What Giuliana accomplishes in *Red Desert* by transforming her fear of the world abstractly perceived into an acceptance of it, is a prerequisite to the artist's own accomplishment, which is to transform that acceptance into a celebration. By the end of the film, Giuliana is not quite at the point where Antonioni is at the beginning—she has learned to fly around the poisonous yellow smoke but has not yet learned to love its yellowness, or its texture or shape. Presumably, this too will come, now that she has abandoned her dreams of escape, be they through suicide, adultery, stowing away, or selling undetermined merchandise in a multicolored shop, and can now concentrate on putting her abstract vision to positive uses.

If we read *Red Desert* as the story of the genesis of a visual style, many of the otherwise troublesome aspects of the film gain new necessity and logic. The storyline itself is minimal; it alone would hardly suffice to recommend the film to our attention. It chronicles the recovery of a middle-class wife and mother from a nervous collapse suffered in the wake of a minor automobile accident. Her hospitalization occurs prior to the action of the film, which begins with Giuliana's visit to the factory where her husband, Ugo, works as an engineer. There she meets Corrado, the factory owner's son, who is in search of workers for a new plant to be opened in Patagonia. Grasping for ways to improve her life after her breakdown, Giuliana attempts to open up a ceramics shop, but her efforts are sporadic and ineffectual. Drawn to Corrado for his seeming sensitivity to her plight, Giuliana accompanies him from Ravenna to Ferrara in search of recruits for the Patagonian venture. A Sunday outing with Ugo, Corrado, and assorted friends promises to become an orgy but ends up instead a crisis for Giuliana, who emerges more convinced than ever of her solitude. While Ugo is on a business trip, Valerio, their son, suffers a temporary, inexplicable paralysis whose equally inexplicable, spontaneous cure sends Giuliana into the arms of Corrado in search of emotional

8. *Giuliana (Monica Vitti) stands before her husband Ugo (Carlo Chionetti, cen-ter) and her future lover Corrado (Richard Harris) in the scene of the pseudo-orgy.*

support. Unconsoled by their lovemaking, Giuliana runs to the shipyards where she momentarily considers stowing away before finally coming to accept her lot.

As this synopsis suggests, Antonioni's storyline is so loosely woven and arbitrary in its progression that we are compelled to look elsewhere for the locus of meaning in the film. The narrative also constantly raises and frustrates audience expectations by flirting with various genres but refusing to settle into any one conventional mode. *Red Desert* is not quite a love story, not quite a psychological case history, not quite an environmentalist or anti-industrialist polemic. The plot itself is full of false starts, dead ends, and unanswered questions, beginning with the workers' strike at the very opening of the film which Antonioni does not see fit to explain or amplify in any way. The curiosity that such a politically charged event naturally arouses is never satisfied, nor are we told what the workers' grievances are, why one man crosses the picket line, and, indeed, most mysteriously, why the plant seems to be fully operant despite a drastically reduced staff. Soon after, the spectacular effusion of steam and noise that envelops Ugo and Corrado as they talk outside the factory is left unexplained. Ugo apparently offers an explanation to a bewildered Corrado, but we cannot hear him for the noise. In a later sequence, we never learn if Valerio's paralysis is a real hysterical episode or an entirely theatrical one. The cry heard by Giuliana and Linda in the seaside cabin also remains an enigma—was it associated with the approaching ship and its unknown contagion? Indeed, all the boats in the film are mysterious: the one in Giuliana's fable to Valerio— a frigate that disappears as inexplicably as it appears and never reveals its purpose—the tanker that materializes like an apparition amid the pine groves of Ravenna; and the one she considers stowing away on toward the conclusion. These narrative loose ends have their verbal equivalents in the many unanswered questions with which the dialogue abounds.

Perhaps the most pervasive and troublesome of all the unresolved mysteries is the origin of Giuliana's neurosis. Is it her unfulfilling family life, or some trauma in her past, or the inhumanity of the technological world to which Giuliana reacts as if she were an exposed nerve, registering its every assault on her fragile sensibility? Antonioni's refusal to cast blame bespeaks not only his general indifference to questions of causality,[25] but also his desire to posit the analogy between Giuliana's vision and his own—an analogy that would suffer from too technical an explanation for her illness. If Giuliana's neurosis were presented as a specific clinical condition attributable to concrete causes and susceptible to a given psychiatric treatment, we would dismiss her vision as just one more pathological symptom, rather than a viable model for Antonioni's own aestheticizing approach.

If visual style is the primary vehicle of meaning in *Red Desert*, and abstraction is its organizing principle, then we can expect that principle to offer the interpretive key to all other elements of the film. Here let us turn to the literal meaning of abstraction as "removal, withdrawal, or separation," or more elaborately, as "the act of considering a thing independently of its associations"[26] and consider how one of the most striking images in the film makes visual style the source of narrative and thematic significance. The outing in Max's seaside cabin has just ended with the ominous arrival of the quarantined boat, and all are making their way to the cars when Giuliana remembers she has left her purse on the doorstep of the cabin. Ugo and Corrado both volunteer to retrieve it, but Giuliana panics at the thought of their approaching the malignant ship. When her anxiety subsides, she turns to regard the company standing dispersed on the quay, enshrouded in a fog which slowly dissolves their contours and threatens to swallow them up. The vision is a terrifying one of separateness and of evanescence, and such is

[25] See Samuels, *Encountering Directors*, pp. 29–30.
[26] *OED* (1933), 1:42.

its power that Giuliana is compelled to rush for the car and drive close to the water's edge in an act more suggestive of a death wish than of the confusion to which she later pleads. Abstraction on the stylistic level becomes alienation on the narrative one—just as images are estranged from their normal contexts, so people are estranged from one another. When Giuliana says to the Turkish sailor, "bodies are separate" (134), she is giving words to the image of fog-enshrouded separateness that characterized her friends on the wharf, while at the same time acknowledging Corrado's recent failure to help her by offering physical consolations for the emotional ones she so desperately requires. The need for intimacy finds an inadequate and self-defeating expression in the desire for sexual conquest that the verbal foreplay in Max's cabin amply illustrates. Mili's nymphomania, Max's predatory pursuits of women in crisis, and the revelers' mechanical concern for increasing their appetites and prolonging their endurance through aphrodisiacs reveal how empty of emotional components their eroticism is. Not surprisingly, Giuliana's and Ugo's sexual drives are completely out of phase—when she awakens from her night terrors and needs Ugo's reassurances, she gets his caresses instead, but when she eats all three quail's eggs and announces, with wonderful absence of guile, that she wants to make love, he pleads the social impropriety of leaving the party so soon.

During the sequence in the cabin, Antonioni reveals what it is that turns sex into empty exhibitionism and keeps people irremediably estranged. Early in the scene, the cry is heard on the soundtrack to which only Giuliana and Linda respond. The others deny hearing it, and Ugo, worst of all, denies its significance. "Scream or no scream, what does it matter?" "No, instead it does matter! Someone screamed" (80), protests Giuliana, granting importance not so much to this proof of her sanity as to the human suffering betokened by the cry. Had the contested sound been a bell or a horn, she probably would not have bothered to insist, but a cry of pain or alarm which falls on the deaf ears of her companions proves once more their ruling defect—the failure of empathy that prevents them from imagining or participating in another's plight. "If you prick me, you don't suffer" (134), Giuliana tells the Turkish sailor at the end of the film, translating this failure of human solidarity into the simplest of physical terms.

But the absence of empathy had been evident throughout the story, from the moment the cold, impassive Ugo was introduced on the screen. His most grievous emotional failure is with regard to Giuliana, the gravity of whose illness he constantly minimizes, happy to believe in the euphemisms and delusions that she and the doctors have conspired to foist upon him. It does not take much to see through this tissue of lies, as Corrado does immediately, but Ugo remains so blind that he is ready to repeat his original error in judgment and embark on another business trip with Giuliana on the brink of nervous collapse, just as he had done on the eve of her accident and hospitalization. In a seemingly trivial detail, Ugo reveals his unwitting cruelty when Giuliana asks how many days he'll be gone. "Five . . . six" (116), he answers with a casualness and an imprecision devastating to a woman who fears abandonment and needs all the certainty she can get.

Even Corrado, who evidences true concern for Giuliana's plight, demonstrates a similar failure of empathy in the treatment he accords prospective members of his crew for Patagonia. He is completely untouched by the idea of breaking up families, answering the men's questions about when they can be reunited with their wives and how often they can speak to them on the phone with official indifference. Perhaps we can excuse his callousness in the face of the men, who dare not betray their true feelings in so public a forum, but when confronted with the raw emotion of one of the wives who would be separated from her husband, Corrado, to our surprise and disappointment, remains impassive. No sooner does he leave the woman's apartment, driven out by the violence of her refusal to be parted from her Mario, than Corrado resolves to seek out Mario himself. Giuliana too is shocked by his insensitivity—so shocked, the screenplay tells us, that she can find no words to contradict him or impede his mission (63). As an itinerant, Corrado embodies the principle of abstraction in the literal sense of the word, constantly denying himself a physical or emotional context by his unwillingness to put down roots. When Giuliana asks Corrado where he's from and he answers with a long list of cities, the effect is at once comic and pathetic, for this is a man perpetually in transit, whose geographic instability precludes the forging of emotional bonds. It is to this sentimental detachment that Giuliana refers when she faults Corrado for traveling so lightly. Giuliana, instead, would take all her belongings for fear that she might return to find that something had changed. But Corrado likes change for its own sake—change of scenery, change of activity, change of "historic ambience," as he pompously tells Max. "I must feel 'spaesato' [literally town-less or villageless] to feel well" (77). Geographical rootlessness is a condition to which Corrado aspires, as Max aspires to a kind of entrepreneurial rootlessness, wandering from one deal to the next in an accumulation of managerial conquests. Indeed, all the characters seem to have accommodated to the emotional inadequacies of their situations by seeking their own particular methods of escape: Linda through the ever-present novel, Mili through promiscuity, Corrado through travel, Max through predatory pursuits of women and property, and Giuliana through neurosis. In a society character-ized by alienation, these remedies seem designed expressly to aggravate the very problems they promise to address. Thus Giuliana is not qualitatively different from the rest of the more functional neurotics who populate the world of the film—she simply takes their escapist tendencies to a pathological extreme.[27] Her illness, which in clinical terms would probably find its closest equivalent in schizophrenia, also exhibits the principle of abstraction which is the guiding idea of the film's aesthetic vision. "You ought to learn how to love," the psychiatrist had told Giuliana. "To love a person or also a thing: your husband, your son, or a job or a dog. . . . But not husband, son, job, dog, trees, river" (61). The doctor's criticism suggests that Giuliana is too diffuse and indiscriminate in her love, that she must be more select and concrete in the objects of her affection, for not all things will love her in return. To love and to be loved universally is an abstract desire dictated less by the identity of specific objects than by the neurotic's need for global approval—a need that is by definition insatiable because its very diffuseness precludes total reciprocity. Giuliana must exchange this abstract, universalizing desire for a concrete, object-appropriate one which rewards selectivity by being returned in kind. This new way of loving will countermand Giuliana's sense of alienation, allowing her to reintegrate herself into reality, according to the psychiatrist's glib prescription for mental health.

In his very title, Antonioni teaches us to read the film abstractly, for it is only on the most general level that "red desert," as a description of industrial Ravenna, makes any sense at all. Like Dante's Santa Lucia who, from the height of the Empyrean, can call the dark wood where the poem begins "a river" because the pilgrim is indeed spiritually drowning in that sylvan setting, Giuliana is able to compare the urban seaport to a desert by virtue of certain shared attributes: desolation, barrenness, and hostility to life. The an-

[27] See Sergio Micheli, "Il personaggio femminile nei film di Antonioni, *Bianco e nero* 28 (January 1967), 6; and Cameron and Wood, *Antonioni*, p. 112. Tinazzi comments that Giuliana's disease extends itself to Mario, the Ferrarese worker, and to Valerio in his pseudo-paralysis. See his *Antonioni*, p. 101.

titype to the red desert of industrial Ravenna is the pink beach
of the fable with which Giuliana amuses Valerio during the
episode of his hysterical paralysis. Indeed, this idyllic interlude constitutes an antifilm within the film, providing a contrast not only to the physical setting of the rest of *Red Desert*, but to its predominant visual style. The industrial city
and pink beach are polar opposites in every way: one is
overcast and grey, the other is lit by radiant sunlight; one is
shot with color and lens distortions, the other in unblem-
ished technicolor; one is spatially congested, the other open
to the horizon; one has foul polluted waterways, the other
has the transparent sea; one is accompanied by electronic
music and industrial noises, the other by Giuliana's narrative
voice or by human song; one is afloat with modern tankers,
the other with an Old World frigate; one is governed by man-
made rhythms, the other by the movements of the sun, and
so on. But more importantly, the fable offers the corrective
to the terrible abstraction of Giuliana's city, for the fairy-tale
island is an organic whole that binds all elements to an establishing natural context and forbids any analytic dismem-
berment of its parts. It is no accident that the protagonist of
the fable is a prepubescent girl who has not yet suffered the
fall into experience that will irrevocably exile her from the
earthly paradise of her island retreat. This is Giuliana's personal myth of Eden, a place where the primal unity between
the self and the world has not yet been split asunder by guilty
knowledge or willful rebellion against the natural order. The
child and the environment live in happy concord, she obey-
ing the rhythms of the sun, the rocks mimicking the smooth
brownness of her flesh, and the mysterious song, half human
and half wild, making literal the metaphor of harmonious
coexistence.

It is against this myth of primal unity and concord that
Antonioni asks us to judge the rest of the film, to take the
true measure of its alienation and abstraction. On the narrative level, correctives for the ills of modern urban living

are nowhere to be found. Political options are rejected out of hand—the strike at the beginning of the film is a feeble, uninspired event which neither binds together a community nor effectuates reform. Since we are not privy to the workers' grievances, we cannot determine the legitimacy of their complaint and can only judge them by the languor and mechanical sloganeering of their demonstration. Similarly, Corrado's spouting of socialistic pieties is so slick and unconvincing that we applaud Giuliana when she replies, "You've put together a nice group of words" (67). Psychiatric solutions to Giuliana's malaise are also discredited. The doctor's suggestion that she accommodate to reality has little to recommend itself when we look for examples of successful social adjustment among the dramatis personae of the film. Indeed, the only character not madly seeking escape is Ugo, but he is exemplary only for those who would equate normalcy with numbness.[28] In Valerio's paralysis, the boy seems to be somatizing his father's temperamental trademark.

The absence of resolutions on the narrative level leads us back to the visual style in search for an answer to the alienation that blights Giuliana's world. It is only aesthetically that Antonioni is able to offer some consolation, and he does so through the use of the objective correlative which posits a continuity between character and setting, between the inner life of the psyche and its outward reflection in the phenomenal world. In *Red Desert*, color assumes this important expressive function, as the title of the film suggests with the chromatic adjective red, distinguishing it from the single, unmodified noun titles of Antonioni's previous trilogy (*L'avventura, La notte, L'eclisse*). This is Antonioni's first color film, and he uses the technique in a highly self-conscious, aggressive way, imposing his own chromatic scheme on all settings, be they landscapes or interiors. Since he refuses to

[28] See Cameron and Wood, *Antonioni*, p. 115.

manipulate color in the laboratory,[29] this means directly painting the backgrounds in order to make the slag heaps dark grey, for example, or Corrado's hotel bedroom pink, or the fruits on the cart outside Giuliana's shop white.[30] Color constitutes so active and autonomous a presence in the film that it makes the environment a character, according to Kauffmann, in dramatic conflict with the protagonists of the film.[31] "Color represents Giuliana's state of mind," Antonioni once agreed in an interview,[32] but Giuliana herself complicates the relationship when she tells Corrado in the shop, "maybe blue is better . . . [for] the walls. And the ceiling green. They are cold colors that shouldn't disturb" (56). Her comments reveal what Antonioni himself has learned about the psycho-physiology of color: that it both reflects and conditions mood.[33] Since chromatic perception is a relational process, it makes color an objective correlative in a dynamic way, bearing passive witness to the character's psychic state, while exerting an active influence over it.[34] "Color does not exist in the absolute," Antonioni explains. "It is always a relationship . . . between the object and the psychological state of the observer, in the sense that both influence each other in turn. That is, the object with its color has a determined influence on the observer and contemporaneously, he sees the color which in that moment he has interest or pleasure in seeing in that object."[35] In an interview with Godard, Antonioni exemplifies this reciprocity in the use of red—a color that was found to incite workers to violence in psychological experiments, and which reflected

[29]See Sarris, *Interviews*, pp. 30–31.

[30]On Antonioni's aggressive use of color, see "Antonioni in Color," *Time*, 19 February 1965, 99.

[31]See Kauffmann, "Red Desert," p. 31.

[32]These are Samuels's words in *Encountering Directors*, p. 30.

[33]Sarris, *Interviews*, p. 29.

[34]On the reciprocity of color and character, see Tinazzi, *Antonioni*, p. 103.

[35]See Di Carlo, "I colori dei sentimenti," in *Il deserto rosso*, p. 20.

the agitation and sexual arousal of the revelers in *Red Desert*. "I would never have done the scene in the shack where they talk about drugs, aphrodisiacs, without using red," he told Godard. "The red puts the spectator in a state of mind that permits him to accept this dialogue. The color is correct for the characters (who are justified by it) and also for the spectator."[36] When Giuliana includes "i colori" (132) in the list of things that frighten her in the environment, she is acknowledging the power of color to reveal and determine character. It is thus no surprise that at moments of acute psychic distress or exaltation, Giuliana hallucinates a welter of colors, or "a stain," as she calls it, literazing the metaphor of the "colors of the sentiments."

Space functions similarly as an objective correlative for Giuliana's state of mind, and when she tries to verbalize her feelings, she often positions herself in spatial settings that corroborate or complement what she is saying. During the visit to the worker's apartment in Ferrara, for example, Giuliana stands framed in a doorway and pushes against its side posts as she discusses her need for firmer psychological grounding. In Corrado's hotel room, she withdraws into a corner when speaking of the desire for a wall of friends to protect her against "something terrible in reality" (133).

The seeming inhospitality of the industrial cityscape to its human populace is thus reversed on the aesthetic level by a continuity which allows that setting to externalize the inner lives of its inhabitants, to make accessible what dialogue and story fail to tell us about them. Such a resolution might strike us as arbitrary and futile for the victims of this society until we realize that Giuliana is on her way to acquiring Antonioni's aestheticizing vision, enabling her to accept and to use what she once feared and fled. Ugo's mechanical accommodation to an industrial world need not be the only road to mental health, nor must Giuliana give up her special vi-

---

[36] Sarris, *Interviews*, p. 30.

sion in order to survive. She need only to master it and put it to the service of aesthetic ends, as she shows she can do through storytelling. Indeed, the tale she tells her son is therapeutic for them both, enabling her to recognize the counterfactual quality of her desires for primal innocence, while it seems literally to cure Valerio, who gets up and walks in the very next scene. Another of Giuliana's stories included in the screenplay but unfortunately cut from the final version of the film tells of a kite whose flight is the collective venture of an entire village. As the craft ascends, the villagers unravel all their fabrics to provide the length of string required for it to reach the stars. The kite survives all manner of threats, both natural and man-made (lightning and missiles) so that the analogies to Giuliana's own psychic state are not far to seek. Such is the therapeutic power of her fictions that one of them, the final one, contains her prescription for mental health, and the germ of the plot for the film which is just drawing to an end. When Valerio asks what happens to the birds who fly through the poisonous smoke, and Giuliana says they learn to avoid it, the solution to her struggle is at hand.

Antonioni's highly abstract, aestheticizing vision may seem worlds away from the concrete, documentary approach of postwar Rossellini or De Sica, for example, and yet the ethical commitment of neorealism is still very much alive in him. Zavattini's notion of a "cinema of inquiry"[37] in search of the truth about contemporary Italy has simply been transferred from the level of theme to that of visual style,[38] but the impulse to reexamine and revise the relationship between the observer and the phenomenal world is still as much a concern for Antonioni as for his neorealist predecessors. Indeed, as Umberto Eco argues, Antonioni's points of departure and arrival are always the world "out there"—the fact that his characters are firmly rooted in a given social class,

[37] See Sandro Petraglia, "Cesare Zavattini teorico del neorealismo," in *Il neorealismo cinematografico italiano*, ed. Miccichè, p. 215.

[38] See Tinazzi, *Antonioni*, pp. 30–31.

profession, geographical and temporal setting,[39] and the fact that Antonioni is always "of his times" according to the realist imperative to contemporary subject matter, means that whatever happens within his autonomous aesthetic framework has a bearing on the extracinematic world, if not the direct, political bearing that the neorealists would have, at least an indirect, exemplary one that teaches us to consider an alternative vision and perhaps a new relationship between the self and the world.

But we have strayed far from neorealism indeed when we realize that Antonioni's primary use of film form as the repository of meaning leads naturally to a self-reflexive cinema which constantly scrutinizes its own language until finally, in *Blow-Up*, it questions the very referentiality of the sign.[40] Yet it is a measure of the strength of the realist impulse in postwar Italian cinema that a filmmaker with Antonioni's formalist tendencies does not withdraw into an art-for-art's sake position, or wallow in metacinematic uncertainties, but that he insists on pursuing an extracinematic truth—not the neorealists' documentary truth, but the "transvaluated" truth of the sentiments and of the vision that registers them. When Antonioni writes of *Red Desert*, "it is a less realistic film from a figurative point of view. That is to say it is realistic in a different way,"[41] he is expressing the paradox of an art that is opaque and self-reflexive on the one hand, didactic and *impegnata* (committed) on the other. If Giuliana's fanciful fiction-making can "cure" Valerio of his paralysis, and her spontaneous miniature parable of the birds circumventing the poisonous fumes can point the way to her own truce with the environment, then angst can become art, and art, in turn, can heal.

[39] See Umberto Eco, "Antonioni impegnato," in *Michelangelo Antonioni*, ed. Di Carlo, p. 70.
[40] See Tinazzi, *Antonioni*, pp. 36 and 55.
[41] See Sarris, *Interviews*, p. 28.

PART III

Return to Social Commentary

9   Olmi's *Il posto*: Discrediting the economic miracle

BECAUSE *Il posto* MEETS all the external requirements of neorealism—nonprofessional cast, location shooting, contemporary subject matter, minimal storyline, social criticism, concern for the common people—and because it avoids the stylistic flamboyance of the great 1950s' auteurs, the film has been hailed as a throwback to early neorealism, a return to the "humble, quotidian reality that for at least fifteen years has been at the root of the vitality of Italian cinema."[1] Ermanno Olmi, with his training as a documentarist and his refusal to work in a commercial film industry wedded to "sword and sandal" films and to sequels of the pseudo-anthropological *Mondo cane* (1962), seems to be the ideal standard-bearer for the neorealist revival.[2] In his sense of the filmmaker's public mission, Olmi demonstrates that he is indeed the moral, as well as the technical heir of 1940s neorealism. "Any reality portrayed on the screen demands that the spectator take responsibility for it," he told Charles Thomas Samuels. "Most films subvert culture because they

---

[1] Lizzani, *Il cinema italiano*, pp. 263–64. For other observations on Olmi's return to the precepts of the early neorealists, see Samuels, *Encountering Directors*, p. 99; Leprohon, *The Italian Cinema*, pp. 201–204; Gerald Mast, *A Short History of the Movies* (New York and Indianapolis: Bobbs-Merrill, 1971), p. 360; Armes, *Patterns of Realism*, p. 201; and *Springtime*, ed. Overbey, p. 30.

[2] Olmi made a series of about thirty "industrial documentaries" from 1953 to 1961 for the Edisonvolta electrical company of Milan. For details, see Lino Miccichè, *Il cinema italiano degli anni '60* (Venice, Marsilio, 1975), p. 192. On his refusal to comply with the commercial film industry, see Gideon Bachmann, "Ermanno Olmi: The New Italian Films," *The Nation*, 25 May 1964, 541.

encourage the evasion of responsibility. In my view, society must be made up of responsible men, for those who do not take responsibility for their own lives are ripe to be led by a dictator."[3] Though less programmatic than the neorealists' *impegno* with its encouragement to direct reformatory action, Olmi's concept of artistic responsibility shares with it the same ethical impulse, which resides at the core of all *engagé* art.[4]

Yet his surface adherence to neorealist technique and his moral affinities with neorealist thought should not blind us to the important differences that separate Olmi from his predecessors and make *Il posto* no throwback at all, but a film very much of its time. When critics speak of him as a latter-day De Sica in his poetic rendering of the ordinary, they imply that Olmi took up where the earlier filmmaker left off with *Umberto D*, carrying forward the unfinished experiment of early 1950s neorealism.[5] Such an approach to Olmi's stylistic ancestry is fraught with difficulties, not the least of which is its dismissal of the very reasons for the movement's decline after 1952. If Olmi indeed takes up where De Sica leaves off, how does he manage to avoid the problems of the filmmakers of the mid-1950s who sought to do just that, with the advantage of greater chronological proximity

[3] See Samuels, *Encountering Directors*, p. 104.

[4] Olmi is emphatic about the imperative to a cinema that forces its viewers to accept moral responsibility for their lives. See his interview with Aldo Tassone in *Parla il cinema italiano*, II, 206–207, 210–11, and 213. Olmi refuses, however, to advocate direct reformatory action since he argues that the human predicament is not amenable to an easy political cure. See the same volume, p. 202.

[5] See Leprohon, *The Italian Cinema*, p. 201; Ferrara, "Neorealism: Today," in *Springtime* ed. Overbey, pp. 222–23. Miccichè sees two traditions at work in post-neorealist cinema: the major, Viscontian postwar mode, and the minor one practiced by Castellani and De Sica. See *Il cinema italiano degli anni '60*, p. 192. On the priority of De Sica's influence over that of Rosselini or Visconti on Olmi's brand of neorealism, see Bondanella, *Italian Cinema*, p. 173. Brunetta, however, finds Rossellini the greater influence. See his *Storia*, p. 652.

to the early neorealists and without the distracting examples of the preeminent fifties auteurs to disrupt the continuity of neorealist influence? In other words, how did Olmi escape the twin traps of rosy realism, on the one hand, and "miserablism"—that wallowing in Roman slums in squalor and despair that had mistaken the outward trappings of neorealism for its inner substance—on the other?[6] Indeed, what kept him from making the kind of mistake that De Sica and Zavattini made with *Il tetto*, their own well-meaning, if tired attempt to continue in the spirit of *Umberto D*? Furthermore, if neorealism first arose in response to a concrete set of historical circumstances, how could the ten years of political and economic changes which separate *Umberto D* from *Il posto* not bring with it the need for aesthetic changes of a corresponding order?

A plot summary reveals the simplicity, even the banality, of subject matter which has prompted critics to see in Olmi the successor to neorealist De Sica. *Il posto* tells the story of Domenico Cantoni, a young man from a working-class family in the small town of Meda, who applies for a white-collar job in a large Milanese corporation. After a long but not very arduous day of examinations in which Domenico meets Antonietta, another candidate for employment, he is awarded a position in the firm. His good luck is compounded by the discovery that Antonietta, too, has been hired. Domenico's hopes are doubly dashed, however, when he is assigned to a department remote from hers, and is temporarily denied the white-collar position of his dreams for an interim job as errand boy. The film reaches its climax at the company-sponsored New Year's Eve party which Domenico attends in the

[6] Films exemplifying this trend include Pasolini's *Accattone* (1961), *Mamma Roma* (1962), and Paolo Heusch's and Brunello Rondi's *Una vita violenta* (1962). On miserablism, see Leprohon, *The Italian Cinema*, p. 195; and Raymonde Borde and André Bouissy, "Le miserabilisme romain," in *Le nouveau cinéma italien* (Lyon: Serdoc, 1963), pp. 18–33.

vain hope of meeting Antonietta. The next day, he is indeed promoted to a clerical post upon the death of a fellow employee.

To take the full measure of the distance separating *Il posto* from early neorealism, let us return to *Bicycle Thief*, since Olmi seems to be bringing some of De Sica's assumptions in that earlier film to their logical conclusions for the Italy of 1961. It is as if we were to visit the Ricci household thirteen years after the events of *Bicycle Thief* to find Antonio not only comfortably employed, but the father of two upwardly mobile sons. In *Il posto*, Olmi offers a visual example of intergenerational mobility as Domenico and his father leave for work one morning, clad in the outfits appropriate to their newly divergent class affiliations. While Domenico wears the fancy new trenchcoat which amounts to a kind of trademark of white-collar elegance (several other applicants for the job were similarly dressed), his father wears the short jacket and beret of the working classes. In an analogous scene from *Bicycle Thief*, both father and son leave for work arrayed in blue-collar attire, since Antonio's job as a poster-hanger represents the pinnacle of his family's class aspirations. Indeed, if Domenico is Bruno grown up, then *Il posto* portrays a world inconceivable to Antonio in 1948, a world in which the job is not just a means of putting bread on the table, but a way of moving up the social scale, of wearing fancy new trenchcoats instead of short jackets and berets. Nor does Domenico's white-collar status represent the height of his family's social ambitions, since his younger brother Franco is being groomed for the even better position to which further schooling will entitle him, at his older brother's expense. When questioned by the boss about why he quit school to come to work, Domenico explains "I have a little brother . . .," suggesting that it is Franco who will take the family's potential for social mobility to its highest realization.

But *Il posto* is far from a celebration of Antonio Ricci's

dream for job security and social status as De Sica portrays it in *Bicycle Thief*. When Domenico finally lands the coveted office position and his eyes open wide in disbelief as the sounds of the mimeograph machine overwhelm the soundtrack, he has belatedly come to realize what Olmi has been intimating all along, that this secure job so vaunted by his parents is simply a way of marking time—the interval between the bells for lunch and for dismissal, or in Domenico's case, the interval between adolescence and retirement.[7] In the phrase "un posto sicuro per tutta la vita" ("a secure position for an entire lifetime") the first part of the proposition negates the second, for the stasis implied by job security is no life at all, but a kind of suspended animation which finds its fitting fulfillment in death. Nothing better demonstrates this criticism than the office itself, whose absence of specified function (we never know what the company produces and what these particular office workers do) makes it an abstract emblem of the bureaucratic life sentence to which Domenico is condemned at the end of the film. Until then, Domenico had been consigned to a temporary position as an errand boy, stationed outside the office proper, waiting for a vacancy to arise within its more prestigious ranks. When the opening occurs, what should be a triumphant moment for Domenico, and for the film, becomes a devastating one, as it brings the awful revelation that death is the dynamizing force of the bureaucracy. Domenico's opportunity comes not because someone has been promoted into a higher department (this apparently is never the case) but because someone has died, and since the order of desks represents the hierarchy of positions within the office, there is a terrific scuffle when everyone advances one place as soon as the dead man's "debris" is removed. Neither does promotion reward merit, nor does it entail new powers and duties—it simply means a better lamp and a desk

[7] Mast notes the grim wit of the human "duplication" that the final image of the mimeograph machine betokens. See *A Short History*, p. 360.

closer to the front.[8] But Olmi puts added bite into this anti-bureaucratic satire by positioning the dead man's desk at the head of the office—the place to which all aspire—in the bitter suggestion that death is the final promotion and the closest biological equivalent to the condition of life in the bureaucracy. Even though the dead man had been a practicing novelist in his spare time, implying a secret life far more vivid and gratifying than that of the workplace, his creative efforts are doomed to suffer the same fate as his office belongings, when the contents of his desk, including Chapter 19 of the novel in progress, are heaped above some file cabinet to be forgotten. Another character for whom the office is the antechamber to death is the pensioner who, after three months of retirement, still comes into work every day, only to nap until minutes before the bell so that he can pride himself on being the first to exit for lunch.

In its antibureaucratic satire, *Il posto* goes beyond a specific institution in a specific social context and finally beyond bureaucracy itself to consider the universal human longing for security and status within a preordained hierarchical structure. Throughout the film, such a need is manifest at the lowest as well as the highest levels of bureaucratic operations. Indeed, the first to demonstrate the differential responses befitting the various gradients of the hierarchy is the doorman, who greets the boss with obsequious bowings and scrapings, answers Domenico in an abrupt and perfunctory way, and dismisses with a shrug of the shoulders the pauper who mistakes the office building for the headquarters of the municipal welfare authorities. In the next sequence, a middle-aged errand "boy" vents his outrage at being asked to do something that he considers beneath his professional dignity. "I may be a page, but I'm not a servant," he explains to his colleague, insisting that his duties do not include getting snacks for the higher-ups. The same two errand boys reappear later

[8] On the meaning of the order of desks in the political context of the office, see Olmi's explanation in Tassone, *Parla il cinema, II*, pp. 202–203.

in the film, just as Domenico is about to receive his job placement, and now they are busy discussing the contents of their sandwiches. Soon after the second introduction to the idle, self-important population of errand boys, we learn that Domenico is temporarily assigned to their ranks, dashing his white-collar hopes for the time, replacing his trenchcoat with the pseudo-military array of the custodial staff. To learn the errand boy's trade, Domenico is apprenticed to Sartori, who enjoys having a captive audience for his platitudinous humor ("my wife kisses me once a month—on payday," "trust anyone—with two heads") and a co-conspirator in his refusal to work ("let the bell ring, when they're tired of ringing it, they'll stop," "let them pick up the mail themselves"). Of all Domenico's superiors, Sartori is the most enviable because the most free, defying bells and summonses, and enjoying the liberty to move about the corridors while his higher-ups are pinioned to their ill-lit desks. The closer to the top of the hierarchy we get, the less happy and the less human the characters become, until we arrive at the baronial boss of the entire technical department who never once deigns to look at Domenico during the interview that will launch his career in the firm. Though this imposing figure is the highest embodiment of bureaucratic authority we see in the film, he is himself only one link in a chain of command that extends into some indefinite bureaucratic "beyond."

Such is the power and mystery of this transcendent governing force that Olmi equates it with the ordering principle of his narration, so that it is seen as responsible for generating the sentimental plot of the film and for blocking its successful resolution. Domenico meets Antonietta because they are both taking the entrance exam for the job and they meet again because they are both hired. When Antonietta whispers to Domenico "we are accepted . . . all those others . . ." looking around at the sadly reduced numbers in the same room that had been so crowded on the day of the exam, the suggestion is that the company's winnowing out process helps to further the protagonist's romantic ambitions as well as his vocational ones. But by assigning Antonietta to a department remote from Domenico's and even worse, by failing to synchronize their schedules, the same invisible bureaucratic intelligence that ordained the couple's meeting presents obstacles to those daily encounters that so nourish the course of affection. Domenico eats one hour before Antonietta, and exits from the plant fifteen minutes after she does so that no sooner is the romantic plot set in motion by the *deus ex machina* of the bureaucracy than it is blocked by the same seemingly superhuman force. When Antonietta fails to appear in the company cafeteria for lunch, a toothless old woman takes an interest in the obviously disappointed Domenico and asks the name and department of his beloved. "Second shift," she concludes, as if giving voice to one of the absolute consequences of natural law. Again, when Domenico awaits Antonietta after work and is met instead by the same old crone who had befriended him at lunch, it is as if the genius of bureaucracy were playing a cruel trick on him, turning the blooming young object of his affections into her antitype in this paragon of experience and physical decay.

One of the anomalies of satire, as Alvin Kernan observes, is its simultaneous pretension to realism and its need to exaggerate, or even distort its subject matter in order to unmask vice.[9] Without the realistic elements, the relationship between satire and its target in the external social order would be considerably weakened, yet without exaggeration, the representation would lose its polemic force. By giving his film the neorealist look, Olmi satisfies the former requirement of the genre, while by stylizing and "storifying" his narration, he is able to realize his satiric assault on the bureaucracy. Upon closer examination, even the film's visual surface exhibits a tension between the straightforward, unobtrusive technique appropriate to realism, and the distorted, exagger-

[9] See Alvin Kernan, *The Cankered Muse: Satire of the English Renaissance* (New Haven: Yale University Press, 1959), p. 23.

ated style required by satire. Three times, for example, Domenico is artificially diminished by a camera which shoots him walking down halls of exaggerated length or facing a boss of exaggerated bulk, in a Kafkaesque commentary on the bureaucracy he is about to join.[10] An aerial shot gives a providential view of the room where the exam takes place, while a low-angle shot idealizes Domenico and Antonietta against the monumental Milanese skyline. Most obtrusive is a *trompe l'oeil* shot of Domenico admiring his errand-boy uniform in what turns out to be a mirror reflection, once the camera backtracks to reveal its trick point of view.

On a narrative level, Olmi posits a similar tension between the rival impulses at the core of the satiric mode. Like a documentary, *Il posto* begins with no credits to distract us from its illusion of reality, showing us instead a boy asleep on a bed in the kitchen of a working-class tenement. In the first words of the film, Domenico's father and mother reveal the conflict between the demands of realism, on the one hand, and those of contrived story on the other. As the father leaves for work, his wife asks him to get some oil, "the usual kind," as if this were any morning in the life of the Cantoni family and we were simply eavesdropping on their daily routine. When Domenico's mother says "the usual kind," she is alluding to the habits and predilections that constitute family life and in so doing, conjures up an entire past, present, and future of small household events which conform to Zavattini's aesthetic of the ordinary.[11] But Domenico's father makes a statement which marks this morning as far from "the usual" and sets the machinery of dramatic plotting in motion. "Make sure he does his best today," he says to his wife, referring to Domenico's candidacy for the job. Though Olmi understates

[10] The Kafka analogy is one of the commonplaces of *Il posto* criticism. See Borde and Bouissy, *Le nouveau cinéma italien*, p. 47, and Tassone, *Parla il cinema*, *II*, p. 202.

[11] On Olmi's preference for "those moments in which nothing happens" and his avoidance of "exceptional moments," see Tassone, *Parla il cinema*, *II*, p. 213.

the dramatic structure of the film by relegating the two most consequential events—Domenico's discovery that he has landed the job, and the death of his colleague—to behind-the-scenes, the film is nonetheless highly "storified," filled with vignettes that imply a wealth of tangential narrations. Among the hordes of job applicants, for example, Olmi manages to single out three characters so vivid that we cannot help fleshing-out in our imaginations the miniature stories suggested by each one. The know-it-all who whispers significantly "psychotechnical exam," as if his mere knowledge of the term made him privy to all kinds of bureaucratic secrets, the mamma's boy whose fur-coated parent squires him through the exam boasting of family "connections," and the older man who insists with exaggerated pride that his name be spelled correctly though he cannot perform the simplest mathematical operations, are all so dramatically suggestive that we cannot resist supplying them with storylines of their own.

Yet even more suggestive are the character sketches of Domenico's potential colleagues whose idiosyncrasies in the office are either explained or complemented by brief narrative forays into their personal lives. It is here that we learn of the novelist's private labors, of Don Luigi's probable ties with the Mafia, of Carletto's operatic exertions at the old folks' home, of the single mother's trials at the hands of her delinquent son, and of the vain man's shame at having his hair cut at home. In this vivid juxtaposition of private story and public life in the office, Olmi's point seems to be that the impersonal, mechanized bureaucracy is made up of intensely human parts, each one capable of generating his or her own versions of *Il posto*, just as the novelist office member quite literally generates stories in his spare time.[12] Thus the stylistic tension inherent in satire between realism on the one hand and contrived dramatic effects on the other finds its thematic

---

[12] On the juxtaposition of these vivid personal vignettes and the drab, routinized workplace, see Bondanella, *Italian Cinema*, p. 174.

equivalent in the tension between the bureaucracy and its implacably human, story-making constituents. It is in the critically acclaimed party sequence that this tension comes to a head, as the guests manage to have a boisterous good time despite the gimmickry and mechanization of the company sponsors.[13] Even though the master of ceremonies admonishes everyone "to have fun" just as the boss might order them to get to work on any other day, and even though the P.A. announces that the front office will allow husbands and fiancés to kiss their partners on the mouth at the stroke of midnight, the revelers still manage to reach a pitch of hilarity and abandon that quite defies the bureaucracy's efforts at control. The party becomes a breeding ground for stories— though not for the particular story of love that Domenico had in mind. Instead, he gets caught in the cross fire of adulterous glances between a self-styled vamp and the escort of a homely young woman. The jilted partner rather good-naturedly takes charge of Domenico and initiates him into the joys of the dance. But when it seems that the human element has finally triumphed over the bureaucracy as the party reaches its height, Olmi's editing suggests otherwise. The cut from the New Year's Eve revelry to the tomblike office—doubly tomblike now that the novelist has died—reveals the victory of bureaucracy and order over the richness and anarchy of human foibles. Appropriately, the film's own narration comes to an end as Domenico is absorbed into the world of the office, abdicating his freedom to choose, to move about, or to participate in the excitement of stories.

Though we have identified with Domenico's romantic hopes all along, Olmi has not let us share his vocational ones, for we have been biased against the bureaucracy from the moment that Domenico set foot in the glass and chrome monolith in downtown Milan. But it is during the course of the entrance exam that Olmi's perspective most obviously and

---

[13] On this celebrated scene, see Leprohon, *The Italian Cinema*, p. 201.

irreversibly splits off from Domenico's.[14] Like any long and involved selection process, its effect is to make the job seem more desirable in the candidates' eyes, while the silliness of the procedure reveals Olmi's judgment of the bureaucracy to which it gives access. The exam includes one simple math question, for which an entire hour is allotted, an essay (we are not made privy to the topic), and the pretentiously titled "psychotechnical" test involving a questionnaire to screen out homosexuals, alcoholics, bed-wetters, and manic-depressives. Domenico falters in the exam when he fails to act in a sufficiently mechanical way, answering "sometimes" to yes or no questions, and anticipating exercise orders ("palms up, palms down") before the orders are actually given. Though Domenico calls the exam "weird" when discussing it with Antonietta at the bus stop, this does not lead him to question the institution that authorizes such a selection process, nor to see the process as a distillation of the governing principles of corporate life. This would be to ascribe Olmi's viewpoint to Domenico in a fusing of perspectives that would prevent the protagonist from playing the naive *eiron* so necessary an agent of the low-norm satire that Northrop Frye describes.[15] But it is this very disparity of perspectives, and by extension, the satiric mode of the film itself, which makes the relationship between *Il posto* and neorealism a qualified one. A cardinal rule of literary and cinematic neorealism had been the abolition of authorial aloofness, which had characterized the prewar arts, now that the commonality of national experiences surrounding Fascism, the Resistance, and reconstruction had mandated a collective voice to recount the stories of the times. It is inconceivable, for example, that Rossellini would ever interpose an ironic distance between himself and Pina, Manfredi, or Don Pietro, for to do so would be to question their individual commitments to freedom and jus-

[14] On Olmi's dual perspective, see Mast, *A Short History*, p. 360; and Liehm, *Passion and Defiance*, p. 203.
[15] See *The Anatomy of Criticism*, p. 226.

9. *Domenico (Alessandro Panzeri, center) waits with the other applicants on the morning of the entrance examination for the job.*

tice, and therefore to impugn the entire Resistance movement which was the sum total of such popular stirrings. There
is in *Bicycle Thief*, however, one episode in which a divergence of perspectives is momentarily introduced, only to be
dismissed in the renewed urgency of our identification with
Antonio's quest. This is the restaurant scene in which the
Riccis are seated next to a wealthy family for whom money
is obviously no object in the pursuit of culinary pleasures.
Though food and drink have restored Antonio's flagging
spirits, he grows morose at the spectacle of such carefree
consumption at the next table. "To pay for a meal like that,"
he tells Bruno, "you'd have to earn . . . I don't know . . .
about a million a month." Though the camera is relentless
in showing the vulgarity and ostentation of these middle-class
family members, Antonio is all admiration for their affluence, oblivious to the political reasons for which De Sica and
Zavattini take them to task. A similar authorial judgment
had been made on the wealthy dispensers of charity at the
paupers' church, but this did not entail an ironic division of
perspectives, for Antonio had no aspirations to their station,
seeing them only as obstacles to his search for the thief. The
family in the restaurant, on the other hand, obviously represents a goal for Antonio's material strivings, and not an
object lesson for him in the abominations of the capitalist
system, as De Sica and Zavattini would have it. Antonio is
neither the Marxist that his membership in the trade union
might suggest, nor the social critic that De Sica's camera is,
but the unquestioning product of a society that rewards power
and wealth with more power and wealth, and excludes those
outside the economic treadmill from ever setting foot on it.
Since he will never accede to the next table in the restaurant,
De Sica need not prolong this momentary disparity between
his perspective, which comes from direct knowledge of the
meaning of affluence, and Antonio's, which comes from the
want of it.

But Domenico will some day be seated at the next table in

the restaurant, and therefore his story invites the sustained split perspective that Antonio's and Umberto D's warranted only fitfully. What revolution never accomplished, the economic miracle did, yet at such an ideological price that the unified neorealist perspective was forever ruptured. The achievement of mass prosperity without the attendant political ideals of justice and equality for which the partisans and the early neorealists fought sets a latter-day neorealist like Olmi apart from his characters, who are so dazzled by the display of consumer items in the shop windows of downtown Milan that they unwittingly sell their souls for more purchasing power. Satire is one of the luxuries of this society whose heroic postwar past forbade a critical perspective on its protagonists, but whose newly acquired prosperity demands it.

If Olmi's cinema is to be compared to De Sica's neorealist work, we would do well then to insist that the younger director be seen not as a throwback to an earlier era, but as a modernizer of it, who understands the aesthetic of *Bicycle Thief* and *Umberto D* and updates it for the Italy of 1961. That internal tendency which spelled the end of orthodox neorealism—the splitting off of the authorial perspective from that of the protagonists, momentarily in *Bicycle Thief*, more frequently and drastically in *Umberto D*, becomes the basis of Olmi's approach in *Il posto* where a lack of shared cultural values makes the early neorealist consensus an impossibility for Restoration Italy.[16]

It is the deterioration of the work ideal which constitutes Olmi's most devastating commentary on the Restoration, given the sovereign status that human labor occupies in the filmmaker's hierarchy of activities. "The world of work, the men

[16] Olmi puts it another way when he departs from the early neorealists in his insistence on authorial intervention. "There are many ways to translate reality: one can hide oneself before it, as the first neorealists do—Rossellini, De Sica—or one can force oneself to give it a meaning through editing. I belong to this second category." Tassone, *Parla il cinema*, II, p. 181.

who work. I think that I'll never tire of this extraordinary theme that subsumes so many others."[17] Olmi's emphasis on the work ideal is a measure of the failure of a society that cannot offer meaningful employment to its populace, substituting bureaucratic busywork for the proud products of genuine human labor. Yet Olmi's point is less to map out revolutionary correctives to the social ills he documents than to use "the medium to explore our problems."[18] "We are living in a particularly historic moment," he told Gideon Bachmann. "We have left behind a rural culture . . . and we are going toward a new civilization which we don't yet understand. . . . The discomfort we feel is caused by the fact that we are not yet capable of mastering the reality we now confront of balancing our spirit with our physical environment. Our new films express this."[19] In Domenico's accession to manhood, Olmi is figuring Italy's economic coming of age, but like the culture that psychologically lags behind its material development, Domenico clings to adolescence. "You're a big boy now. You're going to work," his mother reminds Domenico as he atavistically bickers with his younger brother over the ownership of a schoolbook strap. In his daily commute from the small town of Meda to the big city for work, Domenico recapitulates the creeping urbanization which will transform Italy into a modern, industrialized nation on a par with her neighbors to the north. But Domenico's provincial innocence ill prepares him for life in the big city, where he flounders in the coffee shop and must follow Antonietta's knowledgeable movements in handling cup and saucer. "Domenico suits you," Antonietta says later at the bus stop. "You're old-fashioned like your name." Even Domenico's hometown of Meda is undergoing the change from rural vil-

[17] See *Film*, 1962, ed. Vittorio Spinazzola (Milan: Feltrinelli, 1962), p. 170. According to Brunetta, Olmi is the director most qualified to document the postreconstruction Italian workplace by virtue of his own decade-long employment at Edisonvolta. See his *Storia*, pp. 652–53.

[18] Bachmann, "Ermanno Olmi," p. 542.

[19] Ibid.

lage to bedroom suburb of industrialized Milan.[20] As Domenico and Franco make their way to the train station that first morning, the spectacle of a horse-drawn plow juxtaposes the rural prehistory of the town with its technological present and future. "We live in an atmosphere of uneasiness, of worried expectation," Olmi told Bachmann, "and only through accidental openings do we see a glimmer of our new, future lives."[21] Domenico's future is embodied in the withered, frustrated examples of his new colleagues in the inner office, just as his family past is embodied in his worker father and, still further back, in the peasant ancestors implied by the horse-drawn plow of Meda. "Does the future present itself to you without hope?" the psychologist at the entrance exam had asked. In the final image of the film, Domenico's eyes give their own answer to this question as they contemplate the bitter fulfillment of Antonio Ricci's unrealized dreams.

[20] As Olmi told Samuels, the film is set in the suburbs of Milan, which used to be an agrarian zone. Consequently, Domenico's ancestors were probably farm workers there. See *Encountering Directors*, p. 111. On the urbanization of the peasant population and the consequences of upward mobility, see Olmi's remarks in Tassone, *Parla il cinema, II*, pp. 215–16.

[21] Bachmann, "Ermanno Olmi, p. 542.

I0 Germi's *Seduced and Abandoned*: Inside the honor code

NOTHING COULD BE further from the spare, austere aesthetics of *Il posto* than the teeming, baroque one of *Seduced and Abandoned*, whose density of plot, exuberance of style, and overall triumph of artifice distance it radically from the neorealist revival that Olmi's film was said to herald.[1] Indeed, neorealism is never invoked by critics of *Seduced and Abandoned*, unless it is to lament how far Germi has fallen from the neorealist promise of his early career, or to marvel that someone who could make such ideologically committed films as *In the Name of the Law* (1949) or *The Path of Hope* (1950) could immediately thereafter embark on such blatantly commercial ventures as *The City Defends Itself* (1951) or *The President-Lady* (1952).[2] In *Divorce Italian Style* (1961) and *Seduced and Abandoned* (1963) Germi returned to Sicily, the setting for his two neorealist works, but this time it was to make the films that would give him an international reputation as an entertainer of the first order—a reputation that was to motivate at least one critic retrospectively to see in Germi's neorealist films hints of the commercial concessions and the love of spectacle that marred his early 1950s production and culminated in his great box office triumphs of the 1960s.[3] Indeed, if we look at *In the Name of the Law* and *The Path of Hope* in the light of his later commercial

---

[1] According to Kernan, this crowded, teeming quality is intrinsic to satire. See *The Cankered Muse*, pp. 7–8.

[2] See Gianni Rondolino, *Dizionario del cinema italiano, 1945–69* (Turin: Einaudi, 1969), p. 158.

[3] Thus Bruno Torri sees in the early work of both Germi and De Santis a regressive and vitiating tendency to console and placate audiences by surrendering to their desire for spectacle. See *Cinema italiano*, pp. 38–39.

ventures, we can see how much the neorealist idea was compromised even then by the presence of active, effectual heroes and satisfying resolutions to the most unyielding social problems.[4]

In fact, the happy ending of *In the Name of the Law* is so at variance with the governing precepts of small-town Sicilian life that it contradicts Germi's own expository statements in the publicity material surrounding the film. "For the great part, it is scorched and arid," wrote Germi of Sicily, "a land where men live like anchorites in accordance with ancient, changeless customs."[5] If this is the case, how are we to be convinced that a judge from mainland Italy, newly arrived in the Sicilian town of Capodarso, can liberate the entire populace from subjugation to the combined tyranny of Mafia and feudal control which has victimized the inhabitants for centuries? Yet this is what Germi asks us to believe when the judge, Guido Schiavi, played by the popular star Massimo Girotti, conducts a public murder trial and wins the support of the whole town, as well as its Mafia leaders, to the cause of civil justice and rule by law.[6] The ending is such a falsification of the social and political issues Germi raises that it virtually cancels out the film's original *engagé* stance. When Fellini and Zavattini speak of the immorality, or at least the impropriety, of happy endings, they do so because films that pretend to resolve unresolvable problems lull the public into a false sense of complacency based on the belief that the world will conform to its fictional counterpart on the screen.[7] Germi's *impegno* is thus not only neutralized, but transformed into its ideological opposite in escapist solutions that encourage the public to abdicate responsibility for the real consequences of the problems so blithely dismissed.

Paradoxically, Germi feels no such need to sugar the pill

[4] See Leprohon, *The Italian Cinema*, p. 120.
[5] Quoted in Armes, *Patterns of Realism*, p. 135.
[6] Armes, *Patterns of Realism*, p. 137.
[7] See *Fellini on Fellini*, pp. 150–51; and Zavattini, "Some Ideas on the Cinema," p. 223.

in two unabashedly commercial films of his 1960s satiric production. Though *Divorce Italian Style* and *Seduced and Abandoned* lack the seriousness of neorealist form that typified *In the Name of the Law* and *The Path of Hope*, they do not oversimplify their social themes, nor do they offer facile solutions to the problems they unflinchingly confront. No one lives happily ever after in Germi's satiric Sicilian world, where Peppino Califano seduces and impregnates Agnese Ascalone but refuses to marry her because she is no longer chaste. *Seduced and Abandoned* chronicles the antics of both families to salvage their respective honor according to a code that entitles Peppino to wed a virgin while requiring that Agnese's waywardness be concealed from public notice by marriage to her seducer. To further complicate matters, Peppino is already engaged to Matilde, Agnese's older sister who, according to the Sicilian custom of marrying off daughters in chronological order, must be wed first. Fortunately, the girls' father, Don Vincenzo Ascalone, is able to arrange a hasty match between Matilde and the Baron Rizieri Zappala, an aristocrat fallen on hard times, whose crumbling palace ceiling has failed to hold up under his various attempts to hang himself from it. Except for a few rotten teeth, the Baron makes a presentable partner for Matilde, who accepts his offer of marriage once the new dentures are in place. Peppino, meanwhile, is hiding out in the village of Regalbutto in an effort to escape Don Vincenzo's marital pressures. To avenge his family's honor, Don Vincenzo sends his son Antonio to kill Peppino in a crime of passion that will land him a maximum of five years in jail, but Agnese overhears the plans and reports them to the police. In a tumultuous scene before the local magistrate, Peppino's guilt is established and he is imprisoned. Convinced by his parents that a criminal record would not enhance his career aspirations, Peppino relents and agrees to marry Agnese. Now it is Don Vincenzo's turn to play hard-to-get as he forces the Califanos to make all kinds of public protestations of Peppino's new marital hopes. This involves a carefully staged "kidnapping" of Agnese before the eyes of the entire town. Now it is Agnese who rejects the match in an anguished gesture of self-assertion which results in physical and psychological collapse. Under the strain of it all, Don Vincenzo falls mortally ill, but refuses to let his death impede the nuptials to which Agnese has finally given her assent.

Though marriage may constitute the socially therapeutic ending of classical comic plot structure, as indeed it constitutes an amnesty for all manner of felonous behavior according to the penal code in *Seduced and Abandoned*, it will not offer a future of romantic bliss to Peppino and Agnese, for whom the wedding vows are a capitulation to the tyrannous code of familial honor. When Peppino slips the wedding band on Agnese's finger and she winces, she is reacting as much to the physical pain of too small a ring put on by too rough a husband, as to the emotional pain of consecrating a bad marriage. Nor is the effect of the ceremony limited to the unfortunate couple itself. In a parody of the classical comic ending, which should include all of the society in its affirmation of unity and the renewal of the social contract, Agnese's and Peppino's wedding has the opposite kind of ripple effect, sowing death and destruction in its wake. Thus Don Vincenzo dies, the Baron Rizieri tries once more in vain to hang himself from the crumbling ceiling of his decrepit estate, and Matilde ends up taking monastic vows as a last resort in a mystical version of the wedding ceremony being enacted by her sister and her ex-fiancé. Had he so chosen, Germi could have easily devised a comic ending in the classical tradition which would make his film the entertaining romp in quaint Sicilian social customs that many critics expected it to be. He could have allowed Peppino and Agnese to fall in love after all, so that their forced marriage would coincide with their own deepest wishes, despite the inhuman and mechanical requirements of the honor code. Such a comic ending would make the film an unproblematic consumer item which would exploit Sicilian mores for their entertainment value alone and leave the public free from any distressing afterthoughts about social injustice. But instead, there is no happy resolution to placate the public conscience, and viewers leave the movie theater all the more disturbed because the generic indicators of the film had not prepared them for such seriousness of purpose.

Though critics have faulted Germi for his lighthearted treatment of these grave issues, it is the very incongruity of tone and subject matter that makes his argument so striking and forceful.[8] For Germi, laughter is not an end in itself, it is a weapon used to attack a system whose assumptions are taken to ludicrous extremes the better to demonstrate their folly and vice. "Such people there are living and flourishing in the world—Faithless, Hopeless, Charityless," said Thackeray in *Vanity Fair*. "Some there are, and very successful, too, mere quacks and fools: and it was to combat and expose such as those, no doubt, that Laughter was made."[9]

It is the satiric mode that frees Germi to register the kind of social criticisms he was unable to make in his two avowedly neorealist films. If Germi is an incorrigible crowd-pleaser, as critics suggest, then that impulse to play to the audience which led him to *divismo* and to happy endings in his neorealist films is already discharged in *Divorce Italian Style* and *Seduced and Abandoned* by the gags and the intrigues of the plot. Having entertained his audience through such formal devices, Germi can then allow himself to engage in serious social commentary. Indeed, *Seduced and Abandoned* may be interpreted as Germi's palinode on his neorealist period and as a corrective to the false heroics and the facile resolutions that marred his good intentions in *In the Name of the Law* and *The Path of Hope*. *Seduced and Abandoned* offers a de-

<hr/>

[8]See *Commonweal*, 24 July 1964, 514; Robert Hatch, *The Nation*, 27 July 1964, 40; and Hollis Alpert, *Saturday Review*, 11 July 1964, 22–23.

[9]See William Makepeace Thackeray, *Vanity Fair* (New York: New American Library, 1962), p. 96.

flated, ineffectual, middle-aged version of the handsome young judge who came from the mainland to bring law and order to the Sicilians of *In the Name of the Law.* Whereas the judge in this neorealist film was not only the protagonist of the piece, but its hero in the true sense of the word—potent enough to change centuries of allegiances to Mafia and feudal power—the judge in *Seduced and Abandoned* is relegated to a minor role as a man incapable of replacing the primeval code of honor with anything resembling the rule of law. Though we are not told that he is an outsider to Sicilian culture, his intolerance of the islanders' baroque antics ("let's not dramatize") and his correction of Sicilian usage ("say *pranzo*, not *colazione*" for the noon meal) suggests that he is not a native product of the society he has come to judge. This demoted, powerless, aged version of the hero in *In the Name of the Law* amounts to a retraction, on Germi's part, of his earlier optimism and a surrender to the intransigence of the culture he no longer presumes to see changed.

But this judge represents more than simply a reworking of Germi's cinematic past—he is also a measure of the historical perspective that the filmmaker brings to his social analysis, giving the film deeper neorealist affinities than its slick, commercial surface would ever lead us to expect. By making *Seduced and Abandoned* no mere static representation of social custom, but an explanation of the historic conditions that made Sicily an outpost of reaction, the film conforms to Lukács's and Aristarco's requirements for critical realism. In the title *pretore* (magistrate) displayed prominently on the judge's door, Germi condenses some 2,200 years of Sicilian history—a history of domination by foreign powers and of permanent enmity between the populace and the ruling elite. When the Romans conquered Sicily in 241 B.C. they sent military governors or *praetores* to impose Roman law on the islanders. In the succeeding history of colonial subjugation to wave after wave of foreign rule, the enforcers of the law, be they Arabs, Normans, French, or Spanish, were always seen as outsiders whose interests were not those of the Sicilians and whose authority was borne with indifference, if not outright hostility. In the face of constant external threats to the culture's integrity, Sicilians became rigidly conservative, clinging to their traditions with a tenacity bordering on fanaticism. Even when the island was wedded to the mainland in the Risorgimento, Sicily's habit of cultural introversion remained intact and the age-old suspicions held sway, as Prince Fabrizio of *The Leopard* tells the Piedmontese emissary, Chevally, when the latter comes to inform him of his nomination to a seat in the new national senate. "Having been trampled by a dozen different peoples," Fabrizio says of the Sicilians,

> they consider they have an imperial past which gives them a right to a grand funeral. Do you really think, Chevally, that you are the first who has hoped to channel Sicily into the flow of universal history? I wonder how many Moslem imams, how many of King Roger's knights, how many Swabian scribes, how many Angevin barons, how many jurists of the Most Catholic King have conceived the same fine folly, and how many Spanish viceroys too, how many of Charles III's reforming functionaries! And who knows now what happened to them all! Sicily wanted to sleep in spite of their invocations, for why should she listen to them if she herself is rich, if she's wise, if she's civilized, if she's honest, if she's admired and envied by all, if, in a word, she is perfect?[10]

What for Tomasi di Lampedusa requires a lengthy monologue (and this is only a fraction of the entire passage) Germi achieves in a single quip. While both parties of the Ascalone–Califano feud await a judicial hearing, they temporar-

[10]See Giuseppe Tomasi di Lampedusa, *The Leopard*, trans. Archibald Colquhoun (New York: Pantheon, 1960), pp. 212–13.

ily put aside hostilities as Don Vincenzo exclaims, "We have only one enemy," with an eye to the sign *pretore* on the magistrate's door. Before this embodiment of Roman law, the Sicilian parties to the dispute are united in their suspicion of a foreign ruling authority, preferring to keep silent according to the code of *omertà* and settle their accounts at home. "My family has an unimpeachable reputation," Don Vincenzo boasts later to the judge. "We've had a few violent deaths, but they've always been settled outside the law."

Though the richest in historical implications, the magistrate is by no means the only "foreigner" to watch the action in mute and impotent astonishment. There are two other official figures who share his outsider's perspective: the *carabiniere* marshal whose accent betrays his Roman provenance, and his assistant Bisigato whose youth and Trevisan origins suggest that he is a young draftee doing his military service in the South. If the marshal's extensive knowledge and tolerance of Sicilian folkways make him the spokesman for Germi's point of view within the film, and Bisigato's naiveté makes him the internal embodiment of our own perspective, then it is through their several exchanges that Germi is able to address us in a direct, comic-didactic way. "She says *no* and you write down *no*," the marshal says to Bisigato as the young man records Agnese's deposition. "You think you're in Treviso. Here *no* sometimes means *yes*," and vice versa we might add, after Agnese answers with an anguished affirmative when asked by the magistrate if she consents to the marriage with Peppino. Later, as the marshal and Bisigato deliberately leave town so the carefully contrived kidnapping of Agnese can take place without police intervention, the older officer explains to his assistant, "you are thinking, and you must not think. Marriage extinguishes all crime." When the marshal puts his hand over the Sicilian part of the map of Italy and says "better, much better" (he does so twice in the course of the film) and when Bisigato is surprised by the camera in expressions of shocked disbelief during the hearing before the *pretore*, these reactions become mirrors of our own.

Were our perspective to remain aligned with that of the three non-Sicilian officials, then there would be nothing to detract from our comic pleasure in the machinations of this plot. Nor would there be any substance to the criticism that the comedy is marred by the violence of Don Vincenzo against his pregnant daughter.[11] Indeed, were we able to regard the Sicilians as radically "other," then we would maintain the emotional detachment prerequisite to comic pleasure, as Freud describes it. "The comic is greatly interfered with if the situation from which it ought to develop gives rise at the same time to a release of strong affect," he wrote in *Jokes and Their Relation to the Unconscious*. "For this reason it has been said that the comic feeling comes easiest in more or less indifferent cases where the feelings and interests are not strongly involved."[12] It is Agnese, of course, who does not allow us the luxury of such comic detachment. We sympathize with her not only because she is the sacrificial victim that her name suggests (Agnese = lamblike), but because she dares to violate the codes of her culture, going to the police to report the impending showdown between Peppino and her brother Antonio in defiance of the principle of *omertà*. In the delirium that precedes her final acceptance of the forced marriage with Peppino, she raves about escaping to Milan to become a servant, putting the greatest possible geographical and social distance between herself and her upper middle-class Sicilian roots. But Agnese is also very much of her culture, as Germi suggests during the opening titles of the film where her odyssey through the town weds her visually to it, with her black dress that accents the chiaroscuro effects of the sun-drenched streets, and her Greek profile that exempli-

[11] See Hatch, Review of *Seduced and Abandoned*, p. 40.
[12] See Sigmund Freud, *Jokes and Their Relation to the Unconscious*, trans. James Strachey (New York: Norton, 1963), p. 220.

10. *Agnese (Stefania Sandrelli) breaks the Sicilian code of silence before the law by informing authorities of her brother's intention to murder her seducer.*

fies its tradition of Hellenic beauty. Indeed, only when she conforms to the dictates of her culture do we laugh at her— when she sleeps on a penitential bed of rocks, for example, or when she composes a letter to Peppino written in the purple prose of a sermon against concupiscence ("my sin . . . was to surrender to lust . . ."). It is the ambiguity of Agnese's position as willing victim of her culture, on the one hand, and a willful challenger of it, on the other, that gives Germi's satire its polemic force. Were Agnese merely a victim of the honor code, our comic detachment from her would be complete, and she would remain as remote from us as those other victims, Matilde and the Baron, sharing with them the self-delusions and the illogic that make the Sicilian characters as a group so radically "other." Were she successfully rebellious, however, and had she managed to escape to Milan, or at least to the mainland, according to her delirious wish-fulfillment fantasy, then the impact of Germi's social criticism would be considerably weakened and the film would become quite literally escapist. Instead, as the one Sicilian with whom we can identify, and as the one most tragically victimized by her society, Agnese maximizes the force of Germi's satiric attack.

The resulting sense of *impegno* is not all that allies *Seduced and Abandoned* with its neorealist predecessors. Despite the slick commercial exterior of the film, it shares a formal common denominator with neorealism in the regional theater that played so important a part in the ancestry of *Open City*. Indeed, the closest stylistic analogues to the highly verbal, thickly plotted, gimmicky satires of Germi would be the vernacular comedies of the de Filippos, for example, who make social customs their prime subject matter and local color their source of appeal. Though the brevity and density of its scenes and the plethora of visual jokes would be obstacles to putting *Seduced and Abandoned* on the stage, minor editing and shifts of emphasis would do little to mar the overall dramatic effect, and the theatrical medium might actually enhance the busy, teeming quality of Germi's technique. In fact, *Seduced and Abandoned* is not only good theater, it is also *about* theater—the theatrical nature of Sicilian public life in general, and the theatrical maneuvers necessitated by the honor code in particular. Like Saliena of *Bread, Love, and Fantasy*, Germi's town offers the perfect setting for public spectacle, with its stage-like piazzas, its ready-made audiences at every street corner, and its penchant for gossip and scandal. Don Vincenzo is the stage director par excellence who takes fullest advantage of these indigenous dramatic possibilities for spreading abroad an idealized family image at great variance with the private truths which threaten to dishonor the Ascalone name. Thus the evening promenade serves as a kind of family bulletin in which Matilde's new status as the Baron's fiancée is broadcast to the town. Similarly, the serenade is used to publicize Peppino's courtship of Agnese as Don Vincenzo reveals when he asks the accompanist to turn up the volume on his electric guitar so that the whole town can hear his performance and draw the appropriate conclusions. Furthermore, when Peppino's parents finally agree to his marriage with Agnese, Don Vincenzo makes sure that they voice their consent loudly and openly for the greatest possible public consumption. In a more spontaneous performance, Don Vincenzo orders his family to laugh boisterously after leaving the *pretore*'s office to show their contempt for, and immunity to, such legal procedures. "If you don't laugh, I'll smash your face in," he adds under his breath, marching the family to an ice cream parlor to celebrate their alleged triumph over the law. Of course, the most elaborate staging of all surrounds the kidnapping of Agnese, which is nearly bungled when the wrong Ascalone daughter is seized by Peppino's henchmen. The subsequent reconciliation between the groom-to-be and his prospective father-in-law is just as carefully staged. "First I slap you, then you kiss my hand, then I forgive you," Don Vincenzo tells Peppino before the entire town, which has gathered to witness a religious procession in the piazza outside the Ascalone front door. As the family emerges on the second-story balcony to greet the crowds and to indicate that their honor has been salvaged, Agnese's expression betrays neither joy nor sorrow, but the same remoteness that is painted on the face of the angelic icon being carried in the procession below. Like the statue, Agnese, too, will find her place at the altar as the unwilling bride of Peppino and the sacrificial victim of her family's honor.

Such is the impulse to theatricality that no audience need be present at all to justify a dramatic recitation, as Peppino reveals in his virtuoso one-man performance of guilt and self-abasement. On the pretext of studying, Peppino has cloistered himself in his room with several days' growth of beard on his face and the radio blaring at top volume. "Who are you?" Peppino asks of his image in the cracked mirror above his bureau, "a man or a louse?" "You disgust me," he concludes, spitting at the reflection by way of proof. As if the sleazy, musical commentary were not enough to make us question the depth of Peppino's remorse, the speed with which he responds to the sudden arrival of the prostitutes in town— he requests 5,000 lire of his mother and races to the local hotel to be first in line for their services—casts some doubt on the sincerity of his recent penitential performance. But when Peppino meets his father-in-law-to-be in the lobby of the same hotel, still another performance is required of him. Now he must mask his true motives for being there and act the part of the serious-minded young aspirant to professional advancement, loudly asking the hotel clerk if Dr. Schiavone, his professor of forensic medicine, has arrived. Meanwhile, Don Vincenzo himself had been engaged in a performance of his own in concert with the other town worthies who had gathered to celebrate the prostitutes' arrival. While one self-styled expert in male physiology claims that men have 3,000 bullets to shoot in a lifetime, Don Vincenzo takes this verbal exercise in sexual exhibitionism to another order of magnitude when he argues that a real man shoots one bullet per day between the age of eighteen and sixty, making his arsenal at least five times greater than the earlier speaker would have it. Any slight to personal or family honor is imagined as a public performance before an audience of sneering townspeople. Thus, when Matilde reads Peppino's letter of rejection, her first words are "compromised before the entire town," suggesting that she has internalized the choral voice of the community in her own estimation. This psychic appropriation of public opinion is taken to surrealistic extremes in two nightmare sequences: that of Don Vincenzo in which Agnese, dressed as a harlot, is married to a manacled Peppino in court; and that of Agnese herself who hallucinates repeated confrontations with jeering townspeople as she attempts to return home from court.

It is the code of honor that motivates the histrionics of the external actions as well as the inner psychodynamics of Germi's characters. The psyche becomes a stage on which the self performs for the self and that recitation is judged by the imagined standards of the community at large. The Baron, who is indifferent to appearances—he returns the false teeth bought at Don Vincenzo's expense when he realizes how the Ascalone's are using him to salvage the family name—is simply performing for a higher imagined audience, that of his peers, not that of the local populace. As an aristocrat, albeit one who has fallen upon hard times, the Baron's judging public will entertain standards of honor that go beyond those of white teeth, sweet-smelling breath, and indoor plumbing. "In poverty a man's dignity shines through," the Baron told Don Vincenzo on the latter's first visit to the crumbling palace. Later, when he rejects the new dentures, the Baron explains, "I have a dignity that you can't buy at any price," revising Don Vincenzo's exclusively material notion of honor with a concept of human dignity that transcends external appearances. While Don Vincenzo is content as long as the name

on the front door retains its aura of respectability, despite
the fact that behind the door dwell a pregnant, unmarried
girl imprisoned in her room, a cowardly son who develops
boils at the mere thought of revenge, and another daughter
doubly jilted for reasons she'll never know, the Baron has no
front door at all to hide his abject poverty, nor are there any
window curtains to prevent the neighborhood children from
witnessing yet another failed attempt at baronial suicide.

Eventually, the theatrical metaphor for the honor code gives
way to an even more disparaging one when Don Vincenzo
presents his lawyer cousin with a medical report of Agnese's
condition. "Tumor?" asks the cousin. "No, honor," answers
Don Vincenzo in a rhymed near-equivalent which expresses
Germi's own prognosis for the members of a society prey to
the fanaticism and ill-logic of the honor-crazed. Like the tumor, honor is a terminal illness, as Don Vincenzo's funerary
inscription suggests. The obituary "honor and family" carved
on his tombstone could read as the cause of death, as well
as the ideals to which he dedicated his unnaturally shortened
life. Pathology abounds in the story, in Antonio's boil, in
Agnese's delirium, and in Aunt Carmela's litany of symptoms recited with morbid delight before Don Vincenzo's interview with his lawyer cousin. "Lucky you who can eat and
drink," she tells Don Vincenzo and her husband as she serves
them refreshments. "I have gall bladder problems, rheuma-
tism, high blood pressure, and worst of all, I'm constipated."
As a walking textbook of medical symptoms, not only does
Aunt Carmela demonstrate the hypochondria of a culture
excessively interested in the problems of the flesh, but she
becomes the physical embodiment of the moral decay that
requires the elaborate maskings of honor, respectability, and
family name. At the core of it all is emptiness, deterioration,
and death—the emptiness of Don Vincenzo's funerary bust,
the deterioration of everyone's health—mental, dental, and
otherwise—and the suicide to which the honor-crazed con-
sign themselves, whether intentionally or not. In all the mad

scheming and denying, in all the obsession with morbidity and death, what is forgotten is the promise of new life—that of Agnese's future child and of the couple whose eventual marriage should signify a new start in a renewed social order. It is the vast disparity between what marriage should represent in a classical comedy—reconciliation, unification—and what it represents here—the failure of everyone's hopes but Don Vincenzo's—that constitutes Germi's final satiric blow. In fact, the entire plot can be seen as a parody of classic comic structure wherein the couple's marriage is prevented by a blocking figure, usually that of the woman's father, who is finally brought around to accepting, if not sanctioning, the union. Here, instead, the father does everything in his power to facilitate the union, while the blocking figure proves to be the lover, who refuses to marry the lady he himself has seduced because she is no longer chaste. Such a structural analysis of the way in which *Seduced and Abandoned* parodies classical comedy reveals yet one more aspect of Germi's satire: how the ethos of honor literally works against itself in making Don Vincenzo—the proponent of the marriage—and Peppino—its adversary—enemy agents of the same behavioral code.

Indeed, parody emerges as Germi's predominant expressive technique in *Seduced and Abandoned*, governing both its style and its thematic content.[13] In the scene of Antonio's departure for Regalbutto where he will avenge his sister's disgrace, Germi parodies the conventions of the western, while Don Vincenzo's speculations on the identity of Agnese's seducer are borrowed from the stylistic repertory of the thriller. The film even has moments of self-parody when the four Ascalone women strut down the street to the same tempo and music of the earlier prostitutes' promenade, with all the scathing social commentary that such a comparison implies. More elaborately, the film parodies itself in the replay of the

[13] On the prevalence of parody in the satiric mode, see Frye, *Anatomy of Criticism*, p. 233.

original seduction scene according to Peppino's self-serving account of it before the *pretore*. With the slightest shift in detail, Peppino is able to retell the damning episode in his own favor, making Agnese the sleazy, cigarette-smoking predator that he originally was. It is Peppino's misfortune that the effect of parody in general is to reveal how different, and hence inauthentic, the copy is from the original, and to focus our attention on that disparity. Much of the film's humor is predicated on our awareness of the parodic discrepancy between *Seduced and Abandoned* and its generic exemplars in the thriller, the western, and most importantly, the classic comedy. Germi puts this parodic discrepancy to thematic uses by suggesting that the honor code itself deprives the protagonists of the consolations of a true comic resolution.

Those who argue that *Seduced and Abandoned* is too humorous to support the weight of serious social criticism on the one hand, and too serious to permit untrammeled comic pleasure on the other, have missed the point of Germi's satire, which is to parody the conventions of comedy by showing how the honor code blocks its happy issue. In so doing, Germi is able to make the kind of incisive social commentary that his neorealist films paradoxically lacked. Only by manipulating and exploiting the forms of commercial cinema could Germi at once satisfy the need to entertain that made his Sixties satires products of their times,[14] while registering the social criticism that made them worthy vehicles of neorealist *impegno*.

[14] Accordingly, Miccichè calls Germi "the most inspired and brilliant author of the middle-brow film of the first half of the 60's." See *Il cinema italiano degli anni '60*, p. 80.

II Pasolini's *Teorema*: The halfway revolution

"I CONSIDER MY FILMS realist compared with neorealist film," Pasolini told Oswald Stack in 1968, the year of the release of *Teorema*. "In neorealist films, day-to-day reality is seen from a crepuscular, intimistic, credulous, and above all naturalistic point of view. . . . In neorealism, things are described with a certain detachment, with human warmth, mixed with irony—characteristics which I do not have. Compared with neorealism, I think I have introduced a certain realism, but it would be hard to define it exactly."[1] Hard indeed! For a filmmaker who abhors naturalism, who reconstructs everything, who is wedded to mythic archetypes, dreamwork and wish-fulfillment fantasies, it is difficult to fathom Pasolini's logic in designating himself a realist.[2] Three years earlier, in the famous essay, "The Cinema of Poetry," Pasolini had only complicated matters by calling himself a "mythic realist"—a label so anomalous that the adjective and noun virtually cancel each other out, emptying the phrase of any critical usefulness whatsoever.[3] Indeed, if Pasolini's claim to realism is to have any meaning at all, it must be considered in the con-

---

This chapter is a considerably revised version of an essay entitled "Pier Paolo Pasolini's Poetics of Film," *Yale Italian Studies* 1 (Spring 1977), 184–94.

[1] See Oswald Stack, *Pasolini on Pasolini* (Bloomington, Ind.: Indiana University Press, 1970), p. 109.

[2] Ibid., p. 132. The filmmaker is quite vocal about his hatred of naturalism. Also see ibid., p. 133.

[3] Pasolini calls himself a mythic realist in a coy reference to his influence on Bertolucci, "whose structural realism" is "derived from Rossellinian neorealism and the mythic realism of some younger master." Bertolucci was Pasolini's assistant director in *Accattone*. See "The Cinema of Poetry," in *Movies and Methods*, ed. Nichols, p. 554.

text of his criticism of neorealism. "Literary revolutions," Robbe-Grillet once wrote, "have always been made in the name of realism" even when the style that provokes the reaction is itself avowedly realist.[4] Nor is Pasolini the first to claim credit for the passage from neorealism to realism in the cinema, for this had been Aristarco's strategy in defending Visconti's *Senso* against its neorealist detractors in 1954. Unlike Aristarco, however, Pasolini does not invoke Lukács or the nineteenth-century models of critical realism as correctives to the limitations of neorealist practice. In fact, it is precisely such links to the cultural past that Pasolini deplores in neorealism, seeing in it a stylistic throwback to prewar cultural modes. "I remember criticizing neorealism for not having sufficient intellectual strength to transcend the culture which preceded it," Pasolini told Stack, faulting its aesthetics for being naturalistic in the manner of Verga, crepuscular in the manner of Gozzano, subjective and lyricizing in the manner of the prewar arts in general.[5] "So neorealism is a cultural product of the Resistance as regards content and message but stylistically it is still tied to pre-Resistance culture."[6]

To liberate the cinema from its complicity with prewar modes, Pasolini posits an antinaturalist style which gives his images a mythic, quasi-sacred quality by replacing the deep fields and long takes of the neorealists with flattened planes, frontal shots, a static camera, and a fetishistic attachment to the photographic object.[7] What entitles this style to the realist label is not a theory of history, as it was in the case of Visconti, nor a theory of phenomenology, as in the case of Fellini, nor again a psychological approach as in the case of Antonioni, but a semiotic theory, a theory of cinematic

---

[4] Robbe-Grillet, *For a New Novel*, p. 158.
[5] Stack, *Pasolini on Pasolini*, p. 42.
[6] Ibid.
[7] Pasolini talked frequently of the "need to restore an epic and mythological dimension to life, a sense of awe and reverence to the world." Quoted in Stack, *Pasolini on Pasolini*, p. 9. On Pasolini's camera style, see ibid., p. 132, and Miccichè, *Il cinema italiano degli anni '60*, pp. 168–69.

signs, which makes Pasolini a conscious manipulator of the cinema's built-in powers of realist representation. Far from the notion of an Aristotelian mimesis, which Pasolini explicitly repudiates when he disowns any tendency toward naturalism, this theory argues that the lexicon of film images, or "im-segni" coincides with the infinite number of significant images that make up the real world, as well as the world of memory and dream. Unlike linguistic signs, or "lin-segni," which are finite elements in a code, these "im-segni" are countless, uncodified, and pregrammatical. As such, they give film an oneiric quality "by reason of the elementary character of its archetypes (that is, once again, habitual and consequently unconscious observation of environment, gestures, memory, dreams) and of the fundamental pre-eminence of the pre-grammatical character of objects as symbols of the visual language."[8] Even the most conventional narrative film has this "subfilm" of irrational, elementary, and barbaric imagery, "a naturally hypnotic monstrum," which is responsible for the considerable power and appeal of the medium.[9]

Whereas the writer's is a purely stylistic task in that he or she need only select words from an already established lexicon, the filmmaker's is a double task—first linguistic and then

---

[8] "The Cinema of Poetry," p. 547. It should be noted here that Pasolini's theoretical attempts are highly problematic, "often as ambitious as they are generously confused." See Sandro Petraglia, *Pasolini* (Florence: La Nuova Italia, 1974), p. 78. His semiotic theory is particularly problematic. Though he sides with Christian Metz in arguing that film is a language without a code, this position invites Umberto Eco's criticism that the "universe of action depicted by the cinema is already a universe of signs." Quoted in Antonio Costa, "The Semiological Heresy of Pier Paolo Pasolini," in *Pier Paolo Pasolini*, ed. Paul Willemen (London: British Film Institute, 1977), p. 40. As Costa astutely points out, Pasolini's theorizing is very much at the service of his filmmaking (p. 34). Since Pasolini considers history, language, and literature to be bourgeois institutions, his antibourgeois stance produces a cinema that avoids such mediations in its approach to the real (p. 41). For a comprehensive criticism of Pasolini's semiotics of film, see Teresa De Lauretis, "Language, Representation, Practice: Re-reading Pasolini's Essays on Cinema," *Italian Quarterly* 21–22 (Fall 1980–Winter 1981), 159–66.

[9] "The Cinema of Poetry," p. 547.

stylistic, for the elements must be selected from the infinity of possible images offered by the real and placed in a lexicon before the cinematic process can even begin. Because film language is a direct transcription of these primal, pregrammatical images, it bears a special relationship to reality that no codified language enjoys. Since cinema is "a system of signs whose semiology corresponds to a possible semiology of the system of signs of reality itself,"[10] it is therefore "the written language of reality" whose referentiality is entirely independent of symbolic or conventional mediations.[11] Those filmmakers who honor the cinema's direct semiotic relation to the real, without hiding the "mystic and embryonic" subfilm beneath a rational, narrative surface, are the quintessential cinematic realists, in Pasolini's sense of the term.

In light of his criticism of neorealism, and his semiotics of cinematic signs, Pasolini's claim to a superior realism begins to make some sense. If his cinema is a reaction against the prewar cultural influences on neorealism, especially those of naturalism and crepuscularism, on the one hand, and against those filmmakers on the other hand who deny the oneiric, pregrammatical nature of cinematic signs by imposing a conventional narrative superstructure on them, then Pasolini's answer to both criticisms will be an antinaturalistic style that acknowledges the raw, brute nature of film images by showing how arbitrary the stylistic overlay really is. In *Teorema*, Pasolini achieves this double ambition by purifying his cinematic language of any pretensions to naturalist representation and then making explicit his own, idiosyncratic principles of style. Unlike the storyline of a conventional film, which gives the illusion of the self-sufficiency and inner necessity of its narrative progress, the plot of *Teorema* is completely ar-

[10] *Pasolini on Pasolini*, p. 29.
[11] See "La lingua scritta della realtà," in *Empirismo eretico* (Milan: Garzanti, 1972), pp. 198–226. "When I make a film," Pasolini told Stack, "I am always in reality, among the trees and among people like yourself; there is no symbolic or conventional filter between me and reality, as there is in literature." Stack, *Pasolini on Pasolini*, p. 29.

bitrary and unmotivated, depending upon a mechanism external to the narration to keep it in motion, as Pasolini's title, taken from the discipline of mathematics, immediately suggests. The plot is thus manipulated by an abstract logic, the logic of the theorem, which imposes its own rigid, alien structure on the events of the storyline. Put another way, this obtrusive architecture makes "narrative structure itself the subject of the film, rather than anything it chose to relate" so that the "formal parallelisms create a self-enclosed world where everything has an assigned place in a predetermined structure whose very precision turns the film into a formal creation or, to use Pasolini's words, an 'object' rather than a representation of reality."[12]

In summary form, the plot reveals the schematicism and geometric rigor which amply fulfill the promise of its title: a mysterious visitor enters the life of an upper middle-class family in Milan and makes love to each member of the household, beginning with the servant Emilia, then the artist son Pietro, the mannequin-perfect mother, Lucia, the Oedipally repressed daughter, Odetta, and finally, the industrialist father, Paolo. Midway into the film the guest leaves as mysteriously as he came, and each member of the family proceeds to self-destruct in a way consonant with his or her particular relationship to the visitor. The theorem thus operates with harsh inevitability as the first half of the film sets out the patterns of disintegration to follow.[13] The disappearance of the guest at the exact center of the film creates a perfect bipartite division of the plot, each half of which is subdivided into five equal parts, or corollaries, as the family members act out their individual destinies. When the telegram arrives announcing the guest's departure, an interlude

---

[12] Naomi Greene said this with regard to *Sparrows and Hawks* but it well applies to the aesthetics of *Teorema*. See "Art and Ideology in Pasolini's Films," *Yale Italian Studies* 1 (Summer 1977), 322 and 323.

[13] Thus Adelio Ferrero attributes to the film a "visceral fatalism that runs through it from the first to the last image." See *Il cinema di Pier Paolo Pasolini* (Venice: Marsilio, 1977), p. 102.

follows in which the family members individually confess the totality of their love for him. The order of confession precisely mirrors the order of seduction, and as if this were not symmetrical enough, Pasolini sets each character's self-revelation in the exact location of his previous lovemaking with the guest. Nor do the household members interact with one another, but only with the mysterious visitor who stands detached, and remains opaque, as he brings first joy and then despair into the lives of the five protagonists.

The remoteness of the guest, and his ability to generate a series of similar responses in a number of very different individuals, suggest that he is himself the theorem, the abstract law governing a subset of diverse phenomena. The fact that he is somehow the key to the logic of the film is made visually explicit in two dinner-table scenes. Before his arrival, we see the family of four seated at the table in a disturbingly unbalanced pattern: the father is seated at the head of the table, to his left are two people, to his right is only one. The camera is centered on the father in a way that emphasizes the imbalance of the composition. When the servant Emilia enters with a telegram announcing the arrival of the guest, the suggestion is that his advent will complete the symmetry of the family unit. In fact, the next time we see them at dinner the guest provides the perfect balance of the group, as the father is now flanked by a man and a woman on either side. But the symmetry is soon to be broken, as another telegram is brought into the dining room to be read this time by the guest. He opens it, and utters his only line of dialogue in the entire film: "I have to leave, tomorrow." The physical symmetry provided by his presence is matched by the narrative symmetry of the two telegrams; one anticipating the arrival which will complete the family unit, and one announcing the departure, which will destroy it.

The entire film works on this pattern of mathematical precision. The motif of narrative repetition, of serial seduction, and serial self-destruction, is reflected in the landscapes and cityscapes that Pasolini selects as his cinematic setting. His camera is attracted to endless vistas of tree-lined roads, of factory barracks, of columns and arches, while the family villa is a marvel of classical composition. The mathematical rigor of the camera eliminates any softness, any imperfection, any deviation from the theoretical norm.[14]

But the theorem is more than a formal, stylistic property of the film determining its narrative structure, imagery, and photography. Indeed, its most consequential operations are metaphysical; namely, the systematic way in which the guest elicits each character's most secret desires. During the course of each seduction, he is made privy to his partner's own idealized self-image as expressed in a cluster of images that externalizes the character's hidden longings. When he departs, and the family is bereft of its perfection, each member proceeds to decompose in a parody of the ideal shared with the guest. This is the deepest and most telling pattern of the film, and it unites all the protagonists in a metaphysical theorem of wish-fulfillment and destruction. The guest crystalizes their innermost desires, but without him, these can no longer be satisfied. He has shown the family a dreadful and irresistible truth, and has left them devoid of the means to attain it.

Emilia, the servant who has come into the city from her modest farm in the provinces, is the first to realize her attraction to the young man. She is mowing the lawn as he is sprawled in a lounge chair, reading Rimbaud. Unable to tear her eyes from him, Emilia performs a bizarre series of actions, running back and forth from lawn to house in a crazed and compulsive way. In between these sprints, she stops to look in her bureau mirror, and contemplates her reflection amid postcards of virgins and saints. Pasolini has presented

<hr>

[14]On the geometric precision of Pasolini's camerawork, see Noel Purdon, "Pasolini: The Film of Alienation," in *Pier Paolo Pasolini*, ed. Willemen, p. 47.

her ideal self-portrait in these few images, and her fate as religious martyr is thus inexorably sealed. In strict obedience to the theorem, the guest's departure frees her to pursue this destiny, which includes a return to her native farm, a lengthy vigil in its courtyard, a fast broken only by the eating of nettles, and the performance of several miracles. She cures a leprous child, is levitated above the roof of the farmhouse in cruciform posture, and is buried alive in a construction site, leaving behind her a fountain of tears. This sublime conclusion to Emilia's story suggests her superiority over the middle-class dramatis personae of the film, and exemplifies once more Pasolini's well-known sympathy for the "subproletarians" of the urban shanty towns and the Third World, as well as for the peasant population itself.[15]

Pietro, the artistically inclined son, is the next to succumb. He and the guest must sleep in the same room, due to overcrowding, and end up sharing a bed. Pietro's walls are cluttered with paintings, and the boy's ambitions become explicit as he and the guest lovingly leaf through a catalogue of modern art. Pasolini's camera lingers on several gruesome works by Francis Bacon—animaloid studies for his crucifixion, and decomposing bodies clasped in a lovers' embrace. The last is prophetic of Pietro's destiny, as he repeatedly fails in his attempt to re-create his adored friend through art. He begins by painting frantic portraits, using a predominance of blues, which are the chromatic leitmotif of the guest (blue-eyed and celestial). But as Pietro continues to paint, the realization of his loss overwhelms him, and his art becomes an outpouring of despair. Anger and self-hatred motivate him to acts of violence and desecration as he stands over a blue canvas to urinate. In his final surrender to absurdity, Pietro abdicates all responsibility for his art, closes his eyes, dumps a can of blue paint on a waiting canvas, and hangs it on a

[15] On Pasolini's privileging of Emilia, see Bondanella *Italian Cinema*, pp. 281 and 283.

wall, allowing gravity and chance to govern the resulting design.[16]
It is easy to read into this artistic suicide a self-reflexive Pasolini. Not only does Pietro's name alert us to his autobiographical significance,[17] but so too does his homosexuality, which constituted so important a part of Pasolini's sense of difference. When the guest reveals to Pietro his true sexual inclinations, it is this, as much as his desire for absolute artistic freedom, which prompts the boy to abandon the family as the cornerstone of "straight" bourgeois respectability.[18] But it is in his artistic pretensions that Pietro's autobiographical meaning is most obvious, for he represents a possible alternative for the filmmaker who has contained his own tendencies toward chaos by means of a highly measured, controlled style. When Pietro discovers painting on glass, the celluloid art is not far away. To further the case for an autobiographical reading of Pietro's vocation, it is Giuseppe Zigaina, Pasolini's lifelong friend in politics and the pictorial arts, who is the actual author of the boy's glass painting experiments.

Lucia, the exquisitely wrought mother, is the third to fall. The guest elicits in her a powerful hybrid response, at once maternal and erotic. She is the only family member who is explicitly seductive, presenting herself nude to the guest in the family recreation room. The image complex that triggers Lucia's desire is scattered articles of men's clothing which

[16] As Alberto Moravia puts it "the boy, who is a painter, derails in the direction of the most capricious sterility masquerading as avant-garde art." See *Al cinema* (Milan: Bompiani, 1975), p. 107.

[17] In fact, Purdon finds autobiographic or symbolic meanings in all five of the names. See "The Film of Alienation," p. 44.

[18] Accordingly, Ben Lawton argues that the family is the preferred target of Pasolini's antibourgeois polemic and that sex is the prime weapon with which he wages his campaign. See "The Evolving Rejection of Homosexuality, Sub-Proletariat, and the Third World in Pasolini's Films," *Italian Quarterly* 21–22 (Fall 1980–Winter 1981), 168.

someone has always recently cast off. Her own first stirrings of passion for the guest are subtly suggested by a change of expression as she contemplates his clothes strewn about the room. Lucia looks at them first with the amusement of a mother who enjoys the carelessness of her child, and then with burgeoning passion for the man that child has become. When the guest departs, Lucia is doomed to parody this incident again and again as she picks up and seduces several young men. The first tryst momentarily elicits the combination of maternal tenderness and sexual passion that the guest had aroused in her. But as she notices the clothes strewn about the shabby apartment by her youthful lover, her complacent expression quickly turns to one of panic and loss. Compulsion takes hold of her, and she later picks up two unsavory youths, who lead her to a ditch before an abandoned country church and enjoy her in turn. Lucia's frantic attempt to recover the guest degenerates into an endless series of sordid sexual exploits.

Odetta, the adolescent daughter who is frozen in Oedipal love, finally relinquishes her fixation after the long and grave illness of her father. The guest, who has kindly ministered to the sick man throughout his crisis, becomes the new object of Odetta's obsessive passion. This switch of allegiances takes place one day as the two of them sit quietly on the lawn, attending the father in his convalescence. Odetta suddenly runs into the house, produces a camera, and proceeds to photograph the guest with a compulsion bordering on madness. She then takes him by the hand, and leads him to her monastic bedroom where she reveals to him her Bible—an album of photographs dedicated to her father. When the guest leaves, Odetta devotes herself exclusively to this cult of the past, permanently inhabiting her museum of memories. In her despair, she pores over the treasured album, stops at the new pictures she has taken of her young lover, traces his image with her right hand, and then clenches it in a fist never to be loosened. She falls on the bed in a catatonic fit, making

11. *The guest (Terence Stamp) relieves Paolo's discomfort by supporting the sick man's legs on his shoulders in imitation of a passage from Tolstoy.*

her body itself a frozen image, like the moments of the past that she refuses to release.

The father, Paolo, is the most resistant to the powers of the guest, but his long illness, emblematic of his own inner pathology, finally opens him to the forces of change. Paolo's destiny is contained in a story by Tolstoy, which is read aloud at his bedside, and which he and the guest enact. The passage describes the ministrations of a young peasant, Gerasim, to his ailing master, Ivan Ilich, who can only find relief from his pain when the servant raises his legs and supports them on his strong, young shoulders. The guest performs this rite for Paolo, and the therapy proves effective. After the young man's departure, Paolo experiences an ideological conversion of such intensity that it impels him to relinquish his factory to the workers' control. As further proof of his new antimaterialist stance, he divests himself of all his worldly goods in the train station of Milan, where he takes off his clothes to the amazement of rush-hour crowds.

The theorem is now complete, as each character fulfills the destiny implicit in his or her encounter with the guest. But we have yet to identify this catalytic figure or to explain his power to motivate radical change in the life of this Milanese household. "I made Terence Stamp into a generically ultra-terrestrial and metaphysical apparition," Pasolini said in an interview on BBC television. "He could be the Devil, or a mixture of God and the Devil. The important thing is that he is something authentic and unstoppable."[19] In the very vagueness of his gloss, Pasolini authorizes any number of possible interpretations of the supernatural figure, whose Christological resemblances constitute one obvious aspect of this eclectic divinity.[20] There is an annunciation scene when a postman named Angelino heralds the visitor's arrival, there

[19] In Stack, *Pasolini on Pasolini*, p. 157.

[20] Accordingly, Ferrero calls *Teorema* a "miracle play" (*Il cinema di Pasolini*, p. 96). On the guest as Godhead, see Bondanella, *Italian Cinema*, p. 282.

is the assumption of cruciform postures by the visitor throughout the film, and there is Odetta's final photograph of him that bears a pronounced likeness to a deposition scene. If the guest is, among other things, a *typus Christi*, then Pasolini is taking the doctrine of the Incarnation to its logical extreme in making this character's earthly ministrations primarily sexual ones. Since God embodies his spirit in the flesh to make palpable the abstract operations of divine truth, Pasolini makes such truth accessible to human sensibility in the most intimate of all possible ways. Dante explains that transcendent principles must be given corporeal expression according to the theory of accommodation, by which "Scriptures condescend / to your faculties, and feet and hands / attributes to God, while meaning something else" (*Par.* IV.43–45).[21] Pasolini has given more than hands and feet to his incarnation of divine truth, but in so doing, he is adhering to the tradition which predicates human cognition on sensory perception. Pasolini's God commits the ultimate act of *caritas* by offering himself to man's senses through carnal love.

Not only is the theory of accommodation taken to its logical extreme in *Teorema* but the language of mysticism as well. Union with the divine has been figured in erotic terms throughout the history of Christian thought. Thus by making sexual passion a metaphor for mystical union, the Biblical exegetes were able to transform the frankly erotic Song of Songs into an allegory of divine love, and Dante could establish a continuity between his earthly desire for Beatrice and his longing for the celestial vision made possible through

---

[21] "La Scrittura condescende / A vostra facultate, e piedi e mano / Attribuisce a Dio, ed altro intende" (*Par.* IV.43–45). Purdon, who sees Pasolini's combination of geometric structure and moral concerns in *Teorema* as an allusion to Spinoza's *Ethics*, notes the special relevance of the philosopher's Proposition XIV—Of the Means by which Eternal Things are Known. "We can see that it is above all things necessary to us that we should deduce our ideas from physical things or from real entities." See Purdon, "The Film of Alienation," p. 46.

her agency. Boccaccio parodies the Christian allegorization of eros by reversing the movement from flesh to spirit which typifies the tradition. Rustico's consignment of the devil to Hell through sexual intercourse (*Decameron* III.x) is a prime example of this carnalization of Christian doctrine. Like Boccaccio, Pasolini gives flesh to the disembodied language of mysticism, but the filmmaker's strategy suggests piety, not parody, as he suffuses the sexual act with divine significance.

Yet the analogy between the guest and Christ remains incomplete, for the guest is Christ unresurrected, the Saviour who remains on the cross and whose death is not followed by rebirth into eternal life. This half-realized *imitatio Christi* explains the destructive effect of the guest on the members of the household. While he motivates conversions, urging his disciples to abandon the old way and follow him, these conversions are partial. The guest completes only the first half of the conversion process: that of the *askesis*, and departs before indicating how his converts can remake themselves in his image. He leaves them without a prescription for change, without anything to replace their discarded selves. Lacking a guide, suddenly bereft of sanctifying grace, the family flounders and fails.

A second pattern of allusion gradually emerges. Throughout the film, Pasolini has intercut images of a desert amid the cityscapes of Milan, although it has no place in the physical context of a story about malaise in the urban upper middle classes. Eventually, the motif of the desert gains a cumulative force as it recurs each time a character makes the fateful decision for freedom. The desert becomes the desert of Exodus, and the destiny of the family becomes typologically that of the Jews who wander for forty years in quest of the promised land.[22] As the Jews left Egypt, and relinquished social structure for an unknown salvation, so Pasolini's fam-

---

[22] Pasolini makes this Scriptural allusion explicit in the epigraph to the novel *Teorema*, which contains the quote "God made the people turn, therefore, by way of the desert." Exodus 13:18.

ily has rejected the old norms and opted for change. But this modern Exodus does not have a happy ending, and these Milanese pilgrims are doomed to fail. There seems to be no promised land, and surely no Moses to lead them there. This family remains in the desert, unable to turn back, and unable to arrive.

Pasolini has used both Old Testament and New Testament typology to demonstrate the sorrow of incomplete conversion. The partial Exodus and the partial Atonement both dramatize his anxiety about a contentless freedom. What good is it, he asks, to leave behind the old order only to face a future of infinite alternatives when there is no way to choose among them, no models to imitate, and no guidelines to follow? On the eve of the 1968 upheavals, Pasolini's anxiety in *Teorema* was to be prophetic of the position he would soon take with regard to the protest movement that spread throughout Italy in the aftermath of the uprising in France. He was to see student activism not as a valid extension of "the Maoist cultural revolution by which it was supposedly inspired, but a disguised revolt of the bourgeoisie against itself" and he was to take the side of the police, "sons of the poor" against the spoiled, middle-class perpetrators of revolt.[23] He was to call the young protesters the "unfortunate generation" whose ignorance of cultural tradition doomed them to relive the old mistakes rather than to create the new and vital next chapter that only a dialectic reading of history could authorize.[24]

What is Pasolini's notion of the relationship of the work of art in general, and of *Teorema* in particular, to this world on the brink of violent social change? Is *Teorema* a committed film in the neorealists' sense, or does it constitute a withdrawal from sociopolitical concerns into an art-for-art's sake

[23] Enzo Siciliano, *Pasolini: A Biography*, trans. John Shepley (New York: Random House, 1982), pp. 325 and 326. On Pasolini's application of the label "falsa rivoluzione" to the events of 1968, see Brunetta, *Storia*, p. 661.

[24] Siciliano, *Pasolini*, pp. 348–49.

formalist position? Just as the plot forces us to go beyond
the literal level in our quest for an interpretive key, so too
does the ideological content of the film compel us to look
elsewhere for the source of its logic—this time to the two
textual models (Scriptures and the Tolstoy novella) that Pasolini explicitly invokes. What both allusions suggest is that
Pasolini is indeed appropriating the exemplary status of these
two texts, so that his film will bear witness to a revelation,
according to the Biblical paradigm, and will implicate the
public in its teaching, according to the Tolstoyan one. For
The Death of Iván Ilich is very much a parable on the morally appropriate and inappropriate "readings" of life experience. The story is as much about the other characters' refusal
to accept their own mortality as it is about Ivan's desperate
attempt to do so. The fact that the first part of the narration
is filtered through the perspective of a friend who succeeds
in suppressing the grief that Ivan's death brings him, and the
fact that what interests Tolstoy in Ivan's dying is the series
of cognitive relationships that it generates—Ivan's relationship to his fatal disease, his wife's relationship to her husband's slow demise, his friends' and co-workers' relationship
to it, and so on—reveal that this is a cautionary tale, full of
admonitions about our own relationship to the textual example. When Paolo acts on the knowledge that has come to
Ivan too late—"everything which you have lived by is a lie,
a deception, which conceals from you life and death"[25]—he
proves to be an ideal reader of Tolstoy, one who takes seriously the moral truth that Ivan's wife and friends so strenuously deny. Indeed, *Teorema* too is a parable, and hence it
too makes a moral claim on the viewers to take its teachings
to heart.[26] But the film stops short of the neorealists' *impegno* by refusing to prescribe the new order that will re-

[25] Leo Tolstoy, *The Death of Iván Ilich*, in *The Complete Works of Count
Tolstoy*, vol. 18, trans. Leo Wiener (Boston: D. Estes & Co., 1904), p. 77.
[26] The filmmaker argues this in Petraglia, *Pasolini*, p. 15.

place or regenerate the old.[27] The last sequence of the film shows Paolo stranded in the desert, suspended in the betwixt and between state that was Pasolini's political dwelling place. "For the present," writes Naomi Greene, "all that an Italian intellectual such as himself could do was to bear witness, through the 'pain' within him, a pain born from the struggle to renounce past culture and the impossibility of creating a new one, to a period of unhappy transition."[28]

If we were to accept Pasolini's problematic assessment of himself as a realist, we might qualify the term by calling him a "reactive realist"—that is, one whose style is a reaction to the limitations of neorealism in particular, or to any cinema that denies its semiotic source in the primal images of the real world, the world preceding the codified lexicon of man-made signs. To fulfill the terms of this "reactive realism" Pasolini must continue to experiment with cinematic form, never allowing his language to rigidify into manner or to slip into a conventional mode which would detract from his imagistic source in the real. Though his aesthetic restlessness has been seen as an attempt to reconcile the conflicting ideological and cultural impulses within him,[29] it could also be interpreted as his linguistic response to the realists' mandate to keep renewing the quest for a style which only through constant evolution and self-scrutiny could do justice to the true origin of cinematic discourse. Only then could the cinema assume its proper function as "the written language of reality." Paradoxically, it is by means of his reverential, mythic

[27] Or, as G. C. Ferretti put it, "Pasolini posits in substance the problem of superseding the old 'commitment' by means of an awareness of those *new facts* (and in particular of those ferments of antibourgeois revolt often not embraced or rejected by the organized movements that explicitly claim kinship with Marxism)." Cited in Ferrero, *Il cinema di Pier Paolo Pasolini*, p. 87.

[28] See Greene, "Art and Ideology," p. 318.

[29] See Oswald Stack's introduction to *Pier Paolo Pasolini*, ed. Willemen, p. 1.

approach to film images, rather than the naturalistic approach of the neorealists, that this realists' mandate, as Pasolini saw it, could be fulfilled. Like Paolo at the end of *Teorema*, the realist filmmaker must remain in the desert, ever seeking, but never achieving, the promised land of stylistic and ideological certainty.

$I2$ Petri's *Investigation of a Citizen above Suspicion*: Power as pathology

BY 1969, THE *involuzione* that had typified Italian society since the early fifties had come to an end. The student uprisings of the previous year, the subsequent worker unrest, the mounting protest against Vietnam which crystallized anti-American feeling, and the discrediting of the economic miracle all brought a halt to the complacency and the introversion of the contemporary Italian social order. For the first time since the early period of postwar reconstruction, immediate historical events made their claim on the national attention—a claim which amounted to a mandate for *engagé* art. The success of Costa-Gavras's *Z* provided the Italian cinema with a twofold incentive to political filmmaking: as an adventure in market research, *Z* revealed a public well disposed to politically committed works, and it provided a model for combining *impegno* with spectacle in commercially acceptable proportions. The confluence of external historical events on the one hand, and of internal "industrial" ones on the other, resulted in a spate of films coherent enough in style and didactic intent to constitute the genre of *cinema politico* or *cinema civile*[1] with Elio Petri as its founder, if not

---

[1] In English, the word "civil" usually implies one term in an opposition— civil versus military, civil law versus criminal law, etc. In Italian, it also stands alone as a morally and politically charged term. As Moravia explains it in calling Pasolini a "poeta civile," the adjective applies to one who "commits himself on the . . . historic, political, social front." See "Pasolini, poeta civile," *Italian Quarterly* 21–22 (Fall 1980–Winter 1981), 9.

its foremost practitioner in Italy.[2] That such a genre should be compared to neorealism is hardly surprising, given Petri's early apprenticeship to several neorealist directors, and given the importance of external historical events in the genesis of both movements.[3] Yet it is this understandable tendency to compare the two styles that has led to some unfortunate critical misjudgments with respect to Petri's work—misjudgments that the filmmaker himself seemed to foresee and to stave off as early as 1962, one year after he began making feature films and seven years before he was to inaugurate the genre of *cinema politico*. According to Petri, the difference between the neorealists and the new generation of Sixties filmmakers may be traced to "the differences in the periods in which they and we found ourselves taking our first steps. . . . After the revolution there came a restoration, and the climate of counter-reformations is always suffocating, obscurantist."[4] Using the term *restaurazione* in its double sense, as both the physical rehabilitation of the country and the return of the old values, Petri implies that the new age requires a very different response from the neorealist one engendered by the *rivoluzione* of the 1940s. Though the cinema must continue to fulfill its dissident function, "prodding, enlivening, provoking the critical spirit of the public,"[5] it must address a new historical consciousness which is no longer the repository of postwar revolutionary zeal, but on the contrary, bears all the earmarks of backlash, of *controriforma*. Given the recalcitrance

---

[2] See Torri, *Cinema italiano*, p. 161; and Alfredo Rossi, *Petri* (Florence: La Nuova Italia, 1979), p. 8. On the characteristics of the genre, see Rossi, *Petri*, pp. 10–12.

[3] Petri's entrée into the film world was Gianni Puccini, director of the journal *Cinema* (the forum for much early neorealist thought) and collaborator on Visconti's proto-neorealist film, *Ossessione*. Puccini introduced him to De Santis and the two collaborated on films throughout the Fifties. Petri also collaborated on several films of Puccini and on one with Carlo Lizzani. See Rossi, *Petri*, pp. 118–19.

[4] Quoted in *Film, 1962*, ed. Spinazzola, p. 172.

[5] Ibid., p. 174.

of the postreconstruction social order and the nature of a cinema inextricably wedded to it, the progressive filmmakers, according to Petri, must work within certain prescribed limits—both industrial and stylistic—before they can even hope to win a public hearing. Though not entirely comfortable with the idea, Petri argues that committed filmmakers have no choice but to work within the system and to adopt the cinematic language of the system if they want to address themselves to the masses. "It remains to be seen," Petri told Joan Mellen, "whether we who are to work through the system in order to raise the consciousness of the audience, in spite of the ability of the system to absorb everything, are doing the right thing. What we can say is that all this is a mirror of what's happening now and that we cannot escape it given the way cinema is conceived today."[6]

Petri's desire to reach mass audiences dictates not only a production mode, but a style, remote from the orthodox neorealists'. "The acting and the use of the camera must be a spectacular one," he claims, in a statement that justifies the highly mannered performance of Gian Maria Volonté (the lead in *Investigation of a Citizen* and in several other Petri films) and Petri's own flamboyant, utterly obtrusive cinematographic techniques.[7] "For me the representation must not appear impartial, it must be Brechtian, in the sense that the 'caricatural' element—what Brecht calls 'correction'—must indeed be internal to the structures of the image."[8]

Petri's abandonment of neorealist purity and his seeming capitulation to the demands of a "restoration" film industry are the source of much adverse criticism from the Left.[9] His detractors find a conflict between "the ideological–moral assumptions of the story and its structure—between the 'mes-

[6] Mellen, "Cinema Is Not for an Elite, but for the Masses: An Interview with Elio Petri," p. 10.
[7] Ibid., p. 11.
[8] Quoted in Tassone, *Parla il cinema italian, II*, p. 273.
[9] On anti-Petri criticism from the Left, see Brunetta, *Storia*, p. 696.

sage' that the author would intend to communicate and his mode of communication, between the 'content' (perhaps progressive) and the 'form' (standardized, that is, conservative),"[10] between his "thematic advancement" and his "expressive backwardness,"[11] between his simultaneous obedience to the "imperatives of the market" and to "the divergent ones of ideology."[12] According to the above arguments, which posit the separability of aesthetic form and ideological content, the fact that *Investigation of a Citizen* belongs to the highly marketable genre of the thriller or the *giallo* militates against its function as the vehicle of disinterested social criticism. But if film genres are implicitly ideological to begin with, as Thomas Schatz argues, serving to express and provisionally to resolve the cultural conflicts that threaten the stability of the social order,[13] then Petri's films, according to his critics, are pitting ideology against ideology—the conservative ideology built into his generic forms *versus* the progressive ideology of his stated themes. Though his detractors never explain whether they consider Petri a naive victim of this contradiction who unwittingly sabotages his good intentions by appropriating retrograde forms, or whether they consider him a cunning operator who wants to have it both ways, they fail to consider the possibility that the filmmaker may be manipulating his forms for ideologically responsible reasons.[14] If the "super-cop" variation on the "hardboiled detective" genre requires a protagonist whose "moral sensi-

---

[10] See Miccichè, *Il cinema italiano degli anni '60*, p. 146.

[11] Torri, *Cinema italiano*, p. 158.

[12] Ibid., p. 161. Bondanella concurs with regard to *Investigation* when he objects that "the impact of the film is purchased at a price—a lessening of the work's ideological coherence and historic veracity" (*Italian cinema*, p. 336).

[13] This is one of the emphases of Thomas Schatz's approach to the genre film. See especially his second chapter, "Film Genres and the Genre Film," in *Hollywood Genres* (New York: Random House, 1981), pp. 14–41.

[14] Miccichè argues that Petri puts the mechanisms of spectacle to the service of his "discorso civile," though he does not go on to elaborate this important point. See *Il cinema italiano degli anni '60*, p. 149.

bilities and deep-rooted idealism align him with the forces of
social order and the promise of a utopian urban community,"[15] then Petri's portrait of the psychopathic police chief
utterly subverts the ideological implications of the genre. By
taking all the standard elements of the urban crime film—
slick music, an elegant, modernistic setting, advanced technological apparatus, a handsome, charismatic protagonist, his
loyal staff, efficient bureaucratic machinery, a beautiful "love
interest"—and by pressing them into the service of neofascist
megalomania, rather than of justice and truth (as the genre
has led us to expect), Petri gives his social criticism added
impact. For his indictment goes far beyond the obvious institutional objects of his attack to our own deepest ideological impulses—impulses that conventional narrative genres are
designed to express. By turning one of these genres back on
itself, Petri forces us to examine and revise our own suscep-
tibility to political and media manipulation.

Nor does Petri use surprise tactics to shock us out of our
generic complacency by waiting until the end before explod-
ing the ideological assumptions of the thriller. Early in the
film we sense that this is no ordinary example of the genre
when we learn that it is the chief of police who has committed the murder of the opening scene. And the fact that we
know the *who* and the *how* of the crime from the outset—
the *why* and *what now* remain to be seen—suggests that this
is not a thriller at all, but a film about power, and specifically how power becomes a form of dementia. When the main
character explains to his superiors at the conclusion of the
film that he is the victim of a disease contracted through
prolonged use of power, he is retrospectively glossing the entire action of the story, including his murder of Augusta Terzi,
the ensuing investigation, and his promotion within the police department hierarchy. The main character (I shall call
him "the chief," since he is never named) pursues a bizarre

[15] See Schatz, *Hollywood Genres*, p. 123.

and self-canceling strategy in the wake of the crime, seeking at once to cover up and to flaunt his guilt. Such behavior is attributable to a paradox that lies at the heart of the protagonist's psychopathology: since the chief considers himself above the law, he can commit any crime with impunity, but since his power derives from the authority of the law, he must prove its potency by getting caught and undergoing the appropriate punishment. In the throes of this dilemma, the chief plays a cat-and-mouse game with his pursuers, planting clues and then thwarting the investigation as soon as it threatens to uncover his guilt. Perhaps a more apt analogy, since it will have thematic application later on, would be an erotic one in which the chief conducts a flirtation with discovery, giving his investigators "come hither" signals and then playing hard to get once they have fallen for his enticements. At the very scene of the murder, the chief's approach–avoidance relationship to discovery becomes obvious as he deliberately leaves his signature on the crime while attempting to cover up certain bits of incriminating evidence. Thus he carefully leaves his fingerprints on Augusta's phone, on some glassware, on a bottle of vermouth, and on a wad of 300,000 lire from her bureau, he uses her scented soap to shower with, makes bloody footprints down her corridor, and implants a thread from his garish blue tie on her fingernail. These bizarre acts, which suggest how at home he is amid the evidence of his violence and perversity, are counterbalanced by a halfhearted series of cover-up attempts—he uses a handkerchief to extract a stash of jewels from Augusta's bureau and to open her refrigerator door. Throughout the film, the chief continues to plant clues and then to deflect the investigative pointers that lead to his guilt. He sends a parcel containing incriminating evidence to Patané, the tabloid journalist who gets first scoops from the chief, and telephones him to say, in a barely disguised voice, that the package is on its way. When Patané confronts him with the parcel and the voice identification, the chief uses his power over the journalist to thwart this line of investigation. He threatens Patané with no more privileged information, reminding the journalist that freedom of the press, in this case, would be purchased at a high price indeed.

He uses similar coercive tactics with Panunzio, his assistant and expert on fingerprint analysis. This time, the chief issues a preemptive threat, presenting Panunzio with a file on his cousin Nicola, a Communist activist, before considering what evidence the fingerprint expert has to offer. In a scene verging on the surreal, Panunzio leads the chief into his lab where giant sheets of enlarged fingerprints are suspended from the ceiling like so many laundry items hung out to dry. Of course, all the fingerprints match the chief's, but Panunzio, mindful of the threat of blacklisting made moments earlier, goes to ingenious lengths to explain the ubiquity of his superior's guilty traces. "You weren't feeling well, you remember, so you had a glass of water," Panunzio explains, attributing the fingerprints to the chief's inspection of the murder site in his official capacity.

Unlike Patané and Panunzio, the third victim of the chief's cat-and-mouse strategy is not connected with the world of crime detection or crime reporting at all. He is a poor plumber who happens to pass by the store selling ties similar to the chief's garish blue one. Having commissioned the plumber to buy fifty such ties, the chief identifies himself as a murderer and sends the bewildered man to the police station to do his "civic duty." The plumber obeys, only to be detained for lengthy questioning at the office and to be abused by the chief who psychologically bludgeons the little man into denying the evidence of his senses: that his interrogator is the very man who had identified himself on the streets as a murderer. Where specific professional threats had deflected Patané and Panunzio from the trail, here raw power and the sheer force of institutional authority enabled the chief to prevail over a man armed with unequivocal evidence of his guilt.

The chief's double bind with respect to the law suggests a

profound psychic split which also manifests itself in other aspects of his personality. While his home life is austere, pleasureless, and puritanical, he is irresistibly drawn to Augusta, whose sensuality and decadence represent all that he has sought to repress in himself. When the chief describes the scene of the crime to Patané after visiting it in his official capacity as head of Homicide, his language reflects not only his moral revulsion against Augusta, but against the part of himself that desired her and that made her murder a necessary act of self-purification. This inner tension between his moralizing, puritanical inclinations and the decadent, pleasure-loving ones is externalized in the two sets on which he acts out the drama of his private life. His own apartment could be an extension of the police station with its sterile, ultramodern decor, its lack of color, its scarcity of furniture, and the same picture of the Homicide staff which adorns his wall at the office. Significantly, the most memorable piece of furniture in this setting is his weight-reducing machine, suggesting the punishment that awaits one kind of sensuous overindulgence. Augusta's apartment is the polar opposite of the chief's in every way, from its lush, gauzy atmosphere to its soft, arching lines and its pleasing clutter. Where the chief's apartment is photographed with harsh clarity, Augusta's is shot in soft focus, as if the camera were behind the diaphanous curtains which flutter in the breeze, or were peering through the stained glass windows that suffuse her rooms with an aura of warm color. To emphasize the sense of disorder, her apartment is photographed with no depth of field so that we have only the most confused impression of how the space is organized. Furthermore, we first see this set through the chief's own deranged perspective as the camera presents a series of closeups that dramatize the obsessive and mechanical workings of his criminal intelligence. The jerky editing and the perpetual motion of the camera throughout this scene further exemplify the psychopathology of Augusta's assassin. Indeed, had Pasolini been able to view *Investi-*

gation of a Citizen before writing his "Cinema of Poetry" he might well have included this scene as an example of the "free indirect subjective" technique which allows a director to use his protagonist's neurotic perspective as an alibi for his own abnormal visual style. Since the murder scene offers the most extreme demonstration of this aberrant vision, it sets the tone for the cinematography of the entire film, which maintains its debt to the protagonist's perceptions in its scarcity of establishing shots, its fondness for closeups, and its tendency toward perpetual motion.

Nor is the visual style the only way in which Petri objectifies his protagonist's mental disorder, for the narrative structure also obeys the inner workings of his criminal mind. The story does not progress on a linear path from beginning to end, but proceeds instead in fits and starts, lurching forward and backward according to the combined forces of chronology and reminiscence. The story begins in the middle, with Augusta's murder, and continues with the events of the investigation whose narrative progress is interrupted by six flashbacks to episodes in the chief's relationship with the victim.

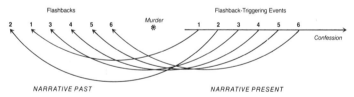

NARRATIVE PAST   NARRATIVE PRESENT

To complicate the structure, the flashbacks are not strictly chronological, but are offered as random memories, triggered by events in the narrative present of the investigation. Through these memories, we are able to reconstruct the events leading up to the murder, so that by the time we reach the sixth and final flashback, we have enough information to understand the opening scene. Such a narrative scheme offers a structural counterpart to the inner division of the chief's psyche, whose past is dominated by Augusta and her voluptuary games, while his present is typified by the all-male, austere, repressed world of the police hierarchy. Musically, this dichotomy is exemplified by Ennio Morricone's two themes, the one whimsical and soft, accompanying his memories, the other tense and perverse, accompanying the investigation.

Of all the flashbacks, the first is the richest in what it says about the psychosexual dynamics of the chief's affair with Augusta. This particular memory is sparked by the discovery of a store of amateur photographs in which Augusta had impersonated the victims of sensational crimes for the chief's camera. Like some sort of demented movie director, he would recite the narrative of each murder while Augusta would pose as the corpse—first as a prostitute found murdered in bed, then as a German stewardess strangled in an airport toilet, later as a singer whose throat was slashed and body covered with records, and finally as a student radical whose mouth was stuffed with 10,000-lire bills. This sadistic montage is striking not only in what it reveals about the perfection of the chief's memory for violent criminal detail, but also in its anticipation of things to come. If we consider the collection of photographs and their explanatory narratives in their entirety, a series of structural resemblances emerges: all the victims are women; all the assailants, men; all the murders have a sexual component; and the circumstances are all metonymically related to the women's vocational status. As the chief's morbid enthusiasm escalates with each new narration, and as he embroiders succeeding ones with more and more vivid detail, it becomes increasingly clear that the climax in this progression of crime photographs will be the one of Augusta's own corpse, and that the entire film is the narration of how this particular photograph came to be. No longer impersonating the victims of violent, sado-sexual crime, Augusta now *is* the victim, and she too is photographed dead amid the trappings of her trade—black silken sheets, a half-read mystery novel, and so on. She too will assume her place in the chief's gory album of memory, and with her photograph, the progression of images comes full circle, beginning and ending with prostitutes slain in bed.

The cumulative effect of the flashbacks is to suggest that Augusta is by no means a passive victim of crime, but that in many ways she is the architect of her own death—a death that she sees as her fate early in the film. "I'll be raped and killed—that is my destiny," she tells the chief in an anonymous phone call predating the onset of their affair. After the murder, Augusta's ghost returns to the chief in a dream and reassures him that "sooner or later it would have happened." And indeed, the progress of this *folie à deux* reveals an ever escalating invitation to lawlessness. "I'll kill you with my own hands," the chief tells Augusta in the fourth flashback as she cuts his tie to ribbons. "You'll conduct the inquiry," she replies. "Would you condemn yourself?" Fascinated by his dual nature as criminal and crime detector, Augusta goads him to run a red light under the very eyes of the traffic officer. "You're above the law and can commit any crime," she gloats, though later on, at the beach, the game goes too far even for Augusta's particular tastes. When she invites the chief to plan a crime and he conjures up a decapitated body, badly decomposed, her delight in the game turns to horror and she rewards him with a mouthful of sand. Decomposing bodies are too real—they destroy the glamor and the mystique of the criminal fantasy world that Augusta has built around their relationship. Her sudden shift in mood has considerable thematic importance as well, for it reveals that Augusta has the same ambivalence toward the chief that he himself has toward legal authority. Just as he wants to be apprehended by the law, while transcending it, she wants to incite him to crime while being spared the violent consequences. As the chief's dilemma comes from his identification with the law, so Augusta's derives from her identification with him. If her power over the chief is to have any meaning, she must be convinced of his omnipotence by subjecting it to continuous tests. Thus the erotic relationship is an analogy for the professional one, not a gratuitous digression into psychosexual deviance, as Pauline Kael suggests, nor a detraction from the political themes, as Stanley Kauffmann argues.[16]

Now we are prepared to interpret the first scene, whose opening words, "How will you kill me this time?" cease to function as pure paradox and instead usher in the logical next episode in a series of simulated crimes. When Augusta rises up under the black silken sheets in what appears to be the moment of her climax but proves instead to be her death throes, this artful confusion is no mere surrender to sensationalism on Petri's part. Indeed, this *is* the consummation of their relationship in its love of violence and foul play, in its escalating incitements to lawbreaking and destruction. Now the chief has realized Augusta's recurrent fantasy by proving his ultimate power over her, and over the legal authority that he represents.

The political implications of this crime are not far to seek. In an inspired juxtaposition, the murder scene is immediately followed by the chief's promotion from the directorship of Homicide to that of the secret police. While explaining his understanding of the continuity between his past and present positions, the chief gives voice to the contortions of his political thought. "Behind every criminal there is a potential subversive," he tells his staff in an inaugural address, "and behind every subversive lurks a criminal." By equating political dissent with crime (they both constitute threats to the established order and they both call forth the law enforcers' suppressive measures) and by stating that suppression is essential to the health of the democratic state, the chief negates the defining characteristic of democracy: its insistence on the

<hr>

[16] See Pauline Kael, "Megalomaniacs," in *Deeper into Movies* (New York: Bantam, 1974), p. 279; and Stanley Kauffmann, *New Republic*, 23 January 1971, 22. Joan Mellen sees yet another relationship between Augusta's sexuality and the chief's political pathology. "Augusta, the Inspector's sensualist victim, is no better than he; she reflects the bourgeoisie which used Fascism to act out vicariously its sadistic impulses." See Joan Mellen, "Fascism in the Contemporary Film," *Film Quarterly* 24 (Summer 1971), 15.

citizens' right to disagree. Ironically, the equation of criminality and subversion, which the chief makes in the interests of his own authoritarian politics, is most directly applicable to his own case. In aspiring to criminal behavior that will prove his impunity before the law, the chief is indeed subverting the entire system of legal authority upon which his own sense of impunity rests. When he says to the head of the wiretapping bureau, "Let's imagine that the Terzi crime had a political motive," that hypothesis indeed proves true, not in the sense that the chief literally intended it (as militant Leftist activism) but in reference to the authoritarian tendencies that lurk within the system and threaten to subvert its democratic safeguards.

In the Kafka allusion that closes the film, Petri makes explicit the ruling assumptions of the authoritarian state. As the chief awaits the verdict of the commissioner and his staff, the following epigraph from *The Trial* appears on the screen. "Whatever impression he makes on us, he is a servant of the Law. He belongs to the Law and is not answerable to human judgment." Petri could have chosen a far less cryptic statement from the same passage in *The Trial* to make his point. "Bound as he is by his service, even only at the door of the Law, he is incomparably greater than anyone at large in the world. . . . It is the Law that has placed him at his post, to doubt his dignity is to doubt the Law itself."[17] Indeed, this passage would have been well suited to the particulars of the chief's logic, for it was Augusta's assaults on his dignity, and hence on the dignity of the authority he represented, which prompted her murder, as he explains to the commissioner in the penultimate scene of the film. But Petri chose instead the more paradoxical formulation of the earlier passage, which exemplifies the way in which the authoritarian system inverts the proper hierarchies of democratic thought. In a true democracy, human judgment has ascendancy over the law, which

[17]Franz Kafka, *The Trial*, trans. Willa and Edwin Muir (New York: Vintage, 1969), p. 276.

functions as its imperfect agent and is open to constant scrutiny by its subjects. The servant of the law stands at the bottom of the democratic hierarchy, accountable to human judgment as its supreme authorizing source. In Kafka's autocratic state, instead, the servant of the law occupies the midpoint of the scale with the law above and human judgment below him. Nor does this middling position imply a mediating function on the part of Kafka's servant, who will neither explain the law to human judgment nor modify it according to human judgment, but will stand as an absolute barrier between the two polar extremes of the hierarchy. The servant of the law is the doorman of Kafka's parable who not only denies the citizen access to the building which houses the law, but cruelly deceives him into waiting all his life for the permission to enter which never comes.

By virtue of his power to determine access to the law, Kafka's doorman, of course, *is* the law—he defines the system as exclusive and undemocratic, in no manner accountable to the citizens it governs. The chief, like Kafka's doorman, has the power to define the very system he allegedly serves by enforcing its laws as he sees fit, confusing his mandate to maintain the public order with a mandate to determine the nature of that order according to his own personal and self-serving ideals.

Like Kafka's unspecified state, Petri's Italy offers no acceptable alternatives to a corrupt and repressive status quo. Though Antonio Pace, left-wing veteran of the '68 uprisings and sometime lover of Augusta, is the only individual able to bring the chief to his knees, Petri does not hold up his revolutionary politics as a model for the new democratic order. Antonio may be an exemplary antagonist to the chief, but when multiplied a hundred-fold, he produces simply masses of arrogant, sloganeering powermongers who can never agree among themselves and who emerge as woefully incapable of piloting the ship of state. As they are disgorged from the police vans and herded into jail, the demonstrators make

12. *Augusta (Florinda Balkan) begs the chief (Gian Maria Volonté) to interrogate her in a scene that reveals the in* loco parentis *operations of the authoritarian state.*

a singularly unappealing impression with their chants, sneers, and macho threats, all of which are given the lie when one of the loudest and most impudent of them is transformed into a cowering traitor under interrogation. Petri's criticism of militant political activism gains historical resonance in the remark of a police officer who notes that the young protesters' last names are the same as those of thirty years before. "Dissidence is like syphilis, it stays in the blood," the officer observes in an analogy that reveals far more than his own intolerance for radical agitators. The criticism applies as much to the fathers as to the sons, to the generation of the Resistance which failed to bring about the lasting social change that would have made it unnecessary for the new generations to fight the same old battles once more. The sons, however, are also to blame for their inability to forge new approaches to old problems and their unimaginative embrace of their fathers' ineffectual political strategies.

But if the father–son relationship explains the failure of the New Left movement in Italy, it is even more applicable to the workings of the authoritarian state. "The population is underage," the chief says in his inaugural address, making explicit the patriarchal function of the state. The parental model for the management of political power becomes even more obvious when Augusta begs the chief to conduct a mock interrogation of her, and to do so with brutality and suspicion—"Be suspicious, like my father," she implores him. Forcing Augusta to her knees, the chief explains that all suspects become children in the face of authority and that he himself becomes the father, and his face becomes that of God. When Augusta accuses him here, and elsewhere, of being childlike, she touches a raw nerve.[18] "You shouldn't have said that," he replies. "*Others* are babies." All this leads us to Wilhelm Reich's theory that the authoritarian personality derives from an upbringing in a patriarchal family whose

[18] For Petri's analogy between sexual immaturity and authoritarianism, see Tassone, *Parla il cinema italiano, II*, p. 250.

disciplinary patterns are so arbitrary and inconsistent that the child can never internalize a standard of conduct but remains dependent upon some external embodiment of power. The authoritarian state, according to Reich, is simply a macrocosm of the lower middle-class patriarchal family whose sons, "apart from a subservient attitude toward authority, develop a strong identification with the father, which forms the basis of the emotional identification with every kind of authority."[19] The primacy of the patriarchal model for the structuring of the authoritarian state explains why the chief, in turn, assumes a childlike role in the face of his superiors, reporting his liaison with Augusta to the high commissioner as a son might offer up his sins to parental judgment. When the commissioner refuses to scold the chief, asking instead "How was she? good?" while photographed in a closeup which emphasizes his cigar and his connoisseur's smile, he becomes the indulgent father who enjoys his son's carousings and thereby welcomes him into "the club." At the end of the film, when the chief daydreams of his hearing before the commissioner and his staff, he becomes a snivelling child to the father grown momentarily severe. Though Petri never makes us privy to the actual resolution of the chief's plight, we are led to believe, by the patriarchal structure of the police power hierarchy, that the whole affair will be treated as a family matter, with no thought of resorting to outside judiciary means.

Significantly, there are no allusions to the family in *Investigation of a Citizen*—a striking omission for a film culture that tends to reflect the familial orientation of Italian life. Augusta and the chief both live alone, and what family bonds

[19] See Wilhelm Reich, *The Mass Psychology of Fascism*, trans. Vincent Carfagno (New York: Farrar, Straus & Giroux, 1970), p. 54. On the application of Reich's theories to the authoritarian personality as it is manifested in recent films about Fascism, see Mellen, "Fascism in the Contemporary Film," pp. 3–4. Petri himself acknowledges his debt to Reich in his interview with Mellen, "Cinema Is Not for an Elite," p. 11.

are mentioned have either been severed, as have Augusta's with her estranged husband, or cause trouble, as do Panunzio's with his Communist cousin. The conspicuous absence of the family in *Investigation of a Citizen* both heightens our awareness of the patriarchal structure of the state, and explains that structure as a compensation for those who are incapable of forging bonds of familial intimacy. Indeed, it is such emotionally inept individuals that Fascism seeks to recruit, according to Joan Mellen, filling the void left by the absent family with a substitute in the form of a patriarchal organ of state.[20]

Since authoritarian personalities know no relationships of peers, the chief can function only in one of two capacities, either as a wielder or as a subject of authority. The shift in roles can be instantaneous, so that when Augusta strikes him in the face, or when Antonio Pace stands up to his bluster, the chief is suddenly disarmed. Neither of these two characters offers an exemplary mode of response for the public with a will to resist the authoritarian tendencies latent in the state, however. Augusta ends up a corpse, and Antonio Pace resembles more a candidate for eventual alienation or terrorist activism than a leader of a new democratic social order. What Petri seems to be advocating is not that we surrender to the authoritarianism in our midst, but that we resist its encroachments through the kind of awareness that films such as his can accord us. Knowledge is not only the chief's primary instrument of power, with his arsenals of files and the latest methods of mechanical surveillance at his disposal, but it is also the public's best weapon against his kind. Augusta and Antonio have power over the chief not just because they can physically or emotionally stand up to his assaults, but because they have privileged information about him: Augusta is privy to his psychosexual weaknesses, and Antonio to incriminating evidence against him (he saw the murderer

[20] See "Fascism in the Contemporary Film," p. 15.

leaving the scene of the crime). What they know by chance or by human contact is far more virulent than what he could ever learn by mechanical or bureaucratic means.

In a society whose New Left and old Right offer unacceptable alternatives to a corrupt status quo, Petri's film stands as an example of the awareness and vigilance necessary to keep democracy alive. That such a film could be made at all attests to the vestigial health of the system—a system whose survival is contingent upon constant public acts of social criticism. Those who deny *Investigation of a Citizen* its claim to *cinema politico* because it offers no concrete prescription for change should recall that neorealism itself was primarily a cinema of indictment or of *inchiesta* whose mandate did not include the making of policy nor the waving of party banners. If by neorealist *impegno* we mean the creation of a political consciousness and a sense of moral responsibility for the social conditions portrayed on the screen, then Petri's film, and the genre of political cinema which it inaugurated, would certainly merit its place among the descendents of neorealism.

For those who would deny Petri his claim to committed filmmaking on the basis of his commercial appeal, a less literal-minded, more open approach to form might indicate otherwise. True, *Investigation of a Citizen* does utilize many of the formal techniques of the conventional thriller, but it turns the genre's ideological assumptions upside down by making the standard macho upholder of social values into society's most insidious enemy—its in-house subverter whose misunderstanding of democratic ideals makes him their unwitting and invisible adversary. Petri's awareness of the dangers of a *cinema di consumo*, which consoles the public and reinforces its most regressive tendencies, is built into the film itself, along with its implied corrective in a cinema of critical self-consciousness. Augusta and the chief are indeed consumers of images, using the remembered and replicated photographs of crime victims as sexual aids or as elements in their shared world of sadomasochistic fantasy. In exposing the abuses to which such image consumption can lead, Petri forbids us any naive, uncritical approach to his own work. "The victim posed for crime photos, taken by an amateur. Puerile. What do you think?" one of the investigators says to the chief on the premises of the crime. Petri asks the same question of his audience, making us active, critical interpreters of his images, and not the passive consumers of his commercial products that the critics would have us be.

In his self-conscious use of conventional form, Petri has incorporated the technical lessons of the contemporary film industry into a cinema that remains ideologically faithful to the neorealists' cause. In so doing, he has laid the groundwork for the *cinema politico* of the 1970s, making possible the commercially viable, yet ideologically committed art of Bertolucci, the Taviani brothers, and Scola.

PART IV

Fascism and War Reconsidered

13 Bertolucci's *The Conformist*: A morals charge

IN *Open City* THERE IS a minor character so loathsome and perverse that we do not even stop to consider his motivation in collaborating with the Nazis. He is the Roman police commissioner who strives to outdo even Bergmann, the Gestapo chief, in hunting down Resistance leaders. The character of this super-collaborator little interested Rossellini, who was far more intent on showing the heroics of the partisan Italians—those who stood up to the Nazi threat and even to Nazi torture rather than surrender their freedom and dignity to a tyrannous state. Rossellini's film bespoke a Manichean division of the world into resisters and collaborators, and the latter were without complexity or human interest (with the exception of Marina, whose betrayal was motivated by sentimental, not political, considerations).

It took the Italian cinema twenty-five years to be able to look back at Fascism and war in a more complicated way, to ask what induced Rossellini's police commissioner to condone, if not to abet, authoritarian rule. In *The Conformist*, Bertolucci tells the other story implicit in *Open City*—that of one man's reasons for collaborating with a murderous regime. Where Rossellini's didactic intent in 1945 was to generate a new Italian society based on Resistance ideals, Bertolucci's emphasis suggests a far darker lesson for the viewing public of 1970. The impulse to consider the phenomenon of collaboration, not of resistance, makes *The Conformist* a cautionary tale—one that enjoins us to heed our history lest we relive its worst moments. "That is why I say *The Conformist* is a film on the present," Bertolucci told Marilyn Goldin. "And when I say that I want to make the public leave with a sense of malaise, perhaps feeling the presence of something obscurely sinister, it's because I want them to realize that however the world has changed, feelings have remained the same."[1]

Despite the radical shift in emphasis that separates Rossellini's film from Bertolucci's, and despite their vast stylistic differences, the works share a moral purpose which locates *The Conformist* in a realist tradition. Bertolucci's desire "to make the public leave with a sense of malaise," to force his viewers to confront their Fascist past and to rethink their relationship to it, constitutes a plea for moral responsibility akin to the early neorealists'. When De Sica said of his first postwar film *Shoeshine* that it was a contribution to the "moral reconstruction of our country," he was arguing not only for a politically activist cinema, but for a morally accountable one.[2] As a reaction to the Fascist film industry and to the ideology it espoused, the neorealists deplored any form of escapism and insisted that the public once more take charge of its political destiny. Similarly, Bertolucci's film may be seen as a parable of what happens when an individual, and by extension when an entire populace, abdicates responsibility for its moral condition. This tropological reading provides not only the interpretive key to *The Conformist*, but its link to the neorealist tradition whose technical divergence from Bertolucci's flamboyant cinema should not blind us to its kindred ethics.[3]

Perhaps the strongest argument for a moral reading of *The Conformist* can be made from a comparison between the film and the eponymous novel by Alberto Moravia. With the ex-

[1] See "Bertolucci on *The Conformist*: An Interview with Marilyn Goldin," *Sight and Sound* 40 (Spring 1971), 66. On the contemporary applicability of *The Conformist*'s themes, see the interview in Jean Gili, *Le cinéma italien*, p. 72.

[2] This quote is discussed at some length in my preface.

[3] On Bertolucci's highly ambivalent relationship to neorealism, see Francesco Casetti, *Bertolucci* (Florence: La Nuova Italia, 1975), p. 28.

ception of the ending, Bertolucci deviates little from Moravia's storyline, which begins with a childhood incident in the life of Marcello Clerici, scion of an upper middle-class Roman family in decay. When the thirteen-year-old Marcello is picked up and propositioned by a homosexual chauffeur, Lino, the child responds with a barrage of gunfire intended to kill his would-be seducer. As an adult, Marcello seeks to obliterate his sense of deviancy by conforming to the social mores and political ideology of 1930s Italy. Accordingly, he marries the unremarkable Giulia and ingratiates himself with the Fascist hierarchy by volunteering for a counterintelligence mission to be carried out in Paris. There he is to insinuate himself into the expatriate underground led by his former thesis advisor, Professor Quadri, and eventually to set up the anti-Fascist leader for liquidation. After an intense and erotically confusing sojourn in Paris with the professor and his bisexual wife, Marcello allows the assassination plot to reach its gory conclusion. The story then flashes forward to the fall of the Mussolini regime as the Clericis, seeking to escape reprisals, are killed by Allied strafing in the countryside near Tagliacozzo.

Moravia's ending is the logical conclusion to a story of inexorable fate: Marcello is marked from the outset by a love of violence and by a feminine sultriness which leads him to be seduced and to react with homicidal vengeance time and again. Though the encounter with Lino was consummated neither sexually nor murderously, it nonetheless dictates the cycles of seduction and destruction he is destined to play out for the remainder of his life. Marcello is portrayed as helpless to ward off this grim fatality, which makes him akin to the Greek hero-victim who, in seeking to escape his destiny, only helps to bring it about. With the deadly strafing on the road to Tagliacozzo, Moravia offers a modern technological equivalent to the *deus ex machina* that intervenes from above to facilitate the plot resolution, while giving his story a final psychological and poetic twist.[4] The disciplinary action that Marcello had continually sought in vain from parents and Church is now finally issued by this agent of divine justice. And, appropriately, it is the gun he had always desired and had earned at such cost, from Lino and from the Fascist authorities, which lowers itself from heaven to bring him his final punitive reward.

Bertolucci has often remarked on the fatalism of Moravia's novel and has likened it to Greek drama in its governing principles. "The destiny of the conformist," he explained, "was like fate in the Greek tragedies"[5] and it is against this very mechanistic approach that the filmmaker is reacting in his adaptation of the novel. Bertolucci opts to replace Moravia's dramatic determinism with psychological determinism. "I prefer that the force of the subconscious take the place of 'fate,' " he told Joan Mellen.[6] Hence Bertolucci's ending eschews the "divine" intervention of American machine-gun fire and insists instead upon Marcello's final moment of psychic self-revelation and self-acceptance. Accordingly, the film ends as Marcello turns toward a young male prostitute with obvious pederastic intent.

Although this denouement certainly privileges the psychosexual determinants of Marcello's character, I find that Bertolucci's critical formulation of the difference between his emphasis and Moravia's is necessarily reductive. It is not simply a question of Moravian fate versus Bertoluccian subconscious, since the subconscious functions importantly in the novel as well, serving as the subterranean and inexorable force against which the textual protagonist must struggle. This is not to deny that Bertolucci has indeed replaced Moravia's

[4] Bertolucci himself invokes the *deus ex machina* comparison in "Bernardo Bertolucci Seminar," *American Film Institute Dialogue on Film* 3 (April 1974), 18.
[5] Ibid.
[6] Joan Mellen, "A Conversation with Bernardo Bertolucci," *Cinéaste* 5 (1973), 22. On Bertolucci's substitution of psychological motivation for fate, see Witcombe, *The New Italian Cinema*, p. 94.

fate with something else. But I would argue that the film is far more interested in the ethical consequences of Fascist adherence than in the psychological causes of it, as an analysis of the ending should indicate.

Prior to Marcello's visual embrace of the male prostitute, he has been wandering about the streets of Rome with his blind friend Italo Montanari, a Bertoluccian addition to Moravia's dramatis personae who functions in the film as the apologist for Fascist ideology and as Clerici's entrée into the secret service. When the two arrive at the Colosseum, they overhear a homosexual flirtation between Lino and the young male prostitute. The spectacle of Lino alive prompts a strange, seemingly demented response in Marcello, who shouts, "Where were you, what were you doing on March 25, 1917?" and again "What were you doing at 4 P.M., October 15, 1938?" The two dates correspond to the various murders for which Marcello believes he is responsible—that of Lino and those of the Quadris—and their linkage reveals the psychopathology of his conformist logic. To atone for the earlier crime, which made him a social outcast in his own eyes, Marcello pledges allegiance to a society in 1938 which requires acts of brutality and murder by its loyal henchmen. This creates the paradox of an atonement that recapitulates the very sin requiring expiation—the equivalent of the physician's homeopathic cure. The logic of Marcello's strategy is verbalized with satiric savagery in the scene of his premarital confession in church. "Blood washes blood," Marcello tells Don Lattanzi. "I confess today the sin I will commit tomorrow." "Are you a member of some subversive group?" asks the priest. "No, I am a member of the organization that hunts down subversives." With this answer Marcello earns Don Lattanzi's full absolution in advance.

It is no coincidence that Lino should be found alive on the very day of Mussolini's deposition. These twin events prove that Marcello's conformist logic is doubly flawed. With Lino alive, Marcello realizes that he never committed the very murder for which the Quadri assassination was to exonerate him. Furthermore, in seeking society's forgiveness, Marcello had never asked *which* society, but had assumed that the Fascist state was absolute, universal, and immutable—not the aberration that history proved it to be. When Marcello discovers the fallacy of his logic, his subsequent ravings reveal the moral disorder at the root of Fascist thought. "His name is Pasqualino Semirama," Marcello announces to random passers-by. "He assassinated a man, a political exile, Professor Quadri, Luca Quadri and his wife, Anna Quadri. He's a pederast, a Fascist." Marcello then turns to Italo and shouts, "he too is a Fascist." By casting the blame for the Quadri murder on Lino, Marcello is performing a very perverse and morally suspect act of logical condensation. The explanation that he had offered in confession—that because he murdered Lino he must murder the Quadris—is shortened to "Lino murdered the Quadris" in a process that conflates the two clauses by making the object of the first one the subject of the second, neatly removing Marcello from the equation (and from all culpability). Such grammatical short-circuiting yields more than gratuitous results, for it reveals the ethical basis of authoritarianism. The agent is not morally accountable for his actions, he is merely the conduit of some external authority whose dictates he follows as a matter of duty. By accusing Lino of murder, pederasty, Fascist allegiance, and later by leveling the last charge at Italo as well, Marcello is disowning responsibility for his crimes in true authoritarian fashion. He is not the author of his moral being.

Marcello's projection of responsibility onto Lino at the end of the film retrospectively organizes an entire pattern of moral abdications. When Manganiello, the Fascist henchman, offers his services to his new boss, Marcello's first orders are to do away with his mother's drug-procuring lover, her Japanese chauffeur Chi. What masquerades as a test of Manganiello's loyalty is really proof of Marcello's cowardice in refusing to avenge his filial honor himself.[7] More importantly, Marcello takes no personal responsibility for joining the Fascist party. Instead, he blames Quadri, whose anti-Fascist teachings at the University of Rome had sustained Marcello until 1928, the year of his mentor's torture and eventual self-exile to Paris. "You left, and I became a Fascist," Marcello explains, thus placing the entire burden of his political apostasy at Quadri's expatriate feet.

Most curious is the way in which Marcello disavows responsibility for the counterintelligence plan that was his very own devising. When the journey to Paris must be interrupted by a stop in Ventimiglia where Marcello will get his final briefing for the mission, he learns that plans have changed. "There is a counterorder from Rome," announces Comrade Raoul. Instead of spying on Quadri, "you must simply eliminate him." Marcello accepts these orders, and the accompanying pistol, undismayed. "This means I have no alternatives," he says with obvious relief that the final decision on Quadri's fate is not up to him. As if Marcello had nothing at all to do with the original conspiracy against Quadri, he greets this command with good grace like the proper functionary that he is.

If Italo Montanari, the blind ideologue, is the embodiment of Fascist theory, then Manganiello is the embodiment of Fascist practice. His name is a play on the Italian word "manganello," meaning club, which suggests his Pulcinella ancestry in the comedia dell'arte. Indeed, our first reaction to Manganiello is an amused one, not unlike the world's first reaction to Mussolini as a posturing, preening buffoon.

---

[7] This is one of Bertolucci's fanciful emendations to the text. Moravia's chauffeur was not Japanese, nor was he eliminated by Manganiello. Bertolucci's modification adds humor and thematic reinforcement to the film. Since "chi" means "who" in Italian, the name provides an occasion for comic equivocation between question and answer. The elimination of Chi proves Manganiello's brutality and Marcello's abdication of responsibility for his misdeeds.

Manganiello provides much of the film's humor, from his chat with the birds in a Parisian park to his hardly inconspicuous trailing of the Clericis and the Quadris on the eve of the assassination. The flash to a Laurel and Hardy photo on the dance-hall window furthers the comic implications of Manganiello's role—he plays the stout, bullying Oliver Hardy to Marcello's slight, sniveling Stan Laurel. However, as Fascism evolved from silly buffoonery in the world's eyes to malignant warmongering, so too does Manganiello's cinematic presence.[8] At the film's climax, he bespeaks the vilest articles of the Nazi-Fascist faith. "Cowards, perverts, Jews. They're all the same. If it were up to me I'd put them against the wall all together. It would be even better to eliminate them immediately, at birth." As a gestural accompaniment to this tirade, Manganiello urinates at the assassination site in the intermission between Quadri's murder and that of his wife.

Throughout the film, Manganiello has articulated the authoritarian defense against moral accountability. After giving Marcello the unwelcome news that Anna Quadri has joined her husband on the journey which is to end in their deaths, Manganiello disowns all blame for the predicament. "I mean I followed instructions to the letter." At two separate moments later in the journey to the assassination site, Manganiello remembers an episode in which the morality of the secret police missions is called into serious question. The fact that Manganiello sees fit to mention the incident twice suggests not only his failure to resolve the issue and his consequent discomfort with it, but also Bertolucci's insistence that we apply the moral lessons of this parable to the assassination that is about to occur. "Do you believe in fate, *dottore?*" asks Manganiello, who then begins to tell of a similar mission in Africa which was followed by a belated counterorder from Rome. So elliptical is this account that it leaves us eager to know more, but our curiosity will be satisfied

---

[8] On the deterioration of Manganiello's character in our eyes, see Robert Hatch's review of *The Conformist* in *Nation*, 5 April 1971, 446.

only much later in the film when Manganiello resumes his
narrative just prior to their arrival at the assassination site.
"In Africa, after so much work, four dead." He discovers it
wasn't necessary. Our commanding officer said 'You've ru-
ined me. You're beasts.' 'This, no,' I answered, 'we're men,
not beasts.' " Of course, Bertolucci implies that the opposite
is true for those who would follow orders regardless of their
moral content. Manganiello's defense (and it is a flimsy one
even in his own eyes, or he would not protest so much) is to
attribute the fourfold murder in Africa to superhuman fate.
When Manganiello argues that it was destined to be, and
that he was merely an agent of the inevitable, he also links
the Quadri murder plot to the principle of divine fatality.
But this very association is given the lie by the astonishing
frequency with which counterorders are issued.[9] If Fascist
authority has the status of superhuman destiny, it must be
absolute and inviolate, not subject to constant change by the
vacillating command in Rome. What emerges from the
shambles of this failed analogy is that orders are as fallible
as the highly uncertain human beings from whom they issue,
and to obey them as if they were divine writ, regardless of
their equivocal morality, is to abdicate one's own human status. Manganiello and his ilk well deserved the opprobrium
of their commanding officer.

In his structuring of the film, Bertolucci offers perhaps his
most powerful illustration of the ethics of Fascist collaboration. Bertolucci has been criticized for his failure to follow
Moravia's linear chronology and he has been accused of an
arbitrary and confusing shuffling of past, present, and future.[10] I would argue instead that such reordering is not only
purposeful, but essential to his moral adaptation of the Mo-

[9]Marcello himself comments on this in the novel. See Alberto Moravia,
The Conformist, trans. Angus Davidson (New York: Playboy Paperbacks,
1982), pp. 126–27.

[10]See, for example, Hollis Alpert, Review of *The Conformist*, *Saturday
Review*, 10 April 1971, 40, and Stanley Kauffmann's review, 10 April 1971,
24.

ravian text. "I thought maybe I need[ed] two times, the present and the past," Bertolucci said of his decision to break up
Moravia's chronological storyline.[11] Accordingly, the filmmaker locates his narrative present in the car ride which takes
Marcello and Manganiello from Paris to the assassination
site on the way to Savoy. During the course of this journey,
which begins early in the morning of 15 October 1938 and
continues until 4 P.M., Marcello remembers the series of events
leading up to his current predicament. These reminiscences
are presented in a complex and disorienting group of flashbacks which take us about two-thirds into the film before
the past catches up with the present and we have enough
information finally to understand the opening sequence. The
narrative exposition is given fitfully in a series of flashbacks
whose order in the film defies any chronological sequencing.
These include 1) a visit to Italo in a radio station; 2) lunch
at Giulia's; 3) a visit to his mother at home and his father in
an asylum; 4) the pseudo-murder of Lino; and 5) the confession in church and the honeymoon journey to Paris. Once in
Paris, the narrative proceeds smoothly, and brings us up to
the dance-hall scene on the eve of the assassination. After
the murder, Bertolucci flashes forward to 25 July 1943, the
day of Mussolini's downfall, for his film's denouement. The
narrative structure, though far more complex than that of
Investigation of a Citizen above Suspicion, may be dia-
grammed in similar fashion.

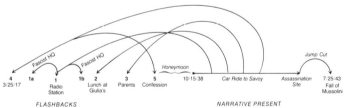

With his very first flashback, Bertolucci introduces us to
the difficulties of his editorial style. We are in the radio sta-

[11] "Bertolucci Seminar," p. 23.

tion as a begrudging Italo congratulates Marcello on his impending marriage. When Italo goes on the air, Marcello dozes off, only to be awakened by a Fascist official who reports that the protagonist's counterintelligence plan is under consideration by the party higher-ups. This dialogue is punctuated by a flashback to Marcello's arrival at Fascist headquarters to submit his plan, and by a flashforward to Fascist headquarters to receive final approval. A later flashback, that of the 1917 encounter with Lino, takes as its point of departure a moment in the narrative present of the car ride to Savoy, but finds its point of return in another flashback—that of the premarital confession in church. T. Jefferson Kline sees in these disorienting editorial techniques Bertolucci's attempt to simulate a dream state—an argument supported by the fact that Marcello's flashbacks often seem to come in the aftermath of his dropping off to sleep.[12] I would argue that the oneiric effects are part of a larger mimetic technique on Bertolucci's part. Like the novel, whose narrator speaks in the third person but whose perspective is exclusively that of Marcello, the film mimics its protagonist's mode of vision. By structuring so much of the film around a series of flashbacks which are the product of reminiscence, Bertolucci establishes Marcello's subjectivity as the source of the camera's perspective. Marcello's cognitive style becomes Bertolucci's, in an example of the free indirect subjective which Pasolini considered the cinematic equivalent of free indirect discourse in literature. If this is indeed the case, then other elements of Bertolucci's style no longer appear to be arbitrary, bravura effects and become, instead, visual analogues of Marcello's mental state. His surrealism (the profusion of walnuts on Raoul's desk, the apples on Marcello's daughter's bureau, for example) the oblique camera angle as Manganiello first

[12] See T. Jefferson Kline, "The Unconformist," in *Modern European Film-makers and the Art of Adaptation*, ed. Andrew Horton and Joan Magretta (New York: Ungar, 1981), especially p. 231.

follows Marcello home, the darkened sets, split-screen effects, and so on[13] all suggest an abnormal, chaotic mental
state—that of a troubled psyche, beset by warring impulses,
which seeks the solace of a strict order imposed upon it from
without.[14] Marcello's rigid body language, typified by robot-
like movements and a total absence of physical spontaneity,
reflects, on a kinesthetic level, his efforts to control the chaos
of his inner psychic state. Accordingly, Italo sees the potential for hysterical collapse in his friend as he admonishes
Marcello several times in the film to "be calm."

Bertolucci's nonchronological structuring of the story does
more than establish Marcello's consciousness as the cognitive center of the film, however. This ordering technique also
says something crucial about the moral and existential consequences of adherence to Fascist thought. By privileging the
car ride, which would merit no attention at all in a sequen-
tial telling of the story, the film is able to concentrate our
attention on the present of decision-making whose results
Bertolucci identifies with Fascism itself. The journey is really
one agonizing process of choice—will Marcello intervene to
save the life of his beloved, or will he watch her murder in
complicitous passivity? By devoting so much attention to the
decision, Bertolucci rejects the Moravian emphasis on inexorable fate and insists instead on Marcello's sovereign free
will. In the novel, there is no car ride to Savoy and, more
importantly, there is no witness of the assassination by Marcello at all—he learns about it after the fact from a newspaper account and then a verbal report by Manganiello (called

---

[13] On Bertolucci's surrealism, see Pauline Kael, "The Poetry of Images,"
in *Deeper into Movies*, p. 345. According to Joel Magny, Bertolucci's style
in *The Conformist* mimics that of the prewar cinematic avant-garde. See
"Dimension politique de l'oeuvre de Bernardo Bertolucci de *Prima della
rivoluzione* à *Novecento*," in *Bernardo Bertolucci*, ed. Michele Estève (Paris:
Minard, 1979), p. 66.

[14] Bertolucci also uses color as an external manifestation of Marcello's
psychic disarray. See Bernard Oheix, "Notes sur les composantes du récit et
de l'image," in *Bernardo Bertolucci*, ed. Estève, p. 118.

Orlando in the text). Instead, Bertolucci's Marcello not only beholds the event, but spends some ten hours in a car trying to decide whether or not to abort the mission.

Like Moravia's Marcello, Bertolucci's could have also stayed in Paris and let the Fascist hit men do their dirty work unobserved. But the phone call by Manganiello informing him that Anna Quadri has joined her husband precipitates Marcello into action. He travels with Manganiello in the initial hope of intervening to save Anna, as proved by his insistence on getting out of the car when Manganiello concludes, "There's nothing we can do for the woman." Marcello's original motives in undertaking the journey are heroic, activist, interventionist ones. In the name of love, Marcello will transcend Fascist allegiances, challenge his killer destiny, and escape to a promised land of freedom and erotic abandon. The dream he recounts to Manganiello dramatizes the romantic impulse that led him to undertake the journey to Savoy. "I was blind. You were driving me to Switzerland to a clinic. It was Professor Quadri who was to operate on me. The operation was a success, I got back my sight and I left with the professor's wife who was in love with me." In this dream, Marcello inadvertently maps out a possible happy ending to the film: a conversion to anti-Fascism, true love, and romantic escape. What Bertolucci is implying here is that Marcello could rewrite his story and become literally the author of his destiny were he to opt for the active heroism that would merit such a narrative reward. Instead, Marcello chooses to sit in cowardly inertia as two people are vilely murdered at his initial behest. The heroic ethos that bade him undertake the journey has evolved into passive, cowardly abdication of responsibility—an evolution suggestive of Fascism itself, where the promise of macho adventurism gives way to the dreary, morally evasive reality of carrying out other men's threats. The car ride to Savoy *is* Fascism in its movement from a seemingly heroic ethos to a passive and cowardly one.

Perhaps the most ingenious of Bertolucci's textual modifications is his insertion of Plato's myth of the cave, for this
not only synthesizes the film's moral arguments, but also le-
gitimizes his cinematographic techniques. From the very outset of the film, the theme of vision has assumed obvious moral
proportions.[15] Italo Montanari, the Fascist apologist, is
sightless, and as his first name suggests, we are to take him
as a personification of an entire populace blinded by Mussolini's untruths. Likewise, Marcello is blind in his dream,
and regains his vision thanks to the surgical intervention of
Quadri. During the scene in Quadri's study where professor
and exstudent retell the myth of Plato's cave, vision is explicitly wed to certain moral and political choices.

> Imagine an enormous tunnel in the form of a cavern.
> On the inside, [there are] men who have lived there
> since childhood, all enchained and obliged to face the
> back of the cave. Far behind them shines the light of a
> fire. Between the fire and the prisoners imagine a wall,
> low, similar to the little stage on which the puppeteer
> has his puppets appear . . . and now try to imagine
> men who pass behind that wall carrying statues of
> wood and stone. . . . What do they [the prisoners]
> see? . . . They see only the shadows that the fire
> projects.

It is the professor who gives the parable its political gloss.
"Shadows, the reflections of things, as happens to you today
in Italy." Meanwhile, Marcello has been unconsciously pan-
tomiming this lesson by raising his arm in the Roman salute
and then turning away from the light of the window to the
wall on which his own silhouette is projected. At the end of
the scene, Quadri suddenly opens the window shutters and
Marcello's shadow dissipates in a visual enactment of the
moment of Platonic enlightenment. Like the dream of restored vision, this triumph of light over shadow alludes to

[15] On the primacy of the visual theme in *The Conformist*, see Magny,
"Dimension politique," pp. 65–66.

the possibility of a happy ending through a conversion to anti-Fascist truth under the aegis of Quadri. But the professor is not the unequivocal hero of the piece, as the Platonic allusion might initially indicate. Instead, further reading of the passage in *The Republic* gives support to Marcello's indictment of his professor's decision to expatriate. Socrates argues that the enlightened must not be allowed to remain aloof, but must share their illumination with their fellow citizens—an implicit condemnation of Quadri's move to abandon Rome and leave his Italian followers to their own devices. In his way, then, Quadri has also abdicated moral responsibility by forsaking the incipient anti-Fascist movement he was supposed to have led.[16] When Giulia announces that Quadri must be a typical intellectual, "negative and impotent," her mindless stereotyping is not without some measure of accuracy.

Retrospectively, the Platonic reference gives philosophic coherence and weight to many of Bertolucci's stylistic and imagistic choices. The sequence in which Marcello receives official approval for his spy mission offers the spectacle of large pieces of statuary—an eagle and the bust of a man—being carried through the ministry lobby. These, then, are the statues positioned on the low wall of Plato's cave and they, like the propagandizing images of Mussolini's rhetoric, will block out the light of the fire to produce those shadows that will be mistaken for the real. Elements of the myth of Plato's cave also recur in the penultimate scene of the film as a bust of Mussolini is dragged over Ponte Sant'Angelo in the wake of the tyrant's deposition. The headlight of a motorcycle which pierces the darkness suggests the illuminating power of anti-Fascist truth to dispel the shadows produced by the imagery of dictatorship.

With the myth of Plato's cave, Bertolucci gives a philo-

---

[16] According to Mellen, "Bertolucci in both *Il conformista* and *The Spider Strategem* (1969–70) condemns the default of intellectuals to devise and lead the necessary resistance to the rise of fascist power." See "Fascism in the Contemporary Film," p. 3.

sophical justification for his lighting techniques throughout the film. His predilection for black backgrounds and for striking chiaroscuro effects is no mere imitation of contemporary film styles of the 1930s, it is also a way of appropriating the moral teachings of Plato's myth. The Roman sequences of the film are considerably darker, suggesting the blighted vision of those prey to Fascist illusions. Light and dark are juxtaposed throughout the film: in the split-screen *mise-en-scène* of the confession, for example, or in the diagonal zebra stripes of Giulia's parlor, which reflect the pattern of her dress and move along the surfaces of the room as if a rhythmical wind were rippling the slats of her Venetian blinds. This zebra-stripe technique is used again, less flamboyantly, but far more momentously, at the assassination site. Here, the woodland setting gives verisimilitude to the alternating bars of light and dark that filter through the tall trees. If we interpret Plato's myth of the cave not as a static confrontation between truth and illusion, but as a dynamic model of conversion, then the light and dark imagery in the murder scene corresponds to the moral choice that besets Marcello. By opting not to intervene on behalf of Anna, Marcello chooses the Platonic shadows rather than the light. Bertolucci shows the moral consequences of this choice in a jump cut to a scene five years later, which is shot in almost total darkness. In fact, a blackout actually does occur some minutes into the scene which has caused this viewer, on several occasions, to suspect a malfunctioning projector. What Bertolucci is showing us in these final dark sequences is how Marcello has fulfilled the negative teachings of Plato's myth by choosing the shadows of Fascist compliance over the bright light of resistance.

The five-year interval between the Quadri assassination and Mussolini's downfall has brought some superficial changes in the direction of Marcello's vaunted normalcy. The Clericis have set up housekeeping in Rome and they have had a daughter, Marta—yet reminders of the atrocity abound. Marta is blue-eyed and blond, unlike either of her parents, but very much like Anna. She is playing dress-up in the final scenes and just happens to be wearing the fox fur that Anna had lent Giulia in Paris, but had not lived long enough to ask for in return. When this blond Marta recites the "Ave Maria" at the prompting of her father, they stand against a wallpaper background of blue heavens and white clouds which suggests the artifice and insincerity of Marcello's belabored normalcy.

Plato's myth is given its most striking and ambiguous enactment in the final scene of the film when Marcello turns toward the male prostitute in acknowledgment of his own repressed desires. The young man lives in a niche in the Colosseum whose source of light and heat is a fire just outside the iron grating that serves as his door. When Marcello gazes upon the young man, fire, niche, and bars provide the equivalents of the setting for Plato's prisoners enchained in the cave. But the moral applicability of the myth is less obvious. Is Marcello embracing the shadows or the light in accepting his latent sexual inclinations? Though his gaze appears to be toward the back of the niche/cave and hence toward falsehood and illusion, his yielding to homosexuality would be a surrender to the truth which he had sought to deny through Fascism and murder—the political "shadows" of the story. By positioning the fire neither to the front nor to the back of Marcello, but to the left side, so that his face remains half in the shadow and half in the light, Bertolucci keeps the ambiguity alive. In so doing, he raises the metacinematic possibilities of Plato's myth and implicates the viewers in its moral challenge. "When you read the *Cave* of Plato's," Bertolucci explains, "the cave is exactly like the theater and the background is the screen and Plato says there is a fire and people walking in front of the fire and the fire projects the shadows in the background of the cave. It's the invention of the cinema."[17] Even without Bertolucci's explanatory gloss, the end of the film forces us to reflect on the illusionism of the me-

[17]"Bertolucci Seminar," p. 21.

dium itself when Marcello turns toward the male prostitute in the final shot. As his eyes seek out his object of desire, they meet our own gaze, breaking the conventional prohibition against looking into the camera and thus destroying the illusion of reality upon which the cinema depends. As he looks upon the young man and upon ourselves in curiosity and desire, he exposes the curious and desirous nature of our own relationship to cinematic illusion. What Bertolucci is telling us, in making this analogy, is to beware of the seductive allure of the shadows on the screen, to perceive them critically, not to endow them with power over us. Fascism worked because people succumbed to illusion, granting moral authority to superior forces which legislated their own ethics and imposed them on a passive, uncritical, irresponsible public. By owning up to the illusory nature of his art, Bertolucci is taking moral responsibility for it and is urging his viewers to accept his fictions for what they are. Bertolucci's plea for moral accountability would lack all credibility without its forthright application to his own filmmaking venture.

Our study of *The Conformist* would be less than thorough were we to ignore the film's title, which Bertolucci wisely chose to borrow from Moravia with all its multileveled meanings and attendant ironies. Indeed, in his very first flashback, Bertolucci offers the perfect visual and aural expression of that social conformity to which Marcello aspires. Three women, identically dressed and coiffed, sing in harmony before the microphone of a radio broadcast studio.[18] In Andrews Sisters fashion, they are individuated neither physically nor vocally as they conform to a collective image which discourages any revelation of difference. The next item on the program, Italo's Fascist apologia, is the ideological equivalent of the immediately previous exercise in

---

[18] For an insightful analysis of this sequence in which the radio station is seen as both the epitome of that normalcy sought by Marcello and an analogue to Plato's cave, see Andrew Britton, "Bertolucci: Thinking about Father," *Movie* 23 (1976–77), 1.

conformist entertainment. In celebrating "the Prussian aspect of Mussolini and the Latin aspect of Hitler," Italo typifies not only the excesses of Fascist rhetoric in general, but the fanciful effort to make two very different regimes conform to one another in a way that denies the individual identity of each. Cinematographically, Bertolucci illustrates this abdication of individual identity in his technique of shooting through glass.[19] At various points in this scene, Italo and Marcello are shot as mere reflections on the transparent partition separating the office from the broadcast studio. Both men have forfeited their titles to individuality—Marcello in his desire to be socially invisible, and Italo in his adherence to an ideology of coercive uniformity.

One of the many ironies of the title is that Marcello's very ambition to conform already sets him apart from the masses whose ranks he hopes to join. "Everyone wants to be different from the others," Italo tells him in the radio station. "Instead, you want to be the same." Throughout the film Bertolucci offers visual proof of how very self-defeating Marcello's efforts at assimilation are. As a child, he was singled out to be the victim of the gang assault which led him to ask protection of Lino. In Paris, as Marcello is being led to his audience with Quadri, he is accompanied by a group of the professor's disciples who form a hostile circle around this accurately perceived enemy of their cause. But the most striking illustration of Marcello's antisocial status is the celebrated farandole in the dance hall of Joinville which culminates the dance imagery throughout the film and bids us look back at its many prefigurations in earlier scenes. Often, during the course of *The Conformist*, dance has served as the moving image of social conformity. In the radio station, the indistinguishable singing threesome do a dance routine in perfect synchrony. Such is their enthusiasm for uniformity

[19] On this technique, see ibid., p. 4; Bondanella, *Italian Cinema*, p. 306; and Richard Roud, "Fathers and Sons," *Sight and Sound* 40 (Spring 1971), 64.

that they they cannot help but dress alike and execute these identical dance steps, even though the medium of the radio is indifferent to the visual aspects of their performance. When Giulia does a similar dance routine to the phonograph record her uncle sent from America, she is conforming to her society's appetite for exotica from the New World.[20] Anna Quadri is also associated with the dance. As a ballet instructor she is allied with classical, humanist culture—a link that Bertolucci has made explicit in several interviews where he has condemned the Quadris' anti-Fascism as stemming from bourgeois, idealist impulses and not from Marxist conviction.[21] Her teaching of ballet would suggest her connection with those very bourgeois cultural values which the Marxist revolution would seek to destroy.

If, by the end of the film, Bertolucci has not succeeded in convincing us of the metaphoric function of his dance sequences, the climactic farandole in the *bal populaire* should seal the argument. The spectacle of so many dancers who give their unconditional assent to a set of rules that govern the movements of each participant offers a perfect metaphor for social conformity. In the flamboyant tango that Anna and Giulia dance together they enact the parodic relationship that homosexuality bears to the social order. Just as the tango is a caricature of seduction, so too does homoerotic love appropriate, sometimes satirically, the conventions of heterosexual passion. Given the nonconformist (or para-conformist) nature of Anna's desire for Giulia, it is fitting that they should dance alone and that the other couples should surrender the floor to them in curiosity and amusement.

For Giulia, whose conventionality would never allow her seriously to entertain Anna's lesbian advances, the farandole

[20] On this scene and its relationship to that of the radio station, see Britton, "Bertolucci," p. 3.

[21] See "Bertolucci Seminar," p. 19; Mellen, "A Conversation with Bertolucci," p. 21; and Goldin, "Bertolucci on *The Conformist*," p. 66. On the shared class background of Marcello and the Quadris, see Bondanella, *Italian Cinema*, p. 304.

13. In his reluctance to join the dance led by Giulia (Stefania Sandrelli) and Anna (Dominique Sanda), Marcello (Jean-Louis Trintignant) dramatizes his outsider's relationship to the social order.

is the true expression of her social being. As a kind of social chameleon, she adapts perfectly to her surroundings, attributing her high spirits now to her Parisian setting. "Ça c'est Paris. Je suis une femme à la page," she says, using French to show how well assimilated she indeed is. With this pronouncement, she begins the farandole in which nearly everyone joins, even the hunchbacked Quadri whose disability does not prevent his entering this rite of social consensus. Among the few who sit out the dance are Marcello and Manganiello, and it is during this interlude that the information required for the assassination plot is exchanged. Since murder, especially the murder of a Resistance leader exiled in France, is the antisocial act par excellence, their abstention from the dance is metaphorically apt. When Marcello is finally forced onto the floor he reacts like a captive, standing alone, moving counterclockwise as the revellers swarm around in the opposite direction. No image could speak more eloquently of his status as social misfit.

What the film's ironies unanimously point to is not the fallacy of its title, but its unexpected referent. Marcello is indeed a conformist, but not to the society whose sanction he so craves. In Moravia's terms, he is a conformist to the fate he sought to escape and in so doing, only hastened to bring about. In Bertolucci's terms he is a conformist to his own psychopathology, ultimately embracing his homosexual leanings, as well as his father's propensity to madness which, though not caused by syphilis, seems nonetheless to have a hereditary source.

Much has been made of Bertolucci's psychosexual explanation for Fascism and this has formed the basis of considerable criticism of the film in the American press.[22] Such objections, however, reflect a serious misinterpretation of Bertolucci's argument, which is not a homophobic one by

[22] See, for example, Jay Cocks, *Time*, 5 April 1971, 86; Kauffmann, review, p. 24; and Kael, *Deeper into Movies*, p. 343.

any means, but which attributes Fascism to the need to deny perceived individual differences of any sort. The etiology of Fascism is not homosexuality—indeed Lino and the male prostitute have nothing in common with the thugs who exterminate the Quadris or the government officials who authorize them to do so. To further vitiate any presumed equivalence between authoritarian and homoerotic tendencies, there is the example of Anna, who is lesbian and anti-Fascist.[23] "Homosexuality is just an element in Marcello's character," Bertolucci explained to Joan Mellen. "Marcello feels different because of his secret homosexuality . . . and when you feel 'different' you have to make a choice: to act with violence against the existing power or, like most people, to ask for the protection of power."[24] Far from insisting that underneath every Fascist lurks a repressed homosexual, Bertolucci presents Marcello's idiosyncratic sexuality as one example of the general need to deny personal differences, which would lead an insecure, threatened individual to identify with an all-powerful state. Upon close analysis, the erotic impulses that subvert Marcello's psychic order are not all homosexual by any means. Of the three characters who arouse his libidinal interest—Lino, the prostitute in Ventimiglia, and Anna—two are women. Though Moravia gives the Anna character the name "Lina," suggesting that it is her homosexuality, or at least her sexual ambiguity, that appeals to Marcello, the writer also associates her with the prostitute in Ventimiglia whose appeal to Marcello is unequivocally feminine. Similarly, in the film, Bertolucci links Marcello's reactions to the prostitute and Anna by having Dominique Sanda

[23] On Anna's lesbianism, see Joan Mellen, *Women and Their Sexuality in the New Film* (New York: The Horizon Press, 1973), pp. 87–91. Mellen errs, however, in seeing Anna as exclusively motivated by her passion for Giulia. I find this reading reductive in its indifference to her political motives, which are to fascinate and confuse Marcello so that he will abandon his homicidal mission.

[24] Mellen, "A Conversation with Bertolucci," p. 21.

play both roles.[25] What Marcello's passions for Lino, harlot, and Anna share is obviously not their homosexual aspects, but their power to disturb his mental balance. Hence his need to destroy them as a way of exorcizing the forbidden impulses they excite in him and of averting the devastating influences these would have on his hard-won self-control. It is no mere coincidence, then, that all three arousers of dangerous passions should have scars on their right cheeks (a wound in Anna's case, for this is where she is fatally shot) and that Lino and Anna should fall in the same positions after being gunned down. Thus the pseudo-murder of Lino shares with the Quadri assassination not the strange logic of atonement that Marcello articulates in the confessional, but the need to exorcize the troubling passions aroused by Lino and Anna— passions that, be they homosexual or otherwise, would destroy his elaborate construct of normalcy and force him to confront the true chaos of his inner psychic state.

Marcello's desire for conformity, therefore, comes less from homosexual anxiety than from fear of any individual difference (or what he would consider deviance) from accepted social practice. Decadent mother, mentally ill father—disruptive passions of any sort—constitute those differences that distinguish Marcello from his compatriots and that prompt his fanatical conformity. Of course, the ultimate irony is that in conforming to a Fascist state, he has simply found on a mass scale the very corruption, psychopathology, and violence that he sought to obliterate in his own soul.

Not surprisingly, the film's title is rich with metacinematic possibilities for so self-conscious a director as Bertolucci. Throughout the film, he revisits the models and influences to which he has conformed during the course of his career and

[25] Sanda also makes a cameo appearance as the mistress of the Fascist minister who approves Marcello's plot. Her ultrafeminine seductiveness in the role underscores the fact that Marcello's sexual preferences are not limited to men.

which have given shape to the present work. Too young to have personal memories of the 1930s, Bertolucci had to rely on cinematic re-creations of those years, so that "my memory was [a] memory of movies."[26] In an interview with Marilyn Goldin, Bertolucci elaborates. "*The Conformist* is lighted like a 1930's studio film, even when we were on location, there were a lot of lights and lighting effects, like that red [during the opening titles] or the rays in Sandrelli's apartment, or the blacks when the professor tells the myth of the Cave."[27] Similarly, in the surrealist moments of the film, Bertolucci is paying his respects to the "most important cultural element during the 20's and 30's."[28] Bertolucci's reconstruction of the Fascist years is thus several removes from any attempt at direct representation and becomes, instead, a personal interpretation of the ways in which Thirties culture saw itself.

In addition to these rather diffuse cinematic references, Bertolucci alludes quite pointedly to two *auteurs*—Godard and Renoir—whose work has had a formative influence on his own.[29] However, these allusions are not offered as homages, but rather as statements of Bertolucci's readiness to challenge and even to reject the cinematic mentors of his past. The in-jokes on Godard are well known: Bertolucci gives Quadri the French filmmaker's phone number, address, and middle name.[30] To further the conceit, he imputes to Quadri a line from Godard's *Le petit soldat*: "The time of reflection is over. Now begins the time of action."[31] The murder of Quadri signifies, on the level of Bertolucci's aesthetic auto-

[26] "Bertolucci Seminar," p. 17.

[27] Goldin, "Bertolucci on *The Conformist*," p. 65.

[28] Mellen, "A Conversation with Bertolucci," p. 22.

[29] On Bertolucci's relationship to Godard and Renoir, see Casetti, *Bertolucci*, pp. 76–77.

[30] See, for example, Lino Miccichè, *Il cinema italiano degli anni '70* (Venice: Marsilio, 1980), pp. 98–99, and Bondanella, *Italian Cinema*, p. 303.

[31] For this attribution, see Casetti, *Bertolucci*, p. 76.

biography, the end of Godard's influence on his own film-making style.[32] With Godard goes the imperative to radical cinema whose limited audience appeal condemned it to total political ineffectuality. (Quadri too was ineffectual in his promulgation of leaflets, not actions, from his expatriate headquarters in France.)

Jean Renoir is invoked twice in the film: once in the far-andole, which recalls the renowned dance sequence in *The Rules of the Game*, and once during the opening titles when a neon sign flashes "La vie est à nous" in a reference to the 1936 film made for the French Communist Party.[33] Though Renoir is not symbolically killed, as Godard is, in *The Conformist*, his model for political cinema is nonetheless repudiated in the finale of the film which both recalls and subverts the corresponding scene in *La vie est à nous*. Renoir's film concludes on a choral note as members of all social classes join in singing "L'internationale" while the crowds in *The Conformist* celebrate Mussolini's downfall by singing two separate songs at once—"L'internazionale" and "Bandiera rossa." The addition of this second song is a cynical stroke of genius on Bertolucci's part, for it reveals the failure of that solidarity of the Left which Renoir's film so triumphantly announced and which the Italian Resistance promoted as its postwar revolutionary hope.[34]

Like Marcello, who goes to Paris to kill off his "spiritual father," so Bertolucci revisits his French models in *The Conformist* and announces his departure from them and from

---

[32] "In that film, 'I kill' Godard," Bertolucci said of *The Conformist*. Quoted in ibid., pp. 9–10.

[33] Bertolucci makes explicit his debt to *The Rules of the Game* in "Bertolucci Seminar," p. 22, while Casetti (*Bertolucci*, p. 76) points out the *La vie est à nous* allusion.

[34] My reading differs from that of Casetti, who sees in the Godard–Renoir allusions Bertolucci's rejection of the former as a model for "marginal" political filmmaking and his embrace of the latter, whose "political cinema" works through "the usual structures" of the film industry. See his *Bertolucci*, pp. 76–77.

their style of political filmmaking.[35] There are no programmatic political solutions, and even if there were, film is not the proper forum for their dissemination. "Cinema rebels against being totally instrumentalized—against being used like a mimeograph," Bertolucci had told Francesco Casetti, and in so saying, had asserted the freedom of his art from bondage to partisan political uses.[36]

Like Marcello, Bertolucci too returns to Rome in search of an alternative to the French model for political filmmaking. And he finds it in Roberto Rossellini, who is never explicitly invoked in *The Conformist*, but whose presence is nonetheless felt in the film's plea for moral accountability. Bertolucci has not been reticent on the subject of Rossellini, and his comments reveal the special importance of the neorealist's filmmaking example. "There is this capacity of having things never too far away and never too close, the ideal distance that his camera has from things and from characters. It is one of the first cases of a truly open cinema."[37] Nor is this notion of an open cinema limited to camera technique alone. "There is an ethic in the style of many directors; for example, for Godard the style is already a way of seeing the world, for Rossellini as well."[38] If film styles have their own built-in morality, then Rossellini's ideal viewing perspective, "never too far away and never too close," suggests an approach that is committed, but not coercive—one that issues an appeal for an activist response without dictating a rigid, ideologically closed program for social change. Rossellini's open cinema asks that we assume responsibility for what we learn from the screen and act according to our own inner

[35] Roud suggests the parallelism of Marcello's and Bertolucci's quests to liberate themselves from their pasts. See his "Fathers and Sons," p. 64.

[36] In Casetti, *Bertolucci*, p. 14.

[37] Quoted in John Bragin, "A Conversation with Bernardo Bertolucci," *Film Quarterly* 20 (Fall 1966), 42.

[38] In ibid., p. 44.

promptings, not to the externally imposed ones of the ideologues.

In *The Conformist*, Bertolucci proves himself an able practitioner of Rossellini's open cinema, accepting full responsibility for the Fascist history he portrays while rejecting programmatic political solutions as inappropriate to the cinema, whose illusionist properties recommend ambiguity rather than didacticism. If Bertolucci's theater is indeed Plato's cave, then the images on the screen will disillusion even as they delude us, calling attention to their shadowy status and admitting their equivocal morality. When Marcello turns to us at the end of the film, he forces us to contemplate our own relationship to the fire and the shadows; in the moviehouse, in the psyche, and in the state. Only then will we be equipped to resist Fascist recurrences—to choose the fire over the shadows, or at least to know that the choice is ours to make.

14 Wertmuller's *Love and Anarchy*: The high price of commitment

ACCORDING TO MUCH Wertmuller criticism, *Love and Anarchy* should have no place in a study of the neorealist impact on postwar Italian cinema. Not only is her antinaturalistic, antimimetic comic style "as far removed as possible from the school of Italian neorealism,"[1] but so too is her ideological teaching, which Pauline Kael finds "reactionary" in its despair over the possibility of social change and its consequent surrender to an unjust status quo.[2] Those critics who would deny Wertmuller's cinema any seriousness of political purpose do so on the basis of her preferred genre and on the kind of public that she chooses to address. Wertmuller's aspiration to a popular cinema, and her use of comedy to that end, are no secret. "I proceeded with great faith in the power of laughter and tears, without fearing to be too obvious or to appear banal, always trying to communicate and entertain and hoping . . . that people would leave my films with problems to think over and analyze."[3] What critics have come

---

[1] William Magretta and Joan Magretta, "Lina Wertmuller and the Tradition of the Italian Carnivalesque Comedy," *Genre* 12 (Spring 1979), 35. The Magrettas attribute Wertmuller's characterizations, plots, language, and directorial style to the grotesque, carnivalesque comic tradition—the tradition that gave rise to the commedia dell'arte, *opera buffa*, and puppet theater. Brunetta also ascribes Wertmuller's cinema to popular narrative modes, calling her "a ballad singer" or professional storyteller whose tales have an "exemplary character." See his *Storia*, p. 708.

[2] See Pauline Kael, Review of *Seven Beauties*, *New Yorker*, 16 February 1976, p. 109.

[3] See Gina Blumenfeld and Paul McIsaac, "You Cannot Make the Revolution on Film: An Interview with Lina Wertmuller," *Cinéaste* 7 (Spring 1976), 7. For further comments by Wertmuller on her desire for a mass

to question, however, is whether the two infinitives—"to communicate" and "to entertain"—can coexist on equal terms in her aesthetics, or whether comic pleasure will prevail, suppressing the doubts and anxieties that her cinema purports to raise.[4]

Though some of this criticism reflects Wertmuller's great commercial success, which makes her suspect in the eyes of the intellectual Left, much of it is warranted by the very comic strategies she uses to bring her ostensibly progressive message to the masses. Humor in itself need not preclude a socially responsible teaching—indeed satire may be one of the more effective methods for registering social criticism in the arts. Wertmuller's comedy is highly topical, engaging many of the most pressing issues of our times—consumerism, bossism, feminism, industrialization, radicalism, ethnicity, recidivism, and so forth. But her professed desire to raise the public consciousness is subverted by her comic technique, which is founded on what I would call "the politics of polarity." This strategy requires that each ideological choice be set in dialectical opposition to another one so that no position will be considered in and of itself, but will exist only in relationship to something else. It is that "something else" which thus defines the original position, allowing no complexity or ambiguity to distract us from the comic tug-of-war. Such a strategy involves an inevitable reduction, distortion, and exaggeration of the issues in order to heighten the dialectic and our comic delight in it. In *All Screwed Up*, for example, the

---

audience, see E. Servi Burgess, "Toward a Popular Feminist Cinema," in *Women and Film* 1, Nos. 5–6 (1974), 6 and 7; and "Look Gideon . . . Gideon Bachmann Talks with Lina Wertmuller," *Film Quarterly* 30 (Spring 1977), 3.

[4] On the problem of reconciling Wertmuller's twin aims, see David Grossvogel, "Lina Wertmuller and the Failure of Criticism," *Yale Italian Studies* 1 (Spring 1977), 171–83. On the affective problems created by Wertmuller's tragicomic mode, see Ernest Callenbach's review of *Everything Ready, Nothing Works*, in *Film Quarterly* 28 (Winter 1974–75), 59.

women's question is reduced to the polar extremes of super-feminist versus super-feminine, where the former alternative is embodied by Biki, a cold, calculating businesswoman, incapable of love, who sleeps with her boss for advancement and plays guru to a commune of young, impressionable women. Biki reduces feminism to mere questions of money and power, making herself the female equivalent of the worst male supremacist. Linda, the wife of a Sicilian immigrant who is prone to multiple births and produces litter upon litter of babies, represents the only alternative to Biki's unfeeling feminism within the world of the film. This polar opposition creates a static system with no gradations and no interplay between the various political options, thus diminishing the opportunities for a fruitful reevaluation of the choices. Such a strategy plays to the deepest biases of the viewing public, particularly to those ill-disposed to feminism, whose preconceptions will surely be reinforced.

Another aspect of Wertmuller's politics of polarity is her use of social stereotypes. The North–South dichotomy is rich with possibilities for her, offering such oppositions as rich versus poor, industrial versus agrarian, European versus Mediterranean, progressive versus conservative, tall versus short, fair versus dark, and so on. But given the virulent northern prejudice against the many immigrants from the South, Wertmuller's ethnic stereotyping takes on unmistakable racist overtones.[5] In *The Seduction of Mimi*, for example, much laughter is generated at the expense of the dark-skinned, curly-headed, primitive, macho, thoroughly Sicilian Mimi who fails to sustain the love of the fair-skinned, red-haired, highly civilized Turinese Fiore. Not only does Wertmuller exploit these stereotypes for comic purposes, but she validates them by insisting, finally, that they cannot be over-

[5] In fact, Brooks Riley, in "Lina Wertmuller: The Sophists' Norman Lear?" *Film Comment* 12 (March–April 1976), attributes Wertmuller's success in the U.S. to "a sense of superiority, not universality, that lets an audience wink at itself at the expense of one more Sicilian idiosyncracy" (p. 49).

come, not even through the most potent erotic and political means.

More distressing is the fact that the politics of polarity can be used to maneuver us into condoning unacceptable moral choices, as Jerzy Kosinski argues in his review of *Seven Beauties*.[6] According to Kosinski, Wertmuller wins our sympathy for a despicable protagonist by making him a cartoon character, and since we have laughed at Pasqualino all along, this tempers our reaction to the monstrosity of his final deeds.[7] Pasqualino's logic is countered by the female commandant of the concentration camp—a character so loathsome that we can hardly identify with her point of view.

> In Paris, there was a Greek who made love to a goose.
> He did it for money, he did it to survive . . . and you,
> you subhuman Mediterranean larva, you even find the
> strength to get an erection. . . . That's why you will
> end up the winners of this war . . . you will be the
> ones who are left . . . you tiny slithering worms . . .
> no ideals or ideas . . . and us, with our dreams of a
> superior race . . . it's far too difficult.[8]

Beset with the polar extremes of Nazi idealism, on the one hand, and the Mediterranean survival strategy on the other, it is obvious that we will side with Pasqualino, regardless of his highly equivocal morality. There is, however, the hint of an alternative in the character of Pedro, the Spanish anarchist who advocates "man in disorder" (295) in contrast to

[6] Jerzy Kosinski, "Seven Beauties—A Cartoon Trying to Be a Tragedy," *New York Times*, 7 March 1976, sec. 2, pp. 1 and 15.

[7] Marjorie Rosen also argues that Wertmuller wins our sympathies for Pasqualino by encouraging us "to respond to the sweet and suffering part of his character rather than to the meretricious." See "Laughing All the Way to the Gallows," *New Times*, 5 March 1976, 51.

[8] *The Screenplays of Lina Wertmuller*, trans. Steven Wagner (New York: Warner Books, 1978), pp. 326–27. Unless otherwise noted, all quotes from the screenplays will come from this edition. Subsequent page references will appear in the text.

Nazi orderliness, and Francesco, Pasqualino's accomplice in
deserting the army, who also has a sense of personal honor
and political integrity. But Wertmuller undercuts these options by making Pedro and Francesco such minor characters
that we have little time to identify with them, and by denying them any heroic stature in death—Pedro drowns in ex-
crement and Francesco pleads to be shot before he becomes
incontinent with fear. Not only does the politics of polarity
in *Seven Beauties* manipulate us into accepting an immoral
position in our preference for Pasqualino's survival tactics
over Nazi idealism, but it insists on the futility of resistance,
which results only in wasted, and undignified, self-destruction.[9]

The most egregious example of Wertmuller's polarization
technique is *Swept Away*, in which sexual tension is used to
heighten the standard geopolitical dialectic. Raffaella is a rich,
northern, capitalist slave-driver while Gennarino is a poor,
southern, Communist slave. But when the couple is stranded
on a desert island, the "natural order" reasserts itself and
the man prevails.[10] Though Wertmuller sophistically claims
that Raffaella really represents the man—artifically elevated
into a position of superiority by society—and Gennarino the
woman,[11] it is the spectacle of voluntary female sexual bondage that remains impressed in the viewers' memories and
not the allegorical meanings that Wertmuller would have us
attach to it.[12] The politics of polarity is once more used to

[9] On Wertmuller's nihilism, which implies that the Allied struggle in World
War II was for naught, that there is no difference between the concentration
camps and Naples after her liberation, see Bruno Bettelheim, "Reflections:
Surviving," *New Yorker*, 2 August 1976, pp. 31–52.
[10] Gina Blumenfeld puts forth this argument in "The (Next to) Last Word
on Lina Wertmuller," *Cinéaste* 7 (Spring 1976), 5.
[11] See Wertmuller's remarks in Blumenfeld and McIsaac, "You Cannot
Make the Revolution on Film," p. 8.
[12] On Wertmuller's dubious feminism, see Ellen Willis, "Is Lina Wertmuller Just One of the Boys?" in *Women and the Cinema: A Critical Anthology*, ed. Karyn Kay and Gerald Peary (New York: Dutton, 1977), pp.
377–83.

reinforce those stereotypes which lie at the root of the public's most regressive social thinking.[13]

This is all by way of saying that critics are right to question Wertmuller's "hybrid radical-popular" cinema[14] and to ask whether her films do indeed succeed in enlightening as they entertain us.[15] There is one Wertmuller film, however, that should be exempt from the blanket criticisms that her cinema has generated. *Love and Anarchy*, it seems, unfairly suffers from comparison with her other, more ideologically compromised films. Since many critics first saw *Love and Anarchy* in close proximity to *The Seduction of Mimi*, *All Screwed Up*, and *Swept Away* when these films were shown as a series in New York, since it also stars Giancarlo Giannini and Mariangela Melato (who appeared in all the films but *All Screwed Up*) and since it shares Wertmuller's recurrent thematic interest in politics and love, the film has naturally been included in an overall consideration of her work. Such a collective assessment does a grave injustice to *Love and Anarchy*, which differs from the rest of Wertmuller's cinema in several respects.[16] Though *Love and Anarchy* partakes of the politics of polarity, as the title immediately sug-

[13] For a scathing critique of Wertmuller's sexual politics in *Swept Away*, see Tania Modleski, "Wertmuller's Women: Swept Away by the Usual Destiny," *Jump Cut*, 10 June 1976, 1 and 16.

[14] See Blumenfeld, "The (Next to) Last Word," p. 50.

[15] In "Look Gideon," Wertmuller argues that she is able to further her didactic intent by keeping her films "open and problematic" (p. 4). Despite her disturbing endings and her refusal of comic closure, however, what remains in the viewer's memory are Wertmuller's slapstick antics and erotic wish-fulfillment fantasies.

[16] Grossvogel also considers *Love and Anarchy* the best of Wertmuller's films to date, "because of its central figure, Tunin, a recognizably human character" ("Lina Wertmuller," p. 180). Since her other films feature puppets and clowns, we are unable to identify with them and therefore are unlikely to take their lessons to heart. Miccichè, on the other hand, feels that *Love and Anarchy*, like Wertmuller's other films, is political only on the surface while maintaining "its substance as a gastronomic product" or consumer item. See *Il cinema italiano degli anni '70*, p. 158.

gests, it does so in ways that avoid the reductivist, exploitative uses to which this strategy was put in other films.
Furthermore, unlike *Seven Beauties*, *The Seduction of Mimi*,
and *All Screwed Up*, *Love and Anarchy* upholds the dignity
and necessity of political activism. Finally, unlike the other
films, which use politics not as an instrument for social
analysis, but as a pretext for the study of interpersonal dynamics, *Love and Anarchy* comments incisively on the historical and ideological context of the Mussolini years.

It would be no exaggeration to say that *Love and Anarchy*
is simply a meditation on its title—on the many ways in which
love and politics interpenetrate, to borrow John Simon's apt
formulation.[17] Here is where Wertmuller's politics of polarity gives way to a far richer, more complex relationship of
terms which are sometimes dialectically opposed, other times
sequentially ordered in an infinite regress of political acts which
are inspired by love, and loving acts which are in turn inspired by politics. Far from heralding yet one more of Wertmuller's dualities, the title sets the terms for a highly nu-
anced and complex study of the interrelationships between
emotional and political commitments.

Set in the early 1930s, *Love and Anarchy* is the story of a
northern Italian peasant named Tunin who witnesses the
murder of his friend, the anarchist Michele Sgaravento, and
resolves himself to carry out the dead man's mission to as-
sassinate Mussolini. After a sojourn in Paris with the anarchist underground, Tunin travels to Rome to make contact
with a prostitute, Salome, who has been cultivating a professional intimacy with Spatoletti, head of Mussolini's secret
service. In the bordello, Tunin meets and falls in love with
Tripolina, who decides to save him from certain death by
not awakening him on the morning of the planned assassination. When Tunin does awaken and realizes that the ap-

---

[17] See his introduction to *The Screenplays of Lina Wertmuller*, p. ix.

pointed hour is long past, he goes beserk, shoots at a platoon
of police during their routine rounds, is captured, tortured,
and bludgeoned to death by Spatoletti and his thugs.
As this plot summary suggests, the most obvious relationship between the two elements in the title is a hostile one.
Eros and politics make mutually exclusive claims on Tunin,
whose passion for Tripolina requires him to cherish life, and
to dedicate himself to the well-being of a single individual,
while his commitment to anarchy requires him to die for an
abstract ideal. In the film's most powerful scene, these rival
claims are embodied by Salome and Tripolina, whose battle
on the bathroom floor is a personification allegory of the
very forces that are ripping Tunin apart. "Look, you little
tart, get the hell out of here," says Salome to Tripolina who
withholds the key to the room where Tunin is sleeping. "This
isn't a romantic love story." "I'm well aware of all these
ideals, all this justice you seek, but you're not going to wake
him!" answers Tripolina. "Is there any justice in this poor
young man going to get himself killed like a dog?" "Of course
he's going to die like a dog," retorts Salome, "but he'd rather
die like a dog than live like one for the rest of his days"
(167). The animal imagery, which has characterized all the
discussions of freedom and human dignity throughout the
film, reveals the diametrically opposed perspectives from which
the two women speak. For Tripolina, the alternative to dying
like a beast for an ideal is the fully humanized life of love.
For Salome, life in an unfree society is even more degrading
than the squalid death her anarchist ideals require. But it is
obvious from this exchange, which takes place early in the
scene, why Tripolina and the claims of love will triumph.
From the very start, Tripolina has been able to steer the discussion away from the substance of the anarchist cause, which
is unarguably just and worthy of adherence, to the suicidal
price exacted of its followers. More important than Tripolina's polemic dexterity in swaying Salome, however, is the
latter's own ambivalence toward Tunin. For Salome's own

anarchist sentiments are deeply tinged with love, as I shall subsequently argue.

This climactic battle between the personified forces of love and anarchy is but the culmination of many minor skirmishes throughout the film. No sooner does Tunin set foot in the bordello than the tension begins. When Salome first asks Tunin what drew him to the anarchist cause and he answers, "Tyrants make me sick," she observes that his attention seems to be focused elsewhere. "It's my thighs, that's what you're looking at, like a hungry child" (102). In a foreshadowing of the final victory of love over anarchy, Tunin decides to accept Salome's offer of her professional services before settling into his own lodgings and preparing for the dangerous mission ahead. But it is Salome herself who later remarks on the incompatibility of erotic and political activism when Tunin asks for a two-day sojourn with Tripolina. "Go make love to your Tripolina," Salome snaps. "You'll see what's going to happen to your aim after a few days of exercise . . . you won't have the strength to pull the trigger!" (157).

We would be wrong, however, to dismiss Tripolina and Salome as simple embodiments of love and anarchy, respectively, for each has motivations and influences that would confound so schematic a reading. Though Tripolina's name would reinforce a strict identification with the erotic principle, its political implications are significant. When Tripolina introduces herself, Tunin comments, "Ah Tripoli, land of love," quoting from the lyrics of a popular song. "Perhaps it was because I always loved Africa, palm trees, and Rudolph Valentino playing the part of the sheik" (121), explains Tripolina. Attributing her choice to exoticism alone, she is oblivious to the political implications of her name, which recalls the capital of Libya, cornerstone of early twentieth-century Italian colonialism and precedent for Mussolini's African campaign of 1934–1936. A totally apolitical creature, Tripolina has unintentionally made herself an advertisement for Fascist imperial aspirations. Thematically, her name has twofold significance. By giving this pesudonym to a prostitute, Wertmuller suggests the connection between the sexual and territorial aspects of Il Duce's appeal—a connection made explicit in Spatoletti's tribute to Mussolini's genitals. "I bet HE has big balls as well, HE could fertilize the entire world" (132).[18] The sexual metaphor for imperialism is literalized later on when one of the whores, Yvonne, notes that bordello business booms on the days of Fascist rallies (140). Tripolina's name hints at darker meanings as well. By giving this nonpartisan character a pseudonym that bears the stamp of Fascist propaganda, Wertmuller shows how the apolitical are nonetheless manipulated and instrumentalized by the wielders of power. Significantly, the song that finally awakens Tunin after Tripolina and Salome let him oversleep is "Tripoli, land of love"—a song used to arouse military enthusiasm for Mussolini's incipient African campaign.

Inadvertently, then, Tripolina becomes an intensely political character whose final act of love—her decision not to awaken Tunin—politically disenfranchises him as surely as any Fascist dictatorship would. Freedom and harmonious social intercourse, the anarchist ideals to which Tunin's desperate mission is directed, are categorically denied by Tripolina's decision to set her desires above her lover's and obstruct the dictates of his free will.[19] Her love results in an abuse of power which, on the microcosmic level, recapitulates the state's most repressive operations. In the name of love, Tripolina "must not only come between him and the oppressor," writes Peter Biskind, "but between him and his own aspirations for self-respect, between him and history and

[18] On Wertmuller's thematic linkage of sexual domination and Fascist rule, see Ernest Ferlita and John May, *The Parables of Lina Wertmuller* (New York: Paulist Press, 1977), p. 43.

[19] For an exposition of anarchist ideals by Errico Malatesta—Wertmuller's most likely source, given her quotation of his sentiments on political assassinations at the end of the film—see his essay *Anarchy* excerpted in *The Anarchists*, ed. Irving Horowitz (New York: Dell, 1964), pp. 73–74 and 85 especially.

life itself."[20] The extent to which Tunin's freedom has been usurped by love is proved by the fact that the crisis of the story belongs entirely to Tripolina and Salome—the man is utterly excluded from the deliberations that determine the narrative catastrophe. Indeed, there is only one sequence in the film when Tunin is able to achieve an absolute balance between the political and amorous claims upon him. This is during the two-day sojourn with Tripolina, which immediately precedes the planned assassination. Tunin can be at once the complete lover, while preparing to be the complete anarchist, for the time when these two identities will be mutually exclusive is yet to come. The perfection of this state is predicated on its transience, as indeed Tunin's peak moment of happiness occurs precisely the night before he is to perform his assassin's mission.[21]

On another level, however, the antagonism between love and anarchy is resolved into continuity and mutual reinforcement when we examine the motivations for political action within the film. Tunin is propelled not by the abstract ideals that drive Manfredi in *Open City* or Quadri in *The Conformist*, for example, but by his passionate devotion to the anarchist Michele Sgaravento, whose death he vows to avenge.[22] Salome's anarchist commitment also derives from love, and it is this which makes her so vulnerable to Tripolina's arguments against awakening Tunin on the morning of the assassination.[23] Tunin's desire to avenge the death of a friend through tyrannicide has its exact equivalent in Sa-

[20]Peter Biskind, "Lina Wertmuller: The Politics of Private Life," *Film Quarterly* 28 (Winter, 1974–75), 16.

[21]On the transience of happiness in Wertmuller's world, see Simon's introduction to the screenplays, p. xi.

[22]The emotional motivations for political actions and the naiveté of the anarchists within the film makes *Love and Anarchy* "a warning against the assumed irresponsibility of the masses, hardly a revolutionary attitude," according to Lucy Quacinella in "How Left Is Lina?" *Cinéaste* 7 (Fall 1976), 15.

[23]On Salome's double love: that of Anteo rekindled by Tunin, and that of "Electra for her Orestes," see Simon's introduction to the screenplays, p. ix.

lome's vindictive resolve. Her fiancé, Anteo Zamboni, had been falsely accused of attempting to kill Mussolini and had been beaten to death as a consequence. Anteo's miserable end, along with Michele's, and with Tunin's mother's definition of an anarchist as "one who kills kings and queens, throws bombs, and is then hung for doing it" (92), provide the element of destiny to which the protagonist's fate will comply.[24] The difference, however, between the mother's definition and the concrete embodiments of it within the film is significant—while Wertmuller's anarchist martyrs all suffer the consequences of their activism, none of them succeeds in performing the first part of the definition.

In the story of Anteo Zamboni, Wertmuller provides both a prophecy of things to come and an insight into Salome's feelings for Tunin. Wertmuller insists that we read the story of Salome's lost love in this double register by including a series of vivid, concrete physical details that reveal its prophetic significance. In describing Anteo, Salome makes mention of his adolescence, acne, forelock, and imploring eyes— features that accord with Tunin's oft-mentioned youth, his flamboyant freckles, tousled hair, and wide-eyed facial expressions. Prophetic, too, is Anteo's death by beating, the brutality of which is underlined by Salome's mention of a prominent Fascist official's physical revulsion at the sight of the victim's disfiguration. Significantly, Salome's narrative is delivered in the immediate aftermath of her lovemaking with Tunin, suggesting the continuity of her feelings for both men. Furthermore, in the climactic dispute with Tripolina just prior to her capitulation, Salome remarks of Tunin, "Of course I love him . . . poor boy, he's fallen in the middle of this political mess . . . just like Anteo, so young, oh . . . my heart breaks when I think of how young they are" (168). By associating the two men, one martyred and the other about to be, Salome stops thinking of the second murder as a cor-

[24] On the prophetic force of this definition, see Ferlita and May, *Parables*, p. 43.

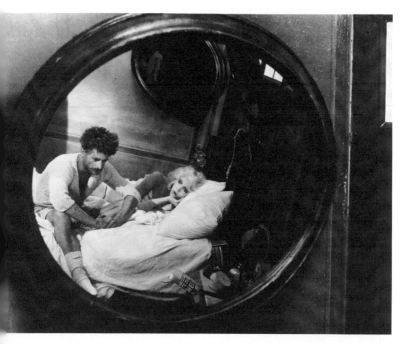

Reflected in the mirror of the bordello bedroom, Tunin (Giancarlo Giannini) listens as Salome (Mariangela Melato) tells how her anarchist commitment springs from the desire to avenge the Fascist murder of her fiancé.

rective for the first, and considers, instead, the wisdom of averting all such violent deaths, according to the apolitical logic of Tripolina.

If anarchy and love conventionally oppose each other on the grounds that one requires an abstract, intellectual commitment while the other requires a concrete, irrational one, Wertmuller subverts such seeming opposition by the very way in which Tunin embodies the principles of the anarchist cause. His is a visceral impulse to political action which, even lacking the motive of personal revenge, would remain at the instinctual level without any need for higher, cerebral justifications.[25] When Salome insists, "you, you're an anarchist" and Tunin responds, "like hell I'm an anarchist. I'm not Michele Sgaravento! I'm Antonio Soffiantini, and that's all" (158), he is setting the terms for an entirely personal, existential, nondoctrinaire partisan allegiance. "I've got no choice but to go ahead with it, even though I'm really not an anarchist . . . I swore I would stop living the way I was, like a slave. I just can't take it any more, not even rats live the way we do. I want to start living like a human being, to stop groveling like a snake in the mud. This one gesture will make me feel like a man again, at last" (159). Tunin's animal imagery here reveals not only his peasant origins, but also the personal philosophy behind his anarchist commitment, which he sees as the only way to reclaim his human dignity. This truth is enacted in the *mise-en-scène* of Tunin's first adult appearance on the screen. He is photographed behind a fence with his cow—a visual reference to his subhuman status under Fascism—while Michele Sgaravento does a little dance outside the fence—gestural proof of his freedom as an anti-Fascist.

Love is seen as the motivating force behind political action

[25] Tunin's nonideological anarchism weakens the political theme of the film according to Colin Westerbeck in his review in *Commonweal*, 9 August 1974, 430–31, and William Pechter in "Watching Lina Wertmuller," *Commentary* 100 (January 1976), 75–76.

not only in the cases of Salome's and Tunin's desires for personal revenge, but in a more general sense as well. "Still, there must be a power of light, a power of love than [sic] would make any person do these acts, above any consideration for personal safety," says Wermuller of her inspiration for the character of Tunin. "And then, in a minute, in thirty seconds, I got thc fccling of a person with this beauty and love inside him."[26] The passion that drives her protagonist, then, is not only his emotional attachment to the slain Michele Sgaravento, but a universalized love, which impels Tunin to combine personal vengeance with humanitarian self-sacrifice. The assassination of Mussolini will fulfill the demands of both these kinds of loves.

Furthermore, Tunin exemplifies not so much a committed member of a radical political movement as an embodiment of the anarchist philosophy itself. "Equal and free, the way we came into the world," says Michele Sgaravento around the fireside of Tunin's boyhood home.[27] By making Tunin a peasant at large in Rome, Wertmuller is not only setting up the terms for a conventional city–country dialectic, but is dramatizing the anarchist truth that natural man is innately just and good, and that it is only organized society, governed by the principles of authority and private property, which corrupts. Accordingly, much of the visual imagery that surrounds Tunin bears out his affinities with the natural world. He lies down in a field of grass near the assassination site as if he were resuming contact with his elemental source. After a harrowing night ride with Spatoletti, Tunin befriends a kitten whose black-and-white spotted fur recalls the peasant's own blotchy coloration. During the country outing, Tunin naturally gravitates to the barn and, when at a loss for words

[26] Quoted in Barbara Garson, "The Wertmuller Ethic," *Ms. Magazine* 4 (May 1976), 72.

[27] Here the published screenplay differs significantly from the soundtrack, which I have chosen to translate directly. I have also had to do this at several other points in the succeeding pages.

with Tripolina, comments on the beauty of the cows.[28] By
virtue of Tunin's instinctual anarchism, then, Wertmuller is
suggesting that freedom and justice are indeed man's birthright and that Fascism is, by contrast, unnatural to the human condition.

Another way in which Wertmuller relates anarchy and love
is to join them in opposition to Fascism and brute sex. The
country outing provides the theater for this foursome of elements as Tunin proves that the anarchist is the tenderest of
lovers while Spatoletti proves that Fascists are the crudest of
flesh-crushers. "If you don't stop I'm going to jump on you
and tear you to pieces, you sexy bitch" (119), Spatoletti announces in the expectation that violence will be as titillating
to Salome as it is to him. Just as Spatoletti's motives for
sleeping with Salome are loveless and territorial, hers are, in
turn, manipulative and exploitative. She wants to glean information about the coming Mussolini rally which Spatoletti, in the guise of boasting, is happy to divulge. Tunin and
Tripolina, on the other hand, make love out of genuine sympathy and physical attraction. Both are small, dark, freckled,
and, more importantly, both share a simple, peasant background, as shown by their reactions to the farmhouse setting
of their first lovers' tryst. Tunin is reminded of his parents'
bedroom and his mother's archetypal mending of socks, while
Tripolina is overcome with tears at the memory of the girl-
hood innocence so betrayed by her current profession. Such
is the power of Tunin's natural affection that it transforms
Tripolina—first into an extreme, self-hating version of the
prostitute that she already is, and then into the innocent
country girl she once was. To formalize this last transformation, Tunin changes her name from the artificial, inadvertently Fascist one which signifies her victimization by an oppressive political and economic system, to Ricciolina, or little
curly locks, which celebrates her own most lovely natural

[28] On Tunin's association with the world of nature, see Giancarlo Giannini's remarks in Rosen, "'Laughing All the Way to the Gallows," p. 47.

attribute. One of the ironies of the anarchy/love versus Fascist/brute sex opposition is that the former dyad emerges as the far more sexy and virile one, despite Spatoletti's constant sexual self-promotion. The women in the film are obviously far more attracted to Tunin's form of masculinity than they are to Spatoletti's, which they merely tolerate for purposes of financial gain or espionage. Spatoletti's name serves as a further commentary on his inferior sexual allure. Like Manganiello in *The Conformist*, whose name is a variant on "manganello," or club, suggesting both his Pulcinella ancestry and his Fascist brutality, Spatoletti's name means "little spatulas," suggesting a similar commedia dell'arte derivation. But the name is not without an obscene double meaning, which the diminuitive "etti" turns into a judgment on his genital prowess. Spatoletti's need to identify with Mussolini's touted masculinity may be seen as a compensation for the sexual inferiority that his name punningly reveals. It is Spatoletti himself who makes the invidious comparison between his performance and Tunin's at the country outing when the anarchist and his beloved tarry in the bedroom. "He's been pumping away for the past three hours," Spatoletti tells Salome as they wait impatiently below. "He must have dried up eventually . . . I'm sure he's fast asleep" (128), concludes Spatoletti by way of calming his competitive sexual anxiety.

So far we have dwelt on the thematic applications of Wertmuller's title, but the dualism also has important implications for a metanarrative interpretation of the film. Early in the battle over whether to awaken Tunin on the morning of the assassination, Salome tells Tripolina, "This isn't a romantic love story, you know!" (167). Her statement sets up the terms for a dialectic of narrative modes, one of which is appropriate to tales of amorous adventure, the other to chronicles of historically true, or historically possible, events. While the "love mode" would be an antimimetic, escapist retreat from the world and would end well, the "anarchy mode" would be a realistic, historically rooted journey into the world and would end badly. The two modes are explicitly juxtaposed in various instances throughout the film. When Salome first brings Tunin to her room, for example, and boasts that it is "a den full of mirrors, the finest in the house . . . it's like a scene from the Thousand and One Nights" (96), she is invoking one of the canonical texts of the romantic storytelling tradition. But ironically, no matter how fantastic, ahistorical, and escapist this allusion may be, it still contains an acknowledgment of that other mode which it seeks to exclude. For Scheherazade tells stories in order to stave off death, just as Tunin lives out his own love story in order to suspend disbelief in the fatal consequences of his mission. Scheherazade's death-defying storytelling is also prophetic of Salome's and Tripolina's hope to save Tunin's life by intervening in the name of the romantic love plot that the young couple would hope to enact. But the second kind of storytelling—the realistic, historically verifiable mode—asserts itself in Tunin's final insistence on becoming an item of chronicle. His refusal to remain in romantic retreat, his public confession of his tyrannicidal intentions, make Tunin's desperate act one of many attempts on Mussolini's life, as Commissioner Pautasso explains to Spatoletti at the end of the film. The final police report, dictated to a typist whose text provides the visuals as the commissioner's voice delivers an incredibly pedestrian account of Tunin's death, reveals the final victory of the second storytelling mode.

> This morning at 10 A.M. in Via dei Fiori, in the notorious brothel, an unidentified man, stricken by a sudden fit of madness, began shooting on a group of policemen who had rushed over to do their job. The man was arrested, but shortly after he was to take his life by repeatedly banging his head against the cell wall. (180)

It has been Wertmuller's task to give urgency and life to this official Fascist "narrative" by constantly pitting its mode against the one dictated by love.

The two storytelling styles are once more explicitly juxtaposed early in the film when Salome persuades Spatoletti to let Tunin join them for the Sunday outing so that he can inspect the site for the planned assassination. "He's acting as if he were Alice in Wonderland," Salome tells Spatoletti of Tunin's reaction to the bordello, "so there's no way that I'm going to leave him here" (114). By invoking Lewis Carroll's exemplar of the fantastic, ahistorical storytelling mode as part of Salome's strategy to further the political intrigue of the film, Wertmuller once more explores their metanarrative relationship. She puts Tripolina's allusion to Valentino's *The Sheik* to similar uses. What Tripolina sees as a straightforward appropriation of the love tradition in popular culture points instead to a political lesson of some asperity: her previously discussed entrapment by the propaganda machine.

But the most poignant example of how love stories give way to political stories is Salome's tale of her martyred Anteo. Told in the mirror room with its Arabian Nights decor, this romance-turned-political tragedy reveals how amorous adventure cannot remain aloof from chronicle, how the latter mode inevitably intrudes on the former one in a way that dictates a permanent "ever after" of political consequences. Anteo's death at the hands of the Fascists prompted Salome's anarchist commitment, which in turn led to her involvement with Tunin, whose martyrdom will lead to further political acts of revenge, and so on. The love story turned historical tragedy generates a potentially open-ended series of private passions seeking public retribution.

The bordello is the appropriate place for this conjunction of romantic and realistic storytelling modes. On the surface, Mme. Aida's establishment belongs solely to the world of erotic retreat—the descendent of Scheherazade's storytelling universe. Thanks to the set of designs of Wertmuller's husband, Enrico Job, the bordello offers a fantastic, cluttered, sensuous, alternative space to the harsh, sterile, rectilinear world of Fascist architecture, as typified by the modernist assassination site.[29] The bordello's twisting corridors suggest infinite recesses where the inexperienced Tunin (and we, the disoriented audience) can easily and pleasurably lose the way. To further the sense of exotic retreat from the real world, Wertmuller gives her prostitutes and their attendants the most improbable, evocative names: Zoraide, Gea, Odette, Yvonne, Isa, Lola. Since these are all obviously pseudonyms, we know that Mme. Aida's prostitutes have shed their outerworld identities when they came into her employ. We are also given the impression that the women remain secluded in the bordello most of the time and are released into the outside world only for that rare moment on Sundays when the Madame treats them to sherbet at Faraglia's.

It is here in our deliberations that we realize how wrong it would be to consider the bordello in terms of the romantic tradition alone. Instead, Wertmuller's "house of tolerance" is highly charged with political meanings. While it is the place where Tunin's amorous adventure unfolds, it also knows the iron hand of Mme. Aida's rule. Though the banter at the prostitutes' dinner table reveals her to be a stock comic figure in her pretentious claims for the prestige of her *maison*, she later turns into a sinister figure who treats her employees like so much property, which must render a maximal return on her investment. When Mme. Aida offers Tunin the exclusive rights to Tripolina for two days in exchange for his removal of a dying man from the premises, she calls her employee "a gold mine" to impress upon Tunin the extent of the monetary loss she is willing to incur on his behalf. Similarly, when questioned during target practice about the vocation of his fiancée, Tunin answers "commerce" in a euphemistic allusion to the special kind of trade which Tripolina carries on. Wertmuller's point here is to remind us that the bordello may indeed be a place of imaginative and erotic retreat from the outside world, according to the romantic

[29] On the contrast between Fascist architectonic order and bordello disorder, see Simon's introduction to the screenplays, p. xv.

tradition, but it is also a real institution, which mirrors the political and economic tendencies of a deeply flawed social order.

It is when we consider the symbolic meaning of the bordello, however, that we encounter the strongest argument for the inadequacy of a purely romantic interpretation of the image. In keeping with a long literary tradition, Wertmuller has made this house of prostitution a figure for Italy in all her anguished history of foreign conquest and moral compromise.[30] "Oh, servile Italy," Dante wrote, "inn of pain / Ship without pilot in a great storm / Not a woman of the provinces, but of a brothel" (*Purg.* VI.76–78).[31] Like Dante, Wertmuller identifies Italy with the whore in her physical beauty, which has been ravished by so many conquerors, and in her willingness to accede to dishonest foreign embraces for immediate personal gain. Thus when Wertmuller gives her prostitutes accents from all over the country, she is doing more than adding linguistic variety to her dialogue, she is making a bitter commentary on Italy's history of whoring for short-term political advantage. Fascism is simply the latest in a series of clients who have enjoyed the willingly surrendered virtue of this desirable, irredeemably fallen land. If the prostitute is indeed an emblem of Italy ready to abandon her integrity to consort with her various conquerors for material gain, then the allusions to heavy bordello traffic on days of Fascist rallies, and to the national obsession with Mussolini's sexuality, gain added metaphoric significance.[32]

However, the way in which *Love and Anarchy* roots itself most firmly in a realist tradition is in its treatment of the

[30] The bordello is also a place of female strength and solidarity in the face of oppression both by their own madam and their Fascist male clients. See Paul Zimmerman's review in *Newsweek*, 29 April 1974, 98; and Marjorie Rosen's review in *Ms. Magazine* 2 (June 1974), 33.

[31] "Ahi serva Italia, di dolore ostello / Nave sanza nocchiere in gran tempesta / Non donna di provincie, ma bordello!"

[32] For the image of Italy as bordello, see Bondanella *Italian Cinema*, pp. 357–58; and Ferlita and May, *Parables*, p. 21.

image of Rome. Like *Open City*, *Love and Anarchy* is very much a Roman film. Not only does all the action take place in and about the city, as the many stills and establishing shots of monumental Rome suggest, but its image undergoes the same process of symbolic recuperation that Rossellini's did in the inaugural film of neorealism. It should be recalled that Mussolini made Rome the centerpiece of his Fascist typology in which his regime was seen to be the fulfillment of pagan antiquity and the Christian Renaissance. Rossellini had to rewrite this Mussolinian typology by making the *anti*-Fascist visionary city the fulfillment of Roman history and by seeing in the past a series of pagan and Christian prefigurations of the ideal to be ushered in by the Resistance. Wertmuller performs a similar act of recuperation throughout *Love and Anarchy*. First and most flamboyant is the night ride of Spatoletti whose drunken ravings offer a caricature of Il Duce's revisionist history of Rome. Wertmuller's setting for this scene provides the perfect spatial occasion for illustrating Fascist typological thought. Indeed, the Campidoglio combines those elements of classical political supremacy and Renaissance genius which Mussolini would see as prefigurations of his own imperial achievement. But Spatoletti's incursions into the Campidoglio suggest not only Mussolini's appropriation of these historical precedents but also his claim to surpass them in glory.[33] "Hail Emperor Marcus Aurelius!" shouts Spatoletti before the equestrian statue of the philosopher-king. "Aren't you a bit worried that one of these days we're going to come up to your horse, take you off it and put a statue of HIM in your place?" (132). Mussolini's aspirations to equal or supplant the second-century Roman emperor explain the iconography of his own equestrian pose in the stills that precede the credits to *Love and Anarchy*. It also makes the motorcycling Spatoletti, who is the Mussolini figure within the film, into a ludicrous, modern, technological parody of the equestrian image.

[33] On Spatoletti's attempts to appropriate "the heroic mythology of Rome's imperial past," see Biskind, "Lina Wertmuller," p. 14.

The Renaissance ideal which is conjured up in Michelangelo's beautiful geometric design of the Piazza del Campidoglio, as well as in the architecture of the three buildings flanking the square, is similarly violated by Spatoletti who sends his motorcycle careening into this elegant, classically proportioned space. And when he climbs into the arms of the statue of Neptune, claiming mastery of Rome, he echoes Mussolini's own pretensions to the pagan and Renaissance glories which the Campidoglio displays. Throughout this scene, however, there is a quiet, unappreciative audience that gainsays all of Spatoletti's bombast and reveals, by extension, the failure of Mussolini's attempt to redirect the history of Rome toward his regime as its fulfillment. Tunin's witness in this scene, as the self-proclaimed representative of the masses, shows how unconvincing Mussolini's typology is and how bent the people are on resistance. In a passage included in the published screenplay but cut from the U.S. version of the film, Tunin says, "You see, what I'm trying to say, Captain, is that perhaps one evening . . . a poor soul . . . say, someone like me who just can't take it anymore. . . . You come along with your fists of steel and the poor soul sinks his knife into your throat" (133–34).

If Wertmuller is arguing for the failure of Mussolini's typological strategy to make his regime the fulfillment of all Roman history, then we would expect her to invoke some version of the event that marked the founding of Il Duce's Rome: his 1922 march on the capital. Though this historical episode is not dramatized in the film, it is nonetheless recalled in a scene rife with hints of popular contempt for Fascist rule. This is the Sunday outing to the same restaurant where Spatoletti and his Fascist cronies had feasted on their way to Rome in 1922. By boasting of his being in the Tamburini regiment from Tuscany,[34] Spatoletti associates himself with the beginning of the Fascist movement—an association that is confirmed by his participation in the march on Rome.

[34] This was one of the first *squadri d'azione* to be formed on behalf of Mussolini's incipient Fascist campaign.

What made the Fascists' stop at the restaurant a memorable one for Romoletto, the innkeeper, was a disfiguring practical joke played on him by one of Spatoletti's fellow Black Shirts. "He was very slow in serving us," Spatoletti explains of Romoletto, "and at one point he said, 'Captain, you must be patient.' Suddenly a knife flashed out of nowhere and his two fingers went flying in the air. Hell, what can you do, we're Fascists!" (118). Since Romoletto's name derives from the mythological founder of the city, his mutilation suggests the foundation of Mussolini's Rome on a brutalized and disabled populace. What is more, this populace is brimming with contempt for its leadership, as Romoletto's next remark makes clear. "I am honored," he says of his injury, "but there's a slight political problem. Whenever I raise my arm in a Fascist salute, it looks as if I'm giving the cuckold sign" (119). Spatoletti, whose wit is somewhat dulled by his Fascist allegiances, interprets the joke as Romoletto's self-deprecating reference to his own disability rather than as the revelation of popular disrespect for the regime that it really is. The cuckold gesture is especially apt, for it refutes Mussolini's macho myth of power in the very same sexual terms in which it was originally cast. Spatoletti had introduced the twin themes of sexual and political conquest early in the scene when he had whacked the buttocks of Romoletto's two daughters and announced, 'Ah, firm and rounded! Lucky for them that in 1922 they weren't ripe yet!" (118). On a symbolic level, the virginal status of these two country girls suggests that indeed all Italy has not prostituted itself to Fascist power, that the Italian popular condition is hardly one of willful and lucrative surrender to authoritarian control. Romoletto, that descendent of the mythic founder of Rome, and his two virginal daughters, thus reveal the popular failure of Mussolini's strategy to refound the city on Fascist premises.

In the penultimate scene of the film, Wertmuller stages the final battle for typological mastery of Rome. It is here that

Spatoletti, like Manganiello in *The Conformist*, abandons all comic pretense and becomes the villainous strong arm of Fascism's punitive threats. As he interrogates a Tunin unmasked of all protective fictions, the two men become visual embodiments of their opposed political positions. Spatoletti is the very image of Fascist order with his slicked-back hair, his impeccable white uniform pulled tightly over his muscular body, his forward-leaning aggressive posture, and his polished rhetoric of interrogation. Tunin, already the victim of Fascist manhandling, is in total physical disarray, with his tousled hair, his loose, sackcloth shirt, his slumping posture, and barely audible, but nonetheless infuriating responses. Though Salome and Tripolina have preempted his will to political action by letting him oversleep on the morning of the assassination, Tunin reasserts that will in the face of Fascist interrogation. And though the two women have denied him the chance to be a hero and to affect the course of history, they have not denied him the human dignity that is his reward for refusing to name his contacts.[35]

All this takes place against the background that has considerable implications for Wertmuller's typological theme. Spatoletti and Tunin are filmed in silhouette before a sunlit panorama of Rome and a statue of the she-wolf suckling the twin founders of the city. Against what Fascism claims to be the fulfillment of Roman history in the image of a perfectly groomed, smooth-tongued, sophisticated agent of dictatorship, Wertmuller presents us with a simple, earthy, unkempt man of the people who holds freedom and human dignity above all considerations of self. It is he, according to Wertmuller, who fulfills the promise of Romulus, St. Peter, and Michelangelo, and not the authoritarian Spatoletti.

[35] On the dignity of Tunin's self-sacrifice, see Ferlita and May, *Parables*, p. 44; and Biskind, "Lina Wertmuller," p. 16. On the other hand, Robert Hatch regretted the film's ending, seeing in it an unfortunate shift in emphasis from "the strength and vulnerability of men and women under pressure" to "the demonstration of Fascist brutality." See his review in *Nation*, 4 May 1974, 574.

Looking back on the Fascist era from the perspective of 1973, Wertmuller, like Bertolucci, felt the need to reinterpret the neorealist vision in light of a postwar history that disappointed the Resistance hopes for a new Italy. While Bertolucci's revisionist strategy required a shift in emphasis from partisans to collaborators, Wertmuller returns to the Rossellinian subject of Resistance. But she does so with none of the heroic illusions that Rossellini had to promulgate in the name of the new society which his film was designed to inspire. Thus, the educated, ideologically coherent Manfredi becomes instead the simple, confused Tunin, just as the solidarity of Rossellini's working-class, anti-Fascist movement gives way to the randomness and ineffectuality of individual anarchist action. Wertmuller's relationship to Rossellini's neorealist heroics is perhaps best expressed in the final scene of her film when Tunin is efficiently beaten to a pulp against a musical soundtrack of inappropriate gaiety. By drawing back from Tunin in these last scenes, Wertmuller refuses to sentimentalize or canonize her protagonist in Rossellinian fashion, while nonetheless expressing admiration for his self-sacrifice. Though *Love and Anarchy* is devoid of those hopes for a new society which so animated Rossellini's vision in *Open City*, Wertmuller still upholds the dignity and necessity of resistance. Tunin may not be Manfredi, nor even Francesco, but he is Wertmuller's celebration of the innate Italian will to freedom and her plea for its continuance.

15 Rosi's *Christ Stopped at Eboli*: A tale of two Italies

IF THE POSTWAR ITALIAN filmmakers can be divided into four generations—those who were active during the neorealist period, those who trained with the great neorealists but came into their own in the Fifties, those whose aesthetic and political formation owed more to the events of 1968 than to any distant memories of war and its neorealist aftermath, and finally those coming of age in the postrevolutionary climate of recent decades—then Francesco Rosi may be said to belong to the important second generation. His neorealist apprenticeship was a particularly intense and binding one. As assistant director to Luchino Visconti, Rosi accompanied the older filmmaker on a stylistic journey that led from the classical neorealism of *La terra trema* to the critical realism of *Senso*.[1] It was perhaps this experience that led Rosi to posit a twofold evolution of neorealism, following Visconti's realist itinerary of those years. "After the first phase of neorealism," Rosi explains,

> there was a second phase which consisted of a time for reflection and a critical examination of the first phase. In the beginning, neorealism involved only the attempt to be a witness to reality, with no critical perspective,

[1] On Visconti's evolving realism, see my chapter on *Senso*. For Rosi's own comments on the lessons he learned from Visconti, see *Le dossier Rosi*, ed. Michel Ciment, (Paris: Stock, 1976), pp. 79–80; Monicelli, *Cinema italiano*, p. 128; Sandro Zambetti, *Rosi* (Florence: La Nuova Italia, 1976), p. 7; Giuseppe Ferrara, *Rosi* (Rome: Canesi, 1965), pp. 157–59; and Tassone, *Parla il cinema, I*, p. 280.

just a desire to record reality. But this was not enough.[2]

Visconti's influence on Rosi, however, was not unproblematic. It propelled him into filmmaking, but it also provided the model against which the young director would have to react throughout much of his career.[3] Rosi's quest for stylistic autonomy, his struggle to free himself from Visconti's example, is what led him to postpone for nearly two decades a long-cherished project: the filming of Carlo Levi's *Christ Stopped at Eboli*. "If I brought it out now [1979] it is because I feel more ready now than I was then to separate myself from a certain neorealist mortgage, which perhaps would have been more difficult to shed when I thought about it the first time, in 1961."[4] Though Rosi does not specify the nature of this "neorealist mortgage," Visconti's presence is not far to seek. In *La terra trema*, Visconti had already confronted and resolved many of the difficulties that Rosi would have to face in filming *Christ Stopped at Eboli*: adapting a major literary work to the screen, directing a large cast of nonprofessionals, establishing the contemporary relevance of historical subject matter, and doing justice to the great geopolitical themes of southern Italian village life. Given the similarities of the projects and the powerful influence of Visconti, it is no wonder that Rosi had to wait years before he could undertake the filming with enough stylistic self-assurance to make it his own.

Nor is this the sole reason for the long delay in making *Christ Stopped at Eboli*. For a director whose constant

[2] Quoted in Gary Crowdus and Dan Georgakas, "The Audience Should Not Be Just Passive Spectators: An Interview with Francesco Rosi," *Cinéaste* 7 (Fall 1975), 6.

[3] Though I do not share Stanley Kauffmann's animus against Rosi and I feel that the critic loads the question when he asks, "Has Rosi been overreacting to Visconti all through his own career?" the query nonetheless suggests the power of the Viscontian model for Rosi. See Kauffmann's review of *Christ Stopped at Eboli* in *The New Republic*, 19 April 1980, 26.

[4] Quoted in Tassone, *Parla il cinema*, I, p. 306.

preoccupation has been "the problem of the South" and whose every film has reflected this all-consuming thematic concern, *Christ Stopped at Eboli* represents a kind of summation, both of the southern question and of Rosi's entire filmmaking career up to that point.[5] Rosi understood the need to conduct his own cinematic forays into this troubled area before he could come to terms with Levi's authoritative treatment of the problem. In addition, *Christ Stopped at Eboli* required emotional ripeness on the part of a director who, in making this quintessentially southern film, was thereby revisiting his own familial past in the cultures of Calabria and Naples.

Though a faithful, even "reverent" cinematic adaptation of the novel, Rosi's *Christ Stopped at Eboli* is nonetheless steeped in originality.[6] "Yes, I gathered the inheritance of Levi's book," Rosi admits, "but only to establish my own personal relationship with the series of problems, be they existential or social, political, cultural, raised by the book."[7] The filmmaker's originality, however, is not confined to his private reworking of Levi's themes. In fact, it is on the level of form that Rosi is most inventive, finding the proper cinematic means to adapt a text that offers little action and even less drama, but which abounds in personal and anthropological insights. Unable to base his adaptive strategy on copious dialogue and action, Rosi turns to the properties of the film medium itself for analogues to Levi's textual meaning.

[5] Tassone observes how this film completes Rosi's exploration of the Italian South. "With this work . . . the Neapolitan director has realized the film 'of' the peasant South that was missing from his twenty-year investigation into the ills of the South." See ibid., p. 275. For Rosi's own comments on how *Christ Stopped at Eboli* constitutes the final statement of the southern question, see the same volume, p. 304. On this pervasive theme in Rosi's cinema, see Jean Gili, *Francesco Rosi: Cinéma et pouvoir* (Paris: Editions du Cerf, 1976), pp. 10ff.

[6] The term "reverent" is Roger Angell's from his review in *The New Yorker*, 5 May 1980, 166.

[7] Quoted in Tassone, *Parla il cinema*, I, p. 292. On Rosi's personalization and modernization of Levi's text, see his comments in the same volume, p. 306. Also, see the interview with Monicelli, *Cinema italiano*, pp. 131–32.

In his attempt to make screenworthy so "interior" a literary source, Rosi reveals the technical ingenuity that will be the subject of close study throughout the following pages. In the framing situation of *Christ Stopped at Eboli*, Rosi makes explicit his cinematic recasting of Levi's text. The film begins and ends in a studio in Turin where an old man, Carlo Levi, contemplates the portraits of those peasants who commanded his sympathies during his year of political imprisonment by Fascist authorities in the southern town of Gagliano.[8] As a way of paying homage to the textual birth of *Christ Stopped at Eboli*, Rosi could have framed his film with images of the middle-aged Levi sitting at a desk in Florence writing his memoirs in 1944. Instead, he depicts Levi as a painter whose advanced age could well place him in the 1970s (the film was released in 1979) and whose visually inspired journey into memory suggests an analogue to Rosi's own cinematic reconstruction. By making his protagonist a painter, then, Rosi not only does justice to the biographical record—Levi was an artist as well as a physician, political dissident, and writer—but he also establishes the medium-specific nature of his adaptation.

At the conclusion of the television version of *Christ Stopped at Eboli*, Rosi returns to the framing situation in Levi's Turinese studio.[9] As the act of contemplation and memory which produced the storyline comes to an end, Levi's eyes close and his head slumps down onto his chest—whether in sleep or death, we never learn. The fact that Levi had died in 1975, shortly before the shooting of the film, and the suggestion that he had been truly alive only during that year of confinement in Gagliano, would make the character's death at the end of his reminiscence a commentary on its supreme per-

[8] Levi was not a left-wing activist, however. He was a member of Giustizia e Libertà, which opposed Fascism from a liberal standpoint. See Witcombe, *The New Italian Cinema*, p. 182.

[9] *Christ Stopped at Eboli* was originally made as a television miniseries to be shown in four segments of one hour each. When the film was released for theatrical distribution, it was cut down to 140 minutes.

sonal importance, as well as a biographical allusion of some poignancy.

Within the film, the protagonist's painterly interests offer several occasions for artistic self-reflexivity. Carlo has finally found suitable lodgings in Gagliano, has hired a housekeeper (no easy task in a culture where women cannot frequent the homes of single men without forfeiting their good reputations), and can now settle down to paint Gagliano life in earnest. A scene set in his living room suggests the representational dilemma that lies at the heart of the film. An easel and palette occupy the extreme foreground of the composition, while in the background toddles Carmellino, the housekeeper's two-year-old-son. At a certain point, Carmellino bursts into tears, frightened by the intense gaze that the portraitist, hungry for models, has fixed upon him. Carmellino's obvious fear in the face of the painter's scrutiny is shared by his mother, Giulia, whose resistance to sitting for her portrait is a prime example of the peasant lore to which she gives voice throughout the film. "I'd be the prisoner of whoever paints me," she argues, in confirmation of the popular power that all societies, primitive and modern, invest in their image-makers. Carlo answers her objection with a sudden slap in the face, proving to Giulia that she is already under his power by virtue of the economic and sexual supremacy that their culture accords him. Her compliance and the ensuing scene of portrait painting suggest the unhappy truth that Levi and Rosi cannot escape—to depict this peasant world is necessarily to objectify it, to exploit it, and to dominate it in ways which may not be as virulent as those employed by the state, but nonetheless reflect the universal tendency to victimize this hapless population. Despite both authors' professed desire to grant peasant culture its dignity and autonomy, this central scene in the book and film reveals the impossibility of overcoming the power hierarchy implicit in subject–object relations. To compensate, Rosi is scrupulous in establishing a respectful distance between himself and the particular world under investigation. He avoids the impulse (so tempting because so natural a part of the camera's function) to probe deeply into the darker recesses of Gagliano life, and play the voyeur.[10] It would be easy for Rosi to sensationalize the strangeness and savagery of peasant existence under the pretext of educating his protected, middle-class public. But to do so would be to burst uninvited into that closed world, to profane the mystery, and to violate that otherness which Rosi, following Levi's lead, so deeply respects.[11] When he finally does coax us into the realm of peasant thought, it is through a slow and gentle motion of understanding, and not through a shocking leap into anthropological difference.

Rosi signals his intent to grant the peasant world its autonomy in the framing situation where he chooses one of the many paintings in Carlo's studio to serve as the background for the opening credits of his film and for all four episodes of the television series. This particular painting spatializes the thematic program of both novelist and filmmaker by figuring a peasant child (probably Carmellino, Giulia's son) whose solemn gaze is directed toward us, while his body turns in the opposite direction. Given its occurrence at the beginning of the film, and given the twisted posture of this figure, the portrait of Carmellino serves a threshold function, which defines the two spaces on either side of the pictorial surface and insists upon their separateness. As the guardian of the gate to this distinct order of experience, Carmellino is heir to the Renaissance tradition of the *sprecher* who beckons the viewer into the world of the painting while defining the boundary between the artwork and the extraaesthetic space of the observer. Unlike his Renaissance ancestor, however, Carmellino issues no easy invitation to follow him. Nor does

[10] On Rosi's restraint, see Roger Angell's *New Yorker* review, p. 165.

[11] On the dignity and respectfulness of Rosi's portrait of the Lucanian peasants, see John Simon's comments in the *National Review*, 30 May 1980, 673.

he forbid us access to his world. He merely warns us, with due solemnity, that this is a serious and somewhat dark journey which we are about to undertake and that we should set our expectations accordingly.

Rosi once complained that the difficulty in adapting a literary text to the screen lay in the lack of a cinematic equivalent for metaphor.[12] In so saying, however, the filmmaker underestimates his own art, which uses one of Levi's chief metaphors—that of space—to great literal and figurative advantage. The paradox of Carlo's political imprisonment—that his psychic life is as freed by it as his physical life is restricted—emerges in a series of spatial analogues throughout the film. Frequent pans of the Lucanian landscape are balanced by claustrophobic renderings of the town square, where the spatial paradox begins to uncover its wealth of figurative applications. The square is lined by aged peasant men whose poverty condemns them to the apathy and immobility that their postures express while the gentry, who have the social and economic run of the town, are prisoners of a subtler tyranny. Their first words to Carlo as he makes his debut in the square reveal the circle of passions that govern their lives: "You should be wary of the evil tongues in town. It's best you frequent no one. . . . Don't accept anything from a woman—neither wine nor coffee. Nothing to eat or drink. They'd put a potion in it. Guess how they're made. With menstrual blood."

"Their passion," writes Levi,

> did not extend beyond the village, encircled by malaria-ridden clay; they were multiplied within the enclosure of half a dozen houses. . . . Penned up in petty souls and desolate surroundings, they seethed like the

---

[12] "The problem is that of visual transformation; literature uses metaphors like keys for knowing reality. The cinema cannot do that." Quoted in *Le dossier,* ed. Ciment, p. 165.

steam pressing against the lid of the widow's saucepan where a thin broth was whistling and grumbling over a low fire. I looked into the fire, thinking of the endless chain of days that lay ahead of me when my horizon, too, would be bounded by these dark emotions.[13]

But for Carlo, the spatial metaphor has only positive applications. His political exile in Gagliano, far from consigning him to the narrow circle of passions that rule the lives of the gentry, opens up new dimensions of self-understanding, revealing to Carlo "the Luciana within each of us" (xi).[14] Since this insight is not one which lends itself to dramatic dialogues, and since Rosi is rightly wary of excessive use of voice-overs, he must rely on Gian Maria Volonté's considerable acting skills to convey Carlo's newly acquired inner freedom. Gestural proof of this achievement marks the final scenes of his Gagliano sojourn where handshakes, ready smiles, and a certain physical *disinvoltura* distinguish the present Carlo from the tense, introverted newcomer of the previous year.

The spatial metaphor is not without a certain topical relevance to Mussolini's imperial aspirations. The campaign in Ethiopia, which constitutes the historical background to the story, is waged on the pretext of conquering a living space, or *spazio vitale*, for the burgeoning population of the Fascist state. When one of the peasants responds to this bit of propaganda by objecting that "taking land from others brings bad luck," he is giving voice less to folk superstition than to the sense of natural justice and universal brotherhood which typify the underclasses. When another peasant argues that Rome should put its money into improving the economy at home, not into making war, he verbalizes what Rosi's camera has been showing us all along—vast stretches of domestic

[13] Carlo Levi, *Christ Stopped at Eboli*, trans. Frances Frenaye (New York: Farrar, Straus & Giroux, 1981), p. 30. All quotes from the novel will be from this edition and subsequent page references will appear in the text.

[14] According to Witcombe, *New Italian Cinema*, p. 184, this "crystallization of the self" is the essence of Levi's book as well as Rosi's film.

land which, with proper care, could indeed become that *spazio vitale* so brutally sought overseas. Criticisms of Mussolini's imperialist exploits pervade the film. During one of the dreary Fascist rallies held in the town square, the mayor (a miniature Mussolini) orates about the seven hills of Rome while Carlo mutters about the hills of Gagliano which "are crumbling, reducing themselves to dust." In a witty, politically damning juxtaposition, the "Americani" of Gagliano (immigrants who had returned home) regale Carlo with stories of their Sunday excursions to the New York countryside for group defecation and choruses of "Viva l'Italia!" This anecdote is immediately followed by a cut to a Fascist rally in which Mussolini's radio speech about the war in Ethiopia is broadcast to the apathetic townfolk, whose scatalogical exploits provide their own commentary on nationalism and the quest for *spazio vitale*.

If the "dynamization of space" and the "spatialization of time" constitute the unique possibilities of the cinema, according to Erwin Panofsky, then it is well equipped as a medium to express the relationship between temporal and spatial values in Levi's text.[15] The title itself reveals how space functions chronometrically when Carlo leaves Eboli for a land where "Christ never came . . . nor did time, nor the individual soul, nor hope, nor the relation of cause to effect, nor reason, nor history. . . . The seasons pass today over the toil of the peasants, just as they did 3,000 years before Christ. No message, human or divine, has reached this stubborn poverty" (4). The distance between Eboli and Gagliano, then, is the distance between a civilization that lives in history and one that stands outside it.

Rosi gives cinematic expression to the historical imperviousness of peasant culture in several key scenes throughout

[15] On the unique properties of the cinema, see Erwin Panofsky's magisterial essay, "Style and Medium in the Motion Pictures," in *Film: An Anthology*, ed. Daniel Talbot (Berkeley and Los Angeles: University of California Press, 1972), p. 18.

the film. As Carlo walks through Gagliano during his first day in residence, he hears band music and the strains of a speech by Italian aviator De Pinedo issuing from one of the primitive side streets of the village. Carlo traces the source of these sounds to the phonograph of the carpenter La Sala, a Sicilian who had settled in America but had returned to Italy out of homesickness and the desire to find a bride. Not only do La Sala's own biography—and those of countless other "Americani" who emigrate only to return home and revert to the old ways—exemplify the resistance of peasant culture to change, but so too does the cinematography of the scene, which ends with the words of De Pinedo's speech, celebrating the irrepressible march of Italian civilization under Fascism, against the visual background of primeval streets cluttered with livestock and woman balancing trays on their heads.

Rosi's other virtuoso cinematic expression of the immobility of peasant culture occurs toward the end of Carlo's sojourn in Gagliano. While the soundtrack broadcasts Mussolini's announcement of the Italian victory in Ethiopia, the camera pans for nearly three minutes over the peasants tilling the land at the foot of the town. Of course, the fieldworkers are oblivious to Mussolini's speech, but even if they were privy to its contents, this would have no effect on their toil. They are doing what they have always done and will continue to do for their historical duration. As Rosi's camera pans over the peasants, it simulates the passage of history over their untouched lives. Peasant indifference to current events provides an ironic visual gloss to Mussolini's claim that "the people gave their blood to build the empire" at the climax of his victory announcement.

In the discrepancy between a soundtrack that celebrates historical progress and visual imagery that defies it, Rosi is able to give cinematic expression to the central argument of Levi's book. The textual thesis is made explicit in the important confrontation between Carlo and Don Luigi over a letter which the mayor has seen fit to censor. "World War I was a war waged by Rome," Carlo had written in the offending passage. "Today peasants die in Abyssinia [Ethiopia] as yesterday they died on the Piave, the Isonzo, for someone else's history, for a history which has nothing to do with them." When Don Luigi answers, "You talk as if there were two Italies," his criticism goes to the very heart of Levi's historical thought.

By dividing Italy into two distinct civilizations and adopting the ahistorical perspective of the second one, *Christ Stopped at Eboli* offers an approach to Fascism which differs markedly from that of other recent films on the subject. Unlike *The Conformist, Love and Anarchy*, or *Night of the Shooting Stars*, which treat Fascism as an historical aberration to be extirpated and corrected by political means, *Christ Stopped at Eboli* considers it a confirmation, by exaggeration, of the rule. For peasant Italy, the difference between the Fascist state and other governmental systems is one of degree, not of kind. All central governments become abstract, remote, arbitrary agents of oppression that remain alien, if not hostile, to peasant interests. "Even after Fascism," Carlo tells his Turinese friends, "petit bourgeois ideology will prevail, either violently or by slow evolution, perpetuating, under new names and banners, the eternal Fascism of Italy." Perhaps the only difference that Fascism makes in the world of the film is that it sets the story in motion by banishing Carlo to Gagliano, but otherwise, the specific form that governmental authority assumes is of no consequence to the peasant populace, which will suffer in varied measure under any directives from Rome.

The "Two Italies" of Carlo's censored letter have their local counterpart in the Gagliano middle class, which identifies with the power of the state, and the peasant population, which labors under the dual scourge of man-made and natural adversity. Few characters in Gagliano escape this Manichean division into oppressive gentry and long-suffering peasantry, except perhaps Don Cosimino, the kindly postmaster, and Don Trajella, the parish priest who partakes of several, mutually exclusive conditions at once. Like the peasants, he suffers from extreme poverty, as Carlo learns when he pays a visit to the squalid living quarters which the priest shares with his mother and a flock of chickens. Don Trajella enjoys none of the privilege attendant upon ecclesiastical service, since his very consignment to Gagliano is in punishment for certain sexual liberties he had taken with his students in days past. Indeed, the priest's disgrace is dramatized in his very first appearance on the screen when the village children pelt him with stones and subject him to a barrage of verbal abuse. Far from the respect and reverence that eclessiastical authority is supposed to inspire in the populace, Don Trajella invites only derision. But, like the Old Testament prophets whose messages so often went unheeded by the masses, Don Trajella retaliates with the considerable invective power at his command. His Latin accusation *profanum vulgus* provides the verbal accompaniment to the visual image of a man in black robes photographed against the background of a crumbling townscape. The scene of the stoning takes place in the ruins of what was once the main square and the old cathedral of Gagliano—both victims of the continual landslides which threaten the very physical existence of the town. When Don Trajella tells Carlo, "This village has fallen from the grace of God," the background offers a topographical equivalent to its falling away from heavenly favor. The landslide not only literalizes the metaphor of the people's religious lapse, it also suggests the *contrapasso*, or divine retribution, which their sins invite.

Though ostracized by the peasants, Don Trajella nonetheless manages to participate in their all-embracing religiosity, which blends Christianity with polytheism, chthonic worship, and natural magic. "Even the ceremonies of the church become pagan rites," according to Levi, "celebrating the existence of inanimate things, which the peasants endow with a soul, and the innumerable earthly divinities of the village" (117). Where Levi's text implicates Don Trajella in the peasant religion by having him lead a procession honoring the black-faced Madonna of Viggiano who was "no sorrowful Mother of God but rather a subterranean deity, black with the shadows of the bowels of the earth, a peasant Persephone or lower-world goddess of the harvest" (118–19), Rosi finds a somewhat different way to dramatize his dual pagan/Christian vocation. He has Don Trajella preside over a ritual plea for rain in which he carries a cross over the fields while imploring the dieties of the earth and sky to end the seasonal drought.

But for all his poverty and participation in peasant rites, Don Trajella is still the instrument of the Church, and as such, he represents that institution which, along with the state, has held the southern underclasses hostage for so many years. In his attempt to foist his authority on the peasants, he is no better than Mayor Luigi Magalone, though the two men are also very much at odds with one another. The priest's relationship with Don Luigi on the one hand, and with his peasant parishioners on the other, is dramatized in the lively scene of Midnight Mass. Having forgotten to bring the text of his sermon (whether by accident or by design, we never learn), Don Trajella pulls a letter out of a crucifix and reads aloud to the congregation. It is a letter from the battlefield which prompts him to rail against war and to call for an end to hostilities. The anti-Fascist import of this sermon is not lost on the mayor, who walks out of the church in a huff and leads his henchmen in a chorus of "Little Black Face," a Fascist propaganda song used to promote the Ethiopian campaign. If Don Trajella has now won our sympathies for his courage in voicing antiwar sentiments and in refusing to sanction Mussolini's imperialist exploits, he soon complicates our feelings by abusing his power over his peasant congregants. Just as Don Luigi uses Fascist rhetoric to serve his own political interests, so Don Trajella uses the mystifications of Church Latin to bolster his own authority over the peasants. "Pax in terra hominibus bonae voluntatis," he intones. "You don't know what that means. It means 'give a little goat to your pastor according to tradition.' Pay the tribute that you owe . . . if you want peace."

Despite his moral ambiguity, Don Trajella's social position is somewhat analogous to Carlo's, and Rosi invites us to compare them when the priest is banished to an even more remote peasant outpost, called Gaglianello, for drunkenness and dereliction of duty. "I'm an exile like you," Don Trajella explains when Carlo comes to visit him in the new parish. But the two men exhibit radically different styles of response to their shared predicament. Don Trajella surrenders to his misfortune, refusing to exercise his considerable erudition, or to paint or write as he had in years past. His inventory of rare books has become a place for chickens to perch and defecate, his paintings remain stashed under the bed, and his writing is limited to satiric epigrams about village life. "In this town, one can do nothing," Don Trajella rationalizes in an abdication of any responsibility for the improvement of his own lot. The priest's inertia serves as a foil (and perhaps as a warning) for Carlo, whose empathy for the peasants threatens to infect him with their perennial sense of defeat. Only when his sister Luisa comes for a visit and exhorts him to act does Carlo rouse himself from his torpor. Though Luisa's activist approach is unrealistic and extreme, it nonetheless provides a needed corrective to Don Trajella's sluggishness and defines an acceptable middle position for Carlo, whose physician's training can be put to modest service in the malarial town of Gagliano. It is here, however, that Rosi must exercise a maximum of restraint in keeping his protagonist from becoming a medical hero and his film from becoming the kind of anthropological fairy-tale that would blunt the force of its social commentary.[16] To dwell on Carlo's

[16] The renunciation of the heroic mode is one of the hallmarks of Rosi's style. See *Le dossier*, ed. Ciment, p. 38.

15. After a year of political imprisonment in the southern Italian town of Gagliano, Carlo Levi (Gian Maria Volonté) gains a deep understanding and respect for the civilization that lies beyond Eboli.

the fearful moans of their owners. The human anxiety about the animals' safety is only surpassed by the peasants' desperate need for the extra meat yielded by nonreproductive livestock. It should be noted here that Rosi considerably modifies the surgical procedure that Levi describes, sparing us the temporary removal of the animal's intestinal tract in search of its second ovary.

The movement from strangeness to understanding and even identification is most evident in the scenes involving Giulia and her explanations of peasant lore. When she refuses to throw out her rubbish in the evening for fear of offending the angel of the doorway, or when she describes the antics of the *monachicchi*—the spirits of the unbaptized young—Carlo smiles the smile of the parent who enjoys the fabrications of a fanciful child. But in a sequence of surpassing lyricism, Giulia teaches him the incantation to win back a faraway heart.[20] As her words continue, the camera shifts from the realistically filmed scene of her recitation, to a fantastically imaged night sky. Against this background, Carlo's voice repeats the incantation, suggesting his own acceptance of its mystery. Listening to Carlo echo the primitive verse in a dialect not his own, the strangeness of it dissipates for us as it had for him and we recognize the universality of this folk wish to harness the stellar powers.

Rosi visualizes this evolution from strangeness to sympathy in the images of Gagliano that introduce and conclude Carlo's sojourn. The filmmaker invites us to compare the two spectacles by setting the arrival and the leave-taking in the rain, and using the same angle of the multifaceted town in both sequences. But the initially forbidding village mass, which appeared to grow out of the crags of the hilltop, now seems like an enchanted castle, gilded by the rays of the sun despite the downpour. For this final image of the transfigured village, I can think of no better gloss than Rosi's own discussion of his symbolic–realist intent in *Christ Stopped at Eboli*.

---

[20] This sequence was edited out of the theatrical version of the film.

Certainly, I am very bound to the sense of the reality of things. Such a sense, however, can be expressed also by transcending the purely real datum. It is what I tried to do in . . . *Christ Stopped at Eboli*, extending the dimension of the real to the value of a symbol.[21]

At the end of the television version of the film, Rosi takes Carlo back to Turin and dramatizes his attempts to explain Gagliano to his sister and their circle of friends. For this public also, the town is a symbol. It is a symbol of the Fascist extension of Bourbon rule, of the maleficence of the capitalist system, of the need for a dictatorship of the proletariat. According to these would-be reformers, the problems of the South are amenable to corrective social action: "land reclamation, irrigation, public works, industrialization, schools and hospitals." In Carlo's civic-minded friends, Rosi may well be figuring those critics of his film (and of Levi's novel) who expect a work of neorealist descent to offer concrete political remedies to the problems at hand.[22] But Carlo insists that such reformatory measures would amount to an internal colonizing of the South—one more imperial conquest by an alien, if well-intentioned, regime. Levi's own solution—that of political autonomy on all levels—so smacks of utopian anarchism that its mere proposal reflects the writer's despair in the possibilities for immediate, practical redress.[23] Levi's and Rosi's emphasis, instead, is on the effort of intercultural understanding that produced the novel and the film. The transfiguration of the image of Gagliano from a squalid, bristling mass to an enchanted castle reveals Rosi's movement away from an investigative neorealism aimed at reformatory action, to one of deep understanding which predicates any hope for social change on self-knowledge and a profound respect for the civilization that lies beyond Eboli.

[21] Quoted in Tassone, *Parla il cinema, I*, p. 283.

[22] On critical attacks from the Left, see Gili, *Francesco Rosi*, p. 144.

[23] On Rosi's refusal to offer concrete political solutions, and his emphasis on clarifying the terms of the problems themselves, see ibid., pp. 18–19, 143.

16 The Taviani Brothers' *Night of the Shooting Stars*: Ambivalent tribute to neorealism

IN THE CASE OF Paolo and Vittorio Taviani, a biographical anecdote speaks eloquently of the part that neorealism was to play in their choice of a profession and in the evolution of their cinematic style.[1] The Tavianis are fond of telling how their commitment to film began the day when they skipped afternoon classes at the San Miniato high school to attend a screening of Rossellini's *Paisan*. "Our decision was made," Paolo Taviani told Jean Gili of their resolve to become filmmakers. "We had understood what we wanted to do with our lives."[2] Though most of the Tavianis' fellow viewers that day were outraged by *Paisan*, the brothers were profoundly moved by its truth to the very war-ravaged conditions that they met daily on the streets of San Miniato. "The public rejected what for us was a shock: to find on the screen what we had just barely left behind in the street."[3] The power of films like *Paisan* for the Tavianis resided not only in their brutal factuality, but in a reading of history that provided the impetus for a postwar activist stance.[4] "The experience [of war and Resistance] had been searing," recounts Vitto-

---

[1] Throughout this section I will treat the Tavianis as an undifferentiated filmmaking unit. By all accounts, they are equal partners in every phase of their work and their theoretical pronouncements are interchangeable. For a discussion of this remarkable symbiosis, see Marco De Poli, *Paolo e Vittorio Taviani* (Milan: Moizzi, 1977), pp. 9–10.

[2] In Gili, *Le cinéma italien*, p. 332.

[3] In ibid.

[4] "Loving neorealism and becoming Marxists were the same thing." Quoted in Accialini and Coluccelli, *I Taviani*, p. 10.

rio, "but we still did not have a way of coming to terms with it. *Paisan* and certain other films of neorealism represented for us one of these means; this cinema was a way of rethinking the entire event and of beginning to give it a meaning for the future."[5] Given their early respect for the cathartic and activist powers of neorealism, it should come as no surprise that the Tavianis' own first film would become a vehicle for exploring and rethinking a local wartime event of considerable significance to them. Thus in 1954, with the help of Cesare Zavattini, the Tavianis made a documentary entitled *San Miniato luglio '44* about the massacre of their townspeople who had sought sanctuary in the local cathedral where they suffered Nazi retaliation for the murder of a German soldier. In both a public and private way, however, the film failed to achieve its therapeutic purpose. Such was the political climate of the mid-1950s in Italy that censors kept *San Miniato luglio '44* from ever reaching a wide audience.[6] On a personal level, the film may have offered the Tavianis a temporary way of coming to terms with this devastating local event, but if so, the solution was short-lived at best, for three decades later, the filmmakers felt compelled to revisit that episode and re-cast it in very different terms. The result of their cinematic return is *Night of the Shooting Stars*, and it is not only the story of the San Miniato massacre, but also of the Tavianis' complicated and ever-changing perspective on the neorealist past.

> Our relationship with neorealism is a love–hate, father–son relationship. Born of a beloved and admired father, we then denied him with the ungrateful violence of sons who realize themselves in the measure to which they destroy the parent. The denial, however, remains always a form of relating. Our formation and

[5] In Gili, *Le cinéma italien*, p. 333.
[6] For an account of this film's censorship, see De Poli *Taviani*, p. 13.

our choice (that is, to make films) are bound to the
love for the cinema in general and for neorealism in
particular.[7]

Though spoken in 1969, this statement of the Tavianis' relationship to neorealism may well be taken as a gauge of the
aesthetic distance they have traveled since *San Miniato luglio
'44*.[8]

In *Night of the Shooting Stars*, the Tavianis are most obviously reacting against the neorealist pretension to documentary reportage, and they do so by calling constant attention to their informing poetic intelligence. *Night of the
Shooting Stars* is thus replete with stylistic "pointers" which
disrupt our suspension of disbelief and insist that we acknowledge the basis of our film-viewing experience in artifice
and illusion. One such pointer is the framing device of *Night
of the Shooting Stars*, which announces, with considerable
candor, the subjective nature of all that is to follow and raises
the question of narrative perspective to the level of a full-
fledged thematic concern. The film's opening titles are projected against the strikingly artificial background of a bedroom whose window opens onto a starry night sky. So ada-
mant are the Tavianis in establishing the fictive status of their
film from the very opening frames that even a studio set is
too naturalistic for their purposes. Thus they resort to a flat
mural painted in unnaturally bright blues and lacking in any
semblance of three-dimensionality. As the credits fade, this
flamboyantly artificial backdrop does not give way to its
credible counterpart in a realistically designed set, but remains stubbornly on screen as a female voice-over only confirms our sense of unreality by describing her narration as a
wish-fulfillment fantasy.

---

[7] Quoted in Accialini and Coluccelli, *Taviani*, p. 10. On the Tavianis' ambivalence toward neorealism, see Bondanella, *Italian Cinema*, p. 176.

[8] For a thorough discussion of the Tavianis' stylistic evolution away
from neorealism, see Vincenzo Camerino and Antonio Tarsi, *Dialettica
dell'Utopia* (Manduria: Lacaita, 1978), pp. 37–43.

> This is the night of San Lorenzo, my love, and the stars
> are going to fall. We Tuscans say that every star that
> falls grants a wish. Wait, don't sleep. You know what I
> wish tonight? To succeed in finding the words to tell
> you of another night of San Lorenzo of many years
> ago.

This proemial promise is rich with interpretive possibilities
for *Night of the Shooting Stars* in its suggestion of regional
rootedness and fidelity to the customs and longings of the
folk. Not only does the superstition implicit in the proem
suggest the cultural convergence of Christianity (embodied
in the allusion to the martyred saint) and paganism, but it
also invokes the image of a unified cosmos in which human
desire is seconded by supernal forces. This primitive world
view makes no distinction between pre-Christian and Christian thought, or between the natural, human, and celestial
spheres, and it is a far cry from the positivist historical outlook that governs most treatments of the subject matter of
Night of the Shooting Stars. By grounding their film in Tuscan folklore, the Tavianis are calling into serious question
the objective claims of World War II histories and, by extension, the documentary pretensions of their cinematic record.

Set in the town of San Martino (a pseudonym for the Tavianis' own San Miniato), *Night of the Shooting Stars* tells of
a Nazi atrocity and the surrounding events which terminate
in the Allied liberation of the area. As the story opens, the
Nazis have mined houses throughout the town and have
warned the citizens to gather in the local cathedral if they
are to escape destruction. A peasant, Galvano Galvani, mis-
trusting Nazi assurances of safety, opts to leave the town in
search of the American liberation army. When he invites
sympathizers to follow, the townspeople are divided in half
as one faction prepares for flight while the other withdraws
to the cathedral. Galvano's group is soon joined by Corrado
and the very pregnant Bellindia, who have celebrated a be-

lated wedding just hours before. Once two of the number are discovered by the Nazi-Fascists and killed, a portion of the group decides to return to San Martino; among them Bellindia and her mother. The Nazis betray their promise and mine the cathedral, whose occupants are either maimed or, in Bellindia's case, killed. Those who stay with Galvano undertake a journey that ends in bloody combat between partisans and Black Shirts in a wheatfield near the banks of the Arno. The survivors spend that night, the night of San Lorenzo, in the hilltop town of Sant'Angelo where they are greeted with the news of the Allied liberation the next morning.

When the storyteller opens the film by asking, "You know what I wish tonight? To succeed in finding the words to tell you of another night of San Lorenzo of many years ago," the Tavianis are pushing to the forefront their own quest for a style which will expose the inadequacies of earlier, neo-realist treatments of World War II history, and in so doing, will commend that history to the new audiences of the 1980s. In making their own night of San Lorenzo wish, the Tavianis are implicitly rejecting their earlier documentary *San Miniato luglio '44*. But the stylistic question posed by the narrative voice-over has, in a sense, already been answered. If the patent artifice of the opening frames had not already revealed the Tavianis' antinaturalist stance, then the stylistic indicators that immediately follow the narrator's wish-making should convince us of their intent. No sooner does she finish her exposition than the camera begins to dolly in on the window until its frame coincides with the photographic frame itself. Though the camera continues its motion until it is well outside the confines of the room, the momentary identification of its visual borders with those of the window is enough to suggest the applicability of an old literary *topos*—that of the chambers of the mind. The metaphoric association of bedrooms with minds and windows with eyes suggests that the Tavianis are here establishing the subjective nature of their cinematic perspective by identifying their viewpoint with the consciousness of the narrator herself. In so doing, they totally subvert the neorealist claim to an objective, authoritative cinematic approach, and their own earlier work that had shared such a premise.

Once the camera has crossed the windowsill, several things happen further to disabuse us of any neorealist expectations for *Night of the Shooting Stars*. As if in response to the titular forecast of a meteorite shower, a star does indeed fall on screen, but the special effect is so willfully amateurish, especially in this age of sophisticated, intergalactic filmwork, that the audience is moved to derision. More importantly, we learn that the eyewitness of the events we are about to observe is the six-year-old Cecilia, whose childishly inappropriate affect (she's delighted that her house has been mined, finds the desperate flight from San Martino the most fun she's ever had, destroys the last two precious eggs in a basket whose other contents she had already accidentally crushed) and misplaced priorities (she's far more concerned with the fate of some valuable earrings than with the fact that her town has been liberated) makes her testimony untrustworthy indeed.[9] To give Cecilia's account a bit more authority, the Tavianis put the narration in the mouth of an adult Cecilia who calls attention to the little girl's testimonial limitations ("I was only six years old. I didn't know if I was afraid or entertained") and who adds details to the story that Cecilia herself could not have known.

It is Cecilia's perspective that provides an alibi for the antinaturalism of the Taviani's style in *Night of the Shooting Stars*.[10] Many examples come to mind, from the story's opening image of the pear tree whose stillness is suddenly

---

[9] This child's perspective allows the Tavianis to indulge their love of exaggeration—a taste that they defend on moral as well as aesthetic grounds. See De Poli, *Taviani*, p. 62; and Tassone, *Parla il cinema italiano, II*, p. 364.

[10] Richard Corliss, for example, calls attention to the "cartoon clarity" of the film's style. See *Time*, 21 February 1983, 80.

and inexplicably shaken by a wind from nowhere, to the fast-motion pacing of the celebrants' dispersal after Corrado and Bellindia are married. Closeups of ears and keys capture the townspeople's reactions of the anticipated mining of their homes. Transitions between scenes are often accomplished by wipes, which make conspicuous the editing process.[11] Central to the Tavianis' antinatural technique is the use of music to determine the rhythms of their cinematography.[12] Thus, it is the urgent staccato of Nicola Piovani's score in the flight scenes which dictates the pacing of the action and the corresponding camerawork. The slow, haunting aria of Wolfram von Eschenbach's hymn to the evening star in *Tannhäuser* is what governs the imagistic movements of the German soldiers' funeral march. (By assimilating this Wagnerian motif into the musical accompaniment of the refugees' most romantic moments later in the film, the Tavianis make unbiased, if ironic, use of this operatic monument to German idealism.) These are only some of the virtuoso stylistic effects that find their justification in the child's point of view.

Though critics have faulted the Tavianis for identifying their perspective with that of a child and then for violating the limits of that perspective, both objections can be refuted on theoretical grounds.[13] If the Tavianis' purpose is to challenge the neorealist pretense to documentary reportage, then the choice of an untrustworthy witness has obvious polemic force. When the adult Cecilia corrects and embroiders her childhood memories, she evidently does so with the help of other people's complementary eyewitness accounts, so that what

[11] According to Pauline Kael, such techniques mimic the operations of memory itself. See her review of the film in *The New Yorker*, 7 February 1983, 120.

[12] On the musical structuring of their sequences, see the Tavianis' comments in Gili, *Le cinéma italien*, p. 359; and Tassone, *Parla il cinema, II*, pp. 359 and 374.

[13] See, for example, Stanley Kauffmann's review in *The New Republic*, 7 March 1983, 24.

purports to be individual reminiscence is really that of the collectivity.[14] The violation of Cecilia's childhood perspective, then, is not the result of authorial slovenliness, nor of bad faith, but rather the proof that memory is never pure, that it is subject to revision according to the subsequent life experiences and needs of the rememberer. Vulnerable as they are to the caprice of personal reminiscence and to the emendation of communal testimony, the events conjured up in the film lose their status as historical fact and take their place among the other items of folklore that make up the collective consciousness of San Martino. Within that repository of popular thought, World War II history finds analogues in folk religious observances and pagan myth, whose precepts are no sooner announced in the film than they immediately become the basis of Cecilia's childhood perceptions. The first and most authoritative spokesman for the communal religion is the country priest who celebrates the wedding of Bellindia and Corrado. His sermon is necessarily brief, for he dare not detain the congregants who have risked their lives to come to the wedding of an army deserter. "Get going," the priest admonishes them. "There's one thing I must say," he adds. "If it's true that the *Dies Irae*, the end of the world, as they call it in Latin, is near—and it's always near—it's also true that each of you, and me too, has the duty to survive." This prophetic utterance is interesting in many ways, not the least of which is its apparently self-contradictory nature. Crisis survival and Apocalypse are two mutually exclusive concepts, unless the priest's reference to the Days of Wrath is to be taken in a purely figurative sense—that is, the Nazi–Allied confrontation will be Armageddonlike in its ferocity. The six-year-old Cecilia, however, takes his allusion literally and she finds visual confirmation of the priest's words in a mural to the side of her pew that depicts the eternally damned

---

[14] See David Ansen, *Newsweek*, 7 February 1983, 69. Pauline Kael discusses the interrelationships of individual memory and communal folklore in her *New Yorker* review of the film.

in attitudes of supreme torment while St. Michael pierces them with his sword. As a measure of the child's belief in the potency of divine justice, and as proof of her transfiguring imagination, the archangel's sword suddenly begins to glow. The seriousness of her gaze is not unremitting, however. When she beholds the image of Satan, cross-eyed in defeat, Cecilia cannot resist crossing her own eyes—whether in sympathy with the vanquished creature or just in childish mimicry, we never learn. Nonetheless, an interpretive framework for the ensuing action has been established in which Allied and Nazi forces are allegorized as the respective bringers of beatitude and damnation.[15]

Musically, the apocalyptic dimension is given twofold reinforcement. Verdi's *Requiem*, which occurs several times on the soundtrack, is replete with allusions to Revelations, while the advent of the Americans is equated with the Second Coming in the pseudo-liberation scene of the story's opening moments. It is the music of "Glory, Glory Hallelujah," bearing witness to the Lord's earthly return, which convinces the townspeople that the Americans are on their way. As they gather on a terrace overlooking the surrounding hills, the strains of "The Battle Hymn of the Republic" suggest to the people that not only are the Americans superior warriors, but that they are able to emerge from battle and produce a fully orchestrated musical accompaniment to their victory march. So convincing is this auditory hoax that one man lifts his hat in greeting, a woman waves her scarf, and an adolescent boy cries out "I see them!"

What this pseudo-encounter with the Americans indicates is the illusory quality of their operations throughout the film. If this phonographic joke is pathetic in its arousal of popular expectations, then the second instance of failed hopes is tragic in its deadly consequences. Mara, the young Sicilian woman

---

[15] On the importance of this mural as an imagistic prophecy of ensuing narrative events, see Richard Blake's review in *America*, 26 February 1983, 154.

about whom we know very little except that she is desperately out of place in Tuscany, rejoices at the news that one unit of the liberating army is composed entirely of Sicilian-Americans. In her eagerness to find them, Mara breaks ranks with the other refugees and runs off into the hills, fully aware that the Nazis have orders to shoot all townspeople caught outside the cathedral. When the fatal shot rings out, Mara imagines that a threesome of approaching soldiers are her compatriots and she addresses them in Sicilian. A conversation follows in which Mara establishes a distant kinship with one of the soldiers and asks him to transport her to relatives in Brooklyn. As if in answer to her plea, another soldier holds up a souvenir bottle containing a miniature Statue of Liberty which, when turned upside down, produces the illusion of snowfall, while the soundtrack intones "The Battle Hymn of the Republic." These few imagined tokens of the promised land will be the only fulfillments of Mara's American dream. She soon loses consciousness as the spectacle of her Sicilian-American saviors modulates into that of the actual German soldiers who have killed her.

Hershey bars and Camel cigarettes provide the iconography of the next meeting with the Americans. Though less illusory than the first several encounters, it nonetheless offers the refugees no help in their quest for safety, since only Cecilia and her young friend Renata ever meet these G.I.'s face to face. Unable to communicate their plight to the soldiers (one of whom is brushing his teeth when the girls approach!) Cecilia and Renata are reduced to sign language. Renata becomes the recipient of the standard American chocolate bar while the unrequited Cecilia exchanges grimaces and cross-eyed expressions with the other soldier until he blows up a condom and gives it to her as a trophy. When the girls return to the site with Galvano and the others, the Americans have vanished. To authenticate the meeting, however, Galvano finds a pack of Camels.

There is more to these three pseudo-encounters with the

Americans than mere irony, or mere illustration of the townspeople's tendency to think in mythic terms. There is also a polemic against that landmark neorealist film which inspired the Tavianis' cinematic vocation and which shares with *Night of the Shooting Stars* its historic subject. Rossellini's *Paisan* is also about the Allied liberation of Nazi-occupied Italy, but it focuses on a variety of intensely personal Italian-American relationships which, according to Rossellini, typified the intercultural dynamics of the liberation campaign. Though a deeply tragic film (there is death, separation, or rampant human misery in five of the six episodes) *Paisan* nonetheless sounded a characteristically idealistic note in its insistence on moments of miraculous communication between representatives of two such radically different civilizations. The title *Paisan* is itself a revelation of Rossellini's thematic ideal, for it implies that the special bond uniting members of the same town or village has been extended to the American liberators. Since the *paese* is the privileged geographic unit in Italy, inspiring loyalties that supersede national or even regional ones in strength, the inclusion of Americans in the inner circle of *paesani* signals the ultimate form of intercultural acceptance.

In its rejection of Rossellini's ideal, *Night of the Shooting Stars* may indeed be considered a *Paisan manqué*. Not only are there no magical moments of Italian-American solidarity, but the Americans are totally absent from the action of the film. We do learn at the end of the story that the area was in fact liberated on the night of 10 August, but that event remains a *deus ex machina* occurrence in the expositional background of the narration. The one interpersonal encounter produces only platitudinous souvenirs (Hershey Bars, Camels, and condoms) and does nothing to promote the salvation of Galvano's refugees. Though the girls and the soldiers do manage to achieve one of those Rossellinian moments of understanding, once established, this channel of communication yields nothing more important than mutual grimace-making, and the breakthrough is without consequence.[16] The scene most reminiscent of *Paisan* is that of Mara's imaginary colloquium with the Sicilian-Americans. Like the first episode in the Rossellini film, a Sicilian girl dies for her momentary desire to commune with the American soldiers. But while Rossellini's Carmela is killed in a heroic attempt to avenge the death of Joe from Jersey and to protect his companions, Mara dies for an illusion, and in vain. This is the Tavianis' most devastating commentary on Rossellini's ideal, for it suggests that the entire premise of *Paisan* is, like Mara's conversation with the soldiers, a wish-fulfillment fantasy.[17]

Night of the Shooting Stars is not only a *Paisan manqué*, it actually reverses the Rossellinian theme. If the neorealist film is about the miraculous extension of the intimate, *paesano* status to a foreign culture, *Night of the Shooting Stars* is about the very absence of that bond within the *paese* itself. Thus the intercultural solidarity of Rossellini gives way to intracultural division for the Tavianis, who see the liberation campaign not as a battle of foreign forces for the military fate of Italy, but as a civil war to determine its political future. The refugees' enemies are not Nazi ghouls who bear Nordic features and utter incomprehensible sounds, but fellow Tuscans whose dialect they speak, whose names they know, and who just happen to be wearing the Black Shirts of Mussolini's Repubblichini rather than the civilian dress of the partisans. Nor are these military allegiances always ideologically determined, as intimated by the abortive conversation between the character Rosanna and her Black Shirt brother, Giuseppe. "Does Mamma know you're with them?"

[16] Kael sees this scene in particular as a spoof not only of *Paisan*, but "of a whole batch of romantic encounters in wartime movies." See her *New Yorker* review, p. 119.

[17] Another link between the Sicilian episode of *Paisan* and *Night of the Shooting Stars* is the meteorite shower which figures importantly in the conversation between Joe from Jersey and Carmela. I am grateful to Ben Lawton for this observation.

she asks as they embrace in the midst of battle. "In Florence . . . ," he begins, but is killed by a partisan before being able to explain what practical circumstances dictated his donning of the Black Shirt after the army disbanded. The internal nature of the war for liberation is evidenced in the very first encounter between Galvano and a Fascist guard. The bishop has just announced the Nazi guarantee of safety for all those who gather in the cathedral as the mines explode through San Martino. Galvano, who instinctively mistrusts Nazi promises, recognizes one of the Black Shirt sentries and tries to sound him out on the subject. "Donati, Donati di Montopoli," Galvano calls him. "I was a guest in your father's house. Your father and I were friends." "You must be Galvano Galvani," he answers, confirming the bond of acquaintanceship and common local lore which often transcends those distinctions of uniform and political affiliations caused by historical accident. "Is it a good idea to go to the cathedral?" asks Galvano, to which Donati gives a double reply. His first impulse is to set himself apart from his interlocutor and to laugh with enough volume to attract his comrades a short distance away, as if to say, in concert with them, "What an idiot you are, Galvano." But when Donati realizes that his cronies are out of earshot, his next impulse is to answer Galvano seriously, in a way that acknowledges the questioner's dignity, and his right to know the truth. Accordingly, the camera has moved back into a long shot, locating both men in the context of the townscape which defines them as sharers in a common cultural heritage. When the camera returns to medium range, we are given Donati's response. "In these times, Galvano, how can one say whether it's a good idea or not." This, of course, is as far as the Black Shirt can go in telling the truth, since a straightforward admission of danger would be a treasonous admission for one wearing Donati's particular colors. But the fact that he has given Galvano no false assurances and that he has exchanged his initial, jeering tone for a serious, admonitory one, suggest that the appeal to cultural commonality has met with a measure of success.

Where that appeal fails, at great human cost, is in the August 10th battle between Resisters and Fascists—a battle that implicates Galvano's refugees who have joined a band of partisans to help them harvest a field of wheat lest it be requisitioned by the enemy. The battle, like its harvest prelude, is also a reaping, but now the fruits are the human lives sacrificed to the seemingly arbitrary military divisions of a people. With all the calling out of names and the meeting of old friends, the battle could almost be considered a reunion, were the two factions not locked in deadly combat. When Nicola grapples with a Black Shirt, for example, it is unclear at first if theirs is an embrace or a death grip. Their verbal exchange, which amounts to "give yourself up," "no, you" and so on, suggests how loath they are to harm one another. And our confusion is only heightened when the Black Shirt seems to walk away unscathed, only to crumple from the knife wound that Nicola has secretly inflicted upon him. Even families are divided by the battle, as Rosanna clasps her brother Giuseppe, who appears among the Black Shirts, while her other brother, Nicola, fights with the partisans. To complicate the intrafamilial division, it is Bruno, Nicola's paragon of anti-Fascist commitment, and the man he would have his sister marry, who shoots and kills Giuseppe.

In mid-battle, the Tavianis interject a slapstick routine which, in less expert directorial hands, would distract us from the horror of the situation, but here only manages to underscore the absurdity of civil war.[18] When enemy groups each seek to aid a casualty, and a request for water is made, the

---

[18] This is also an example of the Tavianis' much noted irony, which enables them to step back from situations and characters in which they have become too emotionally involved. On their use of irony, see Camerino and Tarsi, *Dialettica*, pp. 28–29; Witcombe, *The New Italian Cinema*, p. 202; De Poli, *Taviani*, pp. 64–65; Bondanella, *Italian Cinema*, p. 177; Accialini and Colaccelli, *Taviani*, p. 12; and Tassone, *Parla il cinema*, *II*, pp. 369 and 372.

Black Shirts automatically pass their canteen to the adjacent partisans. Each group then does a doubletake, and bullets, rather than water, become the new medium of exchange. Far from being a pat exercise in black humor, however, or a mere attempt to provide comic relief in the midst of the horror, this sequence acts as a pointed criticism of the unnaturalness of civil war. The Fascist reflex response of compliance has a twofold source: the plea for water is made in a shared language with a familiar regional inflection, and it is an appeal to the universal humanitarian instinct to help others in distress. Only after a moment's reflection is the rational perception of enmity superimposed upon the original, human impulse to solidarity, in a revelation of the perverse and unnatural logic of civil war.

Communal bonds are exploited for sectarian, military purposes by the battle-crazed Fascist, Giglioli di Marzana. "I know you all: Luigi, Giuseppe Lucchesi, and you, Dilvo Senesi," he shouts as a challenge to meet him in one-to-one combat. Dilvo Senesi fatally accepts the dare, and his final words to his assailant express the irrational, if deeply understandable desire to escape mutilation in death. "You've taken my life, Giglioli, why ruin my face?" The request, which Giglioli ignores, is doubly poignant, for Dilvo is the homely young man who has made Cecilia's mother, herself disfigured by a facial birthmark, feel beautiful. "You don't know what it means to be ugly and to feel beautiful," she had told Rosanna, as Dilvo looked on with desire, in obvious disregard for her physical imperfection.

The battle offers only one example of the salutary effect of the cultural links between Black Shirts and partisan sympathizers. The same Giglioli who has slain Dilvo now seems bent on victimizing the six-year-old Cecilia as her mother mourns the young man's death. When Giglioli begins to make his assault, Cecilia closes her eyes, puts her hands over her ears, and repeats the magic incantation, or *filastrocca*, taught her by her mother a short time before.

Marbocchia, marbocchiati	Dirt and soil
San Giobbe aveva i bacchi.	Job had a boil.
Medicina, medicina	Medication, medication
un po' di cacca di gallina.	add some chicken defecation.
Un po' di cane, un po' di gatto,	And dog and cat doodoo,
domattina è tutto fatto.	by tomorrow you'll be through.
Singhiozzo, singhiozzo, albero mozzo	Sigh and moan, stump of tree
vite tagliata, vattene a casa.	severed vine, leave me be.
Pioggia, pioggia, corri corri,	Rise up, run from here,
fammi andar via i porri.	make my warts disappear.[19]

Though literally intended as a cure for warts, the *filastrocca* may be used as a generic exorcism of evil, as Cecilia's mother suggests when she recommends its recitation to ward off imminent danger. Thus, while walking by farmhouses burned and sacked by the Germans, she is impelled by her own anxiety to teach her daughter the incantation. In battle, the *filastrocca* proves remarkably efficacious. No sooner does Cecilia recite it than the ferocious Giglioli shrinks back from her in fear, proving to the child the magic force of the incantation, while proving to us adults the force of a common cultural heritage. What makes Giglioli withdraw is not the occult power of the *filastrocca*, but its evocative power for a man whose provincial Tuscan boyhood obviously afforded ample exposure to this kind of verse. Thus it is by virtue of shared folklore that Cecilia survives and is able to pass on to us her story, and her protective incantation.

The prophecy of Armageddon implicit in the country priest's

[19] This translation is taken from the film's subtitles. Though not literal, it captures the rhythms and the folk wit of the original.

Dies Irae sermon has found unexpected fulfillment in the wheatfield skirmish between Fascists and partisans.[20] Unlike the Biblical contest against the forces of the Anti-Christ, however, the Italian battle does not implicate those alien armies which the popular mind had endowed with superhuman might (the Nazis and Americans) but rather it involves an internal, domestic struggle whose end is collective self-purification. When the Black Shirts finally withdraw and the victorious townspeople are given sanctuary in the village of Sant'Angelo, the apocalyptic suggestion is that the old world has indeed come to an end and that the City of God will duly be established on earth. The refugees' itinerary, from San Martino to the hilltop town of Sant'Angelo, also suggests the completion of a pilgrimage whose goal has been to participate in a higher spiritual order.

Not only does the Christian imagery of the film culminate in the wheatfield confrontation, but so too does the epic theme that was introduced during the primitive postnuptial celebration for Corrado and Bellindia. By way of a toast, an old man recites a passage from Homer which bears full quoting for its relevance to the newlyweds' wartime situation:

> Hector smiled, as did Andromache, the venerable mother. Tenderly the hero coddled his son and lifting him toward the heavens, exclaimed, "O merciful Jove and all ye Gods, deign that this son of mine prove preeminent among the Trojans and valiant in might and when he returneth home from battle let men say, 'His father was never greater,' and may his mother rejoice of that." Hector placed his son in his bride's arms, and moved by both laughter and tears, she had him suckle her fragrant breast.

Not only does this passage celebrate marriage in the obvious affection between Hector and Andromache, but it also antic-

[20] David Denby sees this battle as the fulfillment of the priest's prophecy. See his review in *New York*, 7 February 1983, 75.

ipates the parental roles that Corrado and Bellindia are about to assume. In this scene of fond domesticity, bracketed by acts of paternal coddling and maternal nurturing, Homer interjects heroic and numinous elements in allusion to a three-tiered universe of personal, collective, and divine operations. The lesson is not lost on Corrado and Bellindia, whose familial situation is no less determined by the military events of the day and the overriding dictates of God's providential design.

Given the humble social station of the old man who offers this Homeric toast, it is obvious that his recitation comes not from a classical education, but from the oral tradition of the Tuscan *cantastorie*. Like the folk religion promoted by the Church, classical antiquity offers another popular paradigm for ordering and construing the chaos of contemporary history. That we are to understand the impending battle in epic terms is indicated by the old man's assumption of the name Achilles when the recently sworn-in Resistance fighters are encouraged to adopt pseudonyms to describe their new partisan status. Though the Achilles appellation is greeted with salacious banter about blunted swords, and so on, it is nonetheless to be taken seriously as an expression of one way in which the popular mind interpreted its own wartime experience. Accordingly, when this new Achilles attempts to spear Giglioli with a pitchfork and is killed for his audacity, Cecilia envisions the partisan avengers as ancient Greek warriors who pinion down the Fascist with an entire arsenal of spears. It should come as no surprise, then, that for the folk mentality, populated by classical myths, popular religion, and *filastrocche*—all of which have a credible claim to truth—the struggle for national liberation would simply take its place as another "true" legend among legends.

The title and framing situation of *Night of the Shooting Stars* offers insight not only into the popular mentality through which historical events are filtered, but also into the individual psychologies of the film's dramatis personae. The license to personal desire implied by the titular custom of wishing on stars defines all the characters as wishers, and compels us to interpret them accordingly. For the six-year-old Cecilia, that week in August 1944 which culminated in the liberation of San Martino fulfilled her wildest childhood dreams of adventure, glamor, and even treasure. Though both are over a decade older than Cecilia, Nicola and his sister Rosanna bring similarly childish, or perhaps adolescent, wishes to this night of San Lorenzo. In his return from the battlefields, Nicola has met a fellow soldier Bruno who is resolute in his plan to join the Resistance. Nicola's admiration for Bruno takes the form of love-longings which he projects onto Rosanna, so that when his sister asks "Who is Bruno?" Nicola replies, "A man with whom you should fall in love." Finding Bruno among the anti-Fascist ranks in the wheatfield, Nicola commits himself to the cause and when the new recruits must assume their partisan pseudonyms, the two friends make telling choices: the blond Nicola takes on the appellation Bruno (brunette) while his dark-haired counterpart becomes Biondo (blond). Thus Nicola's wish to take on his friend's identity, an identity predicated on political commitment, finds appropriate fulfillment in the arena of militant partisan activity. Nor is this emulation one-sided, however, for the dark-haired Bruno becomes Biondo not only in ironic defiance of his own coloration, but as a gesture toward Nicola, whose body he watches over in the last frames of the wheatfield scene. This act of *pietas* toward his dead friend suggests that not only will Bruno give Nicola fitting burial, but that his future struggles for the cause will bear the weight of a double commitment.

Rosanna, who has lost one brother to the Fascists and another to the partisans during the wheatfield battle, leaves the site in the Black Shirts' pickup truck—whether as a prisoner or as a volunteer, we never know. Throughout the film she has voiced a variety of conflicting desires, which reflect the utter confusion and disorder of her psychic state. Her first words to Nicola upon his return from the front—"I'm glad that the house will blow up. We'll all move to Florence"— suggest her dissatisfaction with provincial life in San Martino. Nicola's rejoinder, "If it's still there," acts as a criticism of Rosanna's frivolity in indulging her adolescent discontent in times such as these. When the refugees await the demolition of their homes at the well outside San Martino, Rosanna's thoughts take a decidedly different turn. As she anticipates the destruction of her house, she grieves for her past, which is conjured up in a flashback of three typifying moments: her childhood dancing on the dining room table to the encouragement of familial onlookers; her adolescent reading on the living room sofa in the company of Nicola; and her recent wonder at the reflection of her now mature body in the bedroom mirror.

Rosanna links this burgeoning sexuality with political considerations in a way that reveals the confusion and instability of her emotional state. Just as Nicola had wanted Rosanna to fall in love with Bruno—his paragon of partisan activism—she too expresses a similar desire to Cecilia's mother as they take a break from harvesting to hide while German aircraft make their daily rounds overhead. "If the German reconnaissance plane flies over again, one of them [the partisans], I'll say which one, . . . by the end of the summer, I'll no longer be a virgin." This way of formulating her erotic destiny is exceedingly strange, with its mixture of folk reliance on celestial influence and the modern, technological usurpation of that influence by machines of war. Rosanna's hypothesis also makes her political commitment contingent upon some arbitrary act of the heavens (or heavenly invaders) so that both sexually and ideologically, she has abdicated responsibility for her actions. The reconnaissance flight of her prophecy does indeed pass over again, but Rosanna's strangely articulated wish finds reverse fulfillment as she is carried off in the Nazi-Fascist truck, never again to consort with the partisans.

Of course, the most surprising and improbable of all the consummated desires in the film is that of the peasant Galvano for the genteel Concetta, whom he has loved since boyhood. Everything stands in the way of this union, from social distance to moral prohibitions, from the advanced age of both partners to their natural temperamental reserve. But the mutual attraction has been evident throughout the story, in Galvano's obvious solicitude for Concetta's well-being, and in their shy exchange of glances as they discover each other's solitary bliss while bathing in the Arno. What brings Concetta and Galvano together, however, is an accident that reflects the essential rightness of their match in the eyes of the world—they are mistaken for man and wife by their hosts in Sant'Angelo and are lodged in the same bedroom for the night. At the outset of the story, no stranger would have ever associated the peasant Galvano with the elegantly dressed Concetta, who undergoes a double journey during the course of the film: outwardly to Sant'Angelo with the others; inwardly back to the truth of her humble past. Concetta's peasant roots are announced twice in the film—once by Galvano's daughter who invokes the proverb "villano nobilitato non conosce suo parentado" (an ennobled peasant doesn't acknowledge his kin) to explain the lady's contempt for her lowly relations, and a second time, when her own daughter commends her to Galvano with the plea to "leave her at the house of La Meridiana. She was born there." Though Concetta is unable literally to return to her peasant birthplace, since it was burned by the Nazis, she makes that return emotionally by removing the trappings of her socially elevated status. As the journey proceeds, she sheds layer upon layer of clothing, beginning with the veil which she significantly lifts as they pass the burning farmhouse of her youth. At the Arno, in a state of near collapse, she is divested of her cloak and outer garments, so that the formal attire that originally distinguished her from the other refugees is discarded, along with the social privilege it betokened. Her hair in disarray, and her cotton smock soiled by battle, Concetta looks exactly like her co-travelers by the time they reach Sant' Angelo. Given her advanced age, her socially reduced aspect, and her matriarchal authority, we can well understand why Concetta is automatically matched with the group's rustic elder statesman, Galvano.

It is a bold and virtuoso decision on the Tavianis' part to make the climax of their story this scene of senescent romance. For a film public fed on sexual wish-fulfillment fantasies of the most youthful and voluptuous sort, the lovemaking of the two grandparental figures, one of whom is overweight and the other toothless, would be ludicrous viewing fare indeed if it were not for the supreme artistry and tact of the directors, who manage to make this coupling so natural an extension of the action and who enable us to enter so deeply into the characters' sentiments, that we find ourselves saying not only "why not?" but more likely, "of course." The great sympathy we feel for Concetta and Galvano and the genuineness of their affection for one another forbid our stepping back to leer at their caresses or to look on with the emotional detachment of the voyeur. We join with Galvano in the disclosure of the wish he has cherished since boyhood and whose fulfillment has the bittersweet result of revealing to both characters what they had missed for so long. When Galvano tells Concetta, "these things could have happened forty years ago. It would have been better with all my teeth," he is not only apologizing for his physical deterioration but is regretting the lifetime of connubial embraces that their destiny had forbidden. Indeed, the stereotypical farmhouse bedroom where their love scene takes place suggests the bedroom they might have shared these forty years had Concetta not married above her station and left Galvano to dreaming.

But this night of love is as finite and fleeting as the historical events that made it possible. The fresh memories of the wheatfield confrontation ("undress where you like," Concetta says, "after all I've seen, would I be embarrassed by a nude man?") the omnipresent bomb blasts ("we don't know if we'll make it to tomorrow")—these are the extraordinary circumstances that break down the couple's reserve and allow them to fulfill their San Lorenzo longings together. With the morning sun, the liberation, and the consequent return to normalcy, the moment of perfect equipoise between the stars and human desire is over. Aware of this finality, yet reluctant to accept it, Galvano chooses to linger in Sant' Angelo while the others hurry back home. "We're leaving so soon? So suddenly? . . . There's no need to hurry, today, Duilio, let's stay awhile. It's so nice here . . . until it stops raining. We'll all get wet." Such diffidence about weather conditions may strike us as strange in one who has braved the terrors of Fascist assault, German and Allied bombing, and Nazi sanctions against defying the orders of an occupying power, until we see it as Galvano's pretext for prolonging this moment of unimagined bliss.

What keeps *Night of the Shooting Stars* this side of a fairy tale is the fact that it tells not only of wishes come true, but of those that do not—those that meet with agonizing and permanent disappointment. The night of love that so unexpectedly comes to the old couple should have also been a night of love for the young—for Rosanna and Bruno in fulfillment of the former's strange prophecy, for Cecilia's mother and the man who made her feel beautiful, and most of all, for Corrado and Bellindia, whose nuptials would be followed by no wedding night embraces. However, by granting the elders of the story this prerogative, so redolent of youth and new life, the Tavianis make Concetta and Galvano poignant examples of the theme of rebirth which recurs throughout the film.

If *Night of the Shooting Stars* promises wish fulfillments on a collective, as well as on an individual basis, then the twofold Resistance ideal of military liberation and domestic reform may be seen as a desire for national rebirth into free-

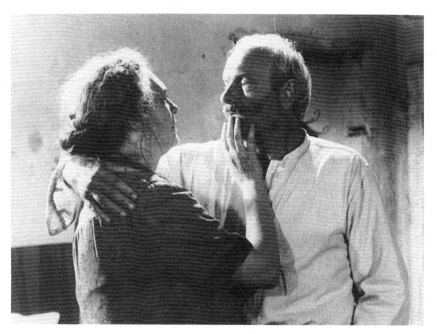

16. *Concetta (Margarita Lozano) and Galvano (Omero Antonutti) find belated fulfillment of their San Lorenzo wishes.*

dom and social justice. The naming ceremony in which the newly enrolled partisans take on pseudonyms suggests that Italy herself is assuming her new identity through them. Two of the chosen appellations are of special importance in this regard. One new recruit of singularly scruffy appearance has a flashback to a scene in church where he performs Verdi's *Requiem* in clean-shaven, well-dressed array. "Requiem, call me Requiem," he says in the wake of this vivid memory which is so rich in meaning for his new anti-Fascist identity. Not only does this character bring his ideal self into the partisan arena—the self that was showcased before his entire community in his solo performance of Verdi—but he associates his Resistance activism with the best that his culture has to offer. The Verdian allusion is itself charged with political significance in the composer's own commitment to a new Italy born from the Risorgimento ferment of the previous century.

Even more significant for the theme of rebirth, both politically and spiritually, is the name assumed by Corrado as he too joins the partisan ranks. In an earlier scene, as he had taken his leave of Bellindia at the foot of San Martino, he had asked his bride, "If it should be born, . . . what name should we give it?" When Bellindia leaves the choice up to Corrado, he follows the tradition of naming his son after his own father. "What was his name?" Bellindia asks the befuddled Corrado, who simply cannot remember. "Good God, what was he called?" When "Giovanni" finally occurs to him, Corrado repeats the name to himself several times, in relief at having recalled it and in the pleasure of passing it on.

When it is Corrado's turn to choose his pseudonym at the partisan naming ceremony, a terrible flashback precedes his decision. We see the end of Bellindia's story as Corrado, who obviously returned to San Martino at the sound of the explosion, pushes the cart with her body on it through the piazza of the stricken cathedral. Giovanni is the name he picks, in an ironic reversal of the passage from *Iliad* 6 which had served as their wedding toast. Unlike the Homeric text in which the affectionate leave-taking preceded the death of Hector, it is the mother and unborn child who die in *Night of the Shooting Stars*, and the father who survives to realize his son's heroic promise in battle (a promise which the Trojan boy, Astyanax himself, never lived to fulfill).

Significantly, it is Corrado who will kill another man's son, the Marmugi boy, who, along with his father, form the deadliest of Fascist twosomes. Perversely fulfilling the Homeric example of father–son heroism in battle, the young Marmugi is hysterical with blood lust and the desire to impress his fanatic parent. Together they bash the head of one of the refugees against a tree, after which the excited Marmugi boy struts about, admonishing the rest of the escapees to return to San Martino, promising that the Nazi-Fascist death squad will return. Good to their word, the killers do indeed come back for the confrontation in the wheatfield, where the Marmugi boy exploits his youth to the detriment of Nicola. Having removed his Black Shirt, this angelic-looking adolescent pops up out of the wheat to distract the solicitous Nicola, who shouts, "Stay down *bimbo*" (an affectionate diminuitive of the already affectionate term *bambino*) only to be shot by the father waiting in ambush.

The young Marmugi's murderous activities are not limited to the isolated victims listed above, however, for he also has a hand in the cathedral massacre, as his presence in front of the building just prior to the explosion suggests. There is justice, then, in Corrado's execution of this youthful accomplice to the murder of his own unborn son. When the older Marmugi pleads for mercy for his child, he does so in the name of the boy's youth. "Kill me, not him—he's only fifteen years old," insists the father, forgetting that the boy's childishness, far from exonerating him, was what made him so effective a killer. Only now does the young Marmugi discard his murderous precocity and act in a way appropriate to his fifteen years, emitting high-pitched squeals of fear as he awaits Corrado's revenge. It is significant, too, that the

Marmugis are given no first names themselves, for they serve as undifferentiated, unitary proof of the proverb, "qual padre tal figlio" ("like father like son") with regard to the Fascist legacy of violent fanaticism. By destroying the filial carrier of the Black Shirt tradition, the Tavianis are prophesying the end of this ideological line of succession.

With the death of the young Marmugi, the Tavianis make way for the rebirth of an Italy in which the ideals of the unborn Giovanni, as expressed in his father's partisan commitment to social justice, can prevail. Indeed, if the night of love enjoyed by Galvano and Concetta is to be more than a mere sentimental adornment to the film, we must see in it an erotic enactment of the Resistance aspiration to a classless society. Accordingly, Galvano's love scene with Concetta offers the most intimate proof of the utter irrelevance of class barriers to full human communication, and as such, it speaks for that Utopian hope which is so characteristic an element of the Tavianis' cinema.[21] Like all Utopias, however, the Tavianis' remains one of the mind, whose points of convergence with the historical order are as rare and as ephemeral as Galvano's night of love.[22]

In a folk culture imbued with religiosity, it would be impossible to limit the theme of rebirth to purely political applications, and this brings us back to the spiritual dimension of the Tavianis' film. *Night of the Shooting Stars* is filled with sacramental moments in which the Christological message of death and resurrection finds repeated expression, both inside and outside Church.[23] Early in the film, a secular communion is performed after the hasty wedding of Corrado and Bellindia. This rite, which celebrates the unity of the *corpus*

---

[21] For a sampling of the Tavianis' ideas on Utopia, see Gili, *Le cinéma italien*, pp. 371–72; and Tassone, *Parla il cinema, II*, pp. 362–63. For critical discussions of their Utopian thought, see Brunetta, *Storia*, pp. 677 and 679, and Witcombe, *The New Italian Cinema*, p. 202.

[22] On the transience of revolutionary moments, see Gili, *Le cinéma italien*, p. 368.

[23] On the sacramental motifs throughout the film, see Blake's review in *America*, p. 154; and the program notes for *Siena Cineforum 19* (1983), 2.

mysticum and of the group participants in it, is followed by the worst of community divisions when one segment of the town believes the assurances of the Nazis and seeks sanctuary in the cathedral, while the other half flees in mistrust. Two more communions are performed in ways that only dramatize the split in the citizenry of San Martino. In fact, what defines Galvano's escapees as a distinct group with its own unique agenda is the rite of bread-baking and the meal preliminary to flight. "We have to do the first kilometers fast. We must have energy," Galvano explains as his followers eat obediently while the other group watches them from the basement steps like so many theatrical spectators.

Galvano's secular, pragmatic bread-breaking has its official, Eucharistic counterpart in the communion performed by the bishop for those who stayed behind. It is extremely important to note that the Tavianis make no moral judgments on the decision of those who remain in San Martino, since they, like Bellindia, have the most valid of reasons for tarrying.[24] Nor do the filmmakers condemn the bishop for the gullibility which makes him, like his parishioners, a vain believer in the moral power of institutions to prevail over wartime criminality. This fatal miscalculation is prefigured in a gaffe that the congregants correct—the bishop's inadequate provision of holy wafers for the multitude of would-be communicants. When Bellindia's mother proposes the substitution of her own bread for the Host, the bishop is quick to accept the expedient and to make the loaves sacramentally acceptable by blessing them on the spot. To cover up for this oversight, and for his own overwhelming sense of inadequacy, the bishop resorts to showmanship, loudly proclaiming this to be "the Day of St. Cyriacus. On this day in the summer of '44 we all together sought salvation in the House of God." As the improvised Host is passed around and the bishop desperately asks his Lord, "do not forsake me now," the Eucharistic ceremony takes on a gravity and a

[24] Kael emphasizes this point in her *New Yorker* review, p. 118.

grandeur that banishes any tendency we might have to judge the congregants' foolishness or gullibility. This ritual of participation in Christ's sacrifice with its promise that death will be followed by eternal life, turns out to be, in many cases, not only Communion, but also Last Rites. The bishop's Mass has become a Requiem for so many of the believers who endowed their prelate with a secular power equivalent to the authority of his spiritual vicarage. Thus it is the country priest's exhortation to survive, with all its rustic urgency and lack of institutional guarantees, which proves effectual, while the bishop's offer of sanctuary under his formal tutelage meets with catastrophe.

The Tavianis' themes of rebirth and new life have their most important sacramental analogues in the informal baptisms that punctuate the film. In the bucolic moment that precedes the wheatfield skirmish, various members of the refugee group bathe in the waters of the Arno—Rosanna and Cecilia's mother only with their feet, Galvano and Concetta in total immersion. But the most significant baptismal moment is the one that ends the story on a note of collective cleansing and initiation into new life. "It's raining and the sun is shining," their hostess informs Galvano and Concetta as she bursts into the bedroom to announce the success of the liberation campaign. Outside, the refugees prepare for their return to San Martino, despite the cloudburst, rather enjoying its cathartic effects. The sin-removing powers of baptism find their poetic equivalent in this rain which frees the refugees from the bloody traces of battle. Thus purified of guilt and set loose from the violence of the past, the pilgrims will be able to return to San Martino and begin their process of social rebirth.

"My story ends here, my love," the narrator concludes. "I don't know if things went exactly this way. Then I was only six years old. But the story is true. And even true stories can sometimes end well." This return to the framing situation of bedtime storytelling is also a return to the problem of style which the Tavianis had posed at the opening of the film. The narrator's epilogue suggests a double polemic against neorealism in a summation of the film's own stylistic intentions. When the adult Cecilia admits her uncertainty about the historical particulars, she calls into question the neorealist claim to documentary reportage, while her observation that some true stories end well argues against the tragic necessity of *Paisan* and neorealist narrative form in general. What the storyteller implies here is that neorealism is not the only qualified vehicle for the conveyance of Resistance history— that it has no monopolistic hold on this, or any other subject matter it might choose to treat. Like all styles, it is a product of a certain cultural need to interpret the historical past and to appropriate it for current uses.[25] In the immediate aftermath of war, the neorealist insistence on a "styleless" cinema fulfilled the exigencies of a society in search of a new truth to oppose the decades of official Fascist bias. Cecilia's contemporary Italy, aware of the relativity of historical interpretation, dramatizes that insight by giving the events of Resistance and war the legendary status so characteristic of regional folklore. Just as legends serve the perennial needs of a culture, so too will this story fulfill the San Lorenzo wishes of the folk, with its heroes, its love longings, its epic action, and its happy ending.[26]

But this is not the film's last word on neorealism. As the camera pulls back it reveals that Cecilia's immediate audience is a slumbering child. "Now sleep, my love. Let me look at you. You're beautiful when you sleep." In making Cecilia's listener a baby who is unable, even when awake, to comprehend her narration, the Tavianis are not further undermining the seriousness of their endeavor, as one critic

[25] For the Tavianis' comments on the contemporary uses of history, see De Poli *Taviani*, p. 70.

[26] Brunetta points out the Tavianis' interest in developing a contemporary epic mode. See his *Storia*, p. 677. On the film as an item of folklore, see Ansen, review, p. 69.

complains, but are forging their most profound link to neo-realism.[27] Like the neorealist films, which bore witness to anti-Fascist truths and argued for their promulgation, *Night of the Shooting Stars* insists on the moral imperative to transmit Resistance history. Nor is one telling in one style enough, for each era requires a new telling in a style appropriate to its own historiographic needs. Even though future generations, figured in the sleeping baby, cannot understand the lesson, it must be constantly reiterated until the proper form is found and the message duly received.

If the Tavianis parody or reject the neorealist model throughout so much of the film, their final frames constitute an unequivocal tribute to the tradition in its argument for the cinematic power to alter our historical course. Though far less sanguine than Rossellini's ideal of a socially formative cinema, the Tavianis' suggestion is that film can at least ward off the coming evil.[28] "Marbocchia, marbocchiati / San Giobbe aveva i bacchi"—these are the adult Cecilia's words as she recites the *filastrocca* that saved her life in the partisan–Black Shirt confrontation. The film, then, is to be the *filastrocca* which will prevent such recurrences by rehearsing the stories of the past, and reinforcing the heroic folk virtues so necessary to the common survival. Significantly, Cecilia ends her *filastrocca* in mid-verse. The exorcism is not over, she warns us—the storytelling and the generational quest for stylistic solutions must go on if we are indeed to stave off Armageddon.

[27] See Kauffmann's review in *The New Republic*, p. 25.

[28] This raises the problem of *cinema politico* and of the Tavianis' complex relation to the genre, which would require another whole essay to resolve. In this regard, the reader is referred to De Poli *Taviani*, pp. 71–73; and Tassone, *Parla il cinema*, *II*, pp. 354–55.

17 Scola's *We All Loved Each Other So Much*: An epilogue

THOUGH CHRONOLOGY ALONE would not dictate that I end this study with *We All Loved Each Other So Much*, thematic and narrative considerations mandate such a position. Not only is Scola's film a retrospective of the very historical period covered in these pages, but it also argues the same thesis: that neorealism was far more than a mere moment in the history of style, that it expressed the popular desire to forge a new national identity based on the ideals of the Resistance, that it sought, accordingly, to play an active political role as agent for reform, and that all serious postwar Italian film owes a debt to this cinematic precedent for social commitment.[1] The inadequacy of a purely stylistic approach is argued by the character Nicola Palumbo, who says of neorealism that "it was the Golden Age of Italian cinema. Films were the only innovative cultural force: Rossellini, Zavattini, Amidei, De Sica, Visconti." In Nicola's claim that "*Bicycle Thief* determined the entire course of my future life," Scola is using one character's highly idiosyncratic relationship to a single film as a figure for the impact of an entire cinematic movement on the life of a national culture.

"The cinema must also collaborate to change the world," Scola himself said of neorealism, echoing Nicola's very sentiments in *We All Loved Each Other So Much*.[2] The difference, however, between Scola and his protagonist is that Nicola begins his cinematic career defending neorealism and

[1] See Scola's comments on the neorealist provenance of all serious postwar Italian film in Tassone, *Parla il cinema, II*, p. 314.

[2] Quoted in ibid., p. 315.

remains faithful to those ideals ever after, while the film-maker starts out as a writer of escapist comedies and only later comes to champion the cinema of *impegno*. Nicola's crusade to teach film history in the schools, to publish his treatise entitled *Cinema as Culture*, to give the medium its due as a powerful social force, finds in Scola a gradual con-vert—one who must first try his hand at entirely frivolous, politically regressive filmmaking before accepting the imper-ative to an ideologically committed cinema. Eventually, by bringing together his celebrated comic style with a serious *prise de position*, Scola becomes in large part responsible for giving the *commedia all'italiana* its social conscience.

In partnership with Ruggero Maccari, Scola was one of the most prolific scriptwriters for the *commedia all'italiana* in the 1950s and early 1960s.[3] He began directing his own screenplays in 1964 with *If You Permit, Let's Talk About Women* starring Vittorio Gassman—a film whose episodic structure, comic-erotic substance, and *divismo* revealed the exclusively escapist aspirations of Scola's early career. By 1968, however, Scola's cinema began to take a more socially re-sponsible turn with *Will Our Heroes Succeed in Finding Their Friend Who Mysteriously Disappeared in Africa?*, a film that heralded what Miccichè calls the second phase of the *com-media all'italiana*.[4] Whereas the first phase of the genre was characterized, according to Miccichè, by "erotic mono-mania," the second was not without "a sociopolitical im-pulse" which suggests a partial return to its neorealist source.[5] Scola's own account of the evolution of the *commedia all'italiana*, from the Fifties to the late Seventies, is so sugges-

[3] See Bondanella, *Italian Cinema*, p. 144; and Brunetta, *Storia*, p. 770.

[4] See Miccichè, *Il cinema italiano degli anni '70*, p. 216. On the pivotal importance of this film in Scola's career, see Tassone, *Parla il cinema*, II, p. 289; and Jean Gili, "22 questions à Ettore Scola," *Ecran*, 15 November 1976, 25.

[5] In *Il cinema italiano degli anni '70*, p. 216. Miccichè calls *We All Loved Each Other So Much* the best example of this second phase of the genre.

tive of the genre's relationship to neorealism that it merits lengthy citation here.

Neorealism . . . can be considered the father of Italian comedy, even if the latter was born precisely as a reaction against neorealism. Neorealism tried to restore the dramatic and authentic face of the Italy of those years, while the Italian comedy, with opposing, solely evasive intentions, tried to fabricate a conciliatory, rural, Don Camillesque Italian picture of "bread" and of "love." The Italian comedy began thus, in a rather false way. Little by little, however, it grew, it took to following ever more closely and critically the progress of society. It registered its changes, illusions, realities, from the "boom" to the "crack," it contributed to corroding some of those taboos of which Catholic Italy is the victim, taboos of family, sex, institutions.[6]

But Scola is not always so sanguine about the power of film to shape a progressive social consciousness. Anxiety about irresponsible uses of the medium and the failure of the masses to apprehend cinematic teachings—these are the filmmaker's preoccupations in *We All Loved Each Other So Much*. If the film should really be entitled *C'eravamo tanto delusi (We Were All So Disappointed)* as Scola once noted,[7] then the cinematic disappointments would constitute one of the three themes on which Scola's film so bitterly reflects. Failed expectations in love and politics are the other two concerns

[6] Quoted in the interview with Monicelli in *Cinema italiano: ma cos'è questa crisi?*, p. 139. For other accounts by Scola of the genealogy of the *commedia all'italiana*, see Tassone, *Parla il cinema*, II, pp. 306 and 314. For further statements by Scola on the reformatory influence of the genre, see Monicelli, *Cinema italiano*, p. 140; and Tassone, *Parla il cinema*, II, p. 309. The filmmaker Mario Monicelli makes similar claims in Tassone, *Parla il cinema italiano*, I, pp. 193–94.

[7] In Tassone, *Parla il cinema*, II, p. 322.

which join to form Scola's commentary on Italian culture from the liberation to the mid-1970s.

We All Loved Each Other So Much is the story of three men, Nicola, Gianni, and Antonio, who fight together as anti-Fascists, but whose postwar lives take them along divergent political, social, and professional paths. Over the ensuing decades, a combination of coincidence and common love interests brings them into brief and sporadic contact. Gianni's story takes him from Pavia, where he earns his law degree after the war, to Rome, where he is apprenticed to a member of the House of Parliament. Early in his Roman sojourn, he encounters Antonio, whose girlfriend, Luciana, is easily seduced by Gianni's superior social status. In the course of his professional activities, Gianni meets the corrupt building magnate Romolo Catenacci and is persuaded to argue his legal defense against multiple charges of criminal violations. Gianni soon drops Luciana in order to make Elide, Romolo's daughter, his bride, thus consolidating his association with the construction tycoon.

At the end of the war, Nicola returns to Nocera Inferiore where he marries Gabriella, bears a son Tommasino, and assumes a position as teacher in a local high school. This family/professional idyll comes to a halt in 1948 when Nicola's controversial political and cinematic tastes put him at odds with the town worthies of Nocera Inferiore. The confrontation takes place at a screening of *Bicycle Thief*, which Nicola defends with some stridency against the retrograde judgments of the local authorities. When Nicola loses his job in consequence, he refuses to seek pardon, choosing instead to leave his wife and child in Nocera Inferiore and pursue a mediocre career as a film critic in Rome. Antonio welcomes his friend into the big city only to watch as he, too, like Gianni before him, romances Luciana.

When Antonio leaves the war zone, it is to resume his job as a hospital worker in Rome. A union activist with Communist allegiances, Antonio is promoted to orderly or demoted to bedpanner according to the political leanings of whoever happens to be directing the hospital at a given time. It is on the wards that he first meets and falls in love with Luciana Zanon, an aspiring actress from Friuli whose straitened circumstances have led to her hospitalization for malnutrition. With Luciana's introduction to Antonio's friends, a serial love life begins which will make her the mistress of Gianni, Nicola, and others, including the anonymous father of her son Luigi. Luciana's career aspirations follow a similar, negative itinerary. From the role of Kathy in *Our Town*, performed in a local theater in Friuli, Luciana becomes an extra in Fellini's *La dolce vita* through the efforts of her unsavory Neapolitan agent, Rinaldo. When Antonio encounters Luciana again after a hiatus of five years, she is indeed at work in the theater, but her status is that of a mere usherette.

"The film is pessimistic," Scola said of *We All Loved Each Other So Much* to Jean Gili. "The reality that it examines is not a reality brought to fruition, [nor is it] a happy reality."[8] Indeed, the film traces the downward trajectory of the hopes for friendship, social rebirth, and cinematic excellence that the opening Resistance episode so fatefully promised. This disappointment of expectations is figured symbolically in the framing action of the film, which begins and ends at Gianni's palatial villa in the outskirts of Rome. Nicola, Antonio, and Luciana, unaware of Gianni's enormous wealth, drive up to his house to return the driver's license he lost at the reunion the previous night. When they realize that the street and number on the license correspond to this luxurious address, they still refuse to accept the evidence of Gianni's Marxist apostasy. "He must be the custodian, gardener, chauffeur," Antonio insists. But when a robed and slippered Gianni strolls out onto the patio, strips down to his bathing suit, and takes a plunge into his pool, the three are disabused of the as-

[8] Quoted in Gili, *Le cinéma italien*, p. 295.

sumed social parity. "Gianni will finish his dive at the end of this story, that began thirty years ago," Nicola tells us after a freeze-frame holds their affluent friend suspended in midair. The entire film becomes a flashback, which explains not only how Gianni amassed his enormous wealth, but why Antonio, Nicola, and Luciana did not. Appropriately, the high point of the dive is followed by a flashback to the Resistance sequence, which represents the apogee of the film's idealism—politically, emotionally, and cinematographically. At the end of We All Loved Each Other So Much, when the three men reunite to sum up their postwar accomplishments, Gianni returns in memory to a Resistance episode in which his insensate body was found and mourned by his comrades. "Gianni was the best of us all," they eulogized, to which the Gianni of the present replies, "It would have been better this way," suggesting that his subsequent life has betrayed its youthful, heroic promise. Accordingly, at the film's end, Gianni finishes the descending arc of his dive, while Antonio makes explicit its symbolic significance by explaining that Gianni "was ashamed at being so reduced, poor thing, figuratively speaking." The paradox is evident when Antonio calls Gianni "poveraccio"—the poor wretch whose riches put him in such ideologically reduced circumstances.

Scola has set an extremely difficult task for himself in We All Loved Each Other So Much if he is to make of it an entertaining yet probing commentary on postwar Italian political and cultural life. To do so, he must first of all make his characters both convincing as individuals and meaningful emblems of Italian geopolitical divisions. Hence Gianni, who comes from Pavia, represents the North; Nicola, who comes from Nocera Inferiore, represents the South (as the Inferiore self-deprecatingly suggests); and Antonio, who comes from Rome, represents central Italy. The characters are also socially representative: Gianni is of the professional bourgeoisie; Nicola is of the intelligentsia; and Antonio is of the working classes.[9] Thanks to the masterful performances of Nino Manfredi, Vittorio Gassman, and Stefano Satta Flores, and thanks to the concreteness of the film medium, whose visual and aural specificity precludes excessive abstraction, these emblematic characters are so credible in their individuality that only when the film is over and the illusion of their reality has dissipated do we reflect on their generic significance.

Scola's second challenge lies in the historical scope of his project: to span thirty years in the stories of three separate characters without lapsing into vignettes or without relying too heavily on such nonvisual devices as the voice-over narration. To keep the film from degenerating into a series of disconnected fragments, Scola employs two techniques. So that the three separate narrative strands can interweave more than just at the beginning and end of the story, Scola introduces the character of Luciana who serves as the occasion for the men to meet, as love rivals, throughout the film. Another way in which Scola achieves unity is by interjecting a series of anniversary events which guarantee continuity, while serving as a measure of the changes that personal and collective histories have wrought. The most obtrusive anniversary sequences are those set in the Half Portion restaurant, Antonio's preferred eating place for obvious budgetary reasons. Gianni has just come to Rome from the provinces, and since he is a poor upstart, he must limit his patronage to the most frugal establishments. This leads him to the Half Portion, where he encounters Antonio seated at one of the tables with Luciana. In this scene, a series of cameo characters are introduced who will become permanent fixtures in the Half Portion and will contribute to the sense of human continuity which each return to the restaurant will afford. One habituée

[9] On the emblematic significance of the three protagonists, see Lawton, "Italian Neorealism," p. 21; Bondanella, *Italian Cinema*, p. 373; Miccichè, *Il cinema italiano degli anni '70*, p. 217.

is an attractive, sad-eyed woman named Margherita who is always telephoning a certain Michele. Since her legendary boyfriend never appears, and since our last glimpse of Margherita is of an aging, heavily madeup alcoholic, still awaiting Michele's return phone call, we infer that this relationship is one of the many disappointments that the postwar years have brought.

Other human fixtures of the Half Portion who recur in the film are the friar who plays the shell game of the "three little saints" (whether for personal enrichment or for the benefit of his Order, we never learn), the seller of black-market cigarette lighters ("interessa l'oggetto?" is his verbal calling card) and the trumpet player whose repertory is limited to a rousing song of the Resistance. The recurrence of these cameo performances in the restaurant and the sense of continuity they provide is made explicit in the last meeting at the Half Portion as Nicola, Antonio, and Gianni name these characters by way of reminiscence.

In the Half Portion, Scola introduces the political and sentimental ideals from which the rest of the action will necessarily fall away. "When you've risked your life with somebody, something remains as if time never passed and you were still there," says Antonio, articulating the theme of friendship to which he alone will remain true. Antonio's mention of temporal stasis in connection with the friendship generated by the Resistance is significant, for it suggests the sad discrepancy between an ideal which should transcend history and the reality of human behavior which is so subject to the whims of circumstance. Unlike Antonio, who remains faithful to a timeless ideal, Gianni and Nicola are creatures of the very historical process they claim to control—through political means, in the one case, and intellectual means in the other. A further irony is that Antonio should celebrate this atemporal ideal in the very setting that serves to measure the passage of time throughout the film.

In the Half Portion Antonio also formulates the political

hopes that the rest of the film will disappoint. "Tomorrow, vote for the Democratic Popular Front," shouts Antonio to the other patrons of the restaurant. When he proposes a toast "that the half portions become full for everyone," the exhortation has a twofold significance. First it situates this scene on the eve of the critical elections between the Christian Democratic party and the Democratic Popular Front. We know from history (and from a later scene) that the political hopes of the Resistance met a crushing defeat at the polls. Secondly, Antonio's toast explains the symbolic significance of the restaurant, which suggests Italy's economic straits in the aftermath of occupation and war. In fact, the Half Portion serves as a barometer of Italian economic circumstances throughout the film. In a scene which takes place in 1959, Antonio invites Luciana to dine with him at the remodeled Half Portion—an occurrence symptomatic of the "economic miracle" of those years. The final reunion of the three friends finds the Half Portion handsomely redecorated, but empty of patrons—the victim of a recovery that makes budget dining obsolete.

Appropriately, the Half Portion offers the setting for Gianni's explicit assessment of his generation's failures. Against the background of the Resistance song, which provides a musical reminder of betrayed partisan ideals, Gianni's indictment proceeds. "Our generation stinks. Just look at Nicola. He abandoned his family and career to scratch out movie reviews, signed Vice [as in vice-president, not vice squad]." Antonio, in his eagerness to preserve the evening's jollity, interrupts in praise of Nicola's productivity ("Oh you're Vice—you write in a lot of newspapers"), and heads off Gianni's forthcoming confession of his own wealth and position. Antonio cannot, however, prevent Gianni from continuing in a more general vein. "For a brighter future," Gianni reflects. "The future has passed and we didn't even notice." It is appropriate, too, that Gianni be the spokesman for this devastating generational assessment. Of the three friends, he was the one best equipped to fulfill the Resistance promise for a new society. When Antonio first introduces Gianni to Luciana at the Half Portion, he sings his friend's praises in a way which predicts the latter's postwar political success. Antonio tells of a partisan encounter with the enemy in which Gianni spoke German and succeeded in securing their collective release. What we learn about Gianni here is that, added to his attributes of intelligence, charm, good looks, and legal expertise, is the ability to speak the language of his adversaries and to strike agreements of a mutually advantageous sort. Gianni is thus perfectly suited for a political career dedicated to the advancement of partisan ideals within the system. If we are to take his character as emblematic of a certain socioeconomic condition, then Scola is expressing, through Gianni, the expectation that the postwar professional bourgeoisie would be the one class most qualified to realize the Resistance promise. When Antonio proposes a toast to Gianni Perego who "will change this society into a more just society," he is acknowledging his friend's superior credentials, as an individual destined for political office, and as a representative of a certain social caste, for fulfilling the partisan hope.

No sooner is Gianni's exemplary status proclaimed, however, than it is immediately called into question by ensuing events. Gianni does nothing to resist his attraction to Luciana—an attraction that is as mutual as it is sudden—despite his acute awareness that in so doing, he is violating a sacred trust. "Which will win, friendship or love?" he muses. "Will we choose to be honest or happy?" The struggle, for Gianni, is obviously less than agonizing, as he wastes no time in wooing Luciana. In fact, the scene in which the two are shown embracing on a nightclub dance floor takes place either the very evening of their meeting in the Half Portion, or soon thereafter, since all this transpires between Antonio's announcement of the election to occur the next day and his announcement of its devastating results. By juxtaposing Gianni's betrayal of his friendship and the electoral defeat of the progressive coalition, Scola blends the interests of narrative economy with the thematic illustration of hopes doubly disappointed. When Nicola began this sequence with the voice-over comment "peace divided us," his literal meaning presaged a darker political significance. Just as the postwar period saw Antonio, Nicola, and Gianni take their separate paths, so too would the cessation of wartime hostilities dissipate the unity that Italians of various regions and classes had achieved during the Nazi-Fascist occupation.

Were Gianni to remain faithful to Luciana, were he to sacrifice in the name of his grand passion, putting it above all other considerations of the self, perhaps we could forgive him his initial betrayal of Antonio. But this love for Luciana proves no end at all for Gianni, who continues his wretched pattern of abandoning relationships for the next attractive proposition that comes along. In his final decision to collaborate with the corrupt building tycoon Romolo Catenacci and to wed this man's daughter in a marriage of convenience, Gianni violates all the ideals of his preceding relationships: those socially progressive ones embodied in his friendship with Antonio, and the grand passion he shared with Luciana.

To trace Gianni's ideological deterioration, Scola uses another anniversary device—that of the roast pork, lowered by crane onto the rooftop of Romolo's latest building project as a birthday celebration. The first pig-lowering ceremony takes place just after Romolo's request that Gianni defend his legally equivocal construction interests. But Gianni is not present at the first birthday celebration because, it seems, he has virtuously declined Romolo's lucrative offer. However, at the next pig-lowering, Gianni is very much in evidence, as the husband of Elide, father of Fabrizio and Donatella, and legal counsel to Romolo's construction empire. Unlike the first pig-lowering sequence, however, this one is in color and the chromatic revelation suggests the allegorical significance of Gianni's relationship with his father-in-law. In both instances the pig is laid out on a cloth which, in the earlier black-and-white scene, escaped our notice, but in the color scene proves to be the flag of Italy. Now, Gianni's wartime facility for speaking the language of his adversary reveals a meaning that is both prophetic and emblematic—prophetic of his temporizing postwar political posture, emblematic of his partnership in Italy's Center-Left ruling regime. Just as the centrist Christian Democrats have had to coalesce with the Socialists, the most influential of the parties of the moderate Left, so too does Romolo Catenacci, embodiment of the status quo, seek alliance with the Left-leaning Gianni. The relationship in both cases is a symbiotic one in which the powerful partner gains the appearance of reformist goodwill while the progressive partner acquires considerable political and financial clout. Lest we assume total equivalence between the two members of the partnership, however, Scola insists that Gianni remain deluded where Romolo does not. The Socialist lawyer practices a high degree of denial even while he defends his father-in-law's fraudulence, by maintaining that once in the system, he will eventually be able to reform it. In a scene of savage confrontation, Gianni argues, "we must make building codes instead of greasing sweaty bureaucratic palms," and when Romolo capitulates, he gloats, "Gianni Perego will change this society into a more just society," in an echo of Antonio's earlier toast at the Half Portion. The reminder, however, serves to underscore the irony of Gianni's reformatory claim, for it dramatizes his ideological slippage from the revolutionary promise of Antonio's toast to his present-day compromise with the powers that be.

But the end of the film reveals the vanity of Gianni's reformist intentions. The Catenacci villa, once teeming with family activity, is now empty save for Gianni and his physically immobilized father-in-law. "The loneliest man in the world is the rich man," wheezes Romolo in a replay of the complaint he had first made to Gianni twenty-five years ago as a bid for the young lawyer's sympathy and services. What then sounded like a sophistic plea for pity now turns into a narrative fact: Gianni and Romolo do indeed live in splendid isolation—an emblematic allusion to the aloofness of the Center-Left leaders from Italian national reality. The subsequent dialogue and a previous image argue powerfully for this allegorical reading of the relationship between Gianni and his father-in-law. "Who can separate us two?" asks Romolo. "You won't escape, and I won't die." Any hopes for the retirement of the Center-Left coalition are effectively quelled by this prophecy, which suggests that the Christian Democrats will rule in perpetuity and that the moderate Marxists will be loath to forfeit the obvious benefits of such an alliance. Scola enriches this allegory by opening the scene with the image of a crane lowering a cage containing Romolo in a wheelchair. Apparently, Romolo has become so weighed down with years and kilograms that he can no longer walk by himself and must depend upon this mechanical conveyance to traverse his own grounds. Of course, Scola is asking us to recall the anniversary sequences of Romolo's birthday in which cranes featured prominently, to lower down pigs. Though Romolo in this last scene is not resting on an Italian flag as the earlier roasted animals had been, the symbolism nonetheless carries over. In all his shrewdness, corpulence, and stubborn refusal to die, Romolo is the Italy of the recovery and Gianni, in his opportunism-masked-as-progressivism, is wedded to him just as the Socialists are locked into a seemingly premanent compromise with the Christian Democratic elite.

If Gianni's relationship with Romolo is indeed an allegory of the Center-Left coalition, then his relationship to his wife, Elide, may be seen in a similarly emblematic way. Whereas Elide is totally smitten with Gianni, his interest in her remains tutorial. She is his to shape and mold into the image of the wife that he feels he so well deserves. This part of the film could be subtitled "The Education of Elide" and as she grows in beauty, literacy, and sophistication, her progress

reflects the course of Italian postwar culture under the aegis
of a Left-leaning intelligentsia. The provincialism and naiveté
of Italy under Mussolini is manifest in Elide's aboriginal state.
She can barely write ("oggi a conoscuto . . . ," she scratches
in her diary), can barely speak ("Lei non salisce?" she asks
Gianni), and is ingenuous to the point of imbecility ("che
bomba" is her face-to-face reaction to Gianni's urbane manner and good looks). In her next appearance, we learn that
Elide is on a diet (Gianni snatches a pastry out of her hand,
warning her against excessive carbohydrate intake) and is
reading Dumas, which she finds exceedingly difficult. The
frumpy, overweight young woman of the first scene is now
a trim, fashionably dressed young matron, though in the next
scene, we see at what expense. Elide must wear a cumber-
some night-brace, which she offers to remove in the interests
of lovemaking. In an allusion to the sexual revolution
with its granting of the female right to erotic pleasure and
its promotion of greater frankness in discussing such matters, Elide looks up from her reading to ask Gianni the
meaning of the term "orgasm." It is in this scene that we
learn how hypocritical Gianni's educational injunctions to
Elide are: she must read "literature" while his texts are limited to newspapers and sports car magazines.

   In Elide's next appearance, the change in set decor speaks
eloquently of her cultural improvement. She is now in her
"Antonioni" phase, so background will define her as much
as it had Giuliana in *Red Desert*. Elide's bedroom, once the
repository of flowers and gilded furnishings, is now all straight
lines, right angles, and starkly contrasting blacks and whites.
As Elide places a larger frame around a smaller, already
framed picture, she explains how Antonioni has given language and legitimacy to her sense of feminine alienation. Since
a lengthy voice-over narration here would disprove Elide's
Antonioniesque claim for the incommunicability of human
sentiments, Scola has her speak into a tape recorder so that
what she is saying is allegedly destined for herself alone.

"There is more warmth in cold objects than in people," she says, fondling a sphere that exemplifies the geometric precision of her Antonioniesque setting. In an observation that prefigures her own postmortem conversation with Gianni later on, Elide wonders if we can find a way of "speaking to the dead. They are everywhere, even in this room." The fact that she confides this message to a tape recorder, whose association with the world of the scientifically verifiable fact contradicts Elide's mysticism, only heightens the silliness of her pretense. The humor of this scene turns to pathos in Elide's next appearance, when the tape recorder is used to rouse Gianni out of his indifference toward this beautiful, emotionally deprived wife. "It's hard to tell you what I must tell you. So I recorded it," confesses Elide, who proceeds to describe her love affair with another man in language borrowed from the sophisticated psychological novels and films which had comprised her program in cultural literacy. Just as he had never listened to his wife in so many years of marriage, Gianni turns off her tape recorder, pleading lateness for work. A distraught Elide, realizing that her husband is incapable of any emotions toward her at all, rushes off in her red sports car to destruction. It is in that same red sports car, now in an automobile cemetery, that Elide returns from the dead to reprimand Gianni for his vanity—"it's you who aren't important, for anyone. Not even yourself"—and for his cultural hypocrisy—"death is sublime. It's obvious you haven't read *Siddharta*. You made me read it, but you never read anything." A slave to two masters—her husband and the paradigms of contemporary culture—Elide lives out a doubly tragic destiny. Unlike Pygmalion, Gianni will not be pleased by his Galatea who, as she achieves the beauty and sophistication he requires of her, embraces cultural models that externalize, and therefore accentuate, her unhappiness. Her impressionable character, and her personal plight, thus make Elide an ideal measure of the cultural progress of the postwar period.

While Elide's perspective is molded by constantly changing cultural norms, Luciana's remains stable and derives from her own self-generated ambition. In her aspiration to the stage, Luciana insists on the dramatic metaphor for the totality of her life's experience. When she and Gianni are first introduced at the Half Portion, Luciana tells us that she immediately fell in love with him, "as in romantic comedies." The simile evolves into a conceit in the scene of Luciana's revival from the drug overdose that was meant to end her life. "It was a rerun of the same play as before," Luciana says to Antonio of her affair with Nicola, "with you, me, and the lawyer. Only the lawyer was a professor, and the play had less success. It lasted only two nights." Luciana's insistence on seeing herself as a diva whose life is a series of passionate love scenes, explains why her sentimental career is such a predictable failure. Her concept of love as transcendent passion may play well in the theater, but it cannot be sustained offstage. Accordingly her romantic expectations lead her into the arms of men like Gianni and Nicola whose relationships with Luciana will necessarily be short-term and hence will preserve their glamor against the erosions of daily life. Thus, Luciana prefers the excitement of running off with Gianni, or the taboo affair with the married Nicola, to the secure and decent love of Antonio, which would make unremarkable stage fare indeed.

It is significant that at the end of the film, when we learn that Luciana has indeed become Antonio's wife, and Gianni makes a slimy attempt at winning her back, she does not invoke the theatrical metaphor for her sentimental life. "Remember when, because of me, you took all those pills?" Gianni recalls, seeking to reestablish the intensity of the days when Luciana saw her experiences in melodramatic terms. "For all those years, I've done nothing but think of you," he confesses. "But I haven't," answers Luciana. "Ten years ago, I married Antonio. I had two children, then a house, a job, never enough money," she explains, shifting the level of dis-

17. *Luciana (Stefania Sandrelli) and Antonio (Nino Manfredi) act out the stage convention that they have just witnessed in a performance of Eugene O'Neill's* Strange Interlude.

cussion from that of theaterworthy passion to the banal stuff of daily life. "But I thought a great love was a great love," insists Gianni. "That's in the past. Since then, I've loved Antonio," answers Luciana, where the Italian "ho voluto bene ad Antonio" suggests the vast differences between the "amore" of Gianni's storybook romance and the genuine affection born of Antonio's and Luciana's long-lived domestic intimacy.

The theatrical metaphor gives rise to a convention within the film that invites a host of metacinematic concerns. After attending a performance of Eugene O'Neill's *Strange Interlude*, Antonio and Luciana discuss the playwright's technique of externalizing the private thoughts of his characters. By spotlighting the character who is to reveal himself or herself, darkening the rest of the stage and having that individual speak, O'Neill is giving his own highly stylized version of the theatrical aside. "They couldn't hear each other's thoughts," Luciana says of the rest of the characters on stage during these soliloquies. "But if we heard them from the last row?" objects Antonio, whose inexperience with the medium causes a certain literal-mindedness. "They heard, but pretended not to. It's a convention," Luciana explains. By making explicit the mechanism of theatrical conventions, Scola is doing several things. He is emphasizing the contractual nature of the aesthetic experience, which involves a tacit agreement between author and public about what constitutes "truth" within the work of art. Antonio is a party to this contract only after the fact, once Luciana explains to him its stipulations and he is able to understand the play retrospectively. Scola makes Antonio's belated understanding an object lesson for us early in the film so that we will enter into the contract immediately and will accept his filmic conventions at once. To underscore the point, Scola borrows O'Neill's convention in the very next scene in the Half Portion where Luciana's and Gianni's mutual infatuation is heralded by spotlights, darkened stage, and the externalization of inner thoughts. Though the same effect could have been achieved by the character's direct address to the camera—a technique Scola already used several times in the film, and will use again—he chooses instead the more elaborate stage device to emphasize his resort to convention. However, the filmmaker has already modified O'Neill's original technique by having Luciana's thoughts overheard, and answered, by Gianni, to demonstrate the mutuality of their burgeoning passion.

When Scola next uses the O'Neill convention, it is to accentuate the repetitive nature of Antonio's betrayal by his companions, who are only too happy to place their sexual interests above loyalty to a friend. The setting is the Half Portion (scene of so many redundancies) where Antonio has brought Nicola for the budget meal that his meager finances require. When Luciana walks in alone, and it is clear that her affair with Gianni is over, the room goes dark, the spotlight shines on Antonio, and he asks, "If you want to start up again, one word is all I need. Yes or no?" But the reciprocity of the convention established in the earlier scene between Luciana and Gianni is here conspicuously absent. When the camera turns to Luciana across the table, the spotlight goes off and we are not privy to the return thoughts of this woman whose indifference to Antonio inures her to his desires.

Variations on the O'Neill convention occur throughout the film. In a purely auditory version of it, we hear Antonio's exaggerated heartbeat (the other character present does not) when Gianni confesses that he and Luciana are in love. Later, spotlighted characters speak alternately on a darkened stage to dramatize an epistolary exchange between Nicola and his wife, Gabriella. Private thoughts are externalized visually in an extremely inventive way in the scene on the Spanish Steps. After a slighted Antonio maligns Luciana, she runs to an instant photo booth, claiming that the director Zampa has requested a picture of her. When Nicola returns to the booth to fetch Luciana and finds her already gone, the newly developed strip of photos comes down the chute. The first shot reveals a relatively composed Luciana, but as they proceed, her expression deteriorates into one of sheer anguish and misery. The series of photos is like the celluloid strip of a filmed study in progressive despair, and it offers, in imagistic shorthand, a summation of Luciana's decline from the beginning of the story until now.

Another variant on the O'Neill convention is Elide's postmortem dialogue with Gianni in the automobile cemetery. Here again we have the spotlight, the otherwise darkened set, and the articulation of private thoughts. But Elide's presence in this scene is a mere projection of Gianni's psyche, so that not only is his part of the dialogue an outward expression of his hidden sentiments, according to the O'Neill convention, but so too is the image of his respondent and her words. The convention now asks us to attribute one character's spoken lines to silent ruminations, while granting the other character, who is as fully embodied as the first, the status of an imaginative construct.

Even more complex is the movie theater scene in which Antonio and Luciana reestablish contact after a hiatus of many years and infidelities. Antonio's original plans for that evening had been to see Alain Resnais's *Last Year at Marienbad* with his current girlfriend, Valeria, but a chance meeting with Luciana in a park caused a change in agenda. Instead, Antonio goes to see Ken Hughes's *Of Human Bondage* in the moviehouse where Luciana is working as an usherette. The setting, which recalls the couple's first evening together at the theater, leads us to expect some version of the O'Neill convention so fruitfully introduced in the earlier scene.[10] Our expectations are indeed fulfilled as the camera shifts back and forth from the images of Laurence Harvey and Kim Novak on the screen to those of Antonio seated in the audience and Luciana standing behind him in usherette garb. Gradually, we come to realize that the dubbed-in voices of Harvey

---

[10] Michael Seitz comments on the connection between these two scenes in his review of the film for *Film Quarterly* 31 (Winter 1977–78), 47.

and Novak have been replaced by those of Antonio and Luciana as they express their own longings in dialogue, which is approximately synchronized with the characters' lip movements on screen. The joke here is that the "dubbing job" done by Antonio and Luciana is no worse nor less convincing than the original Italian dubbing of the English language soundtrack to the film. In this context, the O'Neill convention is used to illustrate the power of the cinema to elicit the viewers' own desires in identifying with the characters on screen.

The recurrence of the O'Neill convention throughout the film has enabled Scola to turn the spotlight on himself as filmmaker and express openly many of the hidden assumptions of his art.[11] The nature of cinematic conventions, the need for public assent, the psychology of the film-viewing experience, and so on—all these subjects of Scola's cinematic self-consciousness are explored through O'Neill's revelational technique. But this constitutes only one of the ways in which *We All Loved Each Other So Much* is a film about filmmaking. Indeed, the movie is as much a cinematic retrospective of the postwar period as it is a political retrospective. Scola's decision to make the cinema itself such an important part of his inquiry offers perhaps the best proof of the medium's centrality in postwar Italian culture. "In Italy, the cinema has always accompanied, articulated, represented, and sometimes even preceded national customs," Scola told Aldo Tassone. "With its capacity to sink the roots of artistic or artisanal inspiration in the soil of reality, the cinema has accompanied, for better or for worse, the progress of Italian society."[12] Of special interest for our study is Scola's finding that it is the *realist* tendency of Italian cinema that makes it so important a cultural protagonist.

[11] Seitz's essay points out the ways in which Scola calls attention to cinematic artifice throughout *We All Loved Each Other So Much*. See ibid., pp. 45ff.

[12] In Tassone, *Parla il cinema, II*, p. 313.

One way in which film history is privileged in *We All Loved Each Other So Much* is by making it an important measure of the passage of time. Thus the *Of Human Bondage* allusion tells us that it is 1964, the mention of *The Eclipse* locates us in the early Sixties, and the making of *La dolce vita* puts us back in 1959. And just as ontogeny recapitulates phylogeny in the biological world, so too does Scola's style in *We All Loved Each Other So Much* evolve in keeping with the film history he traces.[13] Accordingly, the flashback to the Resistance period is handled in the understated, documentary style of the neorealists,[14] the scene of Gianni romancing Luciana in the nightclub recalls a certain genre of 1940s cinematography, and the sequence in which Fellini shoots the Trevi Fountain scene from *La dolce vita* is itself shot with Felliniesque flamboyance to the Nino Rota score. The introduction of color photography into the Italian film industry is illustrated by Scola in the moving scene of the street artist whose black-and-white image of the Madonna and Child, sketched on the pavement, slowly modulates into color to the accompaniment of a swelling musical soundtrack. This scene, which does nothing to further the plot, reminds us that one of Scola's most important referents in *We All Loved Each Other So Much* is film history itself, and that nonnarrative allusions to it are therefore not without thematic justification.

We All Loved Each Other So Much abounds in cinematic quotations, each of which serves to define, in its own way, the mode of Scola's work as a whole. Newsreel footage is included early in the film to document the Allied liberation and De Gaspari's acceptance of a U.S. loan for $100 million, provided he exclude Marxists from high-ranking government

[13] On this evolving stylistic mimesis, see Lawton "Italian Neorealism," p. 21.

[14] As Seitz points out, neorealism is what created our image of the Resistance period. "This may not have been the real world, but it is reality as we remember it in the movies, and this cinematic illusion of reality has formed our historic consciousness" See the *Film Quarterly* review, p. 46.

positions. In addition to adding visual interest to this exposition of historical background, the documentary footage also comments stylistically on the sequence of Resistance activism that immediately precedes it. If the anti-Fascist episode is shot in a manner reminiscent of neorealism, then its juxtaposition with actual newsreel footage reveals, by contrast, the fallacy of the neorealists' claim to eyewitness authenticity and reveals, instead, the style's basis in artifice. Scola uses a similar, contrasting technique again when Luciana's definition of theatrical convention is followed by newsreel footage of the 1948 elections. In this juxtaposition, Scola is suggesting that what separates his film from a work of pure filmic documentation is its very conventionality, as Luciana has just defined the term.

Scola's cinematic cross-references go beyond borrowed footgage to name-dropping, guest appearances, title allusions, and staged re-creations of key works in the history of cinema. Fellini, Mastroianni, and De Sica appear in the film as themselves, while Zavattini, Visconti, Rossellini, Amidei, and Zampa are mentioned in dialogue.[15] Little-known works of celebrated Italian filmmakers are mentioned in Nicola's quiz show appearance. As a way of wooing Luciana, Nicola shows off his cinematic erudition by acting out the Odessa Steps sequence of Eisenstein's *Potemkin* on the Spanish Steps of Rome. Fellini directs a dress rehearsal of the Trevi Fountain scene from *La dolce vita* while Luciana's agent Rinaldo hussles a part for her as an extra. When Antonio appears on the sidelines to stare at Marcello Mastroianni, Scola is able to make a complex commentary on the levels of illusion within his film.[16] The joke, of course, is that Fellini, as he directs the Trevi Fountain scene, is himself being directed by Scola,

[15] On these, and other cinematic cross-references, see Lawton, "Italian Neorealism," p. 21.

[16] On the way in which this staged sequence within a filmed sequence explodes cinema's illusion of reality, see Seitz, *Film Quarterly* review, p. 47. Consult this same page for a list of further cinematic allusions within *We All Loved Each Other So Much.*

so that the great *auteur* who is known for his domineering directorial style becomes himself the creature of this far less celebrated junior colleague.[17]

Perhaps the strongest argument for the importance of the metacinematic theme in *We All Loved Each Other So Much* is that the plot was originally to center on the character of Nicola and on his obsession with the career of Vittorio De Sica (to whom the film itself is dedicated). "We were thinking of the story of a provincial professor who, after having participated in the Resistance, was struck by *Bicycle Thief* during a screening at the ciné-club in his town," Scola told Jean Gili of the original inspiration for *We All Loved Each Other So Much.*

> He abandoned his work, his family, and came to Rome to try to meet De Sica. The film was to be only the story of a long trailing after [De Sica] which lasted thirty years: the character followed De Sica and became for him . . . a veritable obsession. De Sica always encountered him and this man put him in the presence of moral problems, of problems of conscience. De Sica, as we know, produced alternately great works and rather mediocre ones in which he lent himself out as an actor. There was, then, this "talking cricket," this conscience that followed him, reprimanded him, persecuted him, and the film ended with the same phrase as the one which has remained in the definitive version: "We believed we'd change the world and instead the world changed us."[18]

Unlike the final version of the film, which makes politics and the cinema equally responsible for the failure of postwar Italian history to fulfill the social hopes of the Resistance, the initial version was to focus on the cinematic failure alone, as

[17]This paradox was pointed out to me by students in my Italian cinema course at the University of Texas, Fall 1983.
[18]In Gili, *Le cinéma italien*, pp. 291–92.

it was embodied by one of the foremost practitioners of neo-realism. Like Gianni, whose superior promise made his betrayal of Resistance ideals that much more reprehensible, De Sica's neorealist genius, as manifest in *Shoeshine, Bicycle Thief,* and *Umberto D*, made his subsequent descent into commercial filmmaking all the more drastic and disappointing.[19]

Though Nicola's central role in the original story is quantitatively diminished in its final version, his thematic importance is not. From cinematic gadfly, Nicola becomes instead an example of the power of the medium to influence lives.[20] A measure of this cinematic influence is the very outrage it generated in Andreotti and De Gaspari, who faulted *Bicycle Thief* for spreading abroad so unflattering an image of the postwar Italian condition.[21] When Nicola dares to defend *Bicycle Thief* before the town worthies of Nocera Inferiore, who share Andreotti's bias, he personally suffers the consequences of the backlash against neorealism. Relieved of his teaching duties at the local high school, Nicola prefers self-exile to remaining in a town whose authorities support the very retrograde social values that the Resistance sought to depose.

Bicycle Thief again brings disaster into Nicola's life when he appears on the television quiz show "Lascia o Raddoppia" ("Double or Nothing") as an expert on Italian cinema. This sequence extends Scola's study of the formative power of the mass media by reflecting on the omnipresence and influence of television in Italian private life. Accordingly, Nicola's large winnings in the first round of questions make him a hero to the people of Nocera Inferiore who once so maligned their outspoken native son. However, when Nicola

[19] On the theme of De Sica's decadence, see Lawton, "Italian Neorealism," p. 22; and Tassone, *Parla il cinema, II*, p. 295.

[20] Judith Crist notes this in her review of *We All Loved Each Other So Much, Saturday Review*, 23 July ;1977, 47.

[21] For Scola's comments on the threat which neorealism posed to the status quo, see Monicelli, *Cinema italiano*, p. 142.

agrees to appear once more on the show and risk all his prize money in the hope of doubling it, his loss demotes him in the estimation of the townspeople just as surely as the previous week's victory had rehabilitated him. In the aftermath of the television debacle, Scola shows us an auditorium, empty of spectators save a forlorn Gabriella and Tommasino, the familial victims of Nicola's stubborn pride. The setting is identical to the scene of Nicola's altercation with the local authorities after the screening of *Bicycle Thief* many years before, except that now Tommasino is older and his father is absent, seeking an elusive fortune in Rome. But Scola's repetition of the *mise-en-scène* is no mere exercise in comic preciosity—it is a double exemplification of the power of the media to determine the course of human life.

Lest we overlook the second important lesson of the "Lasica o Raddoppia" sequence, let us return to the question on which Nicola falters. Concerning Bruno in *Bicycle Thief*, the moderator asks, "Why does the little boy cry with so much realism?" By way of response, Nicola tells the story of how De Sica filled Enzo Staiola's pockets with cigarette butts and then called the boy a tramp. "The correct answer is something else," cries the moderator. "It's because his father is beaten for stealing a bicycle." Of course both answers are right, though one refers to the technique of filmmaking while the other privileges its narrative content. As Michael Seitz suggests, the discrepancy between the two answers points to the existence of two distinct viewing publics: a sophisticated one that appreciates the artifice on which cinema's illusion of reality is based, and a naive one that interprets the film at face value.[22] It is no accident that Scola should make *Bicycle Thief* the pretext for this kind of polemic, since the neorealist claim to documentary reportage would aggravate the naive public's impulse to identify the filmed image with some extracinematic reality. Therefore, by privileging De Sica's illu-

[22] See Seitz, *Film Quarterly* review, p. 46.

sion-making techniques in *Bicycle Thief*, Nicola is daring to challenge the popular attribution of absolute truth to its neorealist national monuments. No wonder his answer is declared wrong.

Another way in which Scola makes *We All Loved Each Other So Much* a thirty-year retrospective on the history of Italian cinema is in his very casting, for his actors include Aldo Fabrizi of neorealist fame, in addition to those *divi* who appeared in so many Fifties and Sixties *commedie all'italiana* that their names became virtual synonyms for the dominant genre of postwar Italian commercial film production. But it is in the part he chooses for Fabrizi that Scola reveals his bitterest judgment on Italy's social and cinematic failure to fulfill its Resistance ideals. Not only does the obese Romolo Catenacci represent the material and moral monstrosity of the contemporary Italian power elite, but, new layers of fat notwithstanding, we cannot fail to recognize in him the same actor who played Don Pietro in *Open City*.[23] The casting choice has devastating implications for Scola's interpretation of postwar Italian history, since Don Pietro had once carried the full burden of Rossellini's visionary hopes for a new society based on a fusion of Christian and Marxist ideals. Romolo Catenacci's entire being is the very negation of that hope, which is ironically invoked in the birth imagery surrounding Fabrizi's introduction to the screen in *We All Loved Each Other So Much*. When Luciana and Gianni bicycle up to the Catenacci villa, they notice a blue ribbon festooning the gate. "A little boy has been born," Luciana observes. "The handsome little male is me," blusters Romolo as he drags his enormous bulk from his "baptismal" bath in a scene which suggests not new life, but the triumph of overripe flesh—Scola's metaphor for the postwar Italian condition.

[23] Stanley Kauffmann sees in Romolo Catenacci the Aldo Fabrizi of *Open City* but he does not acknowledge in Scola's casting choice a deliberate commentary on the postwar decline of Italian cinema. See his review in *New Republic*, 18 June 1977, 23.

Romolo further attests to the failure of social change and the persistence of the prewar status quo when he lays claim to the title of marquis "by appointment of Mussolini." Indeed, the very name Romolo reveals the intensity of Scola's disappointment in the postwar social order. Like Romoletto of *Open City*, who witnessed Don Pietro's sacrificial death so that he and his young militant companions might carry on the partisan priest's anti-Fascist efforts, Catenacci's first name recalls the founder of Rome. And, appropriately, Scola's character is a real-estate developer—a builder of cities within cities. Unlike Rossellini's young activist who promises to re-found Rome in the image of the neorealist Utopian promise, Catenacci will build luxury apartments out of public funds for low-rent housing, thus converting the state's attempts at social reform into more profits for the already rich. The name Catenacci, meaning door-bolt or padlock, only confirms his association with private property and its exclusivity, in defiance of any movement toward redistribution of the wealth.

Were the film to end with the reunion of Antonio, Nicola, and Gianni at the Half Portion restaurant as they bitterly reflect on their generation's failure to change the world, Scola would deserve the criticisms for political defeatism with which Lina Wertmuller has been charged. But there is a postscript to *We All Loved Each Other So Much* that tempers Scola's pessimism and offers a modest alternative to Gianni's political capitulation, on the one hand, and Nicola's intellectual abdication, on the other. Indeed, it is the humble hospital worker who emerges as the hero of the piece and it is for him alone that the film's title can be applied in the present tense, without irony. For the others, instead, the pluperfect of the Italian verb, *c'eravamo amati*, is only too apt—they *had* loved each other so much, once upon a time, but the unity born of the partisan struggle came to an end after the common enemies were put to rout. For Antonio, instead, that anti-Fascist commitment remained to span the thirty years from the Resistance until the present, inspiring in him a tripartite love: for his comrades, for a woman, and for a cause. Unlike Gianni and Nicola, who each subordinate friendship to sexual attraction, Antonio remains generous to his companions—concerned for their welfare and happy to engineer their final reunion. And where the other two men fail dismally in their relations with women—both in their affairs with Luciana and in their respective marriages—Antonio alone remains loyal to his beloved and forges a successful lifelong partnership with her. Finally, it is Antonio who keeps the Resistance hope alive, not in grandiose ideological gestures or in the bloody activism of a terrorist sort, but in the many small and unglamorous citizen challenges that a democracy requires.[24] Thus the surprise ending of Antonio's love story—the revelation that Luciana is his wife—takes place against the background of a rally for equal access to a public school of limited student capacity. Although Luciana has drawn a low enough number for their child to be enrolled, Antonio puts the needs of the community before his own (just as he has subordinated his individual wishes to those of his friends throughout the film) and proposes that the parents make a collective demand for open admission. Imagistically and musically, Scola goes to considerable lengths to show that such activism is indeed the fulfillment of the Resistance plea for social justice. To beguile the tedium of the all-night vigil before the schoolhouse, a group of parents sing the same song we heard during the newsreel footage of the Allied liberation and during the scenes in the Half Portion restaurant. It is a Resistance song whose lyrics include the lines, "the memory of that day will always keep us united." The song is sung around a campfire reminiscent of the partisan sojourn in the

[24] According to Tassone, Antonio remains true to the cause "because he never entertained too many illusions" (*Parla il cinema, II*, p. 295). On the guarded optimism of this ending, see Scola's comments in Gili, *Le cinéma italien*, pp. 295–96; and Vinicio Marinucci, *Italian Directors: Ettore Scola* (Rome: A.N.I.C.A., n.d.), pp. 13–14. Miccichè, on the other hand, finds this ending hardly edifying, attributing to Antonio an *impegno* of pure will, not of reasoned social analysis. See *Il cinema italiano degli anni '70*, p. 218.

mountains and metaphorically suggestive of impassioned commitment. But for the Professional and the Intellectual who put the cause of the self before all other concerns, the song and the fire have only sarcastic application.[25] For the humble hospital worker, instead, the memory of that day is still alive, both in the selfless love he bears his friends and in this support for the peacetime issue that perhaps most adequately expresses the Resistance hope. In defending the universal right to education, Antonio is committing himself not only to a present of social justice, but to its transmission, through learning, to future generations.

It is significant that we never discover the outcome of Antonio's small battle against the system. Like the contemporary Italian situation it purports to represent, the film remains politicaly open-ended, though it does offer satisfying sentimental closure in the marriage of Antonio and Luciana.[26] The disparity between the film's ideological openness and its conclusive love story thus suggests the dual generic provenance of *We All Loved Each Other So Much*, which owes its plot structure to the *commedia all'italiana* and its social responsibility to neorealism. And if the bleakness of its political commentary is alleviated somewhat by the persistent idealism of Antonio, then its dark reflections on cinema history are similarly, though modestly, brightened by Scola's example of popular filmmaking with a social conscience.[27] The rise of Nino Manfredi's Antonio may not be enough to offset the plunge of Aldo Fabrizi's Don Pietro into

[25] On the egocentrism of Gianni's and Nicola's commitment and on the meaning of the film's title in their regard, see Marinucci, *Scola*, p. 13.

[26] On the political ambiguity of Scola's conclusion, see Lawton, "Italian Neorealism," p. 22. For Scola's own statements on the need for an open-ended, nondogmatic cinema, see *Parla il cinema, II*, pp. 305 and 321.

[27] "I deem it important that, within a 'spectacular' film that will reach millions of viewers, there also be proposed a culturally serious discourse, useful to the movement of ideas." In Tassone, *Parla il cinema, II*, p. 311. For a rephrasing of this idea, see Scola's remarks in Monicelli, *Cinema italiano*, p. 138.

the fleshy depths of Romolo Catenacci, but it nonetheless reveals a film industry still mindful of the neorealist model and still committed to asking difficult questions of itself and of the public it addresses. When Scola ends his film with a quarrel between Antonio and Nicola on the meaning of the expletive "boh," he is doing his humble, comedic part to carry on the neorealist tradition. Though the triviality of the debate reveals Scola's self-deprecating awareness that *We All Loved Each Other So Much* is no *Open City*, his ending is meant neither to diminish the importance of the problems raised by the film, nor to deny its neorealist paternity. Romolo Catenacci may indeed constitute one judgment on the fate of committed cinema in Italy, but his is by no means the only one to gain currency in Scola's film.[28] For Antonio and Luciana prove that the neorealist promise can yet find modest fulfillments in films which may lack definitive solutions to Italy's sociopolitical predicament, but which nonetheless insist on the urgency and appropriateness of the cinematic quest for them.

[28] Bondanella, on the other hand, feels that *We All Loved Each Other So Much* "buried the myth of Italian neorealism" (*Italian Cinema*, p. 374).

Bibliography
of works consulted

Accialini, Fulvio, and Lucia Colucelli. *I Taviani*. Florence: La Nuova Italia, 1979.

Agee, James. Review of *Open City*. *The Nation*, 13 April 1946, 443–44.

Agel, Henri. *Vittorio de Sica*. Paris: Editions Universitaires, 1955.

Alpert, Hollis. Review of *The Conformist*. *Saturday Review*, 10 April 1971, 40.

———. Review of *Seduced and Abandoned*. *Saturday Review*, 11 July 1964, 22–23.

———. "A Talk with Antonioni." *Saturday Review*, 27 October 1962, 27 and 65.

Amidei, Sergio. "*Open City* Revisited." *The New York Times*, 16 February 1947, sec. 10, 5.

Angell, Roger. Review of *Christ Stopped at Eboli*. *The New Yorker*, 5 May 1980, 165–66.

Ansen, David. Review of *Night of the Shooting Stars*. *Newsweek*, 7 February 1983, 69.

Antonioni, Michelangelo. *L'avventura: A Film by Michelangelo Antonioni*. Edited by George Amberg. New York: Grove Press, 1969.

———. *Il deserto rosso*. Edited by Carlo Di Carlo. Bologna: Cappelli, 1978.

"Antonioni in Color." *Time*, 19 February 1965, 99.

Aristarco, Guido. "Esperienza culturale ed esperienza originale in Luchino Visconti." In *Rocco e i suoi fratelli*, edited by G. Aristarco and G. Carancini, pp. 13–47. Bologna: Cappelli, 1960.

Aristarco, Guido, ed. *Antologia di "Cinema nuovo," 1952–1958*. Florence: Guaraldi, 1975.

Aristotle's Theory of Poetry and Fine Art. Translated by S. H. Butcher. New York: Dover, 1951.

Armes, Roy. *Patterns of Realism*. South Brunswick and New York: A. S. Barnes, 1971.

Auerbach, Erich. *Mimesis: The Representation of Reality in Western Literature*. Translated by Willard R. Trask. Princeton, N.J.: Princeton University Press, 1971.

Augustine, St. "De doctrina christiana." *Corpus christianorum*, 32. Edited by Joseph Martin. Tournai: Brepols, 1962.

Ayfre, Amédée. "Néo-réalisme et phénoménologie." *Cahiers du cinéma* 3 (November 1952), 6–18.

———. "Du premier au second néo-réalisme." *Etudes cinématographiques* 32–35 (Summer 1964), 55–72.

Bachmann, Gideon. "Ermanno Olmi: The New Italian Films." *The Nation*, 25 May 1964, 540–43.

———. "Look Gideon . . . Gideon Bachmann Talks with Lina Wertmuller." *Film Quarterly* 30 (Spring 1977), 2–11.

Baldelli, Pio. *Cinema dell'ambiguità*. Rome: La Nuova Sinistra, 1971.

Barbaro, Nick. "*Umberto D.*" *Cinema Texas Program Notes* 12 (Spring 1977), 15–20.

Battaglia, Salvatore. *Grande dizionario della lingua italiana*, vol. 5. Turin: Unione Tipografica Editrice Torinese, 1968.

Bazin, André. *Vittorio De Sica*. Parma: Guanda, 1953.

———. *What is Cinema?* vol. 2. Berkeley and Los Angeles: University of California Press, 1972.

"Bernardo Bertolucci Seminar." *American Film Institute Dialogue on Film* 3 (April 1974), 14–28.

Bettelheim, Bruno. "Reflections: Surviving." *The New Yorker*, 2 August 1976, 31–52.

Biskind, Peter. "Lina Wertmuller: The Politics of Private Life." *Film Quarterly* 28 (Winter 1974–75), 10–16.

Blake, Richard. Review of *Night of the Shooting Stars*. *America*, 26 February 1983, 154.

Blumenfeld, Gina. "The (Next to) Last Word on Lina Wertmuller." *Cinéaste* 7 (Spring 1976), 2–5 and 50.

————, and Paul McIsaac. "You Cannot Make the Revolution on Film: An Interview with Lina Wertmuller." *Cinéaste* 7 (Spring 1976), 7–9.

Bo, Carlo, ed. *Inchiesta sul neorealismo.* Turin: Edizione Radio Italiana, 1951.

Bocelli, Arnaldo. *Letteratura del '900.* Palermo: Salvatore Sciascia, 1975.

Boito, Camillo. *Storielle vane.* Rome: Silva, 1971.

Bondanella, Peter. *Italian Cinema from Neorealism to the Present.* New York: Ungar, 1983.

————. "Neorealist Aesthetics and the Fantastic: *The Machine to Kill Bad People* and *Miracle in Milan.*" *Film Criticism* 3 (Winter 1979), 24–29.

Bondanella, Peter, ed. *Federico Fellini: Essays in Criticism.* New York: Oxford, 1978.

Borde, Raymonde, and André Bouissy. *Le nouveau cinéma italien.* Lyon: Serdoc, 1963.

Bragin, John. "A Conversation with Bernardo Bertolucci." *Film Quarterly* 20 (Fall 1966), 39–44.

Britton, Andrew. "Bertolucci: Thinking about Father." *Movie* 23 (1976–77), 1–14.

Brunetta, Gian Piero. "La migrazione dei generi dalla biblioteca alla filmoteca dell'italiano." *Italian Quarterly* 21 (Summer 1980), 83–90.

————. *Storia del cinema italiano dal 1945 agli anni ottanta.* Rome: Riuniti, 1982.

Brunette, Peter. "Just How Brechtian Is Rossellini?" *Film Criticism* 3 (Winter 1979), 30–42.

————. "Recent Italian Film." *Italian Quarterly* 25 (Spring 1984), 61–70.

Budgen, Suzanne. *Fellini.* London: British Film Institute, 1966.

Burgess, E. Servi. "Toward a Popular Feminist Cinema." *Women and Film* 1, Nos. 5–6 (1974), 6–10.

Callenbach, Ernest. Review of *Everything Ready, Nothing Works. Film Quarterly* 28 (Winter 1974–75), 59.

Camerino, Vincenzo, and Antonio Tarsi. *Dialettica dell'Utopia.* Manduria: Lacaita, 1978.

Cameron, Ian, and Robin Wood. *Antonioni*. New York: Praeger, 1971.

Cannella, Mario. "Ideology and Aesthetic Hypotheses in the Criticism of Neorealism." *Screen* 14 (Winter 1973–74), 5–60.

Cannistraro, Philip V. "Ideological Continuity and Cultural Coherence." *Bianco e nero* 36 (September–December 1975), 14–19.

Canziani, Alfonso, and Cristina Bragaglia. *La stagione neorealista*. Bologna: Cooperativa Libraria Universitaria, 1976.

Capuana, Luigi. *Gli "ismi" contemporanei*. Edited by Giorgio Luti. Milan: Fratelli Fabbri, 1973.

Casetti, Francesco. *Bertolucci*. Florence: La Nuova Italia, 1975.

Chiaromonte, Nicola. "Italian Movies." *Partisan Review* 16 (June 1949), 621–30.

Ciment, Michel, ed. *Le dossier Rosi*. Paris: Stock, 1976.

Cocks, Jay. Review of *The Conformist*. *Time*, 5 April 1971, 86.

Comencini, Luigi. "Li capiva." *Bianco e nero* 36 (September–December 1975), 122–24.

Corliss, Richard. Review of *Night of the Shooting Stars*. *Time*, 21 February 1983, 80.

Crist, Judith. Review of *We All Loved Each Other So Much*. *Saturday Review*, 23 July 1977, 47.

Crowdus, Gary, and Dan Georgakas. "The Audience Should Not Be Just Passive Spectators: An Interview with Francesco Rosi." *Cinéaste* 7 (Fall 1975), 3–8.

Cuccu, Lorenzo. *La visione come problema: Forme e svolgimento del cinema di Antonioni*. Rome: Bulzoni, 1973.

Debreczeni, François. "L'esthétique du néoréalisme." *Etudes cinématographiques* 32–35 (Summer 1964), 73–76.

———. "Origines et évolution du néo-réalisme." *Etudes cinématographiques* 32–35 (Summer 1964), 20–54.

———. "La technique du néo-réalisme." *Etudes cinémato-graphiques* 32–35 (Summer 1964), 114–27.

De Lauretis, Teresa. "Language, Representation, Practise: Re-reading Pasolini's Essays on Cinema." *Italian Quarterly* 21–22 (Fall 1980–Winter 1981), 159–66.

Denby, David. Review of *Night of the Shooting Stars. New York*, 7 February 1983, 72 and 75.

De Poli, Marco. *Paolo e Vittorio Taviani.* Milan: Moizzi, 1977.

De Sanctis, Francesco. *La poesia cavalleresca e scritti vari.* Edited by Mario Petrini. Bari: Laterza, 1954.

———. *Saggi critici.* Edited by Luigi Russo. Bari: Laterza, 1952.

De Santis, Giuseppe, and Mario Alicata. "Ancora di Verga e del cinema italiano." *Cinema*, 25 November 1941, 314–15.

———, and Mario Alicata. "Verità e poesia: Verga e il cinema italiano," *Cinema*, 10 October 1941, 216–17.

De Sica, Vittorio. "Analyzing *Umberto D." The New York Times*, 30 October 1955), sec. 10, 5.

———. *The Bicycle Thief: A Film by Vittorio De Sica.* Translated by Simon Hartog. New York: Simon and Schuster, 1968.

———. "De Sica su De Sica." *Bianco e nero* 36 (September–December 1975), 246–304.

Di Carlo, Carlo, ed. *Michelangelo Antonioni.* Rome: Edizioni di Bianco e nero, 1964.

Doniol-Valcroze, Jacques, and Jean Domarchi. "Entretien avec Luchino Visconti par Jacques Doniol-Valcroze et Jean Domarchi." *Cahiers du cinéma* 16 (March 1959), 1–10.

Estéve, Michele, ed. *Bernardo Bertolucci.* Paris: Minard, 1979.

Etudes cinématographiques 32–35 (Summer 1964).

Evans, Arthur R. Jr. "La croce e il coltello: Malaparte and the March on Rome, A Note on the Rhetoric of Fascism." *Italian Quarterly* 23 (Winter 1982), 47–52.

Farassino, Alberto. *Giuseppe De Santis.* Milan: Moizzi, 1978.

Fellini, Federico. *Fellini on Fellini.* Translated by Isabel Quigley. New York: Dell, 1976.

Ferlita, Ernest, and John May. *The Parables of Lina Wertmuller.* New York: Paulist Press, 1977.

Ferrara, Giuseppe. *Luchino Visconti.* Paris: Seghers, 1963.

―――. *Il nuovo cinema italiano.* Florence: Le Monnier, 1957.

―――. *Rosi.* Rome: Canesi, 1965.

Ferrero, Adelio. *Il cinema di Pier Paolo Pasolini.* Venice: Marsilio, 1977.

Ferrero, Adelio, ed. *Visconti: Il cinema.* Modena: Comune di Modena, 1977.

Focillon, Henri. *Life of Forms in Art.* New York: Wittenborn, 1948.

French, Brandon. "The Continuity of the Italian Cinema." *Yale Italian Studies* 2 (Winter 1978), 59–69.

Freud, Sigmund. *Jokes and Their Relation to the Unconscious.* Translated by James Strachey. New York: Norton, 1963.

Frye, Northrop. *Anatomy of Criticism.* Princeton, N.J.: Princeton University Press, 1973.

Garson, Barbara. "The Wertmuller Ethic," *Ms. Magazine* 4 (May 1976), 71–75 and 128.

Gershman, Herbert S., and Kernan B. Whitworth, Jr., eds. *Anthology of Critical Prefaces to the Nineteenth-Century French Novel.* Columbia, Mo.: University of Missouri Press, 1962.

Giannetti, Louis. *Understanding Movies.* Englewood Cliffs, N.J.: Prentice-Hall, 1972.

Gili, Jean. *Le cinéma italien.* Paris: Union Générale d'Editions, 1978.

―――. *Francesco Rosi: Cinéma et pouvoir.* Paris: Editions du Cerf, 1976.

―――. *Luigi Comencini.* Paris: Edilig, 1981.

―――. "22 questions à Ettore Scola." *Ecran*, 15 November 1976, 22-32.

Goldin, Marilyn. "Bertolucci on *The Conformist*: An Interview with Marilyn Goldin." *Sight and Sound* 40 (Spring 1971), 64–66.

Gramsci, Antonio. *Il Risorgimento*. Turin: Einaudi, 1952.

Greene, Naomi. "Art and Ideology in Pasolini's Films." *Yale Italian Studies* 1 (Summer 1977), 311–26.

Grossvogel, David. "Lina Wertmuller and the Failure of Criticism." *Yale Italian Studies* 1 (Spring 1977), 171–83.

Hatch, Robert. Review of *The Conformist*. *The Nation*, 5 April 1971, 446.

———. Review of *Love and Anarchy*. *The Nation*, 4 May 1974, 573–74.

———. Review of *Seduced and Abandoned*. *The Nation*, 27 July 1964, 40.

Horowitz, Irving, ed. *The Anarchists*. New York: Dell, 1964.

Horton, Andrew, and Joan Magretta, eds. *Modern European Filmmakers and the Art of Adaptation*. New York: Unger, 1981.

Jarratt, Vernon. *The Italian Cinema*. London: The Falcon Press, 1951.

Kael, Pauline. *Deeper into Movies*. New York: Bantam, 1974.

———. Review of *Night of the Shooting Stars*. *The New Yorker*, 7 February 1983, 117–20.

———. Review of *Seven Beauties*. *The New Yorker*, 16 February 1976, 104–109.

Kafka, Franz. *The Trial*. Translated by Willa and Edwin Muir. New York: Vintage, 1969.

Kauffmann, Stanley. Review of *Christ Stopped at Eboli*. *The New Republic*, 19 April 1980, 26.

———. Review of *The Conformist*. *The New Republic*, 10 April 1971, 24.

———. Review of *Investigation of a Citizen above Suspicion*. *The New Republic*, 23 January 1971, 22.

———. Review of *Night of the Shooting Stars*. *The New Republic*, 7 March 1983, 24–25.

————. Review of *Red Desert. The New Republic*, 20 February 1965, 30–34.

————. Review of *We All Loved Each Other So Much. The New Republic*, 18 June 1977, 22–23.

Kay, Karyn, and Gerald Peary, eds. *Women and the Cinema: A Critical Anthology.* New York: Dutton, 1977.

Kernan, Alvin. *The Cankered Muse: Satire of the English Renaissance.* New Haven: Yale University Press, 1959.

Kosinski, Jerzy. "*Seven Beauties*—A Cartoon Trying to Be a Tragedy." *New York Times*, 7 March 1976, sec. 2, 1 and 15.

Kracauer, Siegfried. *Theory of Film: The Redemption of Physical Reality.* New York: Oxford, 1979.

La Polla, Franco. "La città e lo spazio." *Bianco e nero* 36 (September–December 1975), 66–83.

Laura, Ernesto. *Comedy Italian Style.* Rome: A.N.I.C.A., n.d.

Laurot, Edouard de. "*La strada*: A Poem on Saintly Folly." *Film Culture* 2 (1956), 11–14.

Lawton, Ben. "The Evolving Rejection of Homosexuality, Sub-Proletariat, and the Third World in Pasolini's Films." *Italian Quarterly* 21–22 (Fall 1980–Winter 1981), 167–73.

————. "Italian Neorealism: A Mirror Construction of Reality." *Film Criticism* 3 (Winter 1979), 8–23.

Leprohon, Pierre. *The Italian Cinema.* Translated by Roger Greaves and Oliver Stallybrass. New York: Praeger, 1972.

————. *Vittorio De Sica.* Paris: Seghers, 1966.

Levi, Carlo. *Christ Stopped at Eboli.* Translated by Frances Frenaye. New York: Farrar, Straus & Giroux, 1981.

Levin, Harry. *Contexts of Criticism.* Cambridge, Mass.: Harvard University Press, 1957.

————. *The Gates of Horn: A Study of Five French Realists.* New York: Oxford, 1963.

Liehm, Mira. *Passion and Defiance: Film in Italy from 1942 to the Present.* Berkeley and Los Angeles: University of California Press, 1984.

Lizzani, Carlo. *Il cinema italiano 1895–1979*. 2 vols. Rome: Riuniti, 1979.

———. *Storia del cinema italiano 1895–1961*. Florence: Parenti, 1961.

Lukács, Georg. *The Historical Novel*. Translated by Hannah and Stanley Mitchell. London: Merlin Press, 1962.

———. *Realism in Our Time: Literature and the Class Struggle*. Translated by John and Necke Mander. New York and Evanston: Harper & Row, 1964.

Luperini, Romano. *Verga e le strutture narrative del realismo*. Padua: Liviana, 1976.

MacCann, Richard Dyer, ed. *Film: A Montage of Theories*. New York: Dutton, 1966.

Magretta, William, and Joan Magretta. "Lina Wertmuller and the Tradition of Italian Carnivalesque Comedy." *Genre* 12 (Spring 1979), 25–43.

Malerba, Luigi, and Carmine Siniscalco, eds. *Cinquanta anni di cinema italiano*. Rome: Bestetti, 1954.

Marinucci, Vinicio. *Italian Directors: Ettore Scola*. Rome: A.N.I.C.A., n.d.

Masi, Stefano. *De Santis*. Florence: La Nuova Italia, 1981.

Mast, Gerald. *A Short History of the Movies*. New York and Indianapolis: Bobbs-Merrill, 1971.

Materiali sul cinema italiano degli anni '50. Pesaro: Melchiorri, 1978.

Mellen, Joan. "Cinema Is Not for an Elite, but for the Masses: An Interview with Elio Petri." *Cinéaste* 6 (1973), 8–13.

———. "A Conversation with Bernardo Bertolucci." *Cinéaste* 5 (1973), 21–24.

———. "Fascism in the Contemporary Film." *Film Quarterly* 24 (Summer 1971), 2–19.

———. *Women and Their Sexuality in the New Film*. New York: The Horizon Press, 1973.

Miccichè, Lino. *Il cinema italiano degli anni '60*. Venice, Marsilio, 1975.

————. *Il cinema italiano degli anni '70.* Venice, Marsilio, 1980.

Miccichè, Lino, ed. *Il neorealismo cinematografico italiano.* Venice: Marsilio, 1975.

Micheli, Sergio. "Il personaggio femminile nei film di Antonioni." *Bianco e nero* 28 (January 1967), 1–9.

Mida, Massimo, and Lorenzo Quaglietti, eds. *Dai telefoni bianchi al neorealismo.* Bari: Laterza, 1980.

Modleski, Tania. "Wertmuller's Women: Swept Away by the Usual Destiny." *Jump Cut,* 10 June 1976, 1 and 16.

Monicelli, Mino. *Cinema italiano: Ma cos'è questa crisi?* Bari: Laterza, 1979.

Montesanti, Fausto. "Della ispirazione cinematografica." *Cinema,* 10 November 1941, 280–81.

Moravia, Alberto. *Al cinema.* Milan: Bompiani, 1975.

————. *The Conformist.* Translated by Angus Davidson. New York: Playboy Paperbacks, 1982.

————. "Pasolini, poeta civile." *Italian Quarterly* 21–22 (Fall 1980–Winter 1981), 9–12.

Nichols, Bill, ed. *Movies and Methods.* Berkeley and Los Angeles: University of California Press, 1976.

Nochlin, Linda. *Realism.* New York: Penguin, 1978.

Nowell-Smith, Geoffrey. *Luchino Visconti.* New York: Viking, 1973.

Overbey, David, ed: *Springtime in Italy: A Reader in Neo-Realism.* Hamden, Conn.: Archon, 1979.

Pacifici, Sergio. "Notes toward a Definition of Neorealism." *Yale French Studies* 17 (1956), 44–53.

Pasolini, Pier Paolo. *Empirismo eretico.* Milan: Garzanti, 1972.

Pechter, William. "Watching Lina Wertmuller." *Commentary* 100 (January 1976), 75–77.

Petraglia, Sandro. *Pasolini.* Florence: La Nuova Italia, 1974.

Procaccini, Alfonso. "Neorealism: Description/Prescription." *Yale Italian Studies* 2 (Winter 1978), 39–57.

Quacinella, Lucy. "How Left is Lina?" *Cinéaste* 7 (Fall 1976), 15–17.

Quaragnolo, Mario. *Dove va il cinema italiano?* Milan: Pan Editrice, 1972.

Reich, Wilhelm. *The Mass Psychology of Fascism.* Translated by Vincent Carfagno. New York: Farrar, Straus & Giroux, 1970.

Reisz, Karel. "*Umberto D.*" *Etudes cinématographiques* 32–35 (Summer 1964), 162–63.

Riley, Brooks. "Wertmuller: The Sophists' Norman Lear?" *Film Comment* 12 (March–April 1976), 49 and 51.

Robbe-Grillet, Alain. *For a New Novel: Essays on Fiction.* Translated by Richard Howard. New York: Grove Press, 1965.

Rondi, Brunello. *Il neorealismo italiano.* Parma: Guanda, 1956.

Rondolino, Gianni. *Dizionario del cinema italiano, 1945–1969.* Turin: Einaudi, 1969.

———. *Rossellini.* Florence: La Nuova Italia, 1977.

Rosen, Marjorie. "Laughing All the Way to the Gallows." *New Times*, March 1976, 45–53.

———. Review of *Love and Anarchy. Ms. Magazine* 2 (June 1974), 33.

Rossellini, Roberto. *The War Trilogy.* Translated by Judith Green. New York: Grossman, 1973.

Rossi, Alfredo. *Petri.* Florence: La Nuova Italia, 1979.

Roud, Richard. "Fathers and Sons." *Sight and Sound* 40 (Spring 1971), 61–64.

Sadoul, Georges. *Dictionary of Films.* Translated by Peter Morris. Berkeley and Los Angeles: University of California Press, 1972.

Samuels, Charles Thomas. *Encountering Directors.* New York: G. P. Putnam's Sons, 1972.

Sapori, Francesco. *L'arte e il duce.* Milan: Mondadori, 1932.

Sarris, Andrew. *Interviews with Film Directors.* New York: Avon, 1970.

Schatz, Thomas. *Hollywood Genres.* New York: Random House, 1981.

Seitz, Michael. Review of *We All Loved Each Other So Much*. *Film Quarterly* 31 (Winter 1977–78), 45–47.

Siciliano, Enzo. *Pasolini: A Biography*. Translated by John Shepley. New York: Random House, 1982.

Simon, John. Review of *Christ Stopped at Eboli*. *National Review*, 30 May 1980, 673.

Singerman, B. "*Umberto D*." *Etudes cinématographiques* 32–35 (Summer 1964), 165–66.

Sontag, Susan. *On Photography*. New York: Dell, 1980.

Spinazzola, Vittorio, ed. *Film, 1962*. Milan: Feltrinelli, 1962.

Stack, Oswald. *Pasolini on Pasolini*. Bloomington, Ind.: Indiana University Press, 1970.

La table ronde 149 (May 1960).

Talbot, Daniel, ed. *Film: An Anthology*. Berkeley and Los Angeles: University of California Press, 1972.

Tannenbaum, Edward. *The Fascist Experience*. New York: Basic Books, 1972.

Tassone, Aldo. *Parla il cinema italiano, I*. Milan: Il Formichiere, 1979.

——. *Parla il cinema italiano, II*. Milan: Il Formichiere, 1980.

Telotte, J. P. "*8½* and the Evolution of a Neorealist Narrative." *Film Criticism* 3 (Winter 1979), 67-79.

Thackeray, William Makepeace. *Vanity Fair*. New York: New American Library, 1962.

Tinazzi, Giorgio. *Antonioni*. Florence: La Nuova Italia, 1976.

Tinazzi, Giorgio, ed. *Il cinema italiano degli anni '50*. Venice: Marsilio, 1979.

Tolstoy, Leo. *The Death of Iván Ilich*. In *The Complete Works of Count Tolstoy*, vol. 18. Translated by Leo Wiener. Boston: D. Estes & Co., 1904.

Tomasi di Lampedusa, Giuseppe. *The Leopard*. Translated by Archibald Colquhoun. New York: Pantheon, 1960.

Torri, Bruno. *Cinema italiano: Dalla realtà alle metafore*. Palermo: Palumbo, 1973.

Venturini, Franco. "Origini del neorealismo." *Bianco e nero* 11 (February 1950), 31–54.

Verdone, Mario. *Il cinema neorealista da Rossellini a Pasolini.* Palermo: Celebes, 1977.

———. "Colloquio sul neorealismo." *Bianco e nero*, no. 2 (1952), 7–16.

Verga, Giovanni. *I Malavoglia.* Verona: Mondadori, 1968.

———. "Storia de *I Malavoglia*, carteggio con l'editore e con Luigi Capuana con una notizia di L. e V. Perroni." *Nuova antologia* 75 (March 1940), 105–131.

———. *Tutte le novelle.* Vol. 1. Verona: Mondadori, 1967.

Visconti, Luchino. *Visconti, Two Screenplays.* Translated by Judith Green. New York: Orion, 1970.

Walsh, Martin. "*Rome, Open City; The Rise to Power of Louis XIV*: Re-evaluating Rossellini." *Jump Cut*, 20 July 1977, 13–15.

Wellek, René. "Auerbach's Special Realism." *Kenyon Review* 16 (1954), 299–307.

———. *Concepts of Criticism.* New Haven: Yale University Press, 1963.

Wertmuller, Lina. *The Screenplays of Lina Wertmuller.* Translated by Steven Wagner. New York: Warner Books, 1978.

Westerbeck, Colin. Review of *Love and Anarchy. Commonweal*, 9 August 1974, 430.

Wilhelmsen, F. D. "Realism." *New Catholic Encyclopedia*, 1967 ed., pp. 110–13.

Willemen, Paul, ed. *Pier Paolo Pasolini.* London: British Film Institute, 1977.

Witcombe, R. T. *The New Italian Cinema.* New York: Oxford, 1982.

Yeats, William Butler. *Selected Poems and Two Plays of William Butler Yeats.* Edited by W. L. Rosenthal. New York: Macmillan, 1964.

Zambetti, Sandro. *Rosi.* Florence: La Nuova Italia, 1976.

Zavattini, Cesare. "Alcune idee sul cinema." In *Umberto D*, pp. 5–19. Milan and Rome: Fratelli Bocca, 1954.

———. "Some Ideas on the Cinema." In *Film: A Montage of Theories*, ed. Richard Dyer MacCann, pp. 216–28. New York: Dutton, 1966.

Zimmerman, Paul. Review of *Love and Anarchy*. *Newsweek*, 29 April 1974, 98–103.

Index